FROM THE CLOUD OF

Lester Bangs

Marsh--

You know that jive about "If there's a
rock & roll heaven, they must have a
hell of a band"? Don't believe it, pal

All the talent went straight to Hell. All
of it. The big acts up here are Jim Croce,
Karen Carpenter, Cass Elliot, and--
especially--Bobby Bloom! It's a nightmare! If I have to hear that fucking
"Montego Bay" even one more time, I may
kill mysel...(ah, shit, keep forgetting).

Anyway, I apply for admission to Hell
every six months but they keep turning
me down, claiming--dig this: I'm <u>too</u>
<u>good</u> <u>hearted</u>! Write 'em and set 'em
straight, willya? Tell them just what
an asshole I can be when I feel like it,
Tell Uhelszki to do the same. And Marcus.
(By the way, make him cognizant how much
I appreciate his wading through all my old
writhing (with the "h")

Met God when I first got here. I asked him
why. You know, 33 and all. All he said was
"M.T.V." He didn't want me to experience it,
whatever the fuck it is.

Gotta run. Literally. Another herd of
hoary Harp hacks heading here. Playing Zep's
"Stairway" of course. Fucking national
anthem in this burg. Can't believe nobody
here is hip to the Elgins.

Take it from me, Dave. Heaven was Detroit,
Michigan. Who woulda thunk it? —LB

Eternally yours,

Bangs

Psychotic Reactions and Carburetor Dung

Psychotic Reactions and Carburetor Dung

by Lester Bangs
Edited by Greil Marcus

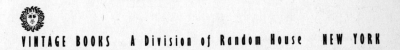
VINTAGE BOOKS   A Division of Random House   NEW YORK

Library of Congress Cataloging-in-Publication Data
Bangs, Lester.
   Psychotic reactions and carburetor dung.
   1. Rock music—History and criticism.   I. Marcus,
Greil.   II. Title.
ML3534.B315   1988   784.5′4′009   88-40180
ISBN 0-679-72045-6 (pbk.)

Manufactured in the United States of America
B987654321

Contents

Introduction and Acknowledgments

"BIO: Lester Bangs was born in Escondido, California, in 1948. He grew up in El Cajon, California, which means 'The Box' in Spanish, where he did things like wash dishes, sell women's casuals, and work as assistant for a husband-and-wife artificial-flower-arranging team while freelancing record reviews and pretending to go to college until 1971, when he moved to Detroit and went to work for *Creem* magazine. In the five years he worked there as head staff writer and in various editorial capacities, he defined a style of critical-journalism based on the sound and language of rock 'n' roll which ended up influencing a whole generation of younger writers and perhaps musicians as well. In 1976 he quit *Creem* to move to New York City and freelance. Since then he has also led two rock 'n' roll bands active on the Manhattan club scene, and began cutting records of his original rock 'n' roll compositions (he writes lyrics, sings lead and plays harmonica, allowing that 'All my melodies are the same melody, and that's a blues'), the first of which, 'Let It Blurt'/'Live,' was released on the Spy label early in 1979. Presently he is preparing an album . . ."

So wrote Lester Bangs a year or two before he died in 1982. The fact of his death demands that any bio be more specific: he was born on 14 December 1948; he died on 30 April 1982, accidentally, due to respiratory and pulmonary complications brought on by flu and ingestion of Darvon. The name of the store where he sold women's casuals was Streicher's Shoes, Mission Valley Shopping Center; his album was released in 1981 on the Live Wire label, credited to Lester Bangs and the Delinquents, under the title *Juke Savages on the Brazos,* though he also thought of calling it "Jehovah's Witness," after the faith his mother embraced following the death of his father in 1955. "Lester said it accounted for his approach as a rock critic," Frances Pelzman wrote me as work began on this book, "because he was always trying to make converts." The fact of death also provokes idle speculation: of all the details he might have included in a one-paragraph autobiography, why did Lester mention that El Cajon means "The Box"? Was it because "box" is old hipster slang for record player, or because the name signified a confinement he thought he could never escape?

It's not easy to write about a dead friend without veering off into melodrama or sentimentality; melancholy might be the most honest tone, but it's the hardest to catch. I should be making a case for the importance of Lester Bangs's work, explaining precisely why those who did not know it in its time should read it, why that work will enrich the life of anyone willing to meet it even halfway on its own terms, and while I believe Lester's writing will do exactly that, I have no heart for the job. It seems condescending, both to the reader and to the writing; it pains me that Lester found it necessary to tout his work on the basis of its influence, real and even overwhelming as that influence was, rather than on the basis of its value. Another self-portrait, then, from about the same time as the first: "I was obviously brilliant, a gifted artist, a sensitive male unafraid to let his vulnerabilities show, one of the few people who actually understood what was wrong with our culture and why it couldn't possibly have any future (a subject I talked about/gave impromptu free lessons on incessantly, especially when I was drunk, which was often, if not every night), a handsome motherfucker, good in bed though of course I was so blessed with wisdom beyond my years and gender that I knew this didn't even make any difference, I was fun, had a wild sense of humor, a truly unique and unpredictable individual, a performing rock 'n' roll artist with a band of my own, perhaps a contender if not now then tomorrow for the title Best Writer in America (who was better? Bukowski? Burroughs? *Hunter Thompson?* Gimme a break. I was the best. I wrote almost nothing but record reviews, and not many of those. . . ." He was half-kidding until the parenthesis began (he never closed it); then he was telling the truth. Perhaps what this book demands from a reader is a willingness to accept that the best writer in America could write almost nothing but record reviews.

I don't really know about the claims preceding the parenthesis. Like thousands of other people, I knew Lester mostly through his writing. We were, perhaps, deep friends, but never close. I was his first editor, at *Rolling Stone* in 1969; after he left California for Detroit and New York, we saw one another half a dozen times, talked on the phone twice as often, corresponded twice more than that. We spoke often of my editing a book of his work; thus this one.

The first bio quoted above is from the manuscript of a collection of Lester's published pieces on rock 'n' roll he prepared in 1980 or 1981. The only publication he had been able to secure had been through a German company, for publication only in German; the working title was "Psychotic Reactions and Carburetor Dung." This is not that book, which never appeared, though the title is the same, the dedication is Lester's, and most of his selections and some of his section headings have been retained; an enormous amount of material has been added, much of it never published before. Lester's book was meant to merely sum up one period in what was to be a long and unpredictable career. (When Lester died, he was about to leave for Mexico to write a novel, "All My Friends Are Hermits," though I don't for a minute believe, as some people far closer to Lester than I ever was have said, that he would have abandoned writing about music.) His book was not meant to define a legacy, which is what this book has to do.

Lester bought his first record (*TV Action Jazz* by Mundell Lowe and His All-Stars, RCA Camden) in 1958; from then on he devoured every piece of sound-bearing plastic he could find. "My most memorable childhood fantasy," he once wrote, "was to have a mansion with *catacombs* underneath containing, alphabetized in endless winding dimly-lit musty rows, every album ever released." About the same time, he became a constant reader; soon after, he became a teenage beatnik. Jack Kerouac and William Burroughs were his heroes and teachers; he bought their myths of dissipation and redemption, dope and satori. Their books and everyone's records made him a writer.

Lester Bangs's first published words, discounting poems in high-school literary magazines, were a review of the MC5's *Kick Out the Jams* LP, *Rolling Stone*, 5 April 1969. It came in over the transom, a brutal, unanswerable attack, because as a rock 'n' roll fan Lester had followed the hype, bought the album, felt cheated and used, and struck back: a good beginning for any critic. (Later he came to love the record and the band, but that was typical: "I double back all over myself," he said in an interview with Jim DeRogatis, who had asked him if his approach to rock 'n' roll was based on the conviction that the music wasn't art: "We can talk about the trash esthetic, all that. . . . Of course it's art.") In June 1969 Lester and I began to work together; in one of the first letters he wrote me (covering the five, ten, fifteen reviews then arriving weekly) he said: "In short, I would like to blow up the whole set and start all over again." And so he did.

Lester published more than a hundred and fifty reviews in *Rolling Stone* (from 1969 to 1973, when editor Jann Wenner banned him for disrespect toward musicians; again in 1979, when record-review editor Paul Nelson demanded his reinstatement), but *Rolling Stone* was never his place of freedom. *Creem,* the rock 'n' roll magazine that grew out of the milieu around John Sinclair's White Panther Party, was that place, at least for a time: it gave Lester space for the farthest reaches of invective, scorn, fantasy, rage, and glee. First as a contributor and soon as an editor, he made the magazine work as a subversive undertow in the inexorable commercial flow of the rock business; along with editor Dave Marsh, he discovered, invented, nurtured, and promoted an esthetic of joyful disdain, a love for apparent trash and contempt for all pretension, that in 1976 and 1977, with the Ramones and CBGB's in New York City and the Sex Pistols in London, would take the name he had given it: punk. He was also a man with a job, covering the scene, scooping up whatever was there: between 1970 and 1976, *Creem* meant more than a hundred and seventy reviews, seventy feature articles, countless picture captions (some of his best work, a demystification of superstars that led as directly to the Ramones and the Sex Pistols as did his reviews and features), countless replies to readers' letters, taking out the trash.

Lester became a figure within the world of rock 'n' roll: within its confines, he became a celebrity. Doping and drinking, wisecracking and insulting, cruel and performing, always good for a laugh, he became rock's essential wild man, a one-man orgy of abandon, excess, wisdom, satire, parody—the bad conscience, acted out or written out, of every band he reviewed or interviewed. He went to an interview ready to provoke whatever band was in town; whatever band was in town tried to provoke him. Thus by the time he moved to New York—to find a burgeoning punk scene that seemed on the verge of fulfilling all his hopes and jeremiads—he was a man to be lionized: a man you could be proud to say you'd bought a drink or given drugs.

Lester had spent his last year of high school on a strange regimen of Romilar cough syrup and belladonna. When a doctor told him he was courting death, he switched to shooting speed. He became an alcoholic, a real one; after many years, he could stink up a room. He stayed away from street drugs (LSD, cocaine, whatever whatever was called at any given time); he never used heroin. Still, he was for a long time his own kind of junkie. In his last year, he had cleaned up; hardly any drugs, little more than a beer, which often brought on a paroxysm of self-hate. He joined Alcoholics Anonymous; he had work to do. I've always believed that the violence of his attempt to change his life left his body shaken, vulnerable to even the slightest anomaly, be it a commonplace bug or an ordinary dose of anyone else's everyday painkiller; that he had shocked his system toward health and that that was what killed him.

In Detroit and especially in New York, Lester had an image to live up to; sometimes he tried to live up to it, and sometimes he fought against it. He doubled back on himself again and again. But the shift in his writing from Detroit to New York is patent. In Detroit he published mostly first drafts, hewing to the Beat line of automatic inspiration; in New York he began to work more slowly, writing a piece again and again, chasing a theme through five, ten times its publishable length, then cutting back or starting over. Moralism in the very best sense—the attempt to understand what is important, and to communicate that understanding to others in a form that somehow obligates the reader as much as it entertains—surfaced at the end of his tenure at *Creem*, and found a field in New York at the *Village Voice*. At the same time he published in obscure fanzines and newsstand slicks and daily newspapers, but his public voice remained stymied, boxed in: he was a rock critic, so what was all this other stuff, all the pages on sex, love, people on the street, philosophy, death, romance? Assigned a 750-word record review, he would sit down at the typewriter and work through the night, through the next day, until he had thousands and thousands of words that he never dared show his editors—some of whom might have struggled to find a way to publish them. Sometimes pieces fluttered rejection slips from slick to fanzine, or even in the opposite direction; sometimes they were lost for good.

In the last years of his life Lester tried to write about everything. In early 1976, in a combative, sarcastic, soul-baring letter to his then boss and nemesis, the late Barry Kramer, publisher of *Creem*, Lester pledged eternal fealty and submission to the magazine that by that time was as much his creation as anyone else's, demanding, over the course of seven thousand words, almost begging for, the $179.07 the magazine owed him. He talked about what he wanted to do, promising that not for a moment would his plans and ambitions interfere with his salaried obligations to edit, write reviews, features, picture captions, replies to readers' letters, to take out the trash: he planned a collection of his *Creem* pieces, and then "a staggeringly

xiv | *Introduction and Acknowledgments*

ambitious cultural commentary that will tie together and explain such disparate phenomena as disco, snuff movies, Roxy Music, Ben Edmonds, Elton John, S&M, *Barry Lyndon,* the popularity of the synthesizer and other synthetic musical instruments, the swinging singles scene and various other currently popular kinds of depersonalized sex, the desire of human beings to turn themselves into machines, *Metal Machine Music, Shampoo, The Passenger,* Donald Barthelme, pet rocks, the inevitability of total world conquest by MOR, the degeneration of language, the lack of any sense of history or culture preceding the New York Dolls on the part of the Joanne Uhelszki generation, the entire span of self-improvement literature/ courses and sensitivity training, Winning Through Intimidation, brutalization as entertainment, the obsolescence of the concept of the avant-garde, the gradual desexualization of a whole generation, including the phenomenon of individuals who prefer drugs to sex consistently, the mindless compulsive drive to dance all night currently sweeping New York City, a (currently in progress) spontaneous and unplanned mass movement on the part of human beings in the West to jettison as many emotions as possible, the deification of numbness and/or the stultifyingly bland, the possible end of civilization as we have known and occasionally treasured it for the past few thousand years, the invisible war beginning right now which may yet rend the entirety of our culture in half, including instructions as to which side you will find yourself on (since it probably will not be your selection, since most people won't figure out what they're becoming until it's too late) and how to locate the nearest branch of the Fifth Column of which I hope to become a leader."

Not that this would interfere with the picture captions: "I've got way too much work to do right now, right here, to really begin such a project on any serious level—if, ultimately, I can pull it off at all. I'm not at all sure that writing Allman Brothers reviews is the proper training for a Spengler."

Here are some of the other books Lester planned to publish:

"Psychotic Reactions and Carburetor Dung: Lester Bangs' Greatest Hits"

"All the Things You Could Be by Now If Iggy Pop's Wife Was Your Mother—A Book of Jive 'n' Verities by Lester Bangs"

"Rock Through the Looking Glass—A Book of Fantasies"

a fantasy biography of the Rolling Stones modeled on Mark Shipper's *Paperback Writer* (requested by a publisher, who lost interest after two hundred pages were completed)

"Lost Generation—American Kids Now in Their Own Words"

"A Reasonable Guide to Horrible Noise"

"All My Friends Are Hermits" (first nonfiction, then a novel)

a book of fantasies about Elvis Presley by various writers

a rock version of A. B. Spellman's *Four Lives in the Bebop Business,* focusing on Brian Eno (two hundred pages completed), Marianne Faithfull, Lydia Lunch, Screamin' Jay Hawkins, or Robbie Robertson, or Danny Fields

"They Invented It (You Took It Over, or Under)," a book on the Beatles (also called "The Firstest with the Mostest")

"Rock Gomorrah—The Scandalous Lies About the Woodstock Nation!" (a collaboration with Michael Ochs, completed, never published)

a book on the everyday lives of prostitutes, much of it written

"Women on Top: Ten Post-Lib Role Models for the Eighties"

a book about Lou Reed and the Velvet Underground

"You Can Live Like a Billionaire on No Income—I Do All the Time, and This Book Tells How"

Sure, no one would want to read most of them; certainly no one would want to read all of them, and had he lived Lester would have written only one or two of them (plus many more), but one of them would have been "All My Friends Are Hermits," his final version of the Spenglerian opus he first limned out in his last year at *Creem,* and that would have been a real book. There are hundreds of pages of it, in dozens of shapes, under

xvi | *Introduction and Acknowledgments*

many headings: only a fraction of what he wrote has found its way into this book, not all under that title.

This book is my version of the work Lester Bangs left behind. It is not a summary, or a representative selection, but an attempt to make a picture of a man creating a view of the world, practicing it, facing its consequences, and trying to move on. This book does not include Lester's first published piece (the MC5 review mentioned above), or his last ("If Oi Were a Carpenter," *Village Voice,* 27 April 1982). In fact it includes none of his writing for *Rolling Stone,* and none of his writing about some of the performers who were for him obsessions, avatars, talismans (the Rolling Stones, Captain Beefheart, Miles Davis, Charles Mingus, the Ramones); it passes over performers who during the long drought years at *Creem* (drought for rock 'n' roll, not for Lester as a writer) appeared to him as signs of life: Black Sabbath, Wet Willie, Roxy Music, Mott the Hoople, the New York Dolls, Patti Smith. Faced with an artist whose work he loved and respected, Lester often wrote poorly, passively: he often fell back, quoting lyrics rather than saying what he thought, replacing ideas with adjectives. This book omits anything from Lester's book *Blondie,* a scabrous, crackling fan-bio he wrote in a few days in 1980; it omits most of the six hundred pages of drafts he wrote for *Rod Stewart,* the fan-bio he published with Paul Nelson in 1981. It includes none of his hundreds of poems or his scores of songs. It omits most of the three million, four million, five million words that were collected for the preparation of this book. But this book is not a record of what Lester Bangs wrote: it is, finally, my attempt to record what what he wrote was about, and what it was worth.

This book was a collaborative project. Ben Catching, Lester's nephew (sometimes so referred to in the pages that follow), is Lester's executor (Lester's beloved mother died a few months before he did), and he made the book possible. John Morthland and Billy Altman are Lester's literary executors; along with RJ Smith and Georgia Christgau, they went through Lester's piles and files and catalogued them. John Morthland did most of the work, indexing, collating pages from all the corners of Lester's rooms and all the years of his writing life; he is the conscience of this book.

Ed Ward spent a week with me sifting through a footlocker full of manuscripts and clippings, making initial selections, beginning preliminary edits. I could not have started without his help. Later, Michael Goodwin and Joan Goodwin aided with final choices. Jim Miller gave crucial advice at a difficult time.

Bill Holdship collected, copied, and indexed everything Lester wrote for *Creem,* down to the last reply to the last reader. Tom Carson and RJ Smith collected and indexed Lester's more than one hundred contributions to the *Village Voice.* Cynthia Rose did the same for his many scattered pieces for London's *New Musical Express.* Robert Hull collected numerous obscure essays and liner notes.

These people also helped: Roger Anderson; Cathy McConnell Ardans; Adam Block; Paul Bresnick; Bart Bull; Bob Chatham; Robert Christgau, who edited most of Lester's work for the *Village Voice;* Diana Clapton; Jean-Charles Costa; Brian S. Curley; Jim DeRogatis; Michael Goldberg; James Grauerholz; Niko Hansen; Klaus Humann; Jimmy Isaacs; Lenny Kaye; Dave Laing; Gary Lucas; Cecily Marcus; Dave Marsh, who edited much of Lester's work for *Creem* and who provided essential support and illumination; Richard Meltzer; Joyce Milman; Phil Milstein; Karen Moline; Glenn Morrow; Herve Muller; Paul Nelson; Michael Ochs; Christine Patoski; Fred "Phast Phreddie" Patterson; Abe Peck; John Peck; Frances Pelzman; Kit Rachlis; Andy Schwartz; Gene Sculatti; Bob Seger; Greg Shaw, who edited and published Lester's "James Taylor Marked for Death" when such a piece would have been unthinkable in any commercial publication, as if it wouldn't be now; Mark Shipper; Doug Simmons; Bill Stephen; Ariel Swartley; Ken Tucker; Steve Wasserman; Steve Weitzman; and Michael Weldon.

Special thanks are due to Nancy Laleau, who as typist did a heroic job with sometimes nearly incomprehensible manuscripts; to Patrick Dillon, who did the same with typescripts; and to Robert Gottlieb, who, when approached about this project, was busy, and so replied briefly: "Of course."

As a writer who has often fantasized his own death, I imagine that all writers fantasize their own deaths. I imagine that they less call forth the praise and regret that might follow their untimely exits than mourn their orphans: all their fugitive pieces, pages, paragraphs, all those things saved, even filed according to some arcane system no one else could ever understand. Looking at my own shelves, no doubt far more neatly organized than Lester's ever were, I can shudder at all the uncorrected reviews, buried malapropisms, and mistakes that stand waiting for whoever might try to make something of them. Lester must have thought the same thoughts, and all I have done is something other than he would have done had he known he was going to die on 30 April 1982, which he didn't.

What I have done is to try and find the work that at once stands on its own and tells a story. One can read this book as an anthology, skipping from here to there and back again, but a story is what it is to me: the story, ultimately, of one man's attempt to confront his loathing of the world, his love for it, and to make sense of what he found in the world and within himself. That the story was cut off does not make it less of a story; it does not make it an impoverished tale. That the story was cut off means that the story is painful. As I worked through my friend's writing, I was for a long time so caught up in the life in the work that it truly was not real to me that he was dead; as I neared the end of the book, as I squirmed over phrasing and choices between one piece and another, the urge to simply ring him up and ask what to do was physical. In those moments, he was less dead than ever, and more dead than he will ever be.

—Greil Marcus
Berkeley, 7 June 1986

Psychotic Reactions and Carburetor Dung

Psychotic Reactions and Carburetor Dung

A Tale of These Times

Run here, my towhead grandchillen, and let this geezer dandle you upon his knee. *While you still recognize me, you little maniacs.* You know the gong has tolled, it's that time again. Now let me set my old brain a-ruminatin', ah, what upbuilding tale from days of yore shall I relate today?

"What's all this shit about the Yardbirds?"

Ah, the Yardbirds. Yes indeedie, those were the days. 1965, and I were an impetuous young squirt, just fell in puppy love first time, she used to push my hand away and sniff, "I'd like to but I don't wanna turn into a tramp." The girls were actually like that in those—

"Ah, cut the senile drool an' get on with the fuckin' archaeology or we gonna de-dandle off yer knee an' go scratch up some action! *Oldster!*"

Okay, kids, okay, just bear with me; no reason to get excited . . . now, as I was saying, it was glorious 1965, and I was starved for some sounds that might warp my brain a little. You see, there wasn't much going except maybe "I'm Henry VIII, I Am"—no, I won't get that one out, I know it sounds good, but believe me . . . we were just stuck in one of those musical recessions we used to have every once in a while, back before we started trading Intra–Solar System package tours. . . . I recollect another mighty sad downer stretch long about the beginning of the seventies . . . 'xcept *that* one lasted so long we damn near dried up an' boycotted records entirely till Barky Dildo and the Bozo Huns showed up to save our souls . . .

"Ahhh, man, how could you like those guys? That stuff was the most reactionary, chickenshit fad in history! I mean, what's so big deal about playing buzzsaw fiddle an' catgut snorkhollerers? Jammin's fine, but those cats even resorted to 4/4 time and key changes! Now I ask you, Grandud, what kind of shit is that?"

All right, all right, I know I shouldna digressed again! From here on out I'm stickin' to the straight facts, and if you sassy tads interrupt me one more time I'm gonna paste one o' yuz right in the mouth!

"Which one?"

Random choice, O seed of my seed, random like everything else in this fuckin' madhouse of a world you guys got which I shall soon be gratefully bowing out of.

"Ahright, go head an' bruise yer knuckles so you can go soak 'em in hot beer, but don't say we didn't warn ya. You oughta know that yer the only old sod around here that Skewey, Ruey and Blooie'll take any crap off of . . . and what's this bowin' out shit? Who's grateful to be dead?"

Well, as a matter of fact, at one time there were a whole lot of marks who were just that. But that's another story. I've gotta get down to this Yardbird saga or we gonna digress ourselves right into the ozone. So listen now an' listen good, and hold your questions till the end.

The Yardbirds, as I said, were incredible. They came stampeding in and just blew everybody clean off the tracks. They were so fucking good, in fact, that people were still imitating 'em as much as a decade later, and getting rich doing it I might add, because the original band of geniuses just didn't last that long. Of course, none of their stepchildren were half as good, and got increasingly pretentious and overblown as time went on until about 1973 a bunch of emaciated fops called Led Zeppelin played their final concert when the lead guitarist was assassinated by an irate strychnine freak in the audience with a zip gun just fifty-eight minutes into his famous two-and-a-half-hour virtuoso solo on one bass note. Then they grabbed the lead vocalist, who was so strung out on datura he couldn't do much but cough "Gleep gleep gug jargaroona fizzlefuck" type lyrics anymore anyway, and they cut off all his hair and stomped his harmonica, gave him a set of civvies (an outsized set of Lifetime Chainmail Bodyjeans, I think it was) and ran him outa town on a rail. Last we heard he was trying to sing "Whole Lotta Love" to a buncha sentimental old hashheads in some Podunk club. Maudlin as hell.

But the Yardbirds, you know, even though they turned it all around they only lasted a coupla years. And some of the imitators they had! Man, I used to get my yuks just *lookin'* at those records! Like when they did "I'm a Man" and made the Top Ten with a mixture of Bo Diddley (ahh, he was this old fat cat cooked up this sorta famous shuffle beat . . . I think it was already passé before you guys were even born. Yeah, fact, when they finally junked the whole idea of a steady bottom pulse altogether I think you guys were still too young to remember the big cultural civil war about it, Jagger ambushin' Zagnose right in the streets and Beefheart taking to the hills of Costa Rica to hide till things cooled down some . . .) and feedback, everybody just blew their wads and flopped over, 'cause all that electro-distort stuff that rocked you guys to sleep when you were first tokin' in your cradles was really unheard-of then, a real earthquake mindfuck. Some people found it vaguely indecent, like the naked nerve inside a wire gleaming all crazy at 'em, but us smokestack whizzband jive cats were hip to the cultural shift right from the start. We were just waitin' for somebody to come along and kick out the jams, yessir . . . oh, that phrase? Yeah, well, that's another one. Yeah, it does have a nice jagging ring, doesn't it. You'll laugh again, but we had a lotta zingy lingo when I was a tad—sharp riffs like "Right on!" and "Peace, brother!" . . . not like all this simpleminded telegraphic shit that passes for communication among you banal brats today. Why, I recall when I was in high school (oh, I told you—that was kind of where they put you when they didn't know what to do with you—when you were too big for the Kiddie Kokoons and too young to go out an' hafta assume what we used to call Manhood, which involved going at the same time every day to some weird building and doing some totally useless shit for hours on end just so you could get some bread and have everybody respect you)—when I was in high school, we used to have some mighty snappy patter. For instance, if somebody did something stupid, we used to say, "Whattaya got, shit for brains?" And another good one was, when you were mad at somebody, you could call 'em "You rotten sack o' shit!" Or a bunch of us, a gang of hoodlums about like you guys, would be driving up to a liquor store to get some Cokes and potato chips, the guy riding shotgun—later, later—would groan, "Mack down!" which meant the act of eating, of course. A few years later some imaginative souls started to call food "munchies," but luckily that moronic term didn't last long.

And even years before that we had a very mysterious incantation: "I don't make trash like you, I burn it!" You could say that and people would get confused. Or kids would, at any rate. I forget just what it signified—I kinda think it was a sort of Zen koan so when you were having a disagreement with somebody you could shoot that 'un their way and their analysis of it could either make peace or end up in a fist fight.

But I'm digressing again. Shit, you kids are right, I'm turning into a waxy-eyed old goat. With shit for brains. Soon as we finish this here anecdotal session I'm gonna go get under the Morphones and sedate my fevered brain an hour or two. I got a date with Delilah Kooch tonite an' I gotta be refreshed if I wanna still be bangin' when the cock crows, Organoil or no Organoil . . . ninety is a year for moderation. But as I was recounting before I wandered down the fleecy path, the Yardbirds themselves didn't hold together for many moons, and when they hit with "I'm a Man" they'd already started gettin' raided (someday I'll tell ya 'bout Paul Revere and the Raiders; hah, you wouldn' even believe me . . .) by little Teeno groups everywhere who immediately recorded windup versions of "I'm a Man" to fill out their debut albums, bands like the Royal Guardsmen, who had two Number One hits with the gimmick of this dog named Snoopy shootin' down old Germans in antique planes, I swear to God, and then punk bands started cropping up who were writing their own songs but taking the Yardbirds' sound and reducing it to this kind of goony fuzztone clatter . . . oh, it was beautiful, it was pure folklore, Old America, and sometimes I think those were the best days ever.

No, I don't just think so, I know they were, been havin' that feeling ever since about 1970 when everything began to curdle into a bunch of wandering minstrels and balladic bards and other such shit which was already obsolete even then. Man, I used to get up in the morning in '65 and '66 and just *love* to turn on that radio, there was so much good jive wailing out. Like there was this song called "Hey Joe" that literally everybody and his fuckin' brother not only recorded but claimed to have written even though it was obviously the psychedelic mutation of some hoary old folk song which was about murderin' somebody for love just like nine-tenths of the rest of them hoary folk ballads. And a group called the Leaves had a killer (that's another word you ought to add to yer little yaksacks) hit with "Hey Joe" and then disappeared after a couple of weird albums, though they did have one other good chart, "Doctor Stone" it was, a real heavy-handed double-entendre dope song. Every other fuckin' record was cram fulla code words for getting stoned for about a year there cause people were just starting to in a big way and it was a big furtive thrill, but the stupid government didn't figure the codes out, FBI and CIA and all, until about four or five years later, at which time they came out with this pompous exposé, this dude who looked like a cross between a gopher and the American Eagle and had a real killer vocal sound took off for this geriatric resort in the desert where people went for the jaded thrill of tossing their money away, he shot out there and delivered this weighty oration intended to let the country in on the secret that drugs and music were related when everybody already knew it anyway, and the whole shebang was hilarious because all the songs he used for examples were old as hell and everybody was already so stoned by that time they didn't need to serenade people into getting high anymore.

But for me and a lotta other folks that point, when nobody cared because everybody'd been converted to the new setup, was precisely where things started to go downhill. Instead of singing about taking tea with Mary Jane and boppin' yer dingus on ol' Sweet Slit Annie it was Help me God I don't know the meaning of life or I believe that love is gonna cure the world of psoriasis and cancer both and I'm gonna tell the people all about it 285 different ways whether you like it or not. And Why is there war well go ask the children they know everything we need to know, and Gee I sure like black folks even if my own folks don't and endless vinyl floods of drivel in similar veins. At that point I started to pack in and resort back to my good old '66 goof squat rock. I got out records like *96 Tears* by Question Mark and the Mysterians, who were mysterious indeed, and re-whooped to jungle juju cackles like "Wooly Bully," which is indescribable and was recorded by a bunch of guys who drove around in a hearse wearing turbans.

That was also when I got back into those junior jiver Yardbirds imitations in a big way. Like there was *Back Door Men* by the Shadows of Knight, who were really good at copping the Yardbird riffs and reworking 'em, and *Psychotic Reaction* by Count Five, who weren't so hot at it actually but ripped their whole routine off with such grungy spunk that I really dug 'em the most! They were a bunch of young guitar-slappin' brats from some indistinguishable California suburb, and just a few months after "I'm a Man" left the charts they got right in there with this inept imitation called "Psychotic Reaction." And it was a big hit, in fact I think it was an even bigger hit than "I'm a Man," which burned me up at the time but was actually cool now that I think about it, yeah, perfectly appropriate. The song was a shlockhouse grinder, completely fatuous. It started out with this fuzz guitar riff they stole off a Johnny Rivers hit that escapes me just now—it was the one just before "Secret Agent Man"—then went into one of the stupidest vocals of all time. It went, let me see, some jive like: "I feel depressed, I feel so bad / Cause you're the best girl that I've ever had / I can't get yer love, I can't get affection / Aouw, little girl's psychotic reaction . . . / An' it feels like this!" and then they'd shoot off into an exact "I'm a Man" ripoff. It was absolute dynamite. I hated it at first but then one day I was driving down the road stoned and it came on and I clapped my noggin: "What the fuck am I thinking of? That's a great song!"

The album (Double Shot DSM 1001) had a killer cover, too—the photo was taken from the bottom of a grave, around the rim of which stood the members of the group, staring down atcha in the sepulchre with bug-eyed malice. Really eerie, except that they were all wearing madras shirts and checkered slacks from Penney's. Which was not so eerie, but a nice touch in the long run. The colors and lettering were nice, too.

The back had four pictures of them: Count Five standing rather awkwardly in Lugosian capes on the lawn in front of an old mansion, trying to look sinister; Count Five on some L.A. dancetime show ravin' it up while a crowd of blooming boppers, presumably cordoned off from their idols, pushed eagerly toward them from the right side of the picture; Count Five in the TV studio; and Count Five loading luggage into the trunk of their car with proper sullen scowls on their faces, gettin' ready for the Big Tour as all popstars must (they probably took it in the manager's wife's station wagon).

Unlike the many asininely obfuscating album jackets of the lamer latter years, when groups started forgetting to put any kind of information on the back except maybe song titles and some phony Kodachrome nature-study which would have them passing around a dying redwood or something, Count Five's first eruption was on its backside just packed with all the essential info. Like the names, nicknames, instruments played, and ages (the oldest were nineteen) of everybody in the band. The song titles looked promising too: aside from two ripoffs from the Who, they were all originals, and with names like "Double-Decker Bus," "Pretty Big Mouth" and "The World," to name only the first three, they could hardly seem to miss.

But chillen, I'm tellin' ya that it took me many weeks of deliberation, and many an hour's sweat hunched over a record counter, before I finally got up the nerve to buy that album. Why? Well, it was just so aggressively mediocre that I simultaneously could hardly resist it and felt more than a little wary because I knew just about how gross it would be. It wasn't until much later, drowning in the kitschvats of Elton John and James Taylor, that I finally came to realize that grossness was the truest criterion for rock 'n' roll, the cruder the clang and grind the more fun and longer listened-to the album'd be. By that time I would just about've knocked out an incisor, shaved my head or made nearly *any* sacrifice to acquire even one more album of this type of in-clanging and hyena-hooting raunch. By then it was too late.

I tried and tried to buy the *Psychotic Reaction* LP—I'd go down to the Unimart stoned on grass, on nutmeg, vodka, Romilar or coming glassy-eyed off ten Dexedrine hours spent working problems in Geometry (I was a real little scholar—when I had the magic medicine which catapults you into a maniacal, obsessive craving for knowledge), I tried every gambit to weaken my resistance, but nothing worked. Shit, I had a fuckin' split personality! And all over a fuckin' *Count Five* album! Maybe I was closer to the jokers' jailhouse than I ever imagined! On the other hand, what else could I or any other loon from my peer group ever possibly become schizoid over *but* a lousy rock 'n' roll album? Girls? Nahh, that's direct, simple, unrationalized. Drugs? Sure, but it'd be them on *me*, "Yer gonna *pay* for messin' with us, boy!," not my own inner wrack of dualistic agony. Nope, nothing more nor less than a *record*, a rock 'n' roll album of the approximate significance of *Psychotic Reaction* (who could contract barking fits from a Stones platter, much less the Beatles?), could ever pulverize my lobes and turn my floor to wormwood. I knew, 'cause I had a brief though quite similar spell of disorientation once over the Question Mark and the Mysterians album! I was at a friend's house, and I was high on Romilar and he on Colt 45, and I said: "Yeah, I bought the Question Mark and the Mysterians album today," and suddenly the equilibrium was seeping from my head like water from the ears after a sea plunge, a desultory vortex started swirling round my skull and gradually spun faster though I couldn't tell if it was a breeze just outside or something right between the flesh and bone. I saw my life before my eyes, and that is no shit—I mean not that I saw some zipping montage from birth to that queasy instant of existential vertigo, but that I saw myself walking in and out of countless record stores, forking over vast fortunes in an endless chain of cash-register clicks and dings at $3.38 and $3.39 and $3.49 and all the other fixed rates I knew by heart being if never on the track team unquestionably an All-American Competitive Shopper, I saw litter bins piled high with bags that stores all seal records in so you won't get nabbed for lifting as you trot out the door. I saw myself on a thousand occasions walking toward my car with a brisk and purposeful step, turning the key in the ignition and varooming off high as a hotrodder in anticipation of the revelations waiting in thirty-five or forty minutes of blasting sound soon as I got home, the eternal promise that *this* time the guitars will jell like TNT and set off galvanic sizzles in your brain "KABLOOIE!!!" and this time at least at last blow your fucking lid sky-high. Brains gleaming on the ceiling, sticking like putty stalactites, while yer berserk body runs around and slams outside hollering subhuman gibberish, jigging in erratic circles and careening split-up syllables insistently like a geek with a bad case of the superstar syndrome.

But that's only the fantasy. The real vision, the real freaking flash, was just like the reality, only looped to replay without end. The real story is rushing home to hear the apocalypse erupt, falling through the front door and slashing open the plastic sealing "for your protection," taking the record out—ah, lookit them grooves, all jet black without a smudge yet, shiny and new and so fucking pristine, then the color of the label, does it glow with auras that'll make subtle comment on the sounds coming out, or is it just a flat utilitarian monochromatic surface, like a schoolhouse wall (like RCA's and Capitol's after some fool revamped 'em—an example of real artistic backwardness)? And finally you get to put the record on the turntable, it spins in limbo a perfect second, followed by the moment of truth, needle into groove, and finally sound.

What then occurs is so often anticlimactic that it drives a rational man to the depths of despair. Bah! The whole musical world is packed with simpletons and charlatans, with few a genius or looney tune joker in between.

All this I saw whilst sitting there in the throes of the Question Mark and the Mysterians frieze, and more, I saw myself as a befuddled old man holding a copy of the 96 Tears album and staring off blankly with the slack jaw of a squandered life's decline. And in the next instant, since practically no time had elapsed at all, my friend said with obvious amazement: "You bought *Question Mark and the Mysterians?*"

I stared at him dully. "Sure," I said. "Why not?"

I realize that this sounds rather pathological—although I never thought so until laying it out here—and the Freudian overtones are child's play, I guess. But what I don't understand is what it all signifies. Don't get the idea that my buying of and listening to records per se has always been marked by such frenzy and disorientation, or even any particular degree of obsession and compulsion. It's just that music has been a fluctuating fanaticism with me ever since—well, ever since I first heard "The Storm" from the *William Tell Overture* on a TV cartoon about first grade. And riding in the car through grammar school when songs like "There Goes My Baby" would come on the radio, and getting a first record player in fifth grade, and hearing for the first time things like John Coltrane and Charlie Mingus's *The Black Saint and the Sinner Lady* and the Stones and feedback and *Trout Mask Replica.* All these were milestones, each one fried my brain a little further, especially the *experience* of the first few listenings to a record so total, so mind-twisting, that you authentically can say you'll never be quite the same again. *Black Saint and the Sinner Lady* did that, and a very few others. They're events you remember all your life, like your first real orgasm. And the whole purpose of the absurd, mechanically persistent involvement with recorded music is the pursuit of that priceless moment. So it's not exactly that records might unhinge the mind, but rather that if anything is going to drive you up the wall it might as well be a record. Because the best music is strong and guides and cleanses and is life itself.

So perhaps the truest autobiography I could ever write, and I know this holds as well for many other people, would take place largely at record counters, jukeboxes, pushing forward in the driver's seat while AM walloped you on, alone under headphones with vast scenic bridges and angelic choirs in the brain through insomniac postmidnights, or just to sit at leisure stoned or not in the vast benign lap of America, slapping on sides and feeling good.

So I finally got the courage of my lunacy and bought Count Five. I guess the last straw was when I read in a Teen Fan magazine (the only recourse then for some hardy listener trying to figure out what's going on with each new sluice of product) that Count Five claimed to have turned down "a million dollars in bookings" because it would have meant that they would have to drop out of college and, said their manager, all the boys realized that getting a good education was the most important thing they could do. What a howl! That really appealed to me, so the next time I perused the album in the racks I snorted, "The boys who went back to school. . . ." That's a certain claim to distinction—imagine Mick Jagger suddenly tripped by an attack of remorse, and right in the middle of a glug of champagne at some jet-set hot spot the ineluctable truth hits him: *You've got to get an education, boy.* You may have millions, but do you think you'll be a popstar all your life? Decidedly not. *What* will you do in those long years of dark autumn? Do you want to end up like Turner in *Performance*, having someone come up and blow your brains out because you can't think of any other diversions at the moment? It's not too late! Get back to the London School of Economics and get that degree. Man must have some form of constructive work to do; otherwise he's an ignoble weasel without meaning. So Mick gulps the rest of his champagne, disengages himself from the sweet thing at his side, and runs off to register. Eventually he earns a degree in Art and when the Stones fold he settles down to teach the drawing of the straight line to a succession of eager moppets. What an example that would be! He might even get blessed by the Pope, or invited to the White House! But of course that will never happen, because Mick Jagger is made of baser clay than Count Five.

I bought the album. It was the same day I got *Happy Jack* by the Who. I rushed home, found in *Happy Jack* a mild satisfaction, gagged at *Psychotic Reaction.*

But *Psychotic Reaction* was the album I kept coming back to. I played it gleefully and often for a year or so until it was ripped off by some bikers, and when I finally found it once more in 1971 in a used record store, man, I up and danced a jig. Then, however, I did something oddly petty and avaricious. It was in the $1.98 rack, right next to things like *Cosmo's Factory* and *Deja Vu,* and somehow that seemed inappropriate to me—it should have been in the 89¢ grab-bag rack where it belonged, right there with all the other down-and-out relics of yore, between *Doin' the Bird* by the Rivingtons, which I also purchased, and *96 Tears,* which was actually there and proved my point, the clerk having had the sense this time to file it where it would be most comfortable (if this personalization bothers you, don't worry: once when I was in the seventh grade I went back to visit the town where I'd lived the year before and get back a copy of the Henry Mancini *Mr. Lucky* soundtrack album which I'd loaned to a friend and failed to retrieve before moving. When I got back home, I put the *Mr. Lucky* album into the record rack next to its old neighbor, the *Peter Gunn* album. Looking down on them sitting there like that, I felt glad for them. I was thinking that the two old friends, among the very first albums I ever bought, must be delighted to see each other again after so long. Maybe they even had some interesting tales to relate).

What I did, then, was to take the Count Five album, the one I'd dug so cool before and wished I still had so many times, and hold it up in the air and say to the store's manager: "What the hell is this thing doing in the $1.98 rack? Nobody's going to pay $1.98 for this!"

He looked at it a second, musing. I seized the time: "How long has this thing been sitting here? I bet it musta sat here a year or two at least, while other albums came and went. It belongs over there! 89¢!"

"Hmmm, I think you're right," he said. "I believe that record—no, the whole band, that's right—is one of the all-time clunkers of history. Yeah, put it over in the 89¢ rack."

"Sold!" I hollered, went over and threw him a buck and rushed out. I had it! The artifact! A stone tablet from Tutankhamen's tomb! A long-lost gem! Priceless—*and I got it for only 89¢!*

Well, rest assured, kids. Time hadn't dimmed the greatness of the Count Five album. In fact, it still hasn't. It sounds just as grungy and jumbled now as it did way back in 1967. I may not have played *Happy Jack* more than five times since that day I bought it, even though I never got rid of it (those Class albums that you just don't get any kicks out of will all reveal their worth and essential appeal *someday,* you always reason—perhaps you yourself must become worthy of them), but I'm gonna rock it up and kick out the jams with *Psychotic Reaction* forever. In the first month after reacquiring it I must've played it ten times, and that's saying something. A poorboy of Port or Tokay, *Psychotic Reaction* blasting off the walls and I would burn with pointless joy as I hopped and stomped around the turntable and couldn't have sat down if I'd tried.

Track for track, you couldn't have found a better deal in a whole year's releases from Warner/Reprise. "Double-Decker Bus" and "Peace of Mind" mashed the Yardbirds into masterpieces as vital as the title hit, the latter for one of the most perfect examples of the rigidly mechanical riff in history, the former for its truly cosmic lyrics ("Well just you walk / Down any street / If you don't see one of us / You're sure to see / A double-decker bus!")

But the real classics on the first Count Five album, while ignored in their own time, might have proven vastly influential if more people had been able to comprehend what the band was doing. "Pretty Big Mouth" was a crunching Tex-Mex street jam, somewhat reminiscent of a Caucasian crew of Red Mountain mariachis, which anticipated the even earthier excursions of their second album and scored with some of the greatest male chauvinist lyrics of all time: "I ended up in the deep deep South / Makin' love to the woman with a real big mouth!"

"They're Gonna Get You," somewhat similarly, was a sprung-rhythm essay in barbershop paranoia, particularly shining by a vocal which veered deliriously between a sullen plaint anticipating Iggy and a cartoon falsetto. But the real crusher was "The World," a clatter whose very monotony buckled under your feet like one of those moving ramps in the crazy house at an amusement park, while the lyrics consisted of a spartan minimum of phrases—"I'll tell the world, you're my girl, you're so fine, you are mine"— crowed in a series of whoops and gnashings goggle-eyed with glee and lunatic pride.

Unfortunately, *Psychotic Reaction* was the only Count Five album to be widely disseminated and recognized in its own time. Double Shot, a company nearly as erratic in promoting West Coast talent as ESP-Disk was handling New York innovators like the Godz, all but buried their second and third releases, giving them promotion and distribution equaled in its myopia and indifference only by Decca's handling of the early Who. The band was lucky enough, however, to have a dynamite manager with the vision to comprehend their potential and enough hardnosed hucksterish drive to eventually land them a contract with Columbia, where they made two more fine albums which, though given the production and promotion they had always merited, still fell flat sales-wise. Ignorant people were still writing them off as nothing more than a Yardbirds rip-off, critics ignored or smeared them with their snidest categorizations, and the sad result was that their most important work has never been given the attention it truly deserves.

Ironically enough, even as the "underground" press and self-appointed arbiters of public taste maintained their conspiracy of silence, it was the very despised trade journals of the "establishment" which first recognized Count Five's achievement in its initial flowering: "Evolving like so many others from their crude beginnings, Count Five has at length distinguished itself as a subtle, sophisticated integration of solid musical workmen creating some of the freshest and least grating sounds in recent memory." That's *Billboard*, talking about Count Five's fourth album, *Ancient Lace and Wrought-Iron Railings* (Columbia CS 9733).

But when *Snowflakes Falling on the International Dateline* (Columbia MS 7528) came out, it blew everybody with *ears*, all the kids fresh and free enough to flip the opinion-mafia the bird, right out the door and all the way to the corner. It featured the unparalleled "Schizophrenic Rainbows: A Raga Concerto," which no one who's sat through its entire 27 minutes will ever be able to forget, especially the thunderous impact of the abrupt and full-volumed entry of George Szell and the Cleveland Orchestra in the eighteenth minute. On this basis alone it must be considered the masterpiece among their albums, though the melancholy "Sidewalks of Calais" which closed side one was also superb, with its remarkable lyrical maturation: "Pitting, patting, trying not to step on the cracks / In Europa, where we saw no sharecropper shacks / Reciting our Mallarmé / Those films with Tom Courtenay / And your hand in mine / On the sidewalks of Calais / Oh no, I shan't forget. . . ."

Unfortunately, that was their last release. After investing so much technology and money in such an ambitious project and being repaid with such total public indifference, both the band and Columbia grew despondent at last, their contract lapsed, and the musicians themselves split for parts unknown, though one, the incredible guitar stylist John "Mouse" Michalski, later emigrated to England and formed the legendary though short-lived Stone Prodigies with several ex-members of John Mayall's Bluesbreakers and Ginger Baker's Air Force. That clutch of titans, as everybody remembers, made one incredible album, *To John Coltrane in Heaven*, then embarked on their record-breaking ten-month tour of the States which was so grueling that afterwards the entire band were committed to rest homes for the rest of their lives.

Between *Psychotic Reaction* and the *Snowflakes* swan song, Count Five produced three other albums, each equally great and each a seven-league step ahead of the last. My favorite has always been their third,

Cartesian Jetstream (Double Shot DDS 1023). Here we had the fullest development of Count Five as a band that was intrinsically and still unqualifiedly rock 'n' roll (one need only give ear to the old Anglo-Saxon madrigals and Felicianoan pseudo-Flamenco of *Ancient Lace and Wrought-Iron Railings* to realize where their true strength lay). Fine and professional, yet intensely driving and almost grungy (sophistication, like history, cannot be braked), it was truly exhilarating music, filled with the wild pulsebeat of creation. Such dynamic originals as "Cannonballs for Christmas," "Her Name Is Ianthe," and "Nothing Is True / Everything Is Permitted" bring me back to it again and again, as does the addition of Marion Brown, alto sax, Sun Ra, piano, and Roland Kirk, bass pennywhistle, on the last track, "Free All Political Prisoners! Seize the Time! Keep the Faith! Sock It to 'Em! Shut the Motherfucker Down! Then Burn It Up! Then Give the Ashes to the Indians! All Power to the People! Right On! All Power to Woodstock Nation! And Watch For Falling Rocks!" That one was a true brain-blitz, and spotlighted some of the most original lyrics of the year.

The only Count Five album to fall totally flat was their second, *Carburetor Dung* (Double Shot DDS 1009). It can truly be said that this was Count Five at their grungiest. In fact, it was so grungy that on most of the songs you could barely distinguish anything except an undifferentiated wall of grinding noise and intermittent punctuation of glottal sowlike gruntings. I suppose the best way to characterize the album would be to call it murky. Some of the lyrics were intelligible, such as these, from "The Hermit's Prayer": "Sunk funk dunk Dog God the goosie Gladstone prod old maids de back seat sprung Louisiana sundown junk an' bunk an' sunken treasures / But oh muh drunken hogbogs / I theenk I smell a skunk." Lyrics such as those don't come every day, and even if their instrumental backup sounded vaguely like a car stuck in the mud and spinning its wheels, it cannot be denied that the song had a certain value as a prototype slab of gully-bottom rock 'n' roll. Other songs, such as "Sweat Haunch Woman," "Woody Dicot," and "Creole Jukebox Pocahontas" validated themselves by emerging slightly from the uniform one-dimensional sloppiness of the rest of the material.

On the other hand, you might be better off not to take my word, but just go into my record library and check the album out for yourself. Dave Marsh loved it (he said: "It's one answer to just how far-out rock can go, one branch's end, and one of the most humanly primitive sets I've *ever* heard. You'd have to be crazy to make music like this, and I'm glad they did it"). Ed Ward told me he'd keep it forever because "it's one of the funniest albums in the history of rock 'n' roll, right up there with *Blows Against the Empire* and *Kick Out the Jams;* how can you pass up something like that?" Although Jon Landau absolutely refused to print a review of it in *Rolling Stone:* "Look man, I'm not in this business in the spirit of some kid who hides in an alley, sticks his feet out and trips the first person who walks by, then laughs his ass off when they fall on their face. Everything connected with this album is wrong. In the first place, it's absolutely horrible, one of the worst monstrosities ever released. Secondly, the group who recorded it are just a front for studio musicians; I know this for a fact. You can't tell me that the same group that recorded 'Iron Rainbows on the International Dateline' or whatever the name of that thing was, whatever it was it was a beautiful piece of work—pretentious, overarranged, overproduced, verbose, egotistical and gauche, but beautiful nonetheless—the glockenspiel player was wailing his ass off for twenty-seven minutes—but you can't tell me that that and *this* pile of crap were done by the same people. This probably *is* the band . . . good riddance. Another thing is that they're on a terrible label. Who ever heard of Double Shot Records? What kind of promotion and publicity do they get? Nada! How many records do they release a year? Who the fuck knows? The last decent act they had was Brenton Wood and that was four years ago. This album, I guarantee, will sell no copies. Just look at the cover: a rusty wheelbarrow, the body of an old Ford with no wheels or engine, and a cottonwood tree in the background. The sun has almost gone down and it's so dark you can hardly see a fuckin' thing. So the title's up there in oxblood-colored letters. Oxblood! And now you come to me and you say we gotta print a review of this album in *Rolling Stone* because it's the only one of its kind and if people don't get it now they may never have a chance to again. And you send this review comparing it to Louis Armstrong, Elmore James, Blind Willie Johnson, Albert Ayler, Beefheart, and the Stooges! All so people will buy it when there's no earthly reason why anybody interested in *music* should. Send the review to *Creem.* Make it the album of the year. Jesus Christ, I used to have some respect for you guys. Now I think you must all be either losing your minds or turning against rock 'n' roll. It's getting to where *Creem* won't even cover an album unless it's either free jazz or so fucking metallic, mediocre and noise-oriented that you'd do as well to stick your ear over a garbage disposal or a buzzsaw. Remember, man: the public ain't buyin' it. No response at all."

Neither Jon nor I nurtured any bad feelings over this, however—it was just that he couldn't stand ineptitude of any kind in music, which was perfectly reasonable, while I dug certain outrageous brands of ineptitude the most! *Carburetor Dung* just may have been the most inept album I ever heard—certainly it was right up there with *Amon Duul* and *Hapshash and the Coloured Coat Featuring the Human Host and the Heavy Metal Kids.* Yes, kids, that was the real title of a real record—I'm given to fabrication of albums sometimes, like if I wish a certain album existed and it doesn't I just make it up, but that one's authentic. *Carburetor Dung* is authentic, too, but Double Shot didn't give it any promotion for a combination of reasons (title, attitudes of various people in both the press and industry, public indifference, and the fact that not one person at Double Shot was ever even willing to talk about it it was so embarrassing). I think it just quietly faded away, like Alexander Spence's *Oar* and so many other notable albums. And as for Count Five, they finally went where all good little bands go—to that big Gas Station in the sky.

"Well, that's all very interesting, keeping us here for the last four hours telling us about the meteoric career of the Carburetor Dungs—"

No, no, *Count Five, Carburetor Dung* was the—

"YEAH, FINE, BUT WHEN THE FUCK ARE YOU GONNA TELL US ABOUT THE YARDBIRDS?!"

Uh, *hrmp*—hmmmmm, yes . . . well, that story'll always be in reserve for another day. Besides, when you get right down to it, Count Five were probably about as important as the Yardbirds, in the long run. It's just that some people are recognized in their own time, and some aren't.

—*Creem,* June 1971

Astral Weeks

Van Morrison's *Astral Weeks* was released ten years, almost to the day, before this was written. It was particularly important to me because the fall of 1968 was such a terrible time: I was a physical and mental wreck, nerves shredded and ghosts and spiders looming and squatting across the mind. My social contacts had dwindled almost to none; the presence of other people made me nervous and paranoid. I spent endless days and nights sunk in an armchair in my bedroom, reading magazines, watching TV, listening to records, staring into space. I had no idea how to improve the situation, and probably wouldn't have done anything about it if I had.

Astral Weeks would be the subject of this piece—i.e., the rock record with the most significance in my life so far—no matter how I'd been feeling when it came out. But in the condition I was in, it assumed at the time the quality of a beacon, a light on the far shores of the murk; what's more, it was proof that there was something left to express artistically besides nihilism and destruction. (My other big record of the day was *White Light/White Heat.*) It sounded like the man who made *Astral Weeks* was in terrible pain, pain most of Van Morrison's previous works had only suggested; but like the later albums by the Velvet Underground, there was a redemptive element in the blackness, ultimate compassion for the suffering of others, and a swath of pure beauty and mystical awe that cut right through the heart of the work.

I don't really know how significant it might be that many others have reported variants on my initial encounter with *Astral Weeks.* I don't think there's anything guiding it to people enduring dark periods. It did come

out at a time when a lot of things that a lot of people cared about passionately were beginning to disintegrate, and when the self-destructive undertow that always accompanied the great sixties party had an awful lot of
ankles firmly in its maw and was pulling straight down. So, as timeless as
it finally is, perhaps *Astral Weeks* was also the product of an era. Better
think that than ask just what sort of Irish churchwebbed haints Van
Morrison might be product of.

Three television shows: A 1970 NET broadcast of a big all-star multiple
bill at the Fillmore East. The Byrds, Sha Na Na, and Elvin Bishop have
all done their respective things. Now we get to see three or four songs from
a set by Van Morrison. He climaxes, as he always did in those days, with
"Cyprus Avenue" from *Astral Weeks*. After going through all the verses,
he drives the song, the band, and himself to a finish which has since become
one of his trademarks and one of the all-time classic rock 'n' roll set-closers.
With consummate dynamics that allow him to snap from indescribably
eccentric throwaway phrasing to sheer passion in the very next breath he
brings the music surging up through crescendo after crescendo, stopping
and starting and stopping and starting the song again and again, imposing
long maniacal silences like giant question marks between the stops and
starts and ruling the room through sheer tension, building to a shout of "It's
too late to stop now!," and just when you think it's all going to surge over
the top, he cuts it off stone cold dead, the hollow of a murdered explosion,
throws the microphone down and stalks off the stage. It is truly one of the
most perverse things I have ever seen a performer do in my life. And, of
course, it's sensational: our guts are knotted up, we're crazed and clawing
for more, but we damn well know we've seen and felt something.

1974, a late night network TV rock concert: Van and his band come
out, strike a few shimmering chords, and for about ten minutes he lingers
over the words "Way over yonder in the clear blue sky / Where flamingos
fly." No other lyrics. I don't think any instrumental solos. Just those words,
repeated slowly again and again, distended, permutated, turned into scat,
suspended in space and then scattered to the winds, muttered like a mantra
till they turn into nonsense syllables, then back into the same soaring image
as time seems to stop entirely. He stands there with eyes closed, singing,
transported, while the band poises quivering over great open-tuned deep
blue gulfs of their own.

1977, spring-summer, same kind of show: he sings "Cold Wind in
August," a song off his recently released album *A Period of Transition,*

which also contains a considerably altered version of the flamingos song. "Cold Wind in August" is a ballad, and Van gives it a fine, standard reading. The only trouble is that the whole time he's singing it he paces back and forth in a line on the stage, his eyes tightly shut, his little fireplug body kicking its way upstream against what must be a purgatorial nervousness that perhaps is being transferred to the cameraman.

What this is about is a whole set of verbal tics—although many are bodily as well—which are there for reason enough to go a long way toward defining his style. They're all over *Astral Weeks:* four rushed repeats of the phrases "you breathe in, you breathe out" and "you turn around" in "Beside You"; in "Cyprus Avenue," twelve "way up on"s, "baby" sung out thirteen times in a row sounding like someone running ecstatically downhill toward one's love, and the heartbreaking way he stretches "one by one" in the third verse; most of all in "Madame George," where he sings the word "dry" and then "your eye" twenty times in a twirling melodic arc so beautiful it steals your own breath, and then this occurs: "And the love that loves the love that loves the love that loves the love that loves to love the love that loves to love the love that loves."

Van Morrison is interested, *obsessed* with how much musical or verbal information he can compress into a small space, and, almost conversely, how far he can spread one note, word, sound, or picture. To capture one moment, be it a caress or a twitch. He repeats certain phrases to extremes that from anybody else would seem ridiculous, because he's waiting for a vision to unfold, trying as unobtrusively as possible to nudge it along. Sometimes he gives it to you through silence, by choking off the song in midflight: "It's too late to stop now!"

It's the great search, fueled by the belief that through these musical and mental processes illumination is attainable. Or may at least be glimpsed.

When he tries for this he usually gets it more in the feeling than in the Revealed Word—perhaps much of the feeling comes from the reaching—but there is also, always, the sense of WHAT if he DID apprehend that Word; there are times when the Word seems to hover very near. And then there are times when we realize the Word was right next to us, when the most mundane overused phrases are transformed: I give you "love," from "Madame George." Out of relative silence, the Word: "Snow in San Anselmo." "That's where it's at," Van will say, and he means it (aren't his interviews *fascinating?*). What he doesn't say is that he is *inside* the snowflake, isolated by the song: "And it's almost Independence Day."

You're probably wondering when I'm going to get around to telling you about *Astral Weeks*. As a matter of fact, there's a whole lot of *Astral Weeks* I don't even want to tell you about. Both because whether you've heard it or not it wouldn't be fair for me to impose my interpretation of such lapidarily subjective imagery on you, and because in many cases I don't really know what he's talking about. He doesn't either: "I'm not surprised that people get different meanings out of my songs," he told a *Rolling Stone* interviewer. "But I don't wanna give the impression that I know what everything means 'cause I don't. . . . There are times when I'm mystified. I look at some of the stuff that comes out, y'know. And like, there it is and it feels right, but I can't say for sure what it means."

> There you go
> Starin' with a look of avarice
> Talkin' to Huddie Ledbetter
> Showin' pictures on the walls
> And whisperin' in the halls
> And pointin' a finger at me

I haven't got the slightest idea what that "means," though on one level I'd like to approach it in a manner as indirect and evocative as the lyrics themselves. Because you're in trouble anyway when you sit yourself down to explicate just exactly what a mystical document, which is exactly what *Astral Weeks* is, *means*. For one thing, what it means is Richard Davis's bass playing, which complements the songs and singing all the way with a lyricism that's something more than just great musicianship: there is something about it that's more than inspired, something that has been touched, that's in the realm of the miraculous. The whole ensemble—Larry Fallon's string section, Jay Berliner's guitar (he played on Mingus's *Black Saint and the Sinner Lady*), Connie Kay's drumming—is like that: they and Van sound like they're not just reading but *dwelling inside of* each other's minds. The facts may be far different. John Cale was making an album of his own in an adjacent studio at the time, and he has said that "Morrison couldn't work with anybody, so finally they just shut him in the studio by himself. He did all the songs with just an acoustic guitar, and later they overdubbed the rest of it around his tapes."

Cale's story might or might not be true—but facts are not going to be of much use here in any case. Fact: Van Morrison was twenty-two—or twenty-three—years old when he made this record; there are lifetimes behind it. What *Astral Weeks* deals in are not facts but truths. *Astral*

Weeks, insofar as it can be pinned down, is a record about people stunned by life, completely overwhelmed, stalled in their skins, their ages and selves, paralyzed by the enormity of what in one moment of vision they can comprehend. It is a precious and terrible gift, born of a terrible truth, because what they see is both infinitely beautiful and terminally horrifying: the unlimited human ability to create or destroy, according to whim. It's no Eastern mystic or psychedelic vision of the emerald beyond, nor is it some Baudelairean perception of the beauty of sleaze and grotesquerie. Maybe what it boils down to is one moment's knowledge of the miracle of life, with its inevitable concomitant, a vertiginous glimpse of the capacity to be hurt, and the capacity to inflict that hurt.

Transfixed between rapture and anguish. Wondering if they may not be the same thing, or at least possessed of an intimate relationship. In "T.B. Sheets," his last extended narrative before making this record, Van Morrison watched a girl he loved die of tuberculosis. The song was claustrophobic, suffocating, monstrously powerful: "innuendos, inadequacies, foreign bodies." A lot of people couldn't take it; the editor of this book has said that it's garbage, but I think it made him squeamish. Anyway, the point is that certain parts of *Astral Weeks*—"Madame George," "Cyprus Avenue"—take the pain in "T.B. Sheets" and root the world in it. Because the pain of watching a loved one die of however dread a disease may be awful, but it is at least something known, in a way understood, in a way measurable and even leading somewhere, because there is a process: sickness, decay, death, mourning, some emotional recovery. But the beautiful horror of "Madame George" and "Cyprus Avenue" is precisely that the people in these songs are not dying: we are looking at life, in its fullest, and what these people are suffering from is not disease but nature, unless nature is a disease.

A man sits in a car on a tree-lined street, watching a fourteen-year-old girl walking home from school, hopelessly in love with her. I've almost come to blows with friends because of my insistence that much of Van Morrison's early work had an obsessively reiterated theme of pedophilia, but here is something that at once may be taken as that and something far beyond it. He *loves* her. Because of that, he is helpless. Shaking. Paralyzed. Maddened. Hopeless. Nature mocks him. As only nature can mock nature. Or is love natural in the first place? No matter. By the end of the song he has entered a kind of hallucinatory ecstasy; the music aches and yearns as it rolls on out. This is one supreme pain, that of being imprisoned a spectator. And perhaps not so very far from "T.B. Sheets," except that it must be far more romantically easy to sit and watch someone you love die than to watch them in the bloom of youth and health and know that you can never, ever have them, can never even speak to them.

"Madame George" is the album's whirlpool. Possibly one of the most compassionate pieces of music ever made, it asks us, no, *arranges* that we see the plight of what I'll be brutal and call a lovelorn drag queen with such intense empathy that when the singer hurts him, we do too. (Morrison has said in at least one interview that the song has nothing to do with any kind of transvestite—at least as far as *he* knows, he is quick to add—but that's bullshit.) The beauty, sensitivity, *holiness* of the song is that there's nothing at all sensationalistic, exploitative, or tawdry about it; in a way Van is right when he insists it's not about a drag queen, as my friends were right and I was wrong about the "pedophilia"—it's about a *person,* like all the best songs, all the greatest literature.

The setting is the same as that of the previous song—Cyprus Avenue, apparently a place where people drift, impelled by desire, into moments of flesh-wracking, sight-curdling confrontation with their destinies. It's an elemental place of pitiless judgment—wind and rain figure in both songs—and, interestingly enough, it's a place of the even crueler judgment of adults by *children*, in both cases love objects absolutely indifferent to their would-be adult lovers. Madame George's little boys are downright contemptuous—like the street urchins who end up cannibalizing the homosexual cousin in Tennessee Williams's *Suddenly Last Summer,* they're only too happy to come around as long as there's music, party times, free drinks and smokes, and only too gleefully spit on George's affections when all the other stuff runs out, the entombing winter settling in with not only wind and rain but hail, sleet, and snow.

What might seem strangest of all but really isn't is that it's exactly those characteristics which supposedly should make George most pathetic—age, drunkenness, the way the boys take his money and trash his love—that awakens something for George in the heart of the kid whose song this is. Obviously the kid hasn't simply "fallen in love with love," or something like that, but rather—what? Why, just exactly that only sunk in the foulest perversions could one human being love another for anything *other* than their humanness: love him for his weakness, his flaws, finally perhaps his decay. Decay is human—that's one of the ultimate messages here, and I don't by any stretch of the lexicon mean decadence. I mean that in this song or whatever inspired it Van Morrison saw the absolute possibility of loving human beings at the farthest extreme of wretchedness, and that the implications of that are terrible indeed, far more terrible than the mere sight of bodies made ugly by age or the seeming absurdity of a man devoting his life to the wobbly artifice of trying to look like a woman.

You can say to love the questions you have to love the answers which quicken the end of love that's loved to love the awful inequality of human experience that loves to say we tower over these the lost that love to love the love that freedom could have been, the train to freedom, but we never get on, we'd rather wave generously walking away from those who are victims of themselves. But who is to say that someone who victimizes him- or herself is not as worthy of total compassion as the most down and out Third World orphan in a *New Yorker* magazine ad? Nah, better to step over the bodies, at least that gives them the respect they might have once deserved. Where I live, in New York (not to make it more than it is, which is hard), everyone I know often steps over bodies which might well be dead or dying as a matter of course, without pain. And I wonder in what scheme it was originally conceived that such action is showing human refuse the ultimate respect it deserves.

There is of course a rationale—what else are you going to do—but it holds no more than our fear of our own helplessness in the face of the plain of life as it truly is: a plain which extends into an infinity beyond the horizons we have only invented. Come on, die it. As I write this, I can read in the *Village Voice* the blurbs of people opening heterosexual S&M clubs in Manhattan, saying things like, "S&M is just another equally valid form of love. Why people can't accept that we'll never know." Makes you want to jump out a fifth floor window rather than even read about it, but it's hardly the end of the world; it's not nearly as bad as the hurts that go on everywhere everyday that are taken so casually by all of us as facts of life. Maybe it boils down to how much you actually want to subject yourself to. If you accept for even a moment the idea that each human life is as precious and delicate as a snowflake and then you look at a wino in a doorway, you've got to hurt until you feel like a sponge for all those other assholes' problems, until you feel like an asshole yourself, so you draw all the appropriate lines. You stop feeling. But you know that then you begin to die. So you tussle with yourself. How much of this horror can I actually allow myself to think about? Perhaps the numbest mannikin is wiser than somebody who only allows their sensitivity to drive them to destroy everything they touch—but then again, to tilt Madame George's hat a hair, just to recognize that that person exists, just to touch his cheek and then probably expire because the realization that you must share the world with him is ultimately unbearable is to go only the first mile. The realization of living is just about that low and that exalted and that unbearable and that sought-after. Please come back and leave me alone. But when we're alone together we can talk all we want about the universality of this abyss: it doesn't make any difference, the highest only meets the lowest for some lying succor, UNICEF to relatives, so you scratch and spit and curse in violent resignation at the strict fact that there is absolutely nothing you can do but finally reject anyone in greater pain than you. At such a moment, another breath is treason. That's why you leave your liberal causes, leave suffering humanity to die in worse squalor than they knew before you happened along. You got their hopes up. Which makes you viler than the most scrofulous carrion. Viler than the ignorant boys who would take Madame George for a couple of cigarettes. Because you have committed the crime of knowledge, and thereby not only walked past or over someone you knew to be suffering, but also violated their privacy, the last possession of the dispossessed.

Such knowledge is possibly the worst thing that can happen to a person (a *lucky* person), so it's no wonder that Morrison's protagonist turned away from Madame George, fled to the train station, trying to run as far away from what he'd seen as a lifetime could get him. And no wonder, too, that Van Morrison never came this close to looking life square in the face again, no wonder he turned to *Tupelo Honey* and even *Hard Nose the Highway* with its entire side of songs about falling leaves. In *Astral Weeks* and "T.B. Sheets" he confronted enough for any man's lifetime. Of course, having been offered this immeasurably stirring and equally frightening gift from Morrison, one can hardly be blamed for not caring terribly much about Old, Old Woodstock and little homilies like "You've Got to Make It Through This World on Your Own" and "Take It Where You Find It."

On the other hand, it might also be pointed out that desolation, hurt, and anguish are hardly the only things in life, or in *Astral Weeks.* They're just the things, perhaps, that we can most easily grasp and explicate, which I suppose shows about what level our souls have evolved to. I said I wouldn't reduce the other songs on this album by trying to explain them, and I won't. But that doesn't mean that, all things considered, a juxtaposition of poets might not be in order.

> If I ventured in the slipstream
> Between the viaducts of your dreams
> Where the mobile steel rims crack
> And the ditch and the backroads stop
> Could you find me
> Would you kiss my eyes
> And lay me down
> In silence easy
> To be born again
>   —Van Morrison

My heart of silk
is filled with lights,
with lost bells,
with lilies and bees.
I will go very far,
farther than those hills,
farther than the seas,
close to the stars,
to beg Christ the Lord
to give back the soul I had
of old, when I was a child,
ripened with legends,
with a feathered cap
and a wooden sword.
                    —Federico García Lorca

                    —*Stranded,* 1979

PART TWO

Blowing
It Up

Of Pop and Pies and Fun

A Program for Mass Liberation in the Form of a Stooges Review, or, Who's the Fool?

PART ONE: ANATOMY OF DISEASE

Like most authentic originals, the Stooges have endured more than their share of abuse, derision, critical condescension and even outright hostility. Their stage act is good copy but easy grist for instant wag putdowns. At first glance their music appears to be so simple that it seems like anyone with rudimentary training should be able to play it (that so few *can* produce any reasonable facsimile, whatever their abilities, is overlooked). While critics have a ball crediting John Cale with the success of *The Stooges,* their first album (as I did), and relegating them to the status of a more than slightly humorous teenage phenomenon, theme music for suburban high school kids freaked out on reds and puberty and fantasies of nihilistic apocalypses, the majority of the listening public seems to view them with almost equal scorn as just one more blaring group whose gimmick (Iggy) still leaves them leagues behind such get-it-on frontrunners in the Heavy sets as Grand Funk, whose songs at least make *sense,* whose act shows *real* showmanship (i.e., inducing vast hordes of ecstatically wasted freaks to charge the stage waving those thousands of hands in the air in a display of marginally political unity 'nuff to warm the heart of any Movement stumper), and who never make fools of themselves the way that Stooge punk does, what with his clawing at himself, smashing the mike in his chops, jumping into the crowd to wallow around a forest of legs and ankles and god knows what else while screaming those sickening songs about TV eyes and feeling like dirt and not having no fun 'cause you're a fucked up adolescent, horny but neurotic, sitting around bored and lonesome and unable to communicate with yourself or anybody else. Shit. Who needs songs like that, that give off such bad vibes? We got a groovy, beautifully insular hip community, maybe a nation, budding here, and our art is a celebration of ourselves as liberated individuals and masses of such—the People, dig? And antisocial art simply don't fit in, brothers and sisters. Who wants to be depressed, anyway?

Well, a lot of changes have gone down since Hip first hit the heartland. There's a new culture shaping up, and while it's certainly an improvement on the repressive society now nervously aging, there is a strong element of sickness in our new, amorphous institutions. The cure bears viruses of its own. The Stooges also carry a strong element of sickness in their music, a crazed quaking uncertainty, an errant foolishness that effectively mirrors the absurdity and desperation of the times, but I believe that they also carry a strong element of cure, a post-derangement sanity. And I also believe that their music is as important as the product of any rock group working today, although you better never call it art or you may wind up with a deluxe pie in the face. What it is, instead, is what rock and roll at heart is and always has been, beneath the stylistic distortions the last few years have wrought. The Stooges are not for the ages—nothing created now is—but they are most implicitly for today and tomorrow and the traditions of two decades of beautifully bopping, manic, simplistic jive.

To approach *Fun House* we've got to go back to the beginning, to all the blather and arbitration left in the wake of notoriety and a first album. Because there is a lot of bad air around, and we've got to clear away the mundane murk of ignorance and incomprehension if we're going to let the *true*, immaculate murk of the Stooges shine forth in all its chaotic prisms like those funhouse mirrors which distract so pointedly. I don't want to have to be an apologist for the Stooges. I would like it if we lived in sanity, where every clear eye could just look and each whole mind appreciate the Stooges on their own obvious merits (even though, granted, in such an environment the Stooges would no longer be necessary—as William Burroughs counseled in one of his lucider epigrams, they really do work to make themselves obsolete). However, since conditions are in the present nigh irremediable mess, with innocent listeners led and hyped, and duped and doped, taught to grovel before drug-addled effeminate Limeys who once collected blues 78s and a few guitar lessons and think that that makes them torch-bearers; a hapless public, finally, of tender boys and girls pavlov'd into salivating greenbacks and stoking reds at the mere utterance of certain magic incantations like "supergroup" and "superstar"—well, is it any wonder your poor average kid, cruisin' addled down the street in vague pursuit of snatch or reds or rock mag newsstands, ain't got no truck with the Stooges?

So, to facilitate the mass psychic liberation necessary, it's imperative that we start with the eye of the hurricane, the center of all the confusion, contention and plain badmouthing, Iggy Stooge himself. Now, I've never met Iggy but from what I've gathered listening to his records and digging the stage act and all, he's basically a nice sensitive American boy growing up amid a thicket of some of the worst personal, interpersonal and national confusion we've seen. I mean, nowhere else but in America would you find a phenomenon like Iggy Stooge, right? I was at one time going to write a letter to Malcolm Muggeridge over in England telling him all about Iggy and the Stooges, but I didn't because I finally decided that he'd just mark it up as one more symptom of the decline of Western civilization. Which it's not. Not *finally,* that is—it may be now, in some of its grosser, semi-pathological trappings, but then look what it came out of. There's always hope for a brighter tomorrow because today's mess spawned stalwart crusaders for something better like Iggy. And, presumably, the rest of the Stooges.

So, Iggy: a pre-eminently American kid, singing songs about growing up in America, about being hung up lotsa the time (as who hasn't been?), about confusion and doubt and uncertainty, about inertia and boredom and suburban pubescent darkness because "I'm not right / To want somethin' / To want somethin' / Tonight. . . ." Sitting around, underaged, narcissistic, masochistic, deep in gloom cuz we *could* have a real cool time but I'm not right, whether from dope or day drudgery or just plain neurotic do-nothing misanthropy, can't get through ("You don't know me / Little Doll / And I don't know you . . .")—ah well, wait awhile, maybe some fine rosy-fleshed little doll with real eyes will come along and marry you and then you'll get some. Until then, though, it shore ain't no fun, so swagger with your buddies, brag, leer at passing legs, whack your doodle at home at night gaping at polyethylene bunnies hugging teddy bears, go back the next day and dope out with the gang, grass, speed, reds, Romilar, who cares, some frat bull's gonna buy us beer, and after that you go home and stare at the wall all cold and stupid inside and think, what the fuck, what the fuck. I hate myself. Same damn thing last year, this year, on and on till I'm an old fart if I live that long. Shit. Think I'll rape my wank-fantasy cunt dog-style tonight.

Pretty depressing, eh? Sheer adolescent drivel. Banal, too. Who needs music with a theme like that? What does it have to do with reality, with the new social systems the Panthers and Yips are cookin' up, with the fact that I took acid four days ago and since then everything is smooth with no hangups like it always is for about a week after a trip? Feel good, benevolent. So what the fuck does all that Holden Caulfield garbage Iggy Stooge is always prattling about have to do with me? Or with art or rock 'n' roll or anything? Sure, we all know about adolescence, why belabor it, why burden "art" (or whatever the Stooges claim that caterwauling is) with something better left in the recesses of immature brains who'll eventually grow out of it themselves? And how, in the name of all these obvious logical realities, can any intelligent person take Iggy Stooge for anything but a blatant fool, wild-eyed, sweaty and loud though he may be?

Well, I'll tell ya why and how. I've been building up through lots of questions and postulations and fantasies, so not one dullard reading this and owning a stack of dated, boring "rock" albums but no Stooge music can fail to comprehend, at which time I will be able to get on to the business of describing the new Stooges album. So here comes the payload. Now, to answer the last question first, because the final conclusion of all Stooge-mockers is definitely true and central to the Stooges: you're goddam right Iggy Stooge is a damn fool. He does a lot better job of making a fool of himself on stage and vinyl than almost any other performer I've ever seen. That is one of his genius's central facets.

What we need are more rock "stars" willing to make fools of themselves, absolutely jump off the deep end and make the audience embarrassed for them if necessary, so long as they have not one shred of dignity or mythic corona left. Because then the whole damn pompous edifice of this supremely ridiculous rock 'n' roll industry, set up to grab bucks by conning youth and encouraging fantasies of a puissant "youth culture," would collapse, and with it would collapse the careers of the hyped talentless nonentities who breed off of it. Can you imagine Led Zeppelin without Robert Plant conning the audience: "I'm gonna give you every inch of my love"—he really gives them nothing, not even a good-natured grinful "Howdy-do"—or Jimmy Page's arch scowl of supermusician ennui?

A friend and I were getting stoned and watching the TV eye's broadcast of the Cincinnati Pop Festival the other night when a great (i.e., useless) idea struck us. Most of the show was boring, concentrating on groups like Grand Funk (endless plodding version of "Inside Looking Out" with lead singer writhing and barking and making up new lyrics like "Oh little honey I need your love so *bad* . . . c'mon, give it to me . . . oh, little mama" etc.) and Mountain (Felix Pappalardi spinning off endless dull solos in a flat distillation of the most overworked elements of Cream's and Creedence's sounds, while fat buckskinned Leslie West thumped guitar and reacted to Pappalardi's piddle with broad, joyously agonized mugging, grimacing and grinning and nodding as if each and every *note* out of Papa's bass was just blowing his mind like no music he'd ever heard before). Well, I watched all this monkey business with one eye scanning the bookshelf for a likely volume to pass the time till Iggy hit the tube, and when he did it was fine—not as good as watching Carlos Santana squint and Cunt Joe spell out "FUCK" in *Woodstock,* mind you, but a fine video spread anyhoo— but the part of the show that intrigued us the most came in Alice Cooper's set (who, however gratingly shrill their amphetamine-queen hysteria, certainly can't be accused of taking themselves seriously—come the revolution, they don't get offed with Pappalardi and West and George Harrison and all them other cats), when Alice crouched, threw his billowy cape over his stringy mop like a monk's cowl, exposing his hormone-plasticized torso, and crept duckwalking like some Chuck Berry from a henbane nightmare to the apron of the stage, where he produced a pocket watch, set it hypnotically in motion, and started chanting in a calm conversational tone: "Bodies . . . need . . . rest"—repeating it at same tempo till finally some (genuinely wise) wiseacre a few bodies into the crowd piped up, "So what?" Good question. What if somebody said "So what?" when Richie Havens started into his righteous "Freedom" number? Of course, the question is stupid since three dozen devout Richie Havens fans would promptly clobber the boorish loudmouth, if not off him completely (in line with the temper of the times, in which case he'd be post-mortemed a pig). But nobody gives a shit what anybody sez to A.C. least of all A.C., who was probably disappointed at not soliciting more razzberries from the peanut gallery, except that a moment later he got his crowd reaction in spades when some accomplished marksman in the mob lobbed a whole *cake* (or maybe it was a pie—yeah, let's say it was a pie just for the sake of the fantasy I'm about to promulgate) which hit him square in the face. So there he was: Alice Cooper, rock star, crouched frontstage in the middle of his act with a faceful of pie and cream with clots dripping from his ears and chin. So what did he do? How did he recoup the sacred time-honored dignity of the performing artist which claims the stage as *his* magic force field from which to bedazzle and *entertain* the helpless audience? Well, he pulled a handful of pie gook out of his face and slapped it right back again, smearing it into his pores and eyes and sneaking the odd little fingerlicking taste. Again and again he repeated the gesture, smearing it in good. The audience said not another word.

The point of all this is not to elicit sympathy for Alice Cooper, but rather to point out that in a way Alice Cooper is better than Richie Havens (even though both make dull music) because at least with Alice Cooper you have the prerogative to express your reaction to his show in a creative way. Most rock stars have their audiences so cowed it's nauseating. What blessed justice it would be if *all* rock stars had to contend with what A.C. elicits, if it became a common practice and method of passing judgment for audiences to regularly fling pies in the faces of performers whom they thought were coming on with a load of bullshit. Because the top rockers have a mythic aura around them, the "superstar," and that's a basically unhealthy state of things, in fact it's the very virus that's fucking up rock, a subspecies of the virus I spoke of earlier which infests "our" culture from popstars to politics (imagine throwing a pie in the face of Eldridge Cleaver! Joan Baez!), and which the Stooges uncategorically oppose as an advance platoon in the nearing war to clear conned narcoleptic mindscreens of the earth, eventually liberating us all from basically uncreative lifestyles in which people often lacking half the talent or personality or charisma of you or I are elevated into godlike positions. Pure pomp and circumstance.

So now you see what I'm driving at, why the Stooges are vital, aside from being good musicians, which I'll prove just as tangentially later. It takes courage to make a fool of yourself, to say, "See, this is all a sham, this whole show and all its floodlit drug-jacked realer-than-life trappings, and the fact that you are out there and I am up here means not the slightest thing." Because it *doesn't*. The Stooges have that kind of courage, but few other performers do. Jim Morrison, of late—how inspiring to see the onetime atropine-eyed Byronic S&M Lizard King come clean stumbling around the stage with a Colt 45 in hand and finally wave his dong at the teeny minions who came there to see him hold both it and his gut in and give them some more vivid production which communicated nothing real but *suggested* everything a fertile pube brain could dredge up! Morrison, def, does not get a pie in the face! He 'fessed up! And even old John Lennon, who for a while qualified for the first and biggest pie (to drown him and Yoko both in slush as ersatz as that which they originally excreted on the entire Western world), has set such a consistent record for absurd self-parody above and beyond the needs of the revolution (like saying "I gave back the MBE also because 'Cold Turkey' was slipping down the charts"—a fine gesture. We won't forget it later, either) that he too qualifies for at least a year's moratorium from the creem guerrillas. But then there's all those *other people*—George Harrison (a giant pie stuffed with the complete works of Manly P. Hall) and that infernal snob McCartney and those radical dilettante capitalist pigs the Jefferson Airplane (it's all right to be a honky, in fact all the Marxists are due for some pies in pronto priority, but to wit on all that bread singin' bout bein' an outlaw when yer most scurrilous illegal set is ripping off lyrics from poor old A. A. Milne and struggling sci-fi hacks, wa'al, the Creem Committee don't cotton to that, neighbor).

Similarly, Mick Jagger gets immediate pie-ority as a fake moneybags revolutionary, and in general for acting smarter and hipper and like more of a cultural and fashion arbiter than he really is. If Jesus had been at Altamont, they would have crucified him, but if Mick Jagger makes me wait forty-five minutes while he primps and stones up in his dressing room one more time and then blames it on some poor menial instrument mover, then me and the corps are goin' stageward with both tins blazing when he does show his fish-eyed mug. And he's far from the worst offender—in fact, as a performing artist, he's one of the least offensive around—his show, with its leers and minces has always been outrageous and foolish and absurd and transcendentally arrogant, yet pretentious only in the best possible way, a spastic flap-lipped tornado writhing from here to a million steaming snatches and beyond in one undifferentiated erogenous mass, a mess and a spectacle all at the same time. You won't catch Mick Jagger lost in solemn grimaces of artistic angst, no sir! So he really is almost as good as the Stooges, in fact anticipated them, but I'd still hate to think of his tantrum if some grinning geek from down in the street tried to commandeer the sacred stage where he jerks out and rips off his rushes. In that sense his whole show is another anachronism, though nowhere near as fossilized as most other rock acts, who will drown in creem and crust before we're through. The plain fact is that 99% of popstars do not have the true charisma, style or stature to hold their bastion (Bastille) stage without the artificial support they've traditionally enjoyed. Most of them, were they splat in the kisser with a pie or confronted with an audience composed of *sane* people demanding calmly (crude militant bullshit is out), "What the fuck do you think you are doing? Just what is all this shit?"—most of your current "phenomenons," "heroes" and "artists" would just fold up a stupefied loss, temperamentally incapable (by virtue of the debilitating spoiled-brat life they've been living, even if they ever had any real pizazz in the first place—the oppressor is fat and weak, brothers!) of dealing with their constituency of wised-up marks on a one-to-one basis. They simply don't have enough personality, enough brains or enough guts, your average popstar being neither very bright nor very aware of much that goes on outside his own glittering substratum, half lodged in fantasy, where ego and preening vanity are overfed and corrode substance like a constant diet of cocaine.

But the Stooges are one band that does have the strength to meet any audience on its own terms, no matter what manner of devilish bullshit that audience might think up (although they are usually too cowed by Ig's psychically pugnacious assertiveness to do anything but gape and cringe slightly, snickering later on the drive home). Iggy is like a matador baiting the vast dark hydra sitting afront him—he enters the audience frequently to see what's what and even from the stage his eyes reach out searchingly, sweeping the joint and singling out startled strangers who're seldom able to stare him down. It's your stage as well as his and if you can take it away from him, why, welcome to it. But the King of the Mountain must maintain the pace, and the authority, and few can. In this sense Ig is a true star of the rarest kind—he has won that stage, and nothing but the force of his own presence entitles him to it.

Here's this smug post-hippie audience, supposedly so loose, liberated, righteous and ravenous, the anarchic terror of middle American insomnia. These are the folks that're always saying: "Someday, somebody's gonna just bust that fucked-up punk right in the chops!" And how many times have you heard people say of bands: "Man, what a shuck! *I* could get up there and cut that shit."

Well, here's your chance. The Stooge act is wide open. Do your worst, People, falsify Iggy and the Stooges, get your kicks and biffs. It's your night!

No takers. They sit there, wide-eyed vegetative Wowers or sullen in a carapace of Cool, afraid or unable to react, to get out there in that arena which is nothing more than life, most often too cowed to even hurl a disappointing hoot stageward. And that is why most rock bands are so soporifically lazy these days, and also why the Stooges, and any other band that challenges its audience, are the answer. Power doesn't go to the people, it comes *from* them, and when the people have gotten this passive nothing short of electroshock and personal exorcism will jolt them and rock them into some kind of fiercely healthy interaction.

Alice Cooper experiments along similar lines, but their routines are really just as old-hat as everybody else's. Flinging dead chickens and carting around props of every size and shape, utilizing splintery deluges of screaming feedback (Velvet Underground, 1965) to attack the nervous systems of the presumably uptight section of the audience whilst raping their libidos with an outrageous blitz of shifting sexual identities and "perversions"— that's just the old *épater la bourgeoisie* riff again, and for all the talk of Artaud and audiences convulsed with certain unstable souls in frothing fits, it still and f'rever will remain that A.C. is putting on a show in the hoary DC manner, and with fewer and fewer people game for sprained sexual sensibilities, since nobody gives a fuck anymore, a seemingly futuristic band like this must fall back on its music, which is too bad, because there's not much happening there outside the context of the act, as their records bear out. So Alice Cooper's slithering around and doing methedrine somersaults in drag, so Jim Morrison finally shows the fans his cock, so what. It's gonna get to the point where Mick Jagger can turn tinkling mandalas across the stage in troilist hubbub with three groupies performing simultaneous services at all his orifices while the Rolling Stones play on a "seemingly" (although the Deep Meaning contingent in each audience will still whisper desperate stabs at what it all Signifies—and the Stones will go on letting it bleed cross the decades into Sun City) unrelated stream of Chuck Berry riffs and Mick comes and the groupies groan and wet sparks fly everywhere like tickertape and no one in the crotch-jaded audience blinks an eye. Mark my words.

So gimmicks have had their day. Where does that leave us now? Where else: with Ig and the Stooges, whom it is finally my pleasure to return to. Because beside the mawkish posturings and nickelodeon emotings of three-quarters of the duds foisted on today's public, the earthy brilliance, power and clarity of Stooge music, though its basic components may resemble those ready-made musical materials lying around in the public domain like Tinkertoys for experimentation by every jerkoff group from Stockholm to San Diego, will nevertheless shine in the dark carnivorous glow of its own genius.

The first thing to remember about Stooge music is that it is monotonous and simplistic on purpose, and that within the seemingly circumscribed confines of this fuzz-feedback territory the Stooges work deftly with musical ideas that may not be highly sophisticated (God forbid) but are certainly advanced. The stunningly simple two-chord guitar line mechanically reiterated all through "1969" on their first album, for instance, is nothing by itself, but within the context of the song it takes on a muted but very compelling power as an ominous, and yes, in the words of Ed Ward which were more perceptive (and more of an accolade) than he ever suspected, "mindless" rhythmic pulsation repeating itself into infinity and providing effective hypnotic counterpoint to the sullen plaint of Iggy's words (and incidentally, Ig writes some of the best throwaway lines in rock, meaning some of the best *lines* in rock, which is basically a music meant to be tossed over the shoulder and off the wall: "Now I'm gonna be twenty-two / I say my-my and-a boo-hoo"—that's classic—he couldn't've picked a better line to complete the rhyme if he'd labored into 1970 and threw the *I Ching* into the bargain—thank God somebody making rock 'n' roll records still has the good sense, understood by our zoot-jive forefathers but few bloated current bands, to know when to just throw down a line and let it lie).

Now *there's* a song just packed with ideas for you, simplistic and "stupid" though it may seem and well be. A trained monkey could probably learn to play that two-chord line underneath, but no monkeys and very few indeed of their cousins half a dozen rungs up on the evolutionary ladder, the "heavy" white rock bands, could think of utilizing it in the vivid way it is here, with a simplicity so basic it's almost pristine. Seemingly the most obvious thing in the world, I would call it a stroke of genius at least equal to Question Mark and the Mysterians' endless one-finger one-key organ drone behind the choruses of "96 Tears," which is one of the greatest rock and roll songs of all time and the real beginning of my story, for it was indeed a complex chronology, the peculiar machinations of rock 'n' roll history from about 1965 on, which ultimately made the Stooges imperative.

PART TWO: BRIEF HISTORY LESSON

I used to hate groups like Question Mark and the Mysterians. They seemed to represent everything simpleminded and dead-endish about rock in a time when groups like the Who and the Yardbirds were writing whole new chapters of musical prophecy almost monthly; certainly we've never known music more advanced at the time of its inception than the likes of "I'm a Man," "Anyway Anyhow Anywhere," "My Generation" and "Shapes of Things." The Yardbirds I especially idolized. Eventually, though, I wised up to the fact that the Yardbirds for all their greatness would finally fizzle out in an eclectic morass of confused experiments and bad judgments, and hardest of all to learn was that the only spawn possible to them were lumbering sloths like Led Zeppelin, because the musicians in the Yardbirds were just too *good,* too accomplished and cocky to do anything but fuck up in the aftermath of an experiment that none of them seemed to understand anyway. And similarly, the Who, erupting with some of the most trail-blazing music ever waxed, got "good" and arty with subtle eccentric songs and fine philosophy, a steadily dilating rep, and all this accomplishment sailing them steadily further from the great experiment they'd begun.

So all these beautiful ideas and raw materials were just lying around waiting for *anybody* to pick them up and elaborate them further into vast baroque structures that would retain the primordial rock and roll drive whilst shattering all the accumulated straitjackets of key and time signature which vanguard jazz musicians had begun to dispose of almost a decade before. By now jazz was in the second stage of its finest experimental flowering, in that beautiful night of headlong adventure before the stale trailoff workaday era which has now set in. The Albert Ayler who is now spooning out quasi-cosmic concept albums cluttered with inept rock ripoffs and sloppy playing was then exploding with works like *Spiritual Unity*'s free-flying Ozark-tinged "Ghosts," and Archie Shepp had not yet passed from *Fire Music* into increasingly virulent Crow-Jim nihilism. Jazz was way out front, clearing a path into a new era of truly free music, where the only limits were the musician's own consciousness and imagination, a music that cut across all boundaries yet still made perfect sense and swung like no music had ever swung before.

Clearly, rock had a lot of catching up to do. We could all see the possibilities for controlling the distortions of Who/Yardbirds feedback and fuzz for a new free music that would combine the rambling adventurousness of the new free jazz with the steady, compelling heartbeat of rock, but the strange part was that nobody with these ideas seemed to play guitar or any of the necessary instruments, while all the budding guitarists weaned on Lonnie Mack and Dick Dale and Duane Eddy and now presumably ready to set out for the unknown were too busy picking up on the sudden proliferation of borrowed, more accessible forms that came with the sixties renaissance. Christ, why go fuck with screaming noise when there were Mike Bloomfield's and George Harrison's newest ideas and all that folk rock to woodshed with?

About this time it also began to look like a decided majority of the rising bands were composed of ex-folkies, as opposed to previous waves whose roots had lain in fifties rock and R&B but never crossed paths with the college mobs of coffee house banjo-pickers, who almost unanimously, from Kingston Trio frat sweaters to hip Baez/Lightnin' Hopkins "purists," looked down their noses at that ugly juvenile noise called rock 'n' roll which they all presumed to have grown out of into more esthetically rewarding tastes (or, in other words, a buncha fuckin' effete snobs).

Well, I never grew out of liking noise, from Little Richard to Cecil Taylor to John Cage to the Stooges, so I always liked rock and grabbed hungrily at the Yardbirds/Who development, expecting great things. Meanwhile, all these folkies who grew out of the jolly Kennedy era camaraderie of "This Land Is Your Land" singalongs into grass and increasing alienation were deciding that the rock 'n' roll stuff warn't so bad: it, not they, was getting better (I'm sure I'm simplifying this a bit, but not much, I fear, not much). So they got electric guitars and started mixing all the musics stored in their well-educated little beans up together, and before we knew it we had Art-rock.

Some of the groups that came out of this watershed were among rock's best ever: the Byrds, the early Airplane, etc. But the total effect, I think, was to set the experiment begun by those second-string English bands back by at least two years. You kept listening for something really creative and free to emerge from all the syntheses, but in the end it mostly just seemed competent and predictable. Raga-rock and other such phases with marginal potential came and went, and the Byrds did a few far-out but seldom followed-up things like "Eight Miles High," while the Stones kept on being great following the trends like the old standbys they had already become. The Airplane hinted at a truly radical (in the musical sense) evolution in *After Bathing at Baxter's*, but the most advanced statement they could seem to manage was the Sandy Bull–like standardized electric guitar raga of "Spare Chaynge." Clearly something was wrong. Rock soaked up influences like some big sponge and went meandering on, but no one in the day's pantheon would really risk it out on the outer-edge tightrope of true noise. 1967 brought *Sgt. Pepper* and psychedelia: the former, after our initial acid-vibes infatuation with it, threatening to herald an era of rock-as-movie-soundtrack, and the latter suggesting the possibility of real (if most likely unconscious) breakthrough in all the fuzztone and groping space jams. Even local bands were beginning to experiment with feedback but neither they nor the names they followed knew what to do with it.

Meanwhile, rumblings were beginning to be heard almost simultaneously on both coasts: Ken Kesey embarked the Acid Tests with the Grateful Dead in Frisco, and Andy Warhol left New York to tour the nation with his Exploding Plastic Inevitable shock show (a violent, sadomasochistic barrage on the senses and the sensibilities of which Alice Cooper is the comparatively innocuous comic book reflection) and the Velvet Underground. Both groups on both coasts claimed to be utilizing the possibilities of feedback and distortion, and both claimed to be the avatars of the psychedelic multimedia trend. Who got the jump on who between Kesey and Warhol is insignificant, but it seems likely that the Velvet Underground were definitely eclipsing the Dead from the start when it came to a new experimental music. The Velvets, for all the seeming crudity of their music, were interested in the possibilities of noise right from the start, and had John Cale's extensive conservatory training to help shape their experiments, while the Dead seemed more like a group of ex-folkies just dabbling in distortion (as their albums eventually bore out).

By the time the Velvets recorded "Sister Ray," they seemed to have carried the Yardbirds/Who project to its ultimate extension, and turned in their third album to more "conventionally" lyrical material. Also, their two largely experimental albums had earned them little more than derision (if not outright animosity) among critics and the listening audience at large. Their music, which might at first hearing seem merely primitive, unmusicianly and chaotic, had at its best sharply drawn subtleties and outer sonances cutting across a stiff, simplistic beat that was sometimes ("Heroin") even lost, and many of the basic guitar lines were simple in the extreme when compared with the much more refined (but also more *defined*, prevented by its very form and purposes from ever leaping free) work of groups like the Byrds and Airplane. I was finally beginning to grasp something.

Sixties avant-garde jazz is in large part a very complex music. The most basic, classic rock, on the other hand, is almost idiotically simple, monotonous melodies over two or three chords and a four-four beat. What was suddenly becoming apparent was that there was no reason why you couldn't play truly free music to a basic backbeat, gaining the best of both worlds. Many jazz drummers, like Milford Graves and Sunny Murray, were distending the beat into a whirling flurry that was almost arrhythmic, or even throwing it out altogether. So if you could do that, why couldn't you find some way of fitting some of the new jazz ideas in with a Question Mark and the Mysterians type format?

It was also becoming evident that the nascent generation of ex-folkie rock stars, like the British beat and R&B groups which preceded them in '64, were never going to get off their rich idolized asses to even take a fling at any kind of free music. They simply knew too much about established musical forms which the last three decades of this century should make moribund, and were too smug about it to do anything else. So the only hope for a free rock 'n' roll renaissance which would be true to the original form, rescue us from all this ill-conceived dilettantish pap so far removed from the soil of jive, and leave some hope for truly adventurous small-guitar-group experiments in the future, would be if all those ignorant teenage dudes out there learning guitar in hick towns and forming bands to play "96 Tears" and "Wooly Bully" at sock hops, evolving exposed to all the eclectic trips but relatively fresh and free too (at least they hadn't grown up feeling snobbish about being among the intellectual elite who could appreciate some arcane folksong), if only they could somehow, some of them somewhere, escape the folk/*Sgt. Pepper* virus, pick up on nothing but roots and noise and the possibilities inherent in approaching the guitar fresh in the age of multiple amp distorting switches, maybe even get exposed to a little of the free jazz which itself seemed rapidly to be fading into its own kind of anachronism, then, just *maybe,* given all those ifs, we might have some hope.

Well, maybe the gods were with us this time around, because sure enough it happened. On a small scale, of course—the majority of people listening to and playing rock were still mired in blues and abortive "classical" hybrids and new shitkicker rock and every other conceivable manner of uninventively "artistic" jerkoff. But there were some bands coming up. Captain Beefheart burst upon us with the monolithic *Trout Mask Replica,* making history and distilling the best of both idioms into new styles undreamed of, but somehow we still wanted something else, something closer to the mechanical, mindless heart of noise and the relentless piston rhythms which seemed to represent the essence of both American life and American rock 'n' roll.

Bands were sprouting and decaying like ragweed everywhere. The MC5 came on with a pre-records hype that promised the moon, and failed to get off the launching pad. Black Pearl appeared with a promising first album—no real experiments, but a distinct Yardbirds echo in the metallic clanging cacophony of precisely distorted guitars. Their second LP fizzled out in bad soul music.

PART THREE: THE OUTLINE OF CURE

And, finally, the Stooges. The Stooges were the first young American group to acknowledge the influence of the Velvet Underground—and it shows heavily in their second album. The early Velvets had the good sense to realize that whatever your capabilities, music with a simple base was the best. Thus, "Sister Ray" evolved from a most basic funk riff seventeen minutes into stark sound structures of incredible complexity. The Stooges started out not being able to do anything else *but* play rock-bottom simple—they formed the concept of the band before half of them knew how to play, which figures—probably just another bunch of disgruntled cats with ideas watching all the bullshit going down. Except that the Stooges decided to do something about it. None of them have been playing their instruments for more than two or three years, but that's *good*—now they won't have to unlearn any of the stuff which ruins so many other promising young musicians: flash blues, folk-pickin', Wes Montgomery–style jazz, etc. Fuck that, said Asheton and Alexander, we can't play it anyway, so why bother trying to learn? Especially since even most of those styles' virtuosos are so fucking boring you wonder how anyone with half a brain can listen to them.

Cecil Taylor, in A. B. Spellman's moving book *Four Lives in the Bebop Business,* once told a story about an experience he had in the mid-fifties, when almost every club owner, jazz writer and listener in New York was turned off to his music because it was still so new and so advanced that they could not begin to grasp it yet. Well, one night he was playing in one of these clubs when in walked this dude off the street with a double bass and asked if he could sit in. Why not, said Taylor, even though the cat seemed very freaked out. So they jammed, and it soon became apparent to Taylor that the man had never had any formal training on bass, knew almost nothing about it beyond the basic rudiments, and probably couldn't play one *known* song or chord progression. Nothing. The guy had just picked up the bass, decided he was going to play it, and a very short time later walked cold into a New York jazz club and bluffed his way onto the bandstand. He didn't even know how to hold the instrument, so he just explored as a child would, pursuing songs or evocative sounds through the tangles of his ignorance. And after a while, Taylor said, he began to hear something coming out, something deeply felt and almost but never quite controlled, veering between a brand-new type of song which cannot be taught because it comes from an unschooled innocence which cuts across known systems, and chaos, which playing the player and spilling garble, sometimes begins to write its own songs. Something was beginning to take shape which, though erratic, was unique in all this world. Quite abruptly, though, the man disappeared, most likely to freak himself into oblivion, because Taylor never saw or heard of him again. But he added that if the cat had kept on playing, he would have been one of the first great free bassists.

The Stooges' music is like that. It comes out of an illiterate chaos gradually taking shape as a uniquely personal style, emerges from a tradition of American music that runs from the wooly rags of backwoods string bands up to the magic promise eternally made and occasionally fulfilled by rock: that a band can start out bone-primitive, untutored and uncertain, and evolve into a powerful and eloquent ensemble. It's happened again and again: the Beatles, Kinks, Velvets, etc. But the Stooges are probably the first name group to actually form before they even knew how to play. This is possibly the ultimate rock 'n' roll story, because rock is mainly about beginnings, about youth and uncertainty and growing through and out of them. And asserting yourself way before you know what the fuck you're doing. Which answers the question raised earlier of what the early Stooges' adolescent mopings had to do with rock 'n' roll. Rock is basically an adolescent music, reflecting the rhythms, concerns and aspirations of a very specialized age group. It *can't* grow up—when it does, it turns into something else which may be just as valid but is still very different from the original. Personally I believe that real rock 'n' roll may be on the way out, just like adolescence as a relatively innocent transitional period is on the way out. What we will have instead is a small island of new free music surrounded by some good reworkings of past idioms and a vast sargasso sea of absolute garbage. And the Stooges' songs may have some of the last great rock 'n' roll lyrics, because everybody else seems either too sophisticated at the outset or hopelessly poisoned by the effects of big ideas on little minds. A little knowledge is still a dangerous thing.

Now, however, that we have cleared up some of the misconceptions and established the Stooges' place in the rock tradition, we can at long last get on to the joyous task of assessing *Fun House.* The first thing you notice about it is that it is much rawer and seemingly more erratic than the first album. In fact, the precise clarity of that set would seem now to be a John Cale false alarm. His influence on it was always apparent: the viola, of course, in "We Will Fall," and the insistent monotonous piano note piercing like weird sleighbells through "I Wanna Be Your Dog" is very reminiscent of the piano solo on the Velvets' "I'm Waiting for the Man." It seems probable now that Cale both made the Stooges' music more monotonous than it really was (although it's still fairly monotonous—it's just that the new monotony is so intensely sustained that you can't get bored), and "cleaned it up" some to make the premiere disc a definite statement, with all of Iggy's vocals absolutely intelligible and the instrumental sections precisely defined, if a bit restrained. The first set, on the whole, sounded almost more like a John Cale Production than whatever band the Stooges might be, and so we who had never heard them live looked forward to the second but nourished serious reservations about their musical abilities. They'd gotten very bad press—Chris Hodenfield had called them "stoned sloths" making "boring, repressed music [which] I suspect appeals to boring, repressed people" (hmmm, certainly would hate to be one of those—whaddaya hafta be, some sick creep to like the Stooges?—well, I guess Grand Funk *is* safer—but, on the other hand, might that not be the defensive reaction of people who're afraid *they* might be sick creeps and read their own nightmares into the Stooge story—just like so many people just absolutely *hated* the Velvet Underground for so long, and still do, one prominent *Rolling Stone* critic asking me when I asked him whether he'd heard *White Light/White Heat:* "Are they still doing fag stuff?"—no, friend, not to worry—they're doing MUSIC). And Robert Christgau wrote of fleeing a room where the Stooges were playing with a pounding headache, desperate to get away from them. Are they really that bad, or is so much critical revulsion an almost sure sign that there's something important going on here? Just like reading about Mighty Quick raising a whole roomful of Movement people to nigh homicidal wrath ("Off the pig band!") at the Alternative Media Conference—anybody who can piss off that many people just by standing on a stage and going through an act, no matter how bad it might be, must have *something* going for 'em.

The first time I played *Fun House* I got very turned off. I had hoped that at least some of the clarity of the first LP would hang on. I put it on, turned it up, and listened through headphones because it was near midnight. Every song sounded exactly the same, the textures seemed mighty muddy, as if the instruments were just grinding on in separate universes, and Iggy's vocals seemed much less distinctive than on the first—more like just any hollering kid. Also, I could make out almost none of the words. The last straw was the instrumental, "L.A. Blues," which closes side two —it just seemed to shriek and groan forever, a stumbling mess of feedback as offensive and pretentious and unmusical as Yoko Ono at her worst. I fell asleep under the phones, awoke to all that noise, jumped up and snapped it angrily off, muttering: "Good god, *enough* of that shit! The truth outs: the Stooges suck."

I played it again the next morning but barely heard it, and threw it aside after that, telling all my friends I thought it was one of the worst albums of the year, a pile of unredeemed shit. The day came a couple of weeks later, though, when a couple of friends came by and *demanded* to hear it. I put it on, grumbling. I was still pissed off because I thought I'd been had, led by hype and production to admire a group who seemed to have no talent whatsoever. And, hotshot rock critic that I fancied myself, it graveled my ass to have to make such a confession.

This time, though, I began to hear the record in a different way. Suddenly, sitting there hearing the music issue from speakers into the open air, it began to make sense. I played it again that night, and finally I was playing it all the time. Eventually I apprehended that the music on *Fun House* is neither sloppy (in the sense that a fuckoff group like Deep Purple is sloppy, cluttering up the songs with all kinds of inappropriate devices, not editing long fumbling solos, and generally behaving as if they don't know what the fuck they're doing) nor inept. It *is* as loose and raw an album as we've ever had, but every song possesses a built-in sense of intuitive taste which gives it an immediacy and propriety. Everything is flying frenziedly around, but as you begin to pick up the specific lines and often buried riffs from the furious torrent, you also notice that no sore thumbs stick out, no gestures half-realized or blatantly ill-conceived. And that's unusual for the school of metallic music which the Stooges supposedly hail from—think of Grand Funk's noxious sludge, Frost clanging along like a brassy fire engine, appealing but just a shade inhuman, the MC5's embarrassing duds like "Starship." The Stooges leave no loose ends—for an exercise in absolute raunch, they're mighty tidy and methodical.

All of which is to say that *Fun House* is one of those rare albums that never sits still quite long enough to actually solidify into what it previously seemed. Not always immediately accessible, it might take some getting into, but the time spent is well repaid. Because properly conceived and handled noise is not noise at all, but music whose textures just happen to be a little thicker and more involved than usual, so that you may not hear much but obscurity the first time, but various subsequent playings can open up whole sonic vistas you never dreamed were there. So you play the record many, many times, slowly making your way to the heartland of its diffuse complexity, then revelling long in its multiplicity, finally growing slowly tired of it months and innumerable playings later since *any* record gets old eventually. It's just that these sounds take longer to learn, thus longer to get tired of than the latest patented technicolor Leon Russell riff from Tuesday's supergroup. The *Free Jazz* album by Ornette Coleman is like this. So is "Sister Ray"—the first time I listened to it the only thing I could really hear was the organ! This Stooges album isn't nearly as complex as either one of those, but then Ornette practically started it all and the Velvets were at that time the most advanced experimental group in the world. What all this means is that the Stooges, as Iggy croons, are learnin' fast.

Each side is like a suite rising in intensity and energy until something just has to give. Side one opens with the Ig's new power anthem: "Down on the street where the faces shine . . . See a pretty thing / Ain't no wall!" A vicious beat like sharp gang boots clicking down the pavement, taut guitars in comparative reserve, and Ig jumping right in with the first of many inchoate vocal interjections. In fact, this album, which seemed at first to bust his true voice for virtual anonymity, reveals a real advance over the cleanly enunciated but comparatively tame singing on *The Stooges*. The oft-leveled criticism that he sounds too much like Mick Jagger came close to real truth there, but now the actual Stooge voice shines in all the glory of its individualistic yawp. True, he started from Jagger just like Dylan started from Woody and Ramblin' Jack—ev'body's gotta start from *some* familiar stoop—but the fact is that Ig has been building steadily from basic

Jaggerisms through a bratty whine (which was brilliant and accounted for not a little of the derision) into a vast adolescent muttering. In *Fun House* the sullen sulker of *The Stooges* has already evolved into a mighty versatile singer—granting, of course, that he still owns no trace of a "good" voice as traditionally accepted (neither does Jagger or Dylan). In fact, he has very little range indeed, more than Question Mark, who talked almost every song like some malevolently emotionless insect from outer space, but probably less than Lou Reed, who also owns basically a flat bark but has lately been trying to teach himself to croon for the subtler songs he's been writing. Iggy still sounds rather sullen, but a leer seems to lurk behind almost every word, and he hardly pouts at all. Mainly he intones the lyrics in the microphone as if with scowling surreptitious pleasure, like some weird kid gang leader phoning in the details of a job to his thugs. And just when you least expect it he flings out one of the bizarre, bestial-sounding nonverbal expletives which are one of the album's hallmarks: wildcat growls (after Roy Orbison?), hawking caws, whoops and shredded gargling threats.

The tempo picks up in band two, "Loose," which is considerably more complex than the opening street-strut. It opens, as do most cuts on the album, with a ragged Iggy shout. The vocal takes on a more grating tone, like a megaphone broadcasting from a meat-grinder, but the words affirm the adolescent stud-swagger of the first song: "I feel fine / I'm a dancin' baby / And you can come / I do believe / I stick it / Deep inside / Stick it deep inside / Cause I'm loose. . . ." Somehow, when Iggy says that, you believe him.

Next is "T.V. Eye," the most relentlessly driving and, for my money, fully realized song on the album. The arrangement is basically that of "Loose" stepped up, but the intensity and conviction of the performance really set it apart. This is the Stooges at their best—jagged, crunching, erratic, but rhythmically right every second of the way. The energy and ferocity which have been mounting steadily all through this side suddenly begin an almost vertical ascent in this song, which comes on like a whirlwind and builds steadily up and up until the tension peaks and there is nowhere left to go but down into the balladic "Dirt."

The lyrics are vintage offhand Iggy imagery, culminating in the usual self-assertion: "See that calf / Down on her back / See that girl / Down on 'er back / She got a T.V. eye on me. . . ." The wild instrumental break which follows shows the album's strongest Velvet Underground influence, sounding very much like the fiercely grinding jet-stream section in the latter leagues of "Sister Ray," just before that musical behemoth's energies peaked, as they also do here, guitars massing in one great bass note throbbing insistently like a hammering heart, and Iggy signing off with a hoarse frenzied scream: "Brothahs! Brothahs! Brothahs!" Whew. Silence. You collapse, spent, then suddenly the sizzling theme starts up again, but it's only a momentary reprise bridging into "Dirt," the long slow closer which brings down the energies mounting the last twelve minutes and packs them back into rumbling undertones.

"Dirt" is a specific ballad of the only stripe possible in this post-romantic era: terse personal assessment and flat-out proposition. "I've been *hurt!* / But I don't care / I've been *dirt!* / But I don't care / 'Cause I'm learnin' . . . learrrnin'. . . ."

"Dirt" 's instrumental track is fine, bitter and somehow proud at the same time, its thematic material seeming to sum up all the adolescent moonings of *The Stooges* and file them away as past history. Iggy, having suffered the sorrows of Young Werther and every other type of freaking frustration, has finally stepped out of the night of inertia into his own strange madmanhood, schooled in blows and ready to take on the world. I wondered why, when the crowd in that TV show hoisted him onto their arms and shoulders, he clenched his fists, puffed out his chest and flexed in the classic Charles Atlas manner (which looks pretty funny when the flexer is a skinny wildeyed kid pouring sweat)—he was rather pugnaciously asserting his newfound resilience and toughness: "Here I am, babies. I, Iggy, have conquered—do your worst."

Side two, like the first, shapes up with steadily rising energies, but the emphasis and pacing is different. "1970" is probably the set's weakest song, not counting "L.A. Blues," which is ungradeable. Somehow the arrangement lacks the tight hysteria of the pieces on side one, and for once the sense of raving disorder seems closer to actual sloppiness than a swirling energy vector. The words echo Chuck Berry's "You Can't Catch Me," but still make it fine as a Saturday night get loose party song, although the song's general haziness and sense of disorientation make you wonder just what sort of party he's going to. Certainly ain't no whooping bash, because while on side one you always know exactly where you are through each electric storm, this one finds Ig and the whole band just sort of wandering around in the murk.

"1970" 's saving grace is the appearance of snazz saxman Steve Mackay, whose work through the whole of this side bears no slighting. For some reason very few young white "rock" sax players can handle jazz forms without getting into one sort of mawkish woodshed parody or another, and when they attempt the free music of the Shepp/Ayler fringe the results regularly sink even lower. Somehow they always seem to end up merely gargling out some most untogether flurry of notes, their fingers skittering carelessly over the keys as if that were all that free jazz, in reality a fierce taskmaster, required. That's all it requires to blow shit, but playing the *real* shit takes a specialized imagination and sense of control. Steve, thank god, has enough of both to make his solos and ensemble fills interesting in their own right, and treads a fine though constantly zigzagging line between the post-Coltrane approach and a great old primitive rock 'n' roll honk.

The title track is next, longest cut, opens with same Ig vocal chorus as "1970," and features a stomping, slamming arrangement that charges right ahead in a blustery delirium. Early on the guitar starts meandering Lou Reed–style behind Iggy's vocal, and Mackay maintains a gutty percussive blat, interspersed with occasional restless flurries of plaintive squawks. The set's most gloriously "sloppy" piece, it creaks and cranks and crackles along like some peglegged Golem hobbling toward carny Bethlehem. The lyrics and Ig's delivery are choice, a vision of delirious kids cascading through garish phantasmagorias of sideshow and steeplechase, with the Fun House seemingly a sort of metaphor for the fully integrated, get-loose life-style, all recited by Iggy with a kind of lunatic glee: "Little baby gurl and little / Bay-buh boy / Covered me with lovin' in a / Bundle o' joy / Do I care to show ya whut I'm / Dreamin' of / Do I dare tuh *fuck* ya / With mah luve?" The "fuck" comes out as a high wheezing whoop, and then he adds: "Evah little baby knows just / What I mean / Livin' in division, in the / Shiftin' sands / I'm callin' from the fun house. . . ."

And finally there's "L.A. Blues," the searing arrhythmic freak-out which drove me to distraction first hearing and which I've since come to kind of dig on its own level as more a steaming, stormy atmosphere than a piece of music. I prefer things that swing or rock or even shuffle— although I've heard many similar freakouts on both rock and jazz albums, and this one beats all of those from other rock bands and most of the jazz. Somehow after a couple of listenings it's not grating, the way Yoko Ono or Archie Shepp's angrier outings or even "European Son" gets grating. The Stooges seem to know what they're doing—most times I rip such aural blitzes off the phonograph posthaste (even a Stooge fan's ears take sensitive exception to some outer-edge tonalities—in fact, I would say that a true Stooge fan, like a true aficionado of Captain Beefheart or the Velvet Underground or Pharoah Sanders, probably has a couple of the ten thousand or so most sensitive ears on the planet, since they are sufficiently developed to appreciate that Stooge magic which so escapes dullards). In fact, the other night I fell in well-stoked with ozone, listened to "L.A. Blues," and it seemed like some vast network of golden metal pulleys rising infinitely into the sky—not that I expect any of the folks around the hearth to heed them kind of psychedelic testimonials. What I do notice through repeated playings is that Iggy is up to some of the album's most abstract vocal tricks here—his voice at times takes on the timbre of one more distorted amplifier, later screams like a wildcat suffering the short end of a boxing match, and at one point sounds as if he is trying to sing through a mouthful of radiator coils. The fading feedback of the song's last minute, however, finds him returning ever so briefly for a signoff reminiscent of Porky Pig's in the old Warner Brothers cartoons: curled up atop the massed metal wreckage of the past five minutes, he's once again the wildcat, considerably quieter now, emitting two low purring yawns, smiling, sleepy, sated.

YOUR MOVE

Well, that's just about it. My labors have been strenuous but thorough, and by rights every last bleary orb running down these last words should be *satorized* and sold on Pop & Co. Yet somehow I still hear a horde of sluggards out there whining: "Are you putting me on?" Or, more fundamentally, haven't the Stooges been putting us all on from Yelp One? And the answer, of course, is Yes. Because, as beautiful Pauline Kael put it in her characteristically epigrammatic way: "To be put on is to be put on the spot, put on the stage, made the stooge in a comedy act. People in the audience at *Bonnie and Clyde* are laughing, demonstrating that they're not stooges—that they appreciate the joke—when they catch the first bullet right in the face."

Some of the most powerful esthetic experiences of our time, from *Naked Lunch* to *Bonnie and Clyde,* set their audiences up just this way, externalizing and magnifying their secret core of sickness which is reflected in the geeks they mock and the lurid fantasies they consume, just as our deepest fears and prejudices script the jokes we tell each other. This is where the Stooges work. They mean to put you on that stage, which is why they are super-modern, though nothing near to Art. In Desolation Row and Woodstock-Altamont Nation the switchblade is mightier and speaks more eloquently than the penknife. But this threat is cathartic, a real cool time is had by all, and the end is liberation.

—*Creem,* November and December 1970

James Taylor
Marked for
Death

PART ONE: KAVE KIDS

All right, punk, this is it. Choose ya out. We're gonna settle this right here. You can talk about yer MC5 and yer Stooges and even yer Grand Funk and Led Zep, yep, alla them badasses've carved out a hunka turf in this town, but I tell you there was once a gang that was so bitchin' *bad* that they woulda cut them dudes down to snotnose crybabies and in less than three minutes too. I mean their shortest rumble was probably the one clocked in at 1:54 and that's pretty fuckin swift, kid. Oh, they didn't *look* so bad, in fact their appearance was a real stealthy move 'cuz they mostly photographed like a bunch of motherson polite mod clerks on their lunch hour, but they not only kicked ass with unparalleled style when the time came, they even had the class to pick one of the most righteous handles of all time: the Troggs.

That's right, the Troggs. Remember? Course I know some a yez wasn't quite outa yer mama's parlors an' into the street yet in 1966, but they *ruled* this set for just one great year, and I can't stop reminiscin' even if I did turn in my chain an' colors a year or two back for a gig in the rags. "Wild Thing" was what most of the dudes and dollies remember 'em by, but they were prolific as a packa Jack the Rippers and even had hearts of blushing awshucks romanticism underneath just like all other genuine tough guys. Their name came from a really farsighted set of British brats who made the dailies by cutting outa all the bringdown brownstones and takin' to the ragged mountains of the Isles to live in *caves*. Some tourists camping out stumbled on them one day in the form of a naked mangy teenager coming round the mountain covered head to toe in grime and filth and shit. On sighting them his panther eyes blazed up and his gnarly jaw dropped and he let out the most bloodcurdling howl heard by human ears since a yard of aeons B.C. at least, and then he *pounced.*

When the campers finally stopped running and came panting and haunted into town, they organized a police party and combed the hills until all the dog-children had been located and brought down, whole scarry tribes of them, naked as niggers in the veldt, and though all were refugees from civil streets and mostly good homes they communicated only in preverbal grunts and yelps and catarrh spasms. What did they eat? Oh, the usual: beasts and fowl of the field cooked on cavern fires, nuts, twigs and berries, no McDonald's or Colonel Sanders because quite naturally all allowances from home were cut off when they shed their threads to run wild in the outback and anyway caves don't have mailboxes or even roads in *that* raw neck of the woods (I didn't even know that terrain so remote and rasty *existed* in Merrie Olde, but it's all true, you can read it in the '65 and '66 papers).

Those papers, in fact, fulfilled their usual function by assigning the primitive clots of lads and lassies a handy monicker—they called them "troglodytes," "troggs" for short, which it sez right here in the notes to the *Wild Thing* album means "one who dwells in caves or creeps in and out of holes or caverns," and one must admit that the name *does* loom more classy and historically, entropically ominous than some jive quickie like "beatnik." And just like the beatnik phase, the enormous promise inherent in the Troglodyte syndrome faded all too quickly, as the prime movers of the Trog scene retreated from the pitiless glare of publicity back (where else?) to Mommy and Daddy's chicken salad and clean sheets and cars, or at the very least beneath the waves to whatever lofts and alleys the *next* (mod-psychedelic) big move was brewing in. To the best of my knowledge, none of them even had the horse sense to apply and capitalize on all that priceless experience as junior jackals by forming caveman rock groups to dress in loincloths and ashes and play guitars made out of bones and bring the Troglodyte Trip to the world. If they had, who knows, we might all be going around right now with de rigueur bones in our noses even in mellow California, and Grand Funk's *Survival* cover would be a big ho-hum at the end of a vast train of pigmy bands, Motown Zulu chiefs and every conceivable stripe of aboriginal entrepreneur trying to cash in (Kim Fowley with his filed teeth a stunningly successful combination Dylan-Spector-Iggy act, the glowering *brujo* spokesman for millions of *ayahuasca*-seething adolescents), the primordial rhythms of the primal Piltdown Pissoffs ripped off repeatedly thru all permutations of capitalist exploi euphemism till we ended at last with prehistoric toothbrushes ("Mon, they just LOVE to brush with a Stone Stiletto! Fits all common filing styles") and a Saturday morning Kirshner cartoon epic about a Paleolithically prepubescent band and their mama called "The Littlest Yeti."

On the other hand, none of that happened, so we can stop our wishful thinking and forget about it (although I still woulda liked to've seen Nancy Sinatra with a bone in her nose). What did happen was that the kave kats became the namesake for the Troggs, who undoubtedly played in some fairly grottolike or grottotious clubs in their coming-up days, but unfortunately never made it to the hills. They *did* have extremely analogous elements in their music that gave listening to it all the appeal of riding a mad bull elephant bareback down into the valley of decision to kick punk Jo Jo Gunne ass right and left. Their music was strong, deep as La Brea without sucking you straight down into the currentless bass depths like many of their successors, and so insanely alive and fiercely aggressive that it could easily begin to resemble a form of total assault which was when the lily-livered lovers of pretty-pompadoured, la-di-da luddy-duddy Beat groups would turn tail just like the tourists before them and make for that Ferry Cross the Mersey. 'Cause this was a no-jive, take-care-of-business band (few of the spawn in its wake have been so starkly pure) churning out rock 'n' roll that thundered right back to the very first grungy chords and straight ahead to the fuzztone subways of the future. And because it was so true to its evolutionary antecedents, it was usually about sex, and not just Sally-go-to-movieshow-and-hold-my-hand stuff, although there was scads more of that in them than anyone would have suspected at first, but the most challengingly blatant flat-out proposition and prurient fantasy. The MC5 might have put you "flat on your back" with "nipple stiffeners" and "wham, bam, thank you ma'am" jams, the Stooges might tie you up in feedback wires while Iggy performed unthinkable experiments on your mind and body, even the Doors might have given you a crawly gust or two, but the Troggs eschewed all trendy gimmicks and kinky theatrics, delivered their proposition with sidewalk directness and absolute sincerity, and came out for any ear that half listens the most powerfully lust-driven outfit in white rock 'n' roll then or now. Just dig their song titles: "Gonna Make You," "I Want You" (which the MC5 ripped off without bothering to credit and essayed a third as convincingly in twice the time), "I Can't Control Myself," "Give It to Me," "I Can Only Give You Everything."

The justice done those great titles in actual practice was almost uniformly stunning. Part of the reason the Troggs ultimately cut their competitors and successors at raw high-energy electro-fertility stomps was their consistent sense of structure and economy—I don't think any of their songs ran over four minutes, the solos were short but always slashingly pertinent, and the vocals were not to be believed. Reg Presley didn't have the Tasmanian-devil glottal scope of an Iggy, but he did have one of the most leering, sneering punk snarls of all time, an approach to singing that was comprised of equal parts thoroughly digested early Elvis, Gene Vincent and Jagger, a way of mauling the lyrics (though without the mannerism of a John Fogerty), crooning and barking not so much in voguish petulance (no pouter he), nor puffing chest to bellow and growl like De Biggest Buck Stud on de Plantation (à la John Kay)—the best way to describe it would be to say that he sounded raspy and cocky and loose and lewd. And the catch was that all this horny aggression was only one side of the story of both performer(s) and material—on the other side of the coin the Troggs excelled at the most shamelessly (and, yes, poignantly) romantic of teenage love songs, manifestos of head-spinning adoration that range from stalwart assurances to Little Honey that their love is stronger than society or even matter and time, to confused, tentative expressions of dumb sky smittenness, to blasts of rage at loss or unfaithfulness that are as relentless in their rage as "Gonna Make You" is in its imperative groin thunder.

To deal with the groin thunder first, since obviously it has the most public appeal and I don't want you dozing off just when I'm getting into the meat of the matter, its most basic expression is obtained in "I Want You," the one the MC5 jerked off to.* This is the Troggs at their most bone-minimal (which is also where they are usually most effective). Like the early Kinks, they had strong roots in "Louie, Louie," which is where both song and guitar solo issue from here. The lyrics are almost worthy of the cave: "I want you / I need you / And I hope that you need me too / I can't

---

*Incidentally, I'm not trying to run down the Five, or write them off as some Trogg trickle. When I reviewed their first album in *Rolling Stone*, I finished by mentioning "the Troggs, who appeared with a similar sex-and-violence thing a couple of years back, and promptly sank into oblivion, where I imagine they are laughing at the MC5," and that of course is as snottily unkind to the Troggs as to the Five. But then, it was the first review I ever had published, and even if more death threats came in after that review than any other save Jann Wenner's *Wheels of Fire* massacre (and most of them from sweet home Detroit), I can see why people privileged enough to be part of the apocalyptic birth of the Five would be enraged. And to compound the irony, *Kick Out the Jams* has been my favorite album or at least one of the two or three most played for about three months now. The MC5 are not the Troggs, and neither were the Stooges, and both can do things that the Troggs would never have dreamed of, but the Troggs *did* have a consistency and sure sense of direction that the other two, the best bands of this sort surviving today, lacked or lost sight of—the Five by their political confusion and bad press, the Stooges by their personal idiosyncrasies and ultimately self-consuming, tailbiting desperation and intensity. The Troggs didn't last long—they were most likely sucked under by economics rather than loss of inspiration—but they existed with a set of problems perhaps light-years removed from those

stand it alone on my own / I want you. . . ." The vocal has a musk of yellow-eyed depravity about it, and the singer sounds absolutely certain of conquest—steady, methodical, deliberate. This is the classic mold for a Troggs stalking song.

"Gonna Make You" is more of the same, Diddley rumbleseat throbbing with sexual aggression and tough-guy disdain for too many words, while the flip side of *that* single, "I Can't Control Myself," begins to elaborate a bit. It opens with a great Iggyish "Ohh, NO!," employs a buckling foundation of boulderlike drums as usual, and takes the Troggpunk's intents and declarations onto a more revealing level. "Yer socks are low and yer hips are showin'," smacks Presley in a line that belongs in the Great Poetry of Rock 'n' Roll Hall of Fame. The number moves past the unrationalized Golem solidity of "I Want You" to begin to hint at the agitation and desperation which will be dealt with more graphically in other songs. "My nerves are breakin' " is the only concession that Presley will make from his monomaniacal drive toward snatch. The Troggs were perhaps the foremost and most consistently male chauvinist group of all time after the Rolling Stones—they were outrageously blatant and repetitive enough about it to fall afoul of old-style radio censors in many places and with more than one record. A two-sided single whose titles were "Give It to Me" and "I Can't Control Myself" was on a collision course with some ultimate puissant bluenose from the start, and sure enough it was banned in America. And really you almost can't blame the Grundys—not when this new pack of slimy Limeys was coming on over the transistors crushed into the ears of freckle-fresh American girls already beleaguered by the Rolling Stones and flicking iguana-tongued insinuations up the aural canals to the effect that if the honeys acquiesce to the hot times the Britishers are proffering, why, "yer knees would bend and yer hair would curl!"

---

faced by rising bands today. They merely had to deliver, and by and large no one ever thought to question or demand more than was proffered. But bands now have to deal with a large and motley scope of attitudes on the part of the audience, have to deal with psychological, social, or "spiritual" vested interests at least as much as business ones, and often the strain of sorting out their image is too much for them. If the MC5 did the songs today that they were doing at revolutionary rallies in 1968, Women's Lib would be literally following them around to commandeer the stage, *kick out* the jams and maybe the Five's asses in the process. If Mitch Ryder gets harassed on May Day in Washington for singing "Devil with a Blue Dress On," you can bet that a reformed Troggs would face lots of trouble in 1971 if they cruised across America's stages laying out such record-breakingly blatant sexism as "Wild Thing" and "Give It to Me," just as it's easy to prognosticate the fracases when the Stones tour America again next spring (if some valiantly addlepated female guerrilla doesn't come within two pubic hairs of claiming the storied Jagger nuts as a war trophy, the political vanguard in this country must have mass mononucleosis).

The conciseness of the Troggs' performances would also lose ground, big buildups and long intros and solos are more than the rage, they're expected down to the last drum solo and interminable blues

Whoo! The cosmically linked collective consciousness of infinitesimal but insistent flickers of nascent lust through downy spring clitorises didn't exactly reverberate from sea to shining sea and ricochet off Saskatchewan and Calexico, but anybody but a born numbnuts could definitely feel it when the wind was up and the static electricity in the air. If you happened to be a sixteen or seventeen-year-old male sagging in the rubberband scrotum of suburban America it braced you, each hearing injected new confidence for however brief a time almost as if some Little Doll had in all phantasmal actuality come pouting up and reached and *grabbed* yer cock for just a minute like you always dreamed of 'em doing sitting in the classroom after lunch computing distances between yourself and the delicate hand swinging freely by the side of the desk in front of you, or even in moments most crazed of what if you just casually slid your hands behind the small of your back down on your chair and extended them aft just a sweet fraction more and started caressing Jean's big golden leg and she'd just sit there being cool pretending that nothing was happening staring straight ahead at the blackboard but getting it feeling it too stirring down where the seam of her crossed legs ended, the whole thing a vast erotic secret between you and her so you might get up at 1:55 and go to your separate last periods without even looking back and in fact never say a thing about it though perhaps maintaining this purely physical relationship like an assignation plotted in the viscera at exactly the same time every day. ... What a pube punk fantasy! But I gotta admit that not only did I devote many fruitful (or at least fulsomely frustrating) institutional hours to such studies a few years back and even in college, *I even actualized the fantasy* as some Maslow moron would say on at least one cockeyed finger-stuttering occasion. It's 9th Grade Dumbbell Math, see, about 1962, and I'm sitting in front of good old mousy, plain Judy Bistodeau (her real name—and she grew up to be a wollapalooza of a drugstore fashion model) with my orang

jam encore. Tempos of many songs would also almost undoubtedly be slowed down, because plodding concrete-slab bass lines are in and the sort of galloping backbeats that the Troggs specialized in are out. So the Troggs would have to modify their natural statement in line with the expectations of the new audience, and as a result their music would probably suffer either technically or spiritually or both. They were definitely a product of a time, albeit a simpler one, and the Five and the Stooges and all the others currently struggling are products of the dislocation that set in with most initial virulence just a few moons past the Troggs. One thing is certain: we need this kind of music, always have and always will, and Grand Funk and *their* progeny aside there will always be someone with the drive and sometime invention to supply it. The Five mangled "I Want You," but their second album was an underrated classic and lots of people think their new *High Time* is even better, and now that the Stooges have disbanded for what may well be the last time, we can only hope that the Five will rise from the rather doldrumish position they've occupied the last year or so and take up their rightful mantle at least as American heirs to everything the Troggs represented and brightest hope to experiment with that gut-pulse and transmute it further into space and exhilaratingly new brands of noise.

arms hangin of course and she's got her pert little feet up on the railshelf under my desk where you're sposed to put your books except I didn't have any cause all I carried then was a pen and a wad of notebook paper in one pocket and a copy of *The Dharma Bums* so I wasn't weighted down and barred from potential vicarious ecstasy by no jiveass junior logarithm trash and her feet made it under the place where I sat and so being the uncommonly aware young sprout that I was I oh so casually tentatively unconcernedly absentmindedly SLOWLY & NERVOUSLY let my left arm swing so my fingers brushed the exquisite surface of her not recently shined light red plain leather junior miss Skool Shoes resentfully bestowed by nickel-niggling parents at Thom McAn the preceding September. I actually *felt* her—or at least an appendage, which is almost the same thing. I had just read the part in J.D.'s *Franny and Zooey* where the chromenose jerkoff college boy dating Franny stops up the snotholes in his trunk by smirking about how on a date he ever-so-artistically kissed Franny's coat collar as if it had some form of sympathetic magic when all he wanted was a fast duck of the dick in and out of Franny's Zen-immaculate honeypot in the back seat. Well, I took all that stuff *seriously,* kissing appendages seemed real romantic to me just like the summer before when I'd sat on the floor in our living room gorging myself on the opportunity to KISS and TONGUE and SUCK on Sandra Wyatt's glorious calf (still the first thing I look at), even the stubble tattling that she was somewhat less than fixed for blades, while she sat in the chair above me holding one of my hands between her knees and watching Saturday Afternoon Wrestling with a slight amusement that only drove me wilder even though I was so intoxicated with her calf and my own muddled conception of what I was doing or supposed to be that I didn't get any farther than maybe the soft backside of one knee that afternoon. (Altho I did get more later—running my hand up her dress to stop at her panties in the back seat of the Jehovah's Witness car afield with *Watchtowers* and *Awake!*s, fiddling about similarly while we watched home movies at her parents' house with *them and my mother all sitting behind us* seemingly absolutely unaware of or indifferent to what in its bald parrot-brained recklessness must have been more than obvious [maybe they were trying to line us up to get married so we'd both be kept out of trouble by each other], feeling pudenda somewhere thru shorts in the back seat on the way home from the San Diego Zoo with my mother and her mother and goofus of a 7th grade brother up front and when I finally navigated to a pressing perch exactly over her sweet box I swiped a sidelong look at her which I've been glad I did ever since because she bit her lower lip with her upper front teeth ever so slightly so briefly and let out the smallest most sweetly near-intangible sigh of new desire—but I never touched her tits or cunt or bush or anything but calves and thighs and cute little round teenflab tummy on the actual skin, and with everything else she allowed she never let me kiss her. I've loved her ever since. She died last year from an overdose of downers.)

But de-digressing part of the way to pick up Math Class Judy once more, I kept sweeping my good old hand under the desk a bit, on the top of her shoe, man how subtle, oh it was nice, it wasn't like being sucked off on mescaline by the Flying Nun while hanging from the top of the Empire State Building guzzling tequila, but it was still nice, and she didn't seem to be complaining so even though my heart was starting to run into peculiar offbeats at odd intervals I made like a real daring dog and actually let it REST on top of her shoe. Still no response. But I was THERE! Home free or close enough at least to begin to think about the top of the Empire State Building and sweet Sally lips in her habit [Editor's note: You forgot that the Flying Nun didn't even debut on TV until several years later, Jerk!]* and fired and flustered I began awkwardly to move my fingers over the surface of the shoe, trying out a few random caresses—one has to set out experimentally and test out a whole slew of new caress moves when dealing with a medium as then-unfamiliar as leather—I at length found the grace to just let my fingers drift and eddy over her little buttons and stitches, venturing out every now and then at just the psychologically appropriate intervals as computed by the abacus in my brain, yes venturing out that crucial extra fraction of an inch to actually touch the slight stretch of foot above the rim of the shoe and under her ankles which interestingly enough didn't seem to hold much appeal for me. She never gave a sign that she was aware of anything, much less irritated, so I pressed my frontiers thinking maybe her foot was asleep and ha what a lucky day this must be for me to stumble into such a treasure trove at least three or four inches of female flesh so I toyed more boldly with her left limb's lower extremity and finally took the shoe in my hand like it was some kind of burgerfried tit and squeezed it deliriously. As soon as I did she mumble-yelled "Ow! What're you doing?!" and indignantly pulled her tantalizing tootsies back to the defantasized zone under her own desk, leaving me not as nonplussed as you might think since we had been at this little charade for the better part of the period and she was getting almost as much out of it for whatever there was to get as I was whether she too was distinctly horny (doubtful) or merely curious and bored (right).

*The editor speaking here is Greg Shaw of *Who Put the Bomp*, in which this piece originally appeared.

So that's the end of the part of the essay entitled WHAT I DID BEFORE I BEGAN TO GET BALLED. I may razor it out at some future date and slide it into my projected erotic autobiography called *Sex Freak* (sequel to *Drug Punk*), but then again I may not since a book like that is probably best written when you're about forty and anyway the sweet vignette just done might feel displaced away from its rightful home herein. And as for what else I did before I began to get balled, well, I used to fill my days with huddling by the record player digging music that fed my nascent sense of sexual identity, like the Troggs. The line that sent me swirling off on that grand tangent ("Yer knees would bend and yer hair would curl") is so effortlessly on-target that I gotta pop a Pabst in sheer admiration and say that the thing it reminds me most of is one of Lightnin' Hopkins's most starkly chilling recordings, a piece called "Buddy Brown's Blues" on the *Blues in the Bottle* album, where he climaxes his ancient quavery Texas moan (after Texas Alexander, his teacher, actually) with a line that made the hairs rise on the back of *my* neck: "I got sump'n to tell you / Make the hair rise on your head / Waall, I got a new way o' lovin' / Make the springs *scrinch* on yer bed!" Are we broaching juju muff potions? I ain't sure, but whether from Troggs or Lightnin' it's pretty strange territory. Although it *is* amazing the consistency with which certain lines and ideas like that will disappear into the cheap whiskey hotel rooms of the old blues South, if indeed they ever originated anywhere but Lightnin's or some colleague's own luridly frying brainpan, only to turn up years later in some song by a punko English rock group who quite possibly (at least I damn fucking well *hope* so) never heard of Lightnin' Hopkins. On the other hand, maybe the theme of sex runs through all folk music (meaning rock and blues and all that other alive shit that doesn't *call* itself Folk Music) in a continuum of parallel strands that reappear endlessly, and the weird claustrophobic promise of dark delights fantasized by an old drunk bluesman can't help but resurface in the once-percolating English music scene as a magnificent teeno lust stalk of an anthemic march.

Now that we've been brassy enough to use a word like "anthemic," we might as well stick our necks out and get even a little more pretentious and note that many of the Troggs' most prurient songs, with their lumberjack-balling-honky-tonk-woman-in-iron-bed-with-screws-loose bum-crash rhythms and drooling "leerics" as *Time* magazine referred to the hits of the Stones in an early smear, are actually just a smidgen beyond the average "Hey, baby! Here I come with a shag haircut and my big Wazoo!" type of composition which jaded fops like Led Zeppelin and virility complexes like John Kay have helped bring to prominence. Many of the Troggs' songs, aside from the fact that they were immediate come-ons and male self-aggrandizement, also seemed to have an extra-excited, almost celebratory quality about them, sexual anthems and sexual whoops that get banned from the radio and get played by their proud owners never at parties for the titillation of giggling cases of arrested development but rather at home alone sitting in front of the speakers so you can pick up that full charge of bravado and self-affirmation even if the basic image is as corny at least as John Wayne; when you're a kid you need stuff like that. And those guitars blast you through the wall, out cross the rooftops 'tween antennas of your neighborhood, straight out of your cell into perfect release in a trophosphering limbo of blizzard noise at last, home free.

An A-OK example of what I'm talking about is "Give It to Me." Structurally, it's pretty standard Troggs fare even if marrow-meltingly great: it builds on another chopped rhythm, a bit of Who influence (early, and that never did anything but good for anybody), and asks for what all the other songs have been asking for in a new way, not even entirely with selfish motives! Dig it, folksies: "Give it to me / Give it to me / All your love / All your love / And I'll know." A very pure song, really. An innocent song. An organic song, better for yer innards than a *gallon* of twigs and berries and crunchy granola. Even a holy song! Because: "When you come I'll be glad / 'Cuz I'll know." Yeah-zoobie, in no way no fay can say them sentiments ain't positive. There has been one other rock 'n' roll song about a girl who couldn't come—Lou Reed's "Here She Comes Now" qualifies for that, I think, with "If she ever comes now now . . . / ah she looks so good / ah she's made out of wood . . ." And I always thought that Buffalo Springfield's "I'll Never Forget You" with that bit of "I just can't seem to get movin', love me a little . . ." was actually about temporary male impotence maybe in the presence of a groupie or someone the poor shmuck cares *too much* about to get it up in his neurotic state.

But this is the only time I've heard a song where the guy was actually being considerate enough to *try* to give his girlfriend an orgasm so she can have a good time too and they can both be satisfied and go down love's highway handinhand with birdies tweettweettweeting in solid pirouettes all round. Man, I just love stuff like that! It gives me faith in the future of the human race. I'm a sucker for sentiment of the right kind—I wouldn't go see *Love Story* or listen to Rod McKuen, but when I hear a song that takes a truly democratic attitude about fucking at last, and this no small thing after all these years of "flat on your back"'s and "Whole Lotta Love"'s, why, I feel like raisin' the flag, tootin' bugles and turning the cornflakes to confetti, and my lady friends share my sentiments too so shut up you cynics who're never satisfied unless the protagonists of a piece of art are utopian androids. It sorta reminds me of the Fugs' "I Want to Know" ("Hunger / Driving me onward / To feel / All of the skin"), a very youthful song of discovery and new nooky. I think I'll start playing it when I get up in the morning.

PART TWO: PARTYIN' WITH THE FREE-LANCE BIGOT

Much the same expansive spirit informs the world-renowned "Wild Thing" with the innate intelligence that makes it not only roll but tower like "96 Tears" and "Wooly Bully" and precious few others above all the peasant poesies of Pop. "Wild Thing, you make my heart sing! / You make everything groovy! / —(sly insinuating whisper) *Wild Thing, I think you move me.* CA-ROMMM! / (slick and loose) *But I wanna kno-ow for sure!* / (down in the furtive glottals again) *C'mon—hold me tight!* / (pregnant pause of vibrating tonsil)—YOU MOVE ME!!!!"

Boys and girls, I mean to say you'd best take that one to HEART— 'cause if your school or hotrod or doper clique ever really *did* get that loose, you would be so heavy you would pierce the very ground and fall through to China where else where they'd put you in a zoo and feed you lentils and rice and all other manner of good green things and Red Guard kats an' kitties would bop down in droves to laugh at yer ten-buck Rod Stewart– style sculpt or tenderly abused and wrinkled black leather jacket. If you take "Wild Thing" to heart and somehow attain its at least Kilimanjaroan level of godawful beauty, you will have so much sheer sheen-gleam of pure fuckin KLASS that your brain will explode like an overheated pan of rabbit gizzards on a prospector's Bunsen and propel you like a teenage Nike skull-first straight outa that fuckin' school past the bells and deals and vice-principals and student stoolies and jock straps and box lunches straight into the blaring sky where I believe we just found ourselves a few pages back whilst listening to "Give It to Me." Well, you're listening to "Wild Thing" now, which is to "Give It to Me" as Charlie Mingus is to a nice boy like, say, Lee Morgan (I'm talking about writing now, I know they play different instruments, wisepuss), so it's gonna put you beyond where the other one put you, not in space because it's not that kind of a song, but how 'bout in, let's say, *East L.A.*, in 1966 natch, blasting down the streets in a souped-up shitcan with some zit-grinnin buddies drinkin the cheapest wine you could find while "Wild Thing" crashes and lunges right thru the radio loud as it'll go out the open windows so everybody can hear it and looking around sonnybitch they all do every car bulbous with noise and rollicking with drunk kids just graduated from high school and taut as high-tension wires just straining out of their bucket seats champing at the bit bursting up into summer like swimmers coming up from a dive to break the surface shoot half out of the water and grin at the sun. It's that kind of a song, 'cause it's about *you* when you had a good time and went mad for real and reared for release 'cause you were too young and naive to know any better. If punk America is dying behind the curdled MSG-free dregs of Hip and all the corny Experiments in New Designs for Living people are trying to get their rocks off and find themselves in, if kids are really too smart and cool to just loon about anymore, if first day of summer means rolling one after another from new lid and plopping hour on hour in front of television or record player instead of tearing into the street and hunting out buddies and leaping and yupping till at least some of the scholastic poison accumulating like belladonna ever since September is plain crazied out of your soul, if all of that's a pipe dream and I'm just an old fart now—cranking out complaints about the New Generation regular as TB spittle—if all that's true, then THE LESSON OF "WILD THING" WAS LOST ON ALL YOU STUPID FUCKERS sometime between the rise of Cream and the fall of the Stooges, and rock 'n' roll may turn into a chamber art yet or at the very least a system of Environments.

I ain't as desperate as I sound, but "Wild Thing" is rock 'n' roll at its most majestic and for all the volume of product we don't have any "Wild Thing"s these days—a few things come close, maybe a Velvets "Head Held High" or Stooges "Little Doll," but even those are created from a standpoint of intellectualized awareness and consequent calculation. I mean, I know when Lou Reed set out to write "Rock & Roll," and that is certainly the least pretentious and most authentic of all the recent songs that take as their subject what is supposedly their form, he set out to write a tribute to the music that, as mentioned in the lyrics, has been sustaining him and his for fifteen going on twenty years now. To approach it from that perspective, though, almost automatically leads to the conclusion that the work is done to some significant extent from a position of detachment or even objectivity. It's a tribute, but in the old days you didn't need "tributes"—there were "Rock and Roll Is Here to Stay," "It Will Stand," "All Around the World," "Rock & Roll Music," all to the last of them a *celebration*. "All around the world / Rock 'n' roll is all they play . . ." was a victory shivaree whooping juicemad all the long night after a *war*. As Ralph Jazzbo Gleason woulda said if he'd been hangin' out on that scene: "We made it. We won." And it was true. All those early songs about rock 'n' roll were successive movements in a suite in progress which was actually nothing more than a gigantic party whose collective ambition was simple: to keep the party going and jive and rave and kick 'em out cross the decades and only stop for the final Bomb or some technological maelstrom of sonic bliss sucking the cities away at last. Because the Party was the *one* thing we had in our lives to grab onto, the one thing we could truly believe in and depend on, a loony tune fountain of youth and vitality that was keeping us alive as much as any medicine we'd ever take or all the fresh air in Big Sur, it sustained us without engulfing us and gave us a nexus of metaphor through which we could refract less infinitely extensible concerns and learn a little bit more about ourselves and what was going on without even, incredibly enough, getting pretentious about it. We didn't exactly know what it meant in the larger, more "profound" scheme of things (although we really did know in our bones and just hadn't gotten around to turning it into a form of scholasticism and self-psychoanalysis yet), but we damn sure knew what we needed.

A while later, though, we got caught up in the whirlwind of Our Consciousness of Ourselves as Our Generation which was the most TNT-packed passel of brats since the *original* troglodytes and all of us started taking steps to move in and keep up (because to do otherwise would be like resigning to refrigerator heaven with Ralph Williams and your mother), to watch all the movings and shakings which passed so fast, to collate and understand and maybe someday get a piece of the action yourself so *you'll* be out there in the Vanguard defining where the trips of Ice Cream Truck America are gonna go next instead of sitting glumly by your record player waiting like a simp for the next phase to be handed down from the Maniacs on high.

The prime effect of this vast intense rush toward a million eddies and vectors of Involvement was that American kids began in progressively larger numbers to take themselves with the utmost seriousness, both as individuals and as a vaguely and mystically defined mass *class,* to take themselves with perhaps the most seriousness they had ever displayed in this country, because for the first time they were relatively free to set their own goals. So everybody put in overtime soul-searching. Everything was scrutinized, dissected, acidized, turned sideways and inside out to gut every last drop of mystery, either that or treated with a kind of wax-paper-filtered reverence, as if mystery and obscurity was the whole show and no one had a right to disturb what was complete and holy in its primal unrationalized objectness. To score this vast combination Renaissance and psychic urban renewal project, however, people turned to rock 'n' roll and later to rock and finally to proudly unclassifiable tissues of offal not worthy of the name of noise, stuff so Nice and careful and positive-thinking (or painfully search-ing) that you wanted to take the records out of the jackets and hang them on the wall like those samplers that Granmaw and Paw used to have in their trailer that said "God Bless This Home" or a Bible verse.

But that's getting off into the usual cranky rant. What I want to get at is what we did to the Rock 'n' Roll Party by making it the soundtrack for our personal and collective narcissistic psychodramas. True, the Party did sort of hibernate for a couple of years there, and then the Beatles/ Stones era brought it back full swing with all sorts of neat additions like Jelly Beans and long hair and the possibility for flamboyant proto-bohemian defiance of all law and order, even the blue laws and friendly orders. People really went crazy in the mid-sixties, it was a rock 'n' roll rampage for a while there even if the initial exhilaration of loosening that came with the onset of the drug revolution was already beginning to give way to more standard-ized forms and manners increasingly threatening to become as oppressive as the worst that had been determinedly tossed behind—perhaps worse, because by the end of the decade it had become obvious that perhaps the one common constant of our variegated and strung-out peer groups was a pervasive sense of self-consciousness that sent us in grouchy packs to ugly festivals just to be *together* and dig ourselves and each other, as if all of this meant something greater than that we were kids who liked rock 'n' roll and came out to have a good time, as if our very styles and trappings and drugs and jargon could be in themselves political statements for any longer than about fifteen stoned seconds, even a threat to the Mother Country! So we loved and loved and doted on ourselves and our reflections in each other even as the whole thing got out of hand and turned into mud and disaster areas and downs and death. If we didn't go to the festivals, too timidly academic or whatever to root with the hogs for three days, we bought books with titles like *Free People,* or (with more patina of importance) *The Making of a Counter Culture,* or for the final Pop sodacounter polemic, *The Greening of America.* These books told us that we were something more than what we might have thought, that our very existence and lifestyle was of vast crucial importance to America and maybe the survival of the planet. So we bought that bilge and started running off in all the directions that people are currently hurtling to Do Something, even if it's only hide out in a commune in the northern woods to pretend you're a visionary who has transcended the problem.

As much as I hate these trends entirely on their own charms and programs, what I hate even more is what they've done to rock 'n' roll. Because the Party's not over yet, but it's come mighty close in the last year or two. The trend toward narcissistic flair has been responsible in large part for smiting rock with the superstar virus, which revolves around the substituting of *attitudes* and flamboyant trappings, into which the audience can project their fantasies, for the simple desire to make music, get loose, knock the folks out or get 'em up dancin'. It's not enough just to do those things anymore; what you must do instead if you want success on any large scale is either figure out a way of getting yourself associated in the audience's mind with their pieties and their sense of "community," i.e., ram it home that you're one of THEM; or, alternately, deck and bake yourself into an image configuration so blatant or outrageous that you become a culture myth. These are not the only avenues to long green and white coke, of course. You can also do something old in a way nobody's thought of lately and mug and writhe a lot onstage so people'll think it's new (Santana); or you can take a lot of old stuff and be very serious about throwing it all together (Chicago) so people won't buy your records just to throw them on or go to your concerts just to get ripped and holler—if not to actually *learn* something, your fans will at least approach your products with unusual respect and the implicit constant reassurance to themselves that it is Good Music, more advanced or important, of so much higher quality than that alleycat racket the teens and proles wallow in.

Or you can play it cool and just get a guitar and start writing songs about easy things, like crises you've remembered in relationships with people you cared for, or what's going on (and I mean *really* going on, like Who are the men that run this country?) in that great wide world outside your window, or even just get up in the morning and open up the fuckin' window, take a toke check the street and write a song about *that.* Any old shit will do, almost literally anything under the sun. Just like shooting monkeys in a barrel.

When I really get dour sometimes I wonder if it'd be possible at *all* to write a song today like, oh, say, "Wild Thing." People are just too superconscious of every creative move made in their lives of infinite possibilities and friendly niceness to do anything anymore that's outside of all contexts or just a simple expression of something with no real ramifications, at least none that the creator consciously put there: if some clown like me wants to come along and tell you that "Wild Thing" is the supreme manifestation of Rock and Roll as Global Worldmind Orgasm plus Antespurt to the Millennium, you have the privilege of laughing in his face and telling him to shut up and go back to his orgone box. But if the *writer* of "Wild Thing" had actually had any considerations in mind even remotely related to that kind of stuff when he sat down and made it up, you can bet it would have been a terrible song. The Troggs probably *were* those clerks they looked like. Quite possibly they understood or ruminated about what they were doing on very limited levels. Because that was all that was necessary. Had they been a clot of intellectual sharpies hanging out in the London avant-garde scene, they would most likely have been a preening mess unless they happened to be the Velvet Underground who were a special case anyway. I really believe maybe you've gotta be *out of it* to create truly great rock 'n' roll, either that or have such supranormal, laser-nerved control over what you are consciously manipulating that it doesn't matter (the Rolling Stones) or be a disciplined artist with an abiding joy in teenage ruck jump music and an exceptionally balanced outlook (Lou Reed, Velvets), or chances right now are that you are almost certain to come out something far less or perhaps artistically more (but still less) than rock 'n' roll, or go under.

About the only places where I could foresee the emergence of a truly vital *rock 'n' roll* band at present would be the most out of the way places in America (and only in America—the only European bands in three years, of the flood we've suffered, to show that they know anything at all about what the music's really about, much less the Party, are Savage Rose and Amon Duul II, who sound like a crazed Gothic-Germanic teenage horror movie fan refraction of the whole early murky psychedelic fuzztone feedback modal music fad; and England can with about two exceptions in the whole fucking commonwealth just sink with the setting of its colonial sun like the new Mu into the ocean as far as rock 'n' roll goes—those Limeys are *really* blundering in the dark, except maybe for Black Sabbath, who are just crass and artless and young enough that they might make it yet if they'd speed their songs up a little and shorten the times), although you can leave out the South pretty much, 'cause all them dumb saltines can play is blues and bluz and blooz and a little soul when the weather lets them far enough out of their torpor to get ambitious (I know I'm talking like a bigot, but being a bigot is fun as long as you don't upset the karmic balance too much so all the negative vibes outweigh the good ones and everybody gets constipated and bummed out; and anyway, even if it is bigotry, it's also true that this time I'm *right*); so unless some rabid new ratpack combination of Question Mark and the Mysterians, the Troggs, the Stooges, MC5 and Bob Seger comes roaring out of some nowhere right-wing cowboy town where it's usually too hot even to drink the beer or do anything much but dodge your parents and the neighbors and the Man and grumble a lot, some real charmer of a town in Arizona (where Alice Cooper was born and created) or maybe Idaho or Arkansas. I'd like to include New Mexico but know it would be fruitless since the goddam place is overrun by wandering hippies turning it into a gigantic combination Cowboy Haight-Ashbury and Spiritual Commune Spa in the desert so some poor kid still playing psychedelic feedback surf licks on his guitar can't even develop naturally without a buncha fuckin world travelers from San Francisco barging in and poisoning his brain with all the latest Crosby-Gravenitis-Taylor & Mitchell drivel which he mighta been able to largely escape if it was a small town with only records in the drugstore and his parents keeping him on a real chintzy allowance until he's old enough to go on tour with his band and become the new Seeds or even the new Hombres.

Other than that the only real hope is Detroit, where the kids take a lot of downs and dig down bands but at LEAST there's no folkie scene and lots of people still care about getdown gutbucket rock 'n' roll passionately because it takes the intolerableness of Detroit life and channels it into a form of strength and survival with humor and much of the energy claimed. And they are still fiercely devoted to the Party because the fatuity rate is incredibly low there, as is the cosmic vibration rate; people tend to have horse sense, which is refreshing, and know what's important; even more than that they know what's absolutely crucial and what's a gaudy ball of gauze.

But all those gauze tissues will continue to have their appeal, because people quite naturally respond initially to the most relatable and reassuring images presented them, and take the time later if at all to sort out the distinctions between package and payload. And with all the sociopsychological baggage accompanying pop music now, it's only natural that true misfits and creeps or just plain ugly people, artists who don't fit in or don't look like they would, should get drubbed with the short end of the shit stick now and then. Times have changed—you could know that Dostoyevsky was a thoroughly despicable person and still read his every word greedily. And even when word began to get out somewhere between *Highway 61* and *Blonde on Blonde* that Dylan might actually have mutated into (or been all along) a nasty little punk who also happened to be the most gifted songwriter of his time, people just shrugged because, after all, it was Dylan.

Nowadays, though, it seems to be getting harder and harder for musical artists to gain true mass acceptance without at least a token mouthing of all the pieties that a large part of this generation totes around with them like a pocket rosary or spare hankie; either that or, as an alternate course, grooming themselves after the by now patented style of the Superperson, expected to capture the public imagination, the extravagant and ostentatious lifestyles that pass for charisma in a time when almost anybody *talks* about charisma but if you think about it there's precious little to be seen. A movie like *Mad Dogs & Englishmen* stacks its whole rationale on the notion that these people are so glamorous and fascinating that we'll be willing to sit still for a long movie of them playing gigs and getting in and out of planes a lot not only because we want to hear the music but also because the way they live and the way they carry themselves is imbued with so much magnetic dynamism that we've just *got* to see them behind the scenes of their concerts and even in their most mundane daily routines. What's ironic about it, though, is that not only do none of the principals in this particular example indicate in the movie that they have personalities of any sort, settling instead merely to parade around in their fancy duds with little stoned smiles, but on top of that audiences everywhere are responding to this narcissistic nonsense with all the enthusiasm and interest the "stars" of the movie have not begun to bother to earn, in fact people will project their own conceptions of these people onto what they are seeing and come back bedazzled. The moral, I guess, is that as long as you carry yourself in the proper noncommittal manner you'll *never* have to do anything else, and your very mysterious impassiveness will implicitly confer all the charisma you'll ever need.

There have always been stars, and stars have always been created, and the public has always lived vicariously through them and invested them with everything that they don't personally have, because the whole point of the thing is to create myths and fantasies anyway. But the difference, I think, is that audiences of the past tended to demand a bit more of their Superpersonalities—i.e., that they *did* have personalities. Even Mick Jagger, who almost certainly is one of the most interesting entertainers to come to prominence in the last decade, doesn't really have to do anything when he appears in a movie, because everybody knows that it's enough for people just to look at him and think about him as the human phenomenon that he is. Unfortunately, though, there's all these other people running around trying to pass themselves off as phenomena when they're actually just random clowns, one classic example being the movie *Easy Rider,* which saw kids all over responding to the two main characters as if they were heroes, when actually neither one showed enough personality one way or another to be called much of anything except boring.

What all this posturing and fake glamour results in is a vast detachment and cynicism on the part of the artists. Since it's impossible to have respect for an audience that'll take just about anything you care to dish out, and the impassive demeanor is so central to the role, a general numbnose is all that can be expected. While the majority of the people buying the records never get close enough to feel the contempt firsthand, those close to the centers of glamour and power often twist the contempt to their own purposes. To use a blatant and obvious example, many of the regulars at the Whisky a Go Go in L.A., the breed of hustlers who hang out in the backroom orbits of visiting stars, will accept almost anything from said star if being recognized by him, even negatively, promises to build their status. British stars of the new shag-and-demi-drag species, especially, are kow-towed to until the point is reached where they could probably get away with anything. Some of the people around the Whisky would probably be glad to let Rod Stewart piss on them if they could actually believe that he would deign to, because they could run right over to their buddies' houses after-wards and say: "You'll *never* guess! Rod Stewart just pissed on me!"

So, for all those winding and long-winded reasons, I expect less from the current music scene all the time. Oh, there are the Van Morrisons and the Bands and even the Randy Newmans and Neil Youngs, and all of them are great, but whichever of them may have been at the Party once maybe half a decade ago, none of them can sit still at the Party right now for more than about one song at a time. And as you get older you get more resigned and so your bigotry kinda slips away—if you think I'm a Johnny Pissoff now, you shoulda seen me in 1968 when everybody was screaming for Cream and Electric Flag and nobody but maybe three people in my whole town paid any attention at all to *White Light / White Heat.* But now I'm real tolerant, even more than your average rock critic. For instance, I could listen to Chicago or Santana anytime, though Ed Ward is starting to anticipate that every time he mentions one of those people I will say I like them with a cornball smile and he just says: "I knew that was coming." To him, of course, they're anathema. I don't think anybody as crass and commercial as they are could possibly be the Enemy. My spleen is reserved for Elton John, James Taylor, all the glory boys of I-Rock. I call it I-Rock, even though I just made up the name, because most of it is so relentlessly, involutedly egocentric that you finally actually stop hating the punk and just want to take the poor bastard out and get him a drink, and then kick his ass, preferably off a high cliff into the nearest ocean.

Matter of fact, if I ever get down to Carolina I'm gonna try to figure out a way to off James Taylor. Hate to come on like a Nazi, but if I hear one more Jesus-walking-the-boys-and-girls-down-a-Carolina-path-while-the-dilemma-of-existence-crashes-like-a-slab-of-hod-on-J.T.'s-shoulders song, I will drop everything (I got nothin' to do here in California but drink beer and watch TV anyway) and hop the first Greyhound to Carolina for the signal satisfaction of breaking off a bottle of Ripple (he deserves no better, and I wish I could think of worse, but they're all local brands) and twisting it into James Taylor's guts until he expires in a spasm of adenoidal poesy.

> EXTRA! TRAGEDY STRIKES ROCK! SUPERSTAR GORED BY DERANGED ROCK CRITIC!! "We made it," gasped Lester Bangs as he was led by police from the bloody scene. "We won."   —*Rolling Stone*

But fantasies and jokes—none of that is really any good. If they just don't seem to be playing your song much right now, well, stop feeling sorry for yourself, scout the terrain and see if we can figure out where to go next. Because there's always gonna be *something* around in the tradition. But fuck the tradition, I want the Party! Too much goddam tradition-worship around here as it is now, that's what's wrong with Creedence Clearwater and half a horde of other wasted talent that could be kickin' off doorknobs and hinges if they weren't so allfired concerned with *respecting* all that stuff from the past and doing things the Right Way as learned from the old farts insteada just kicking their musical asses around the rumpus room until it might begin to sound like something new. And by old farts I mean all the pantheon of geniuses treated with such reverence: Chuck Berry, who might be the greatest songwriter of all time, is an old fart, Little Richard is an old fart, Elvis is Elvis and what he should really do if he was crazy is join the Doors.

The point of such an utterly absurd suggestion is the point of this whole rambling rant, is the point of the Party, and that point is that the Emperors of Rock 'n' Roll are not naked noble savages like we thought they were at all, but the point's not that they wear clothes either, *the point is that the clothes don't fit.* The pants are five sizes too big and with them slingshot suspenders those trousers're liable to hit the sawdust any minute. And those shirts aren't revolutionary battle fatigues, they're polka-dotted bibs, and Christ, that tie, why, wait, *he's actually using a cummerbund for a tie.* And every last one of 'em you think wears glasses, sheeit, that's clear fucking lenses, those are the exact same Bop Glasses that Dizzy Gillespie used to wear when he walked down the streets of Harlem with bubblegum in his mouth blowing up one balloon after another because it kept his lungs in shape and it was a fine way to spend a summer afternoon. I mean, why, fuck, they're all just a buncha fuckin' *clowns.* They don't even have to try to be funny, they just are and can't help it, and it's the grace of their absurdity that makes them geniuses and heroes, just like rock 'n' roll and jazz both were born exactly as Jack Kerouac said of the latter in "History of Bop": "Bop began with jazz, but one afternoon somewhere on a sidewalk in 1939, 1940, Dizzy Gillespie or Charlie Parker or Thelonious Monk was walking past a men's clothing store on 42nd Street or South Main in L.A. and from the loudspeaker they suddenly heard a wild impossible *mistake* in jazz that could only have been heard inside their own imaginary heads, and that is a new art, bop! The name derives from an accident. . . . Lionel Hampton had made a record called 'Hey, Bop-a-Re-Bop' and everybody yelled it when Lionel would jump in the audience and wail at everybody with sweat-claps and jumping fools in the aisles, the drummer vastly booming and belaboring on the stage as the whole theatre rocked. . . ."

It always begins in that glorious "mistake," the crazy unexpected note kicking out sideways to let us loose again no matter what you call it. It reappears periodically every few years, the next new absurd and outrageous squeak that no one could calculate till ten years after it moulders buried under wretched excess in the slowdown twilight, but the Craze will come again in new clothes! And whenever it does it will have about as much respect for all those old farts from the sixties as most of the kids who first awoke to Stones and Yardbird raveups have for those beboppers of Kerouac's nostalgias or for most of the titans from the fifties for that matter! Like a friend of mine who wails lifelong to Velvets Stones MC5 and even gets off marginally on the Grand Funk tapes in his car being nineteen as he is, but when I loaned him my stellar lineup of fifties classics from *Chuck Berry Is on Top* to *For LP Fans Only* he brings them back and says: "I don't know, I couldn't really listen to 'em very much. It just sounds kind of bare without the feedback."

So what're you gonna do? Well, different people have different tastes. That's a fact. And I don't even really much care *what* it is myself at this point, so long as it comes from the Party line. Which is nothing to worry about, because this ain't the kind of party you join or carry around a card for; this is a kind of party you LIVE. And it don't even much matter when you do that, because the Party, though its flame may flicker low and all but gutter in these juiceless times, goes on forever. Any fool could see that those people at the Lionel Hampton concert described by Kerouac were at the Party, and if you've ever heard those old Jazz at the Philharmonic 78s like "Perdido" and "Endido" where Flip Phillips and Illinois Jacquet would tear into those wild jams and end up flat on their backs in the middle of the stage kicking into the air and holding the sax up like a big pacifier and blowing jive blasts past melody while the audience of zootsuiters howled with glee, well, that was 1949, didn't no Little Richard nor any other

Johnny Come Lately invent the Party or even rock 'n' roll for Chrissake because it's all the same shit anyway with just minor differences and names thought up by pensive idiots when what it all boils down to is two things:

Number One, everybody should realize that all this "art" and "bop" and "rock 'n' roll" and whatever is all just a joke and a mistake, just a hunka foolishness so stop treating it with any seriousness or respect at all and just recognize the fact that it's nothing but a Wham-O toy to bash around as you please in the nursery, it's nothing but a goddam Bonusburger so just gobble the stupid thing and burp and go for the next one tomorrow; and don't worry about the fact that it's a joke and a mistake and a bunch of foolishness as if that's gonna cause people to disregard it and do it in or let it dry up and die, because it's the strongest, most resilient, most *invincible* Superjoke in history, nothing could possibly destroy it ever, and the reason for that is precisely that it *is* a joke, mistake, foolishness. The first mistake of Art is to assume that it's serious. I could even be an asshole here and say that "Nothing is true; everything is permitted," which *is* true as a matter of fact, but people might get the wrong idea. What's truest is that you cannot enslave a fool. No way to regiment the heebie jeebies or make 'em walk a straight line. And nothing better to do from here on out, now that we got cybernation and all such like, but just go to the Party and STAY THERE.

Number Two point I wanna make here before wrapping up this pontification which has been all too solemn its own self, is that the time has come for all good men and women to come to the aid of the Party; i.e., DECIDE whether you wanta jump and caper with music that's alive or moulder in the Dostoyevskian hovels of dead bardic auteur crap picking nits out of its navel and so sickly that to see it shake its ass would be a hilarious horror indeed. Well, you don't really have to choose, this is no political party even if others say it is, and anyway the whole mess is just a goddam phase, just like when Kerouac's great gleeful Bop Clowns dancing in the aisles wound down to the Venice, California "beatniks" whose dumbass totems Lawrence Lipton touted in 1959 in *The Holy Barbarians:* "Once you are out of your teens you don't usually dance. You *never* dance in any public place. That's for squares."

Of course not. What you did then instead was sit around in dreary "pads" getting wasted and having big profound discussions for hours on end about the meaning of life, psychoanalysis, the martyrdom of Charlie Parker and materialism in square society. So twelve years later we've come all the way around again except now society has started to bust at the seams so you don't have to be a furtive or blaringly assertive "bohemian" because everybody's a bohemian that smokes grass and now we can sit around in dorms and crashpads and even parents' houses and get wasted and talk about all the stupid things people talk about now with one difference that they don't have as many protocols and taboos as those lard-ass beatniks but there ain't many of them seem to move much more than the former did either and even if they do they're liable to make a big production out of it.

Am I a crank? I feel somewhat like the Uncle Scrooge of pop top journalism; except that twenty-two seems like no age to wear the persona of cantankerous coot so naturally. What's more, the certain self-consciousness of all this makes me a rockcrit auteur, which means James Taylor with a typewriter which means a suicide. Assuming, that is, that I take all this with a solemnity as unrelenting as its style. But the real truth, and it's the only way I could continue to feel positive and even enthusiastic about what I'm doing in this business that they haven't found a name unpejorative enough for yet, is that while I mean every word I say or most of them anyhoo and intend 75% of this kidney pie in total seriousness and passion that's not in the least feigned, I also take it with absolutely no seriousness at all. That is, I believe in rock 'n' roll but I don't believe in Rock 'n' Roll even if I don't always spell it the same way, and I believe in the Party as an exhilarating alternative to the boredom and bitter indifference of life in the "Nothing is true; everything is permitted" era, just as it provided alternatives in the form of momentary release from the repression and moral absolutism of the fifties. The Party is one answer to how to manage leisure in a society cannibalized by it, but it's not bread and circuses either because you can't co-opt jive because jive is the true folk music that liberals can never appropriate or master and only an urban aborigine will understand. And far from being anti-intellectual, the Party is *a*-intellectual; it doesn't make any promises or ask for any field workers. As an answer to the mysteries of life it's a Bronx cheer, and not a dada one either but the kind your uncle Louie used to razz the quarterback with from behind a Schlitz on Saturday afternoon, but as a *way of life* it's a humdinger.

But that Bronx cheer still leads us to questions as to the critic's motivations. *Am I a crank?* Of course. I'm not a crank all the time but I'm a crank right here because dammitall people just got no *spunk* today, a whole society fulla deadbeats being Cool whether it's collegiate doper creeps with their Elton John records or downed-out pubes on the floors of concert halls that if I attended events in them places I'd take a handful of reds before going in the door too. See? I just like people with some Looney Tune in their souls. And seeing how Looney Tune stock has fallen so low and hardly anybody ever goes to the Party anymore except mostly isolated individuals jiving in the privacy of their own rooms which isn't exactly the idea the music's just gotta reflect it and come up Doldrum City. I've tried everything, right here in this fucking diatribe I've tried gratuitous insults, scatology, highschool flashbacks, plain invective, homicidal fantasy in one instance, and even though I feel good about the latter at least I know that no matter how much I rant things ain't gonna get better till it's time for 'em to. And that time will come, make no mistake, it's never been stopped yet, and when our number comes up we can all get back to the Party in the real way we know it should be wailing joy from coast to coast just as Martha and the Vandellas prophesied in "Dancing in the Street": "Callin' out, around the world / Are you ready for a brand-new beat?"

And, until it comes, there's always myth.

PART THREE: TALES OF PRESLEY

If you thought "Wild Thing" was hot, just get a load of "66-5-4-3-2-1." The title is there to make you wonder and trick you. You're supposed to think it's a phone number, like "634-5789" (why did both Wilson Pickett and the Marvelettes have numbers so similar, I've always wondered, and years apart too?—I detect the World Brain at work again), but it's not, and I figured out the *real*, hidden meaning. What it is is a countdown till penile penetration of Reg's girlie's box. The Troggs were kinda deceitful about it because they were getting so paranoid about AM censorship they were almost afraid to put out a record called "Anyway That You Want Me" because the Drake and Gavin stations might think that it was a baldfaced offer of multiple-orifice hanky panky. "With a Girl Like You" was also the subject of some nervousness because obviously "A Girl Like [That]" is a whore, "Girl in Black" had S&M overtones, "I Want You to Come into My Life" was a not-so-clever use of the old randomly selected metaphorical-code-word trick so brilliantly elucidated by Dr. A. Weberman in his recent papers. "Life," of course, is merely ghetto slang for "asshole," as in Sly and the Family Stone's "Life," which was indeed slyly short enough to get by after the band found out that Epic turned thumbs down on them calling their second album and hit single therefrom *Asshole* and "Asshole," respectively. Eyes in the media-filtering offices were a damn sight sharper after the storm of controversy and even high-level executive firings following *that* absurd and unconscionable "leak."

But the Troggs were really starting to chew their cuticles. Suddenly they realized that, like the Fugs and the Velvets and a precious few others, they were so far ahead of their time that they scarcely dared release a single, and if *that* impasse obtained much longer they'd be dead anyway because at the time (1967) singles were crucial. It was obvious that they couldn't use "Night of the Long Grass" because the Comstocks would think it was about that very same Mary whom the Association had "Coming Along" (a classic case of double-exposure simultaneous sex-drug entendre getting by the censors for some reason) just a year or so earlier. But why rattle on with a buncha mundane showbiz tales most of which are pretty much common knowledge anyway on the "In" scene here in, uh, Mill Valley, when we can attend back to the decorously significant historical task at hand, that of sifting all these old Troggs songs to find out if any of 'em are any good or not. So far all of them have been absolutely mind-boggling in their neoclassic radiance, but you never know. I'm not gonna give up until I find at least *one* dud! One blunder, one fall from the lofty heights of their inspiration, one chink in the vast superstructure of this artistic vision which though I have not completed my studies of it I tentatively believe to be at least as profound and enduring as Proust's *Remembrance of Things Past,* excuse me, *A la recherche du temps perdu,* if not the entire oeuvre of Sakyamuni Bach, the Rimbaud of the Bach family. But my scholarly mind has led me down the primrose path of digression again, I fear. In fact, I seem to be digressing all over the place. I don't even remember what I was writing about two pages ago. But what was it, on the other hand, that the most venerable Sir, uh, what's-his-name, said, "Consistency is the hobgoblin of little minds"? So bear with me and stop being such a sissy.

The truly great moment in "66-5-4-3-2-1" arrives when Mr. Presley, who has been counting down to blastoff, or blast-*in,* all through the song, suddenly is stricken with second thoughts: "Someday we'll overdo it / Someday we will go too far / I'll be drained of all my money / And we'll even have to sell my car / 'Cause I know what you want!" Poor kid, hasn't he ever heard of Trojans? Oh well, the British always did have a tendency to be a bit backward, except in their movies, rock 'n' roll 1964–1967 (the last year is definitely cited with reservations), and . . . uh . . . well, they do have Alec Guinness and the Stones and the Troggs. . . . But poor old Reg! What a pickle! Here he is hot to trot and suddenly stricken by a flash that's a surefire dong-wilter: at this moment they are broaching a "big decision" certainly in the running for its gravity with Lou Reed's big decision to shoot smack in "Heroin," except their plight is even more charged and brinksmanshipish because they're poised panting right at each other's urgent portals, while ol' Lou had to go through the whole rigmarole of cooking up, siphoning, tying off, all that junkie shit, before actually committing himself to his Big D (Norman Mailer's Big D was Dallas, and he committed himself to it like a nuthouse; which reminds me that the grapevine also sez that now that former feuds are history ol' Norm and even ol'er LBJ are the fastest friends and spend much time together down on the Pedernales barbecuin', rustlin' steers, fuckin' wimmen, tossin' Humphrey jokes back and forth, and drinkin' like two carpetbaggers what with both of 'em bein' partial to the exact same brand, the name of which I am not at liberty to repeat here because any whisper of payola could fuse like a mountainful of dynamite and find me shitcanned unceremoniously in fact way up shit creek with my rep destroyed by *even one moment's* idle slip of the tongue. . . . Greg Shaw runs a tight ship here at *Who Put the Bomp*, and brooks no jive from any of us from Suzy the secretary to Edmund the Fishing Editor to all the others including me, whose position as a relative greenhorn in this institution is still vague enough to make me nervous: for instance, I have been writing this article for twelve straight hours).

Tuning back in on Reg and his honey again, we see them slumped in the gloom of a flashforward that finds, sure enough, that all the prickly premonitions came true: Taralee (for that is her name) is big with a little Reg or Taralee who from the outer dimensions of his or her abode looks about due to come kickin' into this vale of tears. And vale of tears it is, I wasn't just being literary, because not only was Reg drained of all his money and even had to sell his prize-winning Gorgon-Cammed 387 Torsion Superstock Cord (what does he need with a car in Britain, anyway? Nobody over there under thirty-two has one, or at least nobody young enough to really long for one, so he's probably better off without it and with a clear conscience instead of being a notorious perpetrator of Pig Private Propertyism), but they are scuttling along down in Soho in absolute rags, Reg is intently scanning the sidewalk in search of stray cigarette butts, ha'pences, tuppences, subway tokens, Shell Collect the States and/or Presidents coins, anything to barter for a crust of bread, while Taralee, when one looks close enough to regret it, appears . . . oh, God . . . yes, it is . . . to be slowly . . . expiring . . . of consumption.

Horrible. Reconnoitering the terrain elsewhere we find ourselves in the presence of yet another all-time Troggs poll-topper and a departure from the Hot Pants theme too, which is refreshing by this point. "I Just Sing" is an anthem of loneliness and defiant individuality, a primal scene which finds the pubescent misfit languishing in his bedroom like Iggy's British cousin, finding a way out of the lumpen emptiness of his situation by splitting the maw of silence with the holy healing croak of rock 'n' roll:

"When my luck is down / And I can't think of a thing / I just go to my bed, lay my hands on my head / I open my mouth and I sing / Yeah, I just sing. . . ." It's another year with nothin' to do. Sometimes the only vent in the universe for the tensions and glooms which can barely be understood much less dealt with properly is to just open wide and wail them out. Like when Reg finally pulls himself up from his bed of blues, spruces up and cruises out to the drive-in with his new girl. Now, the one thing that can invariably reverse a streak of down luck is a little sweet stuff, huh? Yup, that's a well-known fact, accepted on four continents (they haven't polled the others yet) as a cure-all transcending Christian Science and even Geritol. Even thinking about it is a perk-up: blood starts pumping with a little more interest, heart a bit less heavy. So they make it to the double Gore Thrill Scare Shock Show at the drive-in, and what do you think happens? Our boy's femme demurs because "that's the only reason you bring me here. When you saw me, you looked at me like you could barely wait to get at me and start bangin' away! Well, there's a lot more to it than that, Reggie. You never think that I might want something better. You never take me out to dinner at a nice place, just to relax—not once! And movies, I'd *love* to go to see some art films, I hear the new Godard's in town, but *no,* it's just drive-ins and balling and balling and drive-ins. I can understand your frustrations and how it's hard for us to get together because you're still living with your parents at twenty-six, but my God we've been to this exact same drive-in every single Friday and Saturday night for the last eighteen months! Monster movies, I'm going crazy, every time I come I'm coming to a goddamned monster movie! I'm coming and I look up and some *creature* is tearing a girl limb from limb! How do you think that makes me *feel?* Rapturous? Well, this is it. I came here tonight with you to tell you: I've met somebody else. His name is Terrence, he's a script consultant for a network—I don't know, he hasn't told me which one yet, we've been going out together only I guess, uh, three weeks now. And he drives a Porsche and, well, he just has so much . . . *savoir faire.* . . . Oh, Reg, I know you *try* to meet my standards, I know you *want* to be suave, but . . . well . . . I'm sorry. What's done is done. Don't cry—don't cry, please. Do you want to go home now?"

No, amazingly enough he didn't wanna—if it'd been me I'da peeled out an' dumped the broad . . . imagine, after all he gave to her, all those years, all those movies, and then she just up and dumps him just like that! Well, I'da dumped her and headed straight for Doc Swifty's Bar. Good riddance. But this poor dumb sucker don't! Instead he decides to stick around and watch the flicks! So while she leans against the far door feeling rather self-conscious, he sits there watching these C-run ghoul pix to cheer himself up! At least that's what she thinks. But actually old Reg had an ace of spades up his sly ol' sleeve: it was an ace bomber of absolutely *atomic* North African marihooch that he had indeed bought at one of the most outrageous prices of the week from a spade down in the West End who grinned from ear to ear like a slit throat all the while. So now, just as the deranged idiot cousin is slurking up out of the depths of the old castle with vengeance in his one bulging eye, ol' Reg ever so casually whips it out, lites up, tokes down. Well, naturally Constance wants to know what it is, poor naif, so he gives her some, in fact he gives her a lot, in fact he gives her so much she don't know which end is up or if the show is on the screen or out zipping tween them stars! She is in the *O-Zone!* Next thing Connie is leaning half out the window trying to stare *through* space and see what's behind it, meanwhile her cute but ample butt is wiggling in wide-open drug delirium, and what happens next? Ask Reg: "When we're out on a date / And you start movin' that thing / It goes to my head and I start seein' red and I sing / Yeah, I just sing!" *Well,* that just blows her out entirely! "What's that?" she whispers. "It's a song!" grins Reg, too proud to play it cool like any cat named Presley should at such a time. "It's a rock 'n' roll song and I wrote it about you!" That did it. I guess you know Terrence just got blown off the set the very next morning, which was just as well anyway cause he was actually a fake and didn't work for no TV network and in fact the Porsche was borrowed from a friend to impress so you *know* he's just a schlemiel behind all that *savoir faire.* Meanwhile, Constance was so entranced with Reg's newly discovered talent that she promptly re-fell in absolute swooning love with him just as she had that first time seven years ago when he was trying to work his way through college selling the *Encyclopaedia Britannica* and came to her house and was invited in to find that both of them were secret maniacal Gene Vincent fans. And now that Reg may wind up even *bigger* than Gene Vincent, what with the Troggs and all, everything should be just hunky dory except unfortunately Connie met a half-Portuguese half-Basque millionaire businessman from Tierra del Fuego with *savoir faire* to spare and what with him having a private jet and all the temptation to bolt was just too much so she did so, briefly breaking Reg's heart until he heard that the smoothie businessman, who was actually a reptilian shark of an amoral manipulator under all the *s.f.*, got bored with her cultural-climbing aspirations and dumped her on a friend in the International Cocaine Set who turned her into a real hype and now she's sunk deep in white slavery and opium addiction in a brothel in Puerto Vallarta which brought Reg down bad for a while till he realized there was nothing he could do about it and started gettin' back to the good times again with all the willing young ladies who breathed a little harder at his precipitate Stardom and many of whom are described both herein and in the songs of the Troggs of course. He even moved out of his parents' house, and he wasn't even thirty yet.

—*Who Put the Bomp,* Winter–Spring 1971

Do the Godz Speak Esperanto?

ESP Records is surely one of the strangest companies (and much of their product among the most elusive) in history. Their records (some of them, anyway) are packaged with all the sturdy solemnity of Folkways library collections, and the cover art has generally been either bizarrely imaginative or unbelievably shoddy. Since 1964, they've introduced such contemporary titans as Pharoah Sanders, Albert Ayler and Gato Barbieri, as well as providing important releases by musicians of stature like Steve Lacey, Bud Powell, Paul Bley, releasing Ornette Coleman's classic 1962 Town Hall concert, bringing Sun Ra back to us after far too long, and coming up with some of the most off-the-wall items in the annals of the music business. Like William Burroughs's stunning readings from *Naked Lunch* and *Nova Express*, a musical adaptation of *Finnegans Wake*, Patty Waters's pre-Yoko album of sixteen-minute-shrieks based on "Black Is the Color of My True Love's Hair," and the *East Village Other Electric Newspaper*—a sloppy, rather cynical "collage" of the radio broadcast of LBJ's daughter Luci's wedding, Ishmael Reed reading from *The Free-Lance Pallbearers*, songs by Tuli Kupferberg of Fugs and Steve Weber of Holy Modal Round-ers ("If I Had Half a Mind," which is one of the great all-time obscure rock croak masterpieces), some good jazz by Marion Brown and fascinating "Noise" by the early Velvet Underground, a witless smattering of camp gossip by Warhol acolytes Ingrid Superstar and Gerard Malanga ("I could turn Steve Reeves on—just like that," brags Ingrid, snapping her fingers), an interminable and equally witless "Interview with Hairy" by Ed Sanders and Ken Weaver pushing their *Playboy*/locker room humor much too far, and Allen Ginsberg and Peter Orlovsky chanting mantras even more interminably though equally as boring. Also, a liner listing of "SILENCE by Andy Warhol, copyright 1932," which must refer to the empty bands leading you in and out of each side. The strong temptation is to call Warhol's spot the highlight of the record, but it *does* have Brown and the Velvets, which was why I bought it. Unfortunately, however, they only got to play for about a minute apiece, and the blaring radio broadcast of Luci's wedding which runs through the whole record all but drowns them out. Not only that, but it's set stereo center, so you can't turn out one speaker to fully absorb that brief moment of primal Velvets. Still, you've got to admit that it's a one-of-a-kind item, and I'll probably keep it forever. My kids might get a kick out of Luci's wedding.

Another interesting ESP album is *Nu Kantu En Esperanto* (Sing Along in Esperanto). I don't know if anybody cares anymore, but there was a brand-new language devised some years back by some genius or maniac, based on several European tongues and phonics. He called it Esperanto, and a foundation was set up to promote its adoption worldwide as the new International Language, wiping out French, English, Swahili, all the others—and part of the rationale behind that proposal was the notion that this would be a way of promoting world peace by sort of manufacturing a Tower of Babel in reverse. If we all spoke the same language, perhaps then we could all get along, no more wars or exploitation, because then we would all understand each other! (I may be simplifying this a bit.) What all this has to do with ESP records is that for a long time, perhaps even today, they had some vague connection with the Esperanto foundation. Until a year or two ago, all ESP releases had a short message about prices and how to order by mail on the back, *translated into Esperanto.* But what's the connection? Do Esperanto speakers dig Ayler and Gato, or even the Fugs and the Godz? Does their knowledge of the new International and so far all but useless Language attune them to the lofty realms where high-energy music soars and William Burroughs croaks out old Doc Benway's lines with perfect snake-oil sonority? Or does Esperanto have some implicit connection with the emergent counterculture, the Life Culture, whatever you want to call it? Will we all speak Esperanto after the Revolution and become true brothers and sisters at last and lay down the gun for good? It's food for thought.

So I have never quite understood the record company called ESP. Warner/Reprise they're not. Cloaked in mystery, inevitably issuing from New York City, they've recorded some of the greatest jazz and most unclassifiable idiosyncrasies of our time. And, periodically, they've made hesitant steps at signing rock talent. But what sort of rock group signs with ESP? The Rascals? The Lovin' Spoonful? No, not even the Mothers or the Velvet Underground. Unchallenged as the most prototypically Underground record company in America, it stands to reason that they would have to sign the most ultra-Underground of Underground groups. So they started with the Fugs in 1966, and the product of the association is a testament to both the genius of the band and the vision of the company. The first two Fugs albums are enshrined forever in the pantheon of heroic rock 'n' roll manias. The inspiration blazing behind songs like "Swinburne Stomp," "Nothing" and "Frenzy" will never again be equalled. I remember buying the *Virgin Forest* album in 1966, staggering back to the record store and asking the girl what their *first* album could be like. "Oh, pretty much like that," she smiled, "except more primitive." *More* primitive? Much more primitive than that and they'd have loincloths and bones in their noses. But, of course, infinite extension in either direction is possible to artists of true vision, so it *was,* and the first real Fugs could likely have made an album that would have taken that slab of backalley primitivism and reduced it to the square root of its nth division, into the yowlings of missing links around the purple fire, and it still woulda been a great, wailing, infinitely entertaining record.

Unfortunately, however, the Fugs were seduced by the big money and technicolor jackets of Frank Sinatra and Reprise, and after that their albums just got worse and worse, until we'd lost yet another great musical yeti forever. Which left us crying up the sleeves of our Bobby Dylan worker shirts and listening to Count Five and Question Mark, but left ESP with a haunted hole where their larger-than-life boogie poets once slouched, and they had to scout around and find somebody fast. Oh, they always had Pearls Before Swine, but who gave a spoonful of swill for them? They were soon to follow the Fugs to the warm fold of the emergent Burbank Adult-Rock cartel, anyway, and if Sanders and the boys never quite fit there the fuckin' place was *made* for P. B. Swine, just find 'em a berth in the stable for snotnose minstrels, right between Arlo and the one reserved for James Taylor.

For a while there it looked like ESP was gonna start a whole line of rock albums, promising to sign the most outrageous and/or untouchable scalawags from Maine to El Cajon. (I even nurtured my own fantasies, blatting my harp and singing "Clark Kent" and "Keep Off the Grass.") Fired by the holy frenzy of the Fugs, I ran right out and tried to steal a copy of Pearls Before Swine. I took a copy of that and the Remains album, which I have never seen and wondered about ever since, and shoved them in my pants and pulled my coat over and walked out and got busted. But

I *believed* in ESP! I went right back soon as my social security check arrived and bought the damn thing, the very same copy I'd tried to lift! Imagine the dent in my artistic sensitivity when I got it home and its pallid putrefaction hit my nostrils! What next—*Albert Ayler Swings Stephen Foster?*

Luckily, however, the Godz came along at about that time, put me back on the right track, and restored my faith in ESP. And it's the Godz I've mainly written this for, because their art has fascinated me for four years—meanwhile absolutely ignored, as so many great artists are, by the rock press and the world at large. They don't take up where the Fugs left off—nobody could do that—but they do sometimes approximate that nth devolution of the Fugs' yawp to the point of squatting dogmen around the cannibal fire. Other times they would remind me of you and me and New York City and the vast vacuous beauty of this crap culture we're fryin' in.

One thing to be said about them is that they may well be the most inept band I've ever heard. I'd almost grant out of hand that they're the most inept *recording* band I've ever heard. And that they are the most inept band with *three* albums to their credit, I cannot deny. Why have they made three albums when so many great, talented, professional, musicianly bands get dumped unceremoniously after one? Because the Godz are brilliant, that's why, and most talented professional musicianly bands are stupid and visionless and exactly alike. Also, perhaps, because most TPMBs don't record for ESP.

So, the Godz are inept. They are also one of the most interesting bands to have survived from the first petal-kissing heydaze of Lovedelia to (presumably) the schizoid present. When I first saw their first album, *Contact High,* I jumped for joy. A new monster from ESP! Then I played it and thought, "Who the fuck do these guys think they're kidding? This is the worst record I ever heard!" And after that I went around for about a year and a half assuring everybody that no matter what kind of atrocity tales they could relate *I* knew what the absolute worst record in history was because I'd heard it! But somehow the memory of that idiot caterwauling kept following me around like the shade of a vision, and one day in 1968 when I saw it remaindered I grabbed and bought it. Man, was it awful! It was so awful I dug it! Not like so-bad-it's-good or any of that camp-kitsch shit—the Godz were onto something. I took it over to my nephew's and he looked at it and said, "How's this?" And I positively beamed, "Oh, man, is that ever *lousy,* oh, it gets *stars* for lousiness!"

"Oh yeah?" he said, getting all excited. "Let's play it!" After all, which would you rather audition first: *Super Session* and the new Butterfield album, or something that gets stars for *lousiness?*

Contact High, though nowhere near the Wagnerian grandeur of the

Fugs, is nevertheless an album like no other before or since. I know, I can hear you snide simps who'd rather listen to what you'd like to call "real music" all out there snorting: "Yeah, because nobody else would wanta do something like that!" And you're right. Most people are too *stupid!* They'd rather go learn Eric Clapton riffs. But the fact remains that the Godz did it and nobody else, and the record lives as an entity unto itself.

As such it is simultaneously a perfect artifact of New York in its period, and probably the Godz' finest album. The only non-snazz aspect of the set is the cornball liner notes by one Marc Crawford: "This is the Godz' truth . . . by four New Yorkers, who don't give a good God-damn whether you dig it or not. . . . But if you want to hear about love and the lack of it by victims unashamed, about hate and too much of it in the world . . . it is a new, honest, emotion-laden telling-it-like-I-feel-it kind of music, which is . . . very American, Lyndon Johnson and the critics notwithstanding. . . . They don't dig mom's apple pie and I've never seen them in church on Sunday."

Boy, they used to drag poor ole LBJ into everything. I bet if he were in now and some cat like David Crosby made a really fucked album and got called on it, he'd probably say that he was so preoccupied by Lyndy's machinations that he couldn't think straight. I don't think the Godz would ever come on so defensive. They may *not* care whether you like it, but they know their music is great, and their whole oeuvre radiates that kind of positive vitality. Marc Crawford probably secretly thought it was shit, himself, superpseudointellectual radiclib that he reeks of. What's more, the Godz don't sing about hate or lack of love, because they know there's too much negativism in the world already; not only that, I bet they *do* like mom's apple pie and mom too because they're too All-American not to. How could a real rock 'n' roller *not* like mom's apple pie for cryin' out loud? And the same goes for Church on Sunday—why'n the fuck d'ya think they called themselves the *Godz?* No, the Godz song is a joyous song of praise for the sun and the moon and all that lives between them.

Their first album, for instance, is a series of elemental celebrations, beginning with "Come On, Little Girl, Turn On," a relatively lengthy (by *Contact High*'s standards—I think the whole album's only about twenty-one minutes long—but then why pad out a perfect production with a bunch of draggy filler?) song exhorting a sweet child of the city to partake of the sacrament for three whole minutes. With Jay Dillon's great psaltery (ain't that some kind of an autoharp?), Jim McCarthy's whinnying harmonica, and the generally rambunctious vocal, the song could hardly miss, even if its form is a bit anachronistic in terms of the Godz' *real* symphonies.

A word should be said about the instrumentation and all that technical folderol. All of them sing, Dillon just plays psaltery here although he'll add piano and organ on *Godz Two,* but Larry Kessler doubles on bass and violin (viola later). A John Cale he's not—in fact he probably never had a lesson —in fact, he may never have *practiced*—but he sure can make that fiddle sing sassy! "Squeak" is his magnum opus, a grinding, grunging violin solo that sounds like he's jamming a non-resined bow on the strings so hard they're buckling against the wood, so you get that great organic sawing creak. I once borrowed a violin from a friend for a few days; I used to play it by holding the bow still and moving the fiddle lightning-fast across it. I'm left-handed. After a while I was even better than Larry, but I never learned his sense of economy—he can grind one note till it sounds like Beethoven, but I'm always sawing all over the damn thing. Just the rambunctiousness of a beginner, I guess.

Jim McCarthy is the guitarist, but he also doubles on plastic flute and harmonica, both of which I play. As a matter of fact, I'm better than him too, but I still really dig his work—I only wish I could sit in sometime. On the only non-original on the album, Hank Williams's "May You Be Alone," he fills in beautifully behind the straight shit-kicker vocal with a marvelous series of Ayler-like plastic flute flurries that squiggle off in all directions yet always remain absolutely appropriate. In Godz music, it's almost impossible to play a wrong note. So what's the point, you say, why can't *anybody* play music like that, why can't you or I? What makes *them* so special?

Well, theoretically, anybody *can* play like that, but in actual practice it just ain't so. Most people would be too stultified—after all, what's the point of doing it if anybody can?—and as for you, you probably ain't got the *balls* to do it, and even if you did, you'd never carry it through like a true Godzly musical maniac must to qualify. You'd just pick it up and tootle a few bars to prove something, and that's entirely different. Me, I could do it because I have been for years, even before I heard of the Godz. All it takes is insane persistence and a total disregard for everything but getting that yawp out if you gotta howl at the moon, and obviously most folks aren't gonna howl at the moon just to prove a point.

But the Godz would! And not to prove a point, but because they *like* howling at the moon! Which is what sets them apart. You gotta *dig* it or it falls flat. Here they are in "White Cat Heat," for instance, not exactly howling at the moon, but yowling like a pack of alley cats in a fur-flying brawl. Notice how it starts out kinda subdued—one guy's even going "Meeoow!" all falsetto-sweet just like mama's very own house tabby! The chickenshit! But then the others start revving up—"SCREEE!

SCRAWWRRR! RRRAAEEIKKHR!"—and before you know it he's as homicidal as the rest! And then dig how it rises to that incredible climax and then dies down in perfect symmetry. Fight's over. And it was a real one, too—you can listen to some of these corny post–*Freak-Out* records, with all these half-ass animal noises and shit, but that's just child's play. When the Godz got into character, they got into it *good,* and those who came to fool around had best just stand aside.

Godz Two is a little bit less raw than the first one—it has more songs, fewer explosions like "White Cat Heat"—but still a great album. Greil Marcus once came to see me when I was playing this album. As soon as he walked in the room, he said: "What's that?"

"It's the Godz!"

"Hhmmmmm," he said, puffing his pipe with that wry look he gets, "so that's the Godz, huh? Well, have fun!" and walked right back out! Sometimes I just don't understand people. Especially since *Godz Two* has at least two all-time Godz classics. "Riffin'," the song Greil walked out on, begins with a Tarzan yell, a wallowing harmonica, "Melons! Get your watermelons!," a hog call, an LBJ imitation, and on through several more political caricatures interspersed with odd punctuation of animal bleatings.

Even better, though, is "Now Song." This is a dead drunk lament featuring viola, guitar, and a truly incredible McCarthy vocal that wheezes and groans and gurgles like an old wino bawling his heart out, finally collapsing in grunts and sobs, right after the heartbreaking words, "This is now-ow-ow, this now-olliew, ow."

This album also found the Godz getting into some relatively conventional material. "Radar Eyes," "Soon the Moon," and "Permanent Green Light" were all dark, droning things, extremely simple but effective with their obsessive drumming, reiterated minor chords and chantlike vocals, and showed the Godz to be getting a rock-bottom groove reminiscent of Tyrannosaurus Rex's initial experiments in elementary electric guitar. There is a certain quality in the approach of a musician not totally familiar with his instrument, a sound found nowhere else. Sometimes less is more. "Soon the Moon," for instance, runs almost entirely on the low vocal chant and the insistent throbbing of one bass string and works perfectly that way, stark and spare to a purpose.

Between the second and third albums, the Godz recorded a single that of course never hit anywhere but should have. Much the best thing they'd ever done, "Whiffenpoof Song" was a real rock 'n' roll record, full in sound, dynamic and driving as the work of a much larger group. It opened with a guitar flourish, then the sad sad lyric echoing pitifully in space: "We are

poor little lambs / Who have gone astray / We are poor little lambs / Who
have lost our way." Then suddenly "BAAH BAAH BAH BAAAAAHH!
BAAH BAAH BAH BAAAAHH! BAAH BAAH BAAH BAH BAAAHH
BAAAHH BAAAAHH!!!" An explosion of martial blasts. And when the
song returns to the plaintive, "We are poor little lambs . . ." you can hear
actual sheep commenting on it (recorded down on the farm? or imper-
sonated once more by the ubiquitous Godz?). Any way you cut it, that's
a great record.

One of the main keys to the Godz' interest is that they are a pure test
of one of the supreme musical traditions of rock 'n' roll: the process by
which a musical band can evolve from beginnings of almost insulting
illiteracy to wind up several albums later romping and stomping deft as
champs. Think of the stiffness and supercool banality of the first Love
album, of the Velvet Underground born in already-fascinating welters of
sheer arrhythmic noise, the Stooges recording their first album when none
of them had been playing their instruments at all for more than two years
or three at the outside. Yet each of these outfits matured into assured
professionalism with astounding rapidity (though less surprising in the case
of the Velvets, who apparently had enough training and background to put
out the slickest sides from the start, but chose to make their early stuff
deliberately simple and cross-cut raw).

The Godz are not in a class with any of those groups, of course—in
fact, most of their music *could* be taken most obviously as downright
insulting—but they always revealed aspirations to rock 'n' roll respectability
and seemed at times on the way to or on the very brink of achieving it. The
first album's "1 + 1 = ?" saw McCarthy attempting the standard Dylan-
Beatles meaningful ballad with plain embarrassing results, but "Radar
Eyes," "Soon the Moon" and "Permanent Green Light" all had genuine
substance however primordial, and "Whiffenpoof Song" and its flip side,
"Travelin' Salesman," firmly set the Godz at a level of a pioneeringly
outrageous exercise in Bizarro. Still no great shakes instrumentally, they had
ingeniously surmounted their limitations with solid, methodical arrangements and full vocals. They were exciting to think about because they
promised to break through and become even more outrageous by dynamit-
ing all the stupid Standards by which esthetic-minded critics and tech-
nique-bound musicians sought to raise rock from pigmy squawl to
Art-Form.

Sadly, they blew the chance in the worst possible way. *The Third
Testament* is a lame, psychedelically stereotyped, even smug album that
sounds like everything their detractors might ever have accused the Godz

of being. Where the amusical rampages of earlier albums showed fiendish genius, the ones here are utterly obvious, echoing several of the most gimmicky banalities of acid-rock where the early Godz prophesied them. There is the unedifying mindlessness (genius mindlessness is something far different) of the alphabet-recitals "ABC" and "KLM," and side one is nearly engulfed by "First Multitude," a muddy collage of divers taped music, random clatterings and half-coherent gurglings patterned after "Revolution #9" and several other similar atrocities by more commercial groups, ending with the standard high nasal chant: "The mind, the mind, the mind. . . ."

Bad as it is, though, "First Multitude" comes close to being the best thing here. Its very murkiness makes it work in the event of certain types of delirium, and delirium being commoner and more diversified than ever these days there's probably a place for it in more than one dark decelerating rush. Maybe.

There ain't no maybe in the rest o' these babies at all, though, with one beautiful exception. Because with "First Multitude" out of the way, the balance of the album belongs to an unblinking succession of straight songs in the "1 + 1 = ?" vein, done with apparent sincerity and uniform mediocrity. "Ruby Red" almost makes it on the basis of strong, moody melody and lyrics, but the performance is so awkwardly earnest it's just sad. The greater Godz yowled and muttered with real authority but they just don't have the vocal cords for conventional work ballads. "Like a Sparrow" also comes close with its combination of Van Morrison's Spanish Harlem phase and Beach Boys "Bu-diddit, bu-diddit" chorus, but again, sounds like Thursday night in somebody's living room, and not much of a Thursday night at that. And "Walking Guitar Blues" delivers with a straight face lines like: "Just my guitar and a song / The policeman said move along / I wondered what have I done wrong? / Since when did they outlaw song?"

Such sniveling pieties would have been tromped into cackling refractions by the Godz of old, and that primal sense of humor is evidenced on one song here. "Woman" is a Larry Kessler classic, a cracked-rhythm fit of macho breast-beatings that hilariously parodies the perennial cliché of super-emotive growl and slur from Eric Burdon to the latest pasty-faced British bluesband yammering on with dipshit explicitness about how they're gonna *ball* their Little Schoolgirl: "I wuz—(halt, grunt, heavy-breathing hesitation)—uh-walkin' with my woman / An' I said, uh . . . Woman . . . I really . . . love yuh . . . An' I said I love yuh becuz—(halt, grunt)—of whutcha have. An' you know whutcha have, woman—you got my, you got my soul—yeah . . . you got me—a long time ago . . . Took

muh mind—and you tole me it wuz—(agonized second)—all *right.*
And that I—wuz—*outa*—*sight*—That's what you said—Ohh, woman—
you—wommmmmmmmmun—ungh—Woommmununummmmmuhn-
nnnn . . . erg . . . unghhh . . . (sniff, choke) . . . yeah . . . you make it,
uh, like you make it *young,* you make it, like you make it all *fun*—you
know—when it's young it's all fun . . . oh wow, what am I talking about?
. . . wummmmunnn . . ."

The more you listen to that piece, the more it sounds not only like
Burdon and the Bobby Plants and Bear Hites but seems even to suggest
the shade of fifties posturings handed down by Brando and James Dean,
that whole fumbling, mumbling, brooding, sweaty Dimwit as Virility routine. Maybe the Godz' approach in their greatest work, from "White Cat
Heat"'s fencepost tracas through "New Song"'s wino to this song, boils
down to a kind of Method School of rock 'n' roll. Instead of taking on the
usable components of the inchoate howl of the jungle or the gurgle of
the stooping slob and integrating them into the standard framework of the
rhythm 'n' riffs, the Godz macheted their larynxes all the way through to
be those alley cats, derelicts and hooligans, just as Method actors once tried
to "become" trees by standing with their arms twisted out.

I don't know if the Godz are still in operation. *The Third Testament*
leads one to doubt it, though they may surprise us tomorrow with an album
even more lamely conventional. They might even turn up recording for
Warner/Reprise. (Some of that company's applecheeked minstrels aren't
that far ahead of the Godz in folk-ballad sophistication and guitar technique, and their wilder stylings could conceivably appeal to as large an
audience as Wild Man Fischer's.)

It would be truly mind-bending, though, if they could somehow stay
together to come back from their latest descent into near-total obscurity
with further elaborations on that saber-toothed rending of the rational ear
which they pioneered, and even more bounteous a blessing if they balanced
it with still more anthemic hotrods of the sterling clarity and coherence of
"Whiffenpoof Song." Who knows, they might even enter the mainstream,
get bought and plugged and amped-up and *Circus-*magazined and end up
touring with the next British five-man poetic-rockabilly-blues Sensation of
the Year, then back to New York to record under Glyn Johns with various
contractually anonymous You Know Whos sitting in and end up with bad
reviews in *Creem* 'cause:

What profiteth a Godz if he gain the world and lose his loon-lunging
soul?

None of that is likely to come to pass, of course—maybe the Godz were for all their primal potency very limited and specific, sent here to do their work and go. At their best, they made the craziest of the touted Crazies look like bluesjam diddlers, and few indeed have made it to their Cheshire outpost on the limb even yet. At least one thing's absolutely certain—after them, the planet will never whistle, hum, yodel or even sing in the shower quite the same again. They've turned us all to Godz yowling freer than we ever dreamed, and every yowl and squeak and whinny is a hymn of praise to their ancient eminence.

—*Creem,* December 1971

PART THREE

Creemwork—Frauds,
Failures, and Fantasies

Chicago at Carnegie Hall,
    Volumes I, II, III & IV (1972)
Black Oak Arkansas: Keep the Faith (1972)
White Witch (1972)
John Coltrane Lives (1972)
The Guess Who: Live at the Paramount (1972)
James Taylor: One Man Dog (1973)
The Incredibly Strange Creatures Who
    Stopped Living and Became Mixed-Up Zombies,
    or, The Day the Airwaves Erupted (1973)
Jethro Tull in Vietnam (1973)
Screwing the System with Dick Clark (1973)
Slade: Sladest (1973)
My Night of Ecstasy with the J. Geils Band (1974)
Johnny Ray's Better Whirlpool (1975)
Barry White: Just Another Way
    to Say I Love You (1975)
Kraftwerkfeature (1975)
David Bowie: Station to Station (1976)

Chicago at Carnegie Hall, Volumes I, II, III & IV

I like this album because it's on Columbia. I trust them, I believe in their product, because Columbia is the General Motors of the record industry. They consistently come up with the best of everything: best logo, best lettering in artists' names and album titles, best photography, best cardboard. I know some thankless souls are now talking as if the whole wide universe belonged to the Kinney Corporation and Columbia were just a doddering old has-been, but I believe in sticking by my friends. I mean, which has more prestige to you—a box of Kix or Cheerios?

But being on Columbia isn't the only thing that makes *Chicago at Carnegie Hall* a classic. If you balk at buying by brand alone, another surefire way of gauging the worth of an album is to take a gander at the grooves themselves. Notice the light and dark patterns. If there are more light patterns than dark ones, it means that the grooves are wider, which means in turn that the record is heavier because there's more music crammed into each groove. Not only does this album weigh in at 3.23 pounds, but it's so jampacked with sounds that it's got grooves wide enough to satisfy even the most picayune of connoisseurs. Anybody that tells me it's not the heaviest album of the year just doesn't know his math.

Loving *Chicago at Carnegie Hall* as much as I do, though, I still don't play it very often. In fact, I've only played it once since I got it, and never intend to play any of it again. But then, I don't really have to; it is sufficient unto itself, an existing entity, and playing it too much would only put smudges and scratches on its pristine surfaces. So who cares if it's Chicago's worst album? Does it really matter that the songs sound exactly like they do on the studio albums except for being immeasurably more sodden and stuffed with long directionless solos? Or that the brass arrangements sound like Stan Kenton charts played backwards? Or that as technically competent as Chicago may be, there are just too many times when you can hear all the parts better than the whole?

Decidedly not. And for those of you who recognize the essential need for an album such as this, and don't want to defile your own copies even by breaking the shrinkwrap, I will list the highlights of the eight sides:

▪ In the "free form" piano intro to "Does Anybody Really Know What Time It Is?" Robert Lamm is introduced as "Mr. Chops," deriving from the fact that his roommates jokingly called him "Chopin" in college, and then goes into a solo equal parts Roger Williams, "Slaughter on Tenth Avenue," and "Cast Your Fate to the Wind."

▪ In "It Better End Soon—Second Movement," Walter Parazaider takes off on a long and wildly eclectic flute solo, starting with "Morning Song" from Grieg's *Peer Gynt* suite, shifting abruptly into "Dixie," to cheers from the audience, and thence to "Battle Hymn of the Republic," complete with martial drum-rolls.

▪ For the "preaching" vocal improvisation in the Fourth Movement of "It Better End Soon"—"We've gotta do it right / Within this system / Gonna take over / But within this system"—the They Got the Guns But We Got the Numbers Award.

▪ Listening to "I'm a Man" on the radio, feeling fine, knowing you don't have to buy or play the whole set to know what's good on it.

▪ Wondering whether "Anxiety's Moment" is a ripoff of "Moonlight Sonata" or "Unchained Melody." Wondering whether it matters.

If there's one thing Chicago's got, it's variety. They also have no trace of originality, but I don't think that matters very much either. They saw a void, they came and they filled it. With putty and plaster of Paris, but they *did* fill it. And if you think that's any small potatoes, just check out the *Billboard* or *Record World* or *Cash Box* charts, where their first album is still riding high after two and a half years. Until very recently none of their albums had ever left the charts. They have conquered this world, and will do it again with this Christmas-timed album, which has exactly the same songs as their others except for the inclusion of a new one about Richard Nixon. It will be the obvious present for people to grab for young kin they don't know too well, and since it retails for enough that they're only gonna have to sell about a copy a store to do a million bucks' worth of biz, it should become a gold record almost on the day it's released. In fact, at this point there's only one further pinnacle for Chicago to scale:

When they get to *Chicago VII*, they can release a *seven*-record set, with one entire album for each member of the group—a whole record of nothing but Peter Cetera's bass, another of Lee Loughnane on trumpet, etc.—playing a forty-minute version of "Does Anybody Really Know What Time It Is?" and then we can get seven record players, and have the greatest concert of all time.

—*Creem*, February 1972

Black Oak Arkansas:
Keep the Faith

When Black Oak Arkansas's first album was released, I made the mistake of listening to it one time and writing a fulsomely imagistic review while under the influence of amphetamines, praising it to the skies. A bit later a very good friend of mine called me up long distance and said: "Well, Lester, I just bought the Black Oak Arkansas album on the basis of that review you wrote, and I just wanted to tell you that they *suck!*"

A few months ago I saw them on tour with Grand Funk, and while I felt that the lead singer's twerpy attempts at Dr. John–ish mumbo-jumbo in a wretched pseudo–Captain Beefheart voice were godawful, the three guitarists and rhythm section were full, exciting, dense and driving all the way. By the time this album came out, however, I had become so sick of this wimp dubbed Dandy's growly pullulations that I could hardly stand to listen to it and only half-jokingly suggested to somebody that "I wish somebody would shoot that fuckin' lead singer in that group."

Okay. Record reviews start to get precious and self-aggrandizing when they become too autobiographical, but the point of all this is that I have listened to the record some more, and while I *still* think Dandy is just about as obnoxious as he can be I'm starting to like it, and not just for the instrumental work either. I read a story once in the *Atlantic Monthly* where the faculty at Yale or someplace was meeting up with this bunch of student radicals led by Mark Rudd, and one professor was heard to remark, "Why, that Mark Rudd is so obnoxious I can't stand to be in the same room with him," and another professor, who sympathized a bit more with Rudd and the *Ruddniki,* said, "Yes, but you could have said the same thing about

Tom Paine." So I say the same thing about Dandy. There is a point where some things can become so obnoxious that they stop being mere dreck and become interesting, even enjoyable, and *maybe because they are so obnoxious.*

Eric Burdon is (was?) a good example of this. Certainly Eric has been since he switched from the straight blues of the early Animals to art rock one of the most pretentious, mawkish, ballooned burlesques of a singer-songwriter in human history, not to mention a racist. But, with the exception of his merely bar-band-boring work with War, he has always managed to put together good bands, write interesting songs and, more than that, be infinitely entertaining for precisely the bozo that he is.

Dandy doesn't have Eric's gift for brilliantly gauche social commentary, but he comes damn close. *Keep the Faith* (subtitled "The Teachings of Black Oak Arkansas") continues and amplifies his juju-hosannah riff, and comes complete with ancient leather volumes of the Bible, the *Bhagavad Gita, The Teachings of Buddha,* and Hesse's *Siddhartha* depicted on the cover, and if the music didn't sound so much like the raunchier side of Springfield-Grape folkrock shot full of crank and turned into a crazy mechanical guitar loop, the lyrics would almost make you think it was 1967 again, what with lines like: "We're just what you need, good solid wood. We're your power to make evil curl, together we'll make and shape our new world. We're God's children so don't forget, paradise is just around the corner and we'll get there yet. Then we'll give ya all our love; we'll try our best. For after all, our love is what we want to give."

But it's not 1967 at all, it's, uh, it's a new day so let a soul man come in and do the popcorn, I mean something new is blowing in the wind: "We're your freedom, we're your son. We shine a light for everyone. We're your happiness, we're your joy. Your Revolutionary All-American Boys!"

Yes, the times they have a-changed. At the Free John Sinclair rally in Ann Arbor last December, John Lennon said, "So flower power didn't work, so let's try something new," and when Big John says it you know something's going on. Black Oak Arkansas certainly don't sing about dipple-dappled crystal leaf-vein patterns in the dewy spiderwebs of your mind—they sing about "Fever in My Mind" and about earthquakes. In "The Big One's Still Coming," the hot shot of this album which has so much strychnine in it it's like an acid flashback all by itself, Dandy takes the apocalyptic motif running through all of the songs here and turns it into a vision of imminent natural catastrophe: "We're havin' an earthquake / We're goin' insane / A California earthquake / Has been shakin' our brains." Fortunately, however, he also recognizes that all these seemingly horrific cataclysms and disasters can be turned around into something resembling a real cool time, if you think about it and exercise the proper karmic manipulations ("But mystic thoughts can only fly to another plane"), can be harnessed and ridden cross the crumbling spires of Babylon to glory: "California earthquake / Shakin' our heads / Yeah we're havin' an earthquake / On our waterbeds."

And that's kind of how I feel about this album. It reminds me of the scene in Billy Wilder's *One, Two, Three* where the Commies in East Berlin torture and brainwash a captured spy by strapping him in a chair and forcing him to listen to Brian Hyland's "Itsie Bitsie Teenie Weenie Yellow Polka Dot Bikini" 789 times played at 78 rpm with the spindle through a hole punched in the record just a half-inch from the center, so it gives out with a mind-destroying back-and-forth whine, sort of like a wah-wah in fact. After listening to all the psychedelic, studio-artistic, electronic, filtered, altered, phased and played-backwards music of the past six or seven years, with Black Oak Arkansas and Dandy's tattered tonsils capping it all, I think that I could tell my old high school civics teacher that I would be immune to at least this form of Communist brainwashing. I would probably tap my foot.

—*Creem,* May 1972

White
Witch

A big part of punk rock is the Great American (or English, really) Teen Sublimation Riff. Everybody wants to get laid 'twixt twelve and twenty, thinks about it round the clock in fact, but most of their cogitation is neurotic energy-drain stuff, with the result that we get Two Major Punk Rock Schools. One overcompensates for teen neurosis with exaggerated displays of macho arrogance driven home by vengeful hard-on bass lines (Troggs being supreme archetype), while the other just freaks out, submerging the whole thing into highly involved, murky drug-lyric double entendres. Acid-ecstasy-transcending-body-in-one-fell-spurt. Come-on-little-honey-puff-this-joint-o'-mine-and-you'll-see-things-differently—that kind of stuff.

Until recently, that is. That was mid-60s trippy dippy wank-off, now times have changed and everybody's blasé about drugs; there's gotta be something new to help keep these poor virgins from having to sing about fucking and blow it by revealing their rank inexperience. We can't write 'em off, because they're at least 40% of what rock's all about. Only one in twenty thousand has the nervy genius of Iggy or Jonathan of the Modern Lovers and is willing to sing about his adolescent hangups in a manner so painfully honest as to embarrass the piss out of half the audience.

Solution, dammit! Not bisexual or gay rock, because only Limeys can really bring that off and besides, these guys ain't gay, they're goofed up and stuck in between. Okay, I got it. Kozmik. Mystik Okkult Jujube Ragas. Mumbo Jumbo Merlin Mush. Look at the back cover of this album: now observe the dude standing on the left. It is ineluctable fact that beneath all that makeup, silk, Beelzebeads and hoodoo-voodoo drag, lies a true dork. One look confirms it. He could be standing in a gray thin-lapeled suit on an Astronauts album a decade ago; or nervous under a brand-new Beatle pudding-bowl halfway between then and now; or solemn in his Nehru jacket with a New Delhi Tourist Throwrug hanging on the wall behind him a year or two later; or sullenly spaced behind a Heavy blues guitar in 1968 . . . well, the great tradition never dies, so here he is now, made up like an acid transvestite, and not only is his masculinity not compromised a whit but he's unmistakably that same dork, the one that used to sit in the seat right in front of you in Driver Training and fart all the time. The rest of the band is no different.

What do they sound like? Great! Grunge noise and mystikal studio abstractions, better than most of Black Oak's stuff, vocals and organ and other things quite Deep Purple, and if you've got any sense of humor or no standards at all you'll love 'em.

—*Creem*, October 1972

John Coltrane
Lives

The whole thing started so simply. I never meant for it to end up in this bog of complications.

I was sitting around one Monday evening, jamming and drinking port with my buddies Roger and Tim. We are starting this Stooges-type rock band which has at various times been named such things as Crime Desire, Cannibal Rape Job, Romilar Jag, and Cigar Box Joe Bob & the Clap, and is currently called National Dust, since we are going through our down-to-rudimentals period. Tim plays rhythm guitar, Roger sings and blows flute, and we have a couple of other cats not present this evening on lead and bass, although our drummer recently split because we were too far out for him. I blow harp and sing lead on some tunes. This night we were rehearsing some of my new killer originals such as "Please Don't Burn My Yoyo," "A Race of Citizens," "He Gave You the Finger, Mabel," "After My Misspent Youth," and "Barracuda Anthem," which was my own revolutionary juvenile delinquent philippic.

> Hey motherfucker!
> Hey motherfucker!
> All you do is sit on your can
> Get out in the streets and prove you're a man
> We been sittin' still too long
> It's time to pull the lever
> On the ones that stole the ground from unborn feet forever!

Rehearsing with just three band members and only one guitar was not the easiest chore in the world, but it got looser as we got drunker, and just as things really began to cook I was seized with an inspiration that seemed brilliant at the time but was to have a dire denouement. Huffing and shrieking through my Hohner Marine Band, I gazed around Roger's room strewn with smudged manuscripts, tattered skin mags, half-empty bottles, and records with wine stains in the grooves, and suddenly I saw, leaning dusty in a corner, an old alto sax that Roger had borrowed from his brother-in-law months ago with the intention of branching out from flute and never quite gotten around to.

Instantly I dropped the harp, which was such a limited palette for an experimental artist anyway, and snatched up the horn. Just holding it in my hands and toying with the keys was like a revelation, flashing me back to my high school days and lessons on another borrowed alto. Sitting in the practice room of the music store with the patient, plodding instructor trying to teach me scales and embouchure, when all I wanted to do was cut loose with a searing Bronx blast that would blow the roof off the place. A saxophone has always been a symbol of power with me, ever since the days I first sat chilling and rocking to things like John Coltrane's *Africa/Brass* while staring in awe at the pictures of the man on the jacket, awash in yellow and purple lights, blowing the truest testament in history through that big honking horn.

Days home from school faking flu I would put Trane on loud as my Sears Silvertone could blare, and stand up on a hassock reading Allen Ginsberg's "Howl" at the top of my lungs, pretending I was in a North Beach or Greenwich Village coffeehouse. Music fueled me, although I was just dimly realizing that I was at core a verbal child. In the shower I wailed and whammed at imaginary keyboards, drums, later guitars, but most especially saxes, emulating my heroes with twenty-minute atonal ragas that soared to their stormiest climaxes when the hot water ended.

I also took lessons at various times on real guitars, pianos, trumpet, drums and the aforementioned sax, never meeting with much success because I was always too fired with the imperatives of inner song to bother learning music book drivel like "Old Black Joe" and "My Bonnie." Afternoons with the alto I would practice scales for five or ten minutes, feel them sliding ineluctably into improvisations, wail awhile and then light a Chesterfield, settle back hunched in my chair with my axe lying casually on my crossed legs, fingers of one hand still at the keys, listening to my Jackie McLean records, dreaming. Later I began to smoke grass and in the random, perfect riffings of euphoria actually sorted out Gershwin's "Summertime." I joined a Johnny and the Hurricanes type band for one afternoon; couldn't play "Night Train" or "Let's Get One," but sure did wail, even if the reed was cracked and its tip chipped and bitten away a good half-inch.

The reed on Roger's brother-in-law's alto was new but stiff and dusty and had probably never been used. A "professional" musician would have taken it off the instrument and sucked it until it was limber enough for proper tone, but I was in too much of a hurry to bother with any of that Juilliard conservatory shit. Something infantile about sucking on a piece of wood, anyway. I just hauled the damn thing up from the corner and started working out, HONK! BLAT! SQUEEEE!, rippling fingertips working the keys, gravel vocalisms tearing out, experimenting with loud rhythmic redundancies on one or two notes, bop jive crossbreeds between Illinois Jacquet and Albert Ayler and licks akin to Stooges guitar riffs. Sounded great to me, and Roger and Tim were enthusiastic as hell at first but after ten or fifteen minutes they seemed to grow a little weary, stopped playing and sort of stared at lint on the carpet or the silent "Dick Van Dyke Show" TV screen between glugs on the port. Not that that bothered me in the slightest; the flow of my high-energy inspiration is so constant and sustained that I don't really expect any of my peers to keep up with me. Now if it was *Trane* or *Pharoah* I was riffing with . . .

Anyway, the evening ended in utter confusion as we all got so drunk we passed into that sometimes blissful, sometimes disastrous state of ambulatory unconsciousness where you have to make phonecalls the next morning for your own edification, hoping you haven't stumbled into some absurd gaffe. I vaguely recall Tim driving me home as I kept yammering and yelping through the sax, becoming less coherent with each note, until at last I was blowing a single pure true note with a vocal laugh running through it, pausing only for breath. Tim yelled at me to shut the fuck up, to which I replied, "You must be kidding," and only stopped to scoop myself out of the car, drag myself up the stairs of my apartment house and fall fully-dressed into total oblivion on my bed.

That night I had a strange and wonderful dream. It was one of the best dreams of my entire life. I was in a vast auditorium modeled after the little theatre of my old junior college, filled to the dusty windows with people, and all alone on the stage I stood with my sax, fingering and blatting it every which way, blowing out the crassest garble that even I had ever heard. The audience was getting restless, and a few minor mutterings were beginning to be heard. But suddenly I began to have a very strange feeling, and I realized all at once that it was the hand of Ohnedaruth himself passing coolly over my brow. In that instant I was stuck with the divine insight that the way to play *more* is to play *less*, that I was overblowing and dissipating my energies. So I relaxed, and began to apply both breath pressure and finger movements in a calmer, more deliberate, meditative manner. And that was when the breathiest, most sublime tune began to emanate from my instrument, from *me*. It was fantastic, it was a holy moment. I sounded exactly like Pharoah Sanders. The audience sat hushed in awe. The gentle, strong current of the melody wound on and on, growing more godlike with each measure, was so intense it was almost post-emotional. At its peak I realized that, through the windings and turnings of song, I had somehow begun to play "The Girl from Ipanema." But it sounded just as holy.

I woke up the next day with one of the more notable hangovers of the month and a memory made of Swiss cheese. The sight of the saxophone leaning up 'gainst the wall of my own bedroom dumbfounded me, and I immediately called up Roger and demanded: "What the fuck's this saxophone doing at *my* house?"

"Don't ask *me!*"

"Well, what the fuck happened last night?"

"I was gonna ask *you* that!"

There was no hope of cognition. It's that bad Gallo port; it'll fry your brain just like a wino's. That's why all us teenagers like it so much. Roger said maybe he and Tim would be over to drink and watch some TV a little later, and I hung up and set about trying to get myself together. I don't usually drink in the morning, but today the quality of my hangover was so extraordinarily intense that I was nearly blind, and spent about three-quarters of an hour walking around the house in circles and staring at the purplish black fuzz in the air before deciding to break down and break into the Jack Daniel's for breakfast. It was good, too, and as my head began to clear I sat in the rocking chair by the living room window playing with the sax and remembering my Jackie McLean days. Finally I put my mouth to the embouchure and gave an experimental "TOOT!" Not bad. Gradually, mindful of the throbbing in my head, I began to rip off a few barnyard squawks.

Suddenly I saw a wizened shadow pass on the shade beside me. I stopped playing, quietly stood up, lifted one of the blinds ever so slightly and peered out. There stood my landlady, all four feet of white-haired crone, leaning on her cane right in front of the door to my apartment, listening. I laid the sax down and sat back in my chair with my hands folded in my lap, not making a sound. At length she went away.

I had had trouble with this old apparition before. Ever since the previous managers, a retired couple, had left when the husband had a heart attack, and Mrs. Brown had taken over, she and I had been at loggerheads. The first time it was quite civil. I was playing *The American Revolution* by David Peel and the Lower East Side at top volume, and she came and so sweetly told me that another tenant had complained. Fine. I turned down. The next time it was Sir Lord Baltimore: I listened to a whole side with headphones and speakers both on before realizing that she had been banging on the door with all her strength for twenty minutes. When I answered it she launched into a tirade rife with threats of eviction, but my blood was fired with Sir Lord Baltimorean feedback and I just screamed at her and slammed the door.

All this was complicated by two things. One was her son, a baby-faced weakling of the type that always has a purple swath through his stubble after he shaves, who married the bitchiest Student Council socialite of a blonde from my high school and spent much of his time in loud fights with her. It amused the whole building to hear her browbeat and him whine, and she always won. It was clear that he was still tied to his *madre*'s apron strings, because they accepted free rent from his mother, even though it was plain that his wife hated her (although in truth it seemed like she hated the whole world).

The other factor making it difficult for me to kick out the jams in peace was that the apartment right under the one occupied by myself and my own sainted mother was rented to somebody else I went to high school with, namely one of the stupidest, ugliest pugs I ever knew, named Butch Dugger, and *he* just happened to have grown up to be a cop. A kid who lived in the apartment house told me once that Dugger had been heard saying that he remembered me from school, had never liked me, and now had sworn that he was going to "get me," his words.

Now, I'm not particularly paranoid. All I know is that one night when I had a friend over juicing it up, my friend tapped me on the shoulder right in the middle of "Sister Ray" and when I took off my headphones he said that somebody was banging on the front door. When I opened it there were *four* cops standing there in uniform, claiming that somebody, they wouldn't say who, had complained about the noise, and since it was after ten o'clock on a Sunday evening they would have to take my name. My room was still full of marijuana fumes and my friend was stoned on reds, so I told them who I was to get them out of there, and they left.

But that was all in the past, and I didn't have any dope in the house now, and besides it rankled me that my landlady should stand outside my door spying on me in the United States of America where a man has the right to play free jazz at high noon. I had heard other tenants talking about how both she and her son had been caught at odd hours, stooping slightly by people's windows, listening to see what went on within.

I sat and mulled it awhile, reaching the halfway point in my fifth of

Jack's, and then I called my girlfriend up on the phone for a little fun. Her sister answered, and I didn't say a word but launched immediately into a squealy version of "Mary Had a Little Lamb" on the horn that would have done Yusef Lateef proud. She was shocked at first, thinking it was a crank call I guess, but when I told her who it was she handed the phone to Candy, my girlfriend, and I repeated my performance.

By the time I was halfway through the first rendition, though, the landlady had come galloping up, or as close to a gallop as one can get with a chrome cane, and commenced to bang unremittingly on the door with her gnarled fist. It made a pretty good rhythm track, in fact, but Candy and her sister couldn't hear that. When I started playing for Candy, Mrs. Brown began to yell: "Hey, in there! Stop that racket and open this door right now!"

But I finished my recital, Candy laughing, and told her to hold on a second. I answered the door with axe in hand. The landlady was fuming: "What are you doing in there?"

"I'm practicing my saxophone," I said with a smile of innocence, holding it out a bit so she could see. She was not mollified.

"Are you havin' a drunk party in there?"

Now I started to get mad. Every goddam time she interrupts me she accuses me of having a "drunk party," and the worst part is she never does it when I actually am having one. Once she called me up and said this on a Sunday afternoon while I was watching a rather flighty college professor who looked like Woody Allen play piano sonatas by an obscure homosexual composer and then explain their programmatic content in purple prose, on TV. "No," I bristled, adrenaline rising, "I'm just playing my sax as you can fucking well see!"

She put her foot half on the doorsill and half on the carpet, leaning in. "Don't use that language and tone with me, young man!"

"Don't try to barge into my apartment like that, I didn't tell you you could come in here! You're trespassing!" We were both getting a bit crazy now. We had been dreaming of this confrontation for months, though I was gone much of the time, attending drunk parties in Los Angeles. She served: "I thought I'd got you outa here, you young scamp!"

"Well, you old bitch," I cackled, my eyes fairly popping out of my head, "you didn't!"

"Ooohh," she seethed, waving her pallid little fist and brittle old arm in the air, "I, I, I'll smack you!"

"Go ahead!" I howled. I was really starting to get into it. I could see myself now, suing a crippled 78-year-old woman for assault and battery.

"I'll call the *police!*"

"*On what charge?*" I brayed.

"Disturbing the peace . . . disturbing my apartment house!"

"Bullshit," I said. "Anyway, why don't you just shut up and get outa here and stop bothering me. I'm leaving in two weeks and then I'll never have to look at your ugly face again."

"I give you *three days* to get out!"

"Fuck you, you can't do that!"

She was really frustrated; she began to reach for things. "I'll tell your mother what you do!"

"So what?"

"I'll get my *son* to come up here and *beat you up!*"

"Ahh, your faggot son won't do nothin'," I snarled, and slammed the door. She left, and I went back to the phone where Candy waited in perplexity: "What was all that?"

"Nothing," I laughed. "My landlady is really crazy." Though I was certainly not in the best shape myself. My hangover had me trembling all over, and there was a slight tremor in my voice.

But I knew everything was going to be all right. I didn't play the sax anymore, though as I kept drinking I ran through endless fantasies of further confrontations with her. Eventually Roger and Tim arrived, and we went out for more booze, although Tim was back to his old regimen of reds and whites. In fact as he proudly brought his stash out to show us he fumbled, dropping the bag. The little pills rolled and scattered everywhere, and in his condition he only managed to retrieve about three-fourths of them. I made a note of the ones that rolled under the couch and the chair, planning to gather them later.

After putting what he found of his stuff away, he picked up the sax. I had already told them about the scene with the landlady, and Tim blew a few farting honks. Roger jumped on him: "Don't do that, man, we don't want a hassle here."

"Yeah," I said, "what are you gonna tell my landlady if she comes back to the door?"

"Why, hand it to her and say, 'Here, if you think you can play any better, go ahead and try!' "

"No," we both yelled at him, "no! Let's just be cool." And being cool, he and Roger started a quiet jam on guitar and flute. I listened at first, sipping my Jack's and water, but the more I listened the more I wanted to play too, and finally, seized by the muse and drink, I yelled "Fuck it!" And picked up the sax and started to wail.

It took her even less time to arrive this time than the last. She'd probably been sitting in her apartment, just like me, wondering when we'd get a chance to tangle again. How romantic. She was banging with both fists now, hollering at the top of her lungs. I answered the door, as before, with the sax still in my hands. But this time, Trane laid his hand on my brow once more, and I didn't need paltry words to reply.

"I *told* you about that racket—"

HONK!

"I'm not going to put up with any more of—"

HONK! HONK! HONKHONKHONKSQUAKSQUONK!

"Will you put that damn thing down and listen to—"

SQUEEEE-ONK! SHKRIEEEE! GRRUGHRRGLONK-EE-ERNK!

I advanced on her with it, backing her out the door, pausing only for breath. She turned and fled. "All right," she gasped, running to the door of her apartment and opening the screen. "I'm gonna call the police."

I don't know what got into me. Partially it was the booze, partially the dream I'd had the night before, partially pure inspiration and rage at the abridgement of my inalienable right to jam. I chased her down the balustrade, wailing all the way, and right into her apartment. I ran up to her as she was dialing the phone, and smiled at the look of terror in her eyes as I advanced on her, blowing like a hurricane. Rock out!

I stood right over her, jiving and honking in her face as she leaned farther and farther back, dropping the phone and grimacing in fright. She never lost her cane, though.

"What's the matter here, ma'am?"

It was Butch Dugger himself, standing in the doorway in his shirtsleeves with a half-eaten tuna sandwich in his hand, roused from TV on his day off from work.

"This boy," she panted, "he's attacking me! He's like a mad dog! Get him off!"

"Right away, ma'am," said Butch through clenched teeth, laying his tuna sandwich next to a porcelain tulip on her living room table. And he came up and strong-armed me from behind, grabbing my arms and twisting them up behind my head so that I dropped the sax with a clatter on her carpet. As he was pushing me out the door, I saw her go to the kitchen, get a napkin and put it under the sandwich. And I heard him tell her to call the police station and tell Officer Betancourt that Officer Dugger said to come out.

He pushed me down the stairs and face first onto the lawn and I felt his knee in my back. As I lay there chewing crabgrass I heard a screen door slam; his wife was bringing him his handcuffs. Still keeping his knee in my back, he put them on me and then got up. I could see Roger and Tim across the street, moving quietly in the direction of their car. They weren't looking at me. I didn't blame them.

A minute later a gold-fleck patrol car came roaring up, two cops jumped out and ran over, as if there were some major emergency. One had his nightstick out. Mrs. Brown must have made quite a phone call. Dugger spoke: "Here 'e is. Assault with intent to commit bodily harm, maybe attempted rape, maybe something else. Watch out for 'im, he's a sick one. I think he's been taking LSD. I'm gonna go down and get a warrant—I think I've smelled marijuana fumes comin' outa that apartment before."

So they took me and they booked me, for assault and eventually possession of dangerous drugs, and threw me in the tank. I sat down and lit a cigarette, and a tough-looking black dude about thirty years old bummed one from me. "Whut you in for?"

"Being ahead of my time."

He just looked at me. For a second I thought he was going to laugh, but he didn't. "Yeah," he said. "Me too."

—*Creem,* November 1972

The Guess Who: Live at the Paramount

Lately some people have begun to assert that, what with 1967 so far gone and all, ain't nothin' cosmic anymore. They say that rare evanescent psychic Pez drop has gone out of contemporary life. But I Know Different. Ever since last Thursday, when I was awakened at five o'clock in the morning by a bolt of lightning striking the streetlight in front of my house, creating such a big boom, with a slowly fading aftermath hiss so close to the one at the end of "A Day in the Life," that I was sure the Russkies or the Chinks had dropped the Bomb on us at last. I just lay there waiting for the shock wave to come and snort me up.

I stayed that way for about fifteen seconds, and when I was finally and absolutely convinced that it definitely was not coming, I got up and played the sixteen-minute version of "American Woman" on the new Guess Who album recorded live in Seattle, Washington. In the process of auditioning this performance for the first time, I was hit by not one but two of the first true *flashes* I could remember having in, oh, it must be at least four years. I realized simultaneously that:

1. The Guess Who is God.

2. Burton Cummings is the rightful and unquestionable heir to Jim Morrison's spiritual mantle.

I saw the Guess Who do this version of "American Woman" live a year ago, and I have never been more offended by a concert. Just as he does on the record, Burton Cummings indulged himself in a long, extremely cranky rumination on Yankee Yin, in a sort of fallen-out Beat poetic style:

American bitch
American cunt
American slut
American lesbian
American schoolgirl
American housewife
American beaver

etc., etc., etc. Wouldn't *you* be offended by this Canuck creep coming down here taking all our money while running down our women? *Sure* you would! Until you realized, as I did, eventually, that that kind of stuff is exactly what makes the Guess Who great. They have absolutely no taste at all, they don't even mind embarrassing everybody in the audience, they're real punks without even working too hard at it. This was all brought home when I went to see them a couple of months ago and got offended all over again by a song which had Cummings hollering: "I got cocaine and morphine too / Lots of stuff to get you all high . . ."

I mean, these guys just don't know when to quit! That's what puts 'em so far ahead of everyone else. They'll say anything. What do you think "diesel fixer, fixed a diesel, diesel fixed me, what a weasel" means? Do you care? No! Do you love it anyway? Sure!

This album, as far as I can tell, is the Guess Who's magnum opus so far. "Woman" alone, starting with a long sloppy medium tempo blues, proves that Burton can improvise the best gauche jive lyrics since the Lizard King himself. Who else but Burton or Jimbo would have the nerve to actually begin a song with the line "Whatchew gonna do, mama, now that the roast beef's gone?" Then he actually has the gall in the course of his rant to list every last way that the American Woman just totally submits to and serves him, and proceeds to dump on her for "messing your mind"! Man, that is true punk; that is so fucked up it's got class up the ass. And on top of all that, he's getting into some great, lazy, uncontrolled scat singing and he plays harmonica better than anybody since Keith Relf.

In case you wondered about the drug commercial, it's in a song called "Truckin' Off Across the Sky," the main character of which is the Grim Reaper. There he is, head and shoulders looming over yonder bluff, grinning, outstretched arms holding bags of you-know-what. Positively the best drug song of 1972. And this may well be the best live album of the year. Fuck, all them old dudes wearing their hip tastes on their sleeves: get this and play it loud and be the first on your block to become a public nuisance.

James Taylor:
One Man Dog

Today I am a pud.

When in the course of rock drought you cast about desperately for something to listen to, why not let your defenses down and try James Taylor? I know he wears his neuroses on his sleeve, solicits his audience's sympathy, and holes up in a Martha's Vineyard bungalow far more than is healthy for any growing boy (most of this album was recorded there, in fact), and he's probably got lots of fans who empathize with him so much they'd like to curl up into foetal balls and contract till they disappear.

On the other hand, everybody needs a little vicarious pain. Where would the Velvet Underground be without Lou Reed's angst? Or Black Sabbath buffs without Ozzy Osbourne's insomnia? Right. So what makes James any different? That he was a spoiled rich kid, makes it with Carly Simon (woo woo) and sings wimp? Well, that's not enough.

In the first place, wimp's just as valid as anything else on the radio if you just dig it for the totally meaningless, dunced-out trash that it is, just like you dug things like Eric Burdon and War. In the second place, James Taylor's a real *punk*, when ya get right down to it. He never had any shame in the first place; he just sits around and gets fucked up all the time, just like most of us, and I betcha when he's not being a Sensitive Genius he's a getdown dude who don't give a shit about nothin'. Just look at him on the cover of *One Man Dog*, out in a canoe with his mutt, wearing a necktie even which is a cool move at this point in time. Or those pictures of him at the McGovern benefits, in an oversize sportcoat, another throwback: hell, he ain't trying to con anybody.

But, you say, I still can't listen to the record inside. Bullshit! It's a very nice record. It's easier to listen to than lots of these hotshit Rock And Roll albums like the new Black Sabbath or side two of *Exile on Main Street.* It flows smooth as Sioux Bee straight in one ear and . . . stops off for a bit of contemplation.

Because this ain't James bragging about being in the nuthouse, or bellyaching about having to be a star. It's James at home, a one-man parade indeed, and as such a monolithic archetype for our time. He doesn't care about anything in particular except himself, the love he's found, his dog, and the lanes and pastures in his neighborhood which he finds great contentment ambling through.

The songs are short and there's lots of them, almost twice as many as any other album on the racks. Why? Why waste space with repeated choruses, instrumental breaks (except in the fadeouts, and the instrumentals, which are also present and precisely as awful as Black Sabbath's), boring jams, or any of that flapdoodle? Isn't it enough for them all to have nice, lulling melodies and inoffensive lyrics? James may not look like an economical man, but he is actually a real cheaper by the dozen conservative when it comes to creation. Lifestylewise, as I said, he's a punk. It may, in fact, be just this irresolvable dichotomy which has been ripping the boy apart lo these years. So come on outa the closet, James; stop trying to be the J. D. Salinger of the count-out culture, slouch on down and drool by the lamppost and the bar with the rest of the wetbacks. You'll be an even greater American and more of an inspiration than you are now.

—*Creem,* February 1973

The Incredibly Strange Creatures Who Stopped Living and Became Mixed-Up Zombies,

or, The Day the Airwaves Erupted

I'm perusing *TV Guide* and I see this title, number two of the three movies that KTTV in L.A. programs all night, which have provided such unsung therapy over the years and are interspersed with Ralph Williams and that other benign used-car-lot yokel with My Dog Storm. I had to watch it. I mean, there's movies and MOVIES! Allowing for the fact that even stations in L.A. and N.Y. can only buy so many films, there's still an awful lotta spiff items that them damn channels've got and only show once in a gnu's lifetime, and lots more that they've never bought or never show! Which is grounds for a People's uprising in any man's book.

In L.A., Albert Zugsmith's classic *The Beat Generation* is screened about once a year even though any movie with Mamie Van Doren deserves reprogramming at mathematical intervals.

But how often have you seen a *real* gasser like *Teenagers from Outer Space* or *The Blob* with Steve McQueen (he didn't play the Blob like James Arness played *The Thing*, but the title song *was* sung by the Five Blobs and released as a single on Columbia: "It creeps / And leaps / And glides and slides across the floor . . .")?

These opuses are true rock 'n' roll movies, buried under a conspiracy of *baldheaded short-haired jellyfish biting tricky Dicky pricks rite now!* Who didja think programmed all that jive on the tube from Farm Report to National Anthem—the Mod Squad? No! The very same fascist nebbishes that keep you from buying juice in highschool, diggin' sounds after hours and smokin' your bamalam and walking down the street stark noble savage naked to the world! And I say it's time we rose up outta our remote control chairs and DID something about it! Crazed TV to the TV Crazies!

BOOB TUBE LIBERATION FRONT STORMS
CBS, ABC, PBS & QUAKING INDEPENDENTS
FROM COAST TO COAST

Left-Wing Fanatics Burn Film Libraries, Make Demands
FCC Declares Maoist Plot, Calls In Nat'l Guard

WASHINGTON, D.C. (UPI)—FCC Commissioner Susskind said today that the recent outbreaks of violence and vandalism against TV stations in every state of the Union were the actions of a vast conspiratorial network "whose extensiveness staggers the imagination of any reasonable man." The Commissioner stated further that the network was populated mainly by heroin addicts, students driven psychopathic by the use of hallucinogenic drugs, politicized shakedown artists, and prostitutes of both sexes— "junkies, sickies, trickies and quickies," as the Commissioner quipped—led by an elusive cabal of disgruntled dropouts from the Weathermen on special orders from Red China.

The Commissioner further stated that as dire as the threat might appear, the Government was already taking steps to "locate these bacteria, with the aid of the great microscopes of the FBI and CIA, and administer appropriate medication. And if I may extend my metaphor, gentlemen, said medication's application will prove much more analogous to that in commercials for Raid or No Bugs M'Lady, and the fate of the viruses inferred from such, than any kind of light-humor spot pushing antihistamines which come on like a crew of house-painters trapping the sympathetically polka-dotted personification of a summer cold as played by Morey Amsterdam in a corner of the nasal passages. Because we are not dealing with Morey Amsterdam, gentlemen, we are dealing with the Plague."

On other fronts in what Senate Majority Leader Mansfield called "the nation's worst crisis since the assassination of JFK," independent stations in Paw Paw, Michigan, Clovis, N.M., and Nome, Alaska were seized in yesterday's series of guerrilla assaults, leaving only seven stations nationwide still free, the names and locations of which the FCC Commissioner refused to divulge.

At last report, the station in Paw Paw was showing nothing but old "Popeye," "Bugs Bunny," and "Donald Duck" cartoons interspersed with 1952 episodes of "Dragnet" and "Inner Sanctum."

The Clovis station aired absolutely nothing but long-haired young people drifting through the studio, taking off their clothes, engaging in sex acts and shouting strings of obscenities at the camera. After approximately five hours of this, viewers said, they seemed to tire and started running at the camera making faces. Forty-five minutes later all that could be seen was a group of them slouching against the walls, lounging on couches and the floor, smoking marijuana and drinking wine and occasionally burping or gesturing obscenely toward the camera. At some point in the early hours of the morning, viewers said, a bug-eyed, fidgety young man appearing to be in a state of compulsive drug hysteria began a harangue which was delivered so rapidly and sounded so incoherent that few viewers could make out more than two or three successive words at any given time. The harangue continued for thirteen hours, and was reportedly brought to an abrupt halt when two burly, bearded conspirators walked onto the set, seized the unfortunate youth and strong-armed him off, after which he was not seen again.

A sort of coup seemed to take place, as the hippie-types who had predominated were largely replaced by what Commissioner Susskind called "less crypto, more avowedly political groups." There followed a spate of political speeches along New Left themes, by members of the American Communist Party, Progressive Labor Party, Black Panthers, Women's Liberation, Gay Liberation and others. Few of the speeches lasted more than two minutes and none were concluded. Viewers reported that each one was engulfed in such a rising tide of verbal abuse approximately a minute after it began that the proceedings dissolved into a round of shouted charges, countercharges and slogans. An independent poll in the area reported that viewer "ratings" were highest at that point. It is also reported that later the delegates of the various political organizations attained some semblance of order, and that the speeches and debates which followed, although entirely Left-oriented, are still continuing. Unfortunately, details of their exact nature were still unavailable at press time, because the "ratings" had dropped so low that the pollsters had not yet found even a single household still tuned in.

In Nome, the commandeered station was reportedly showing nothing but old commercials and newscasts run backwards, with a soundtrack comprised of Redd Foxx records and old rhythm and blues "party" (sex-oriented) songs superimposed on them.

Stations in other parts of the country are showing propaganda films from Communist countries and groups and broadcasting readings from Chairman Mao by hirsute under-thirties. Others screen nothing but Andy Warhol films, or "home movies" or "underground films" made by the guerrillas themselves. In San Francisco a rock group called the Grateful Dead has been playing an uninterrupted concert for ten days and, even more amazingly, a song entitled "Turn on Your Lovelamp" for the last four straight days, round the clock. One channel in Los Angeles is currently featuring a gentleman of indeterminate age named Kim Fowley, engaged in unprintable acts with a girl who doesn't look older than 14 and a boa constrictor, while "singing" in a warbling monotone. Another channel broadcasts nothing but "Jesus Freaks"—longhaired hippie youngsters claiming conversion to Christianity—proselytizing, beating tambourines and singing songs 24 hours a day.

This trend has been noted at many stations across the country. Another L.A. channel features nothing but Buddhist chanting, endless and uninterrupted, with no breaks for breath, commercials or the "no-broadcast" hours required each week by the FCC Code. This too has been seen in more than one community, although there are a variety of sects and chants involved on different channels.

Largest viewer response, however, was gleaned by yet another L.A. station, which declared its aim, almost immediately after being seized by guerrillas, to be the chronological broadcasting of every motion picture in history. They began at 2:43 A.M. on May 11th with *The Great Train Robbery,* and continued without pause for commercials or announcements. Runners have been observed driving up to the back doors regularly in delivery trucks presumably carrying cans of film. At press time they had reached the year 1927, and viewer response was reportedly unprecedented, as vast numbers of California citizens rearranged schedules and even quit their jobs to build their lives around the station's output. As a shocking side effect, Los Angeles County Hospital reported a sharp upsurge in the number of admissions for nervous collapses, in most cases brought on by viewers so obsessed with the station's round-the-clock cinematic history that they resorted to artificial stimulants to keep up with it, which as *Times* critic Charles Champlin observed is ridiculous if not insane, since even if the rebels are not turned out of the studio by authorities (and the station's owner is so pleased by viewer response that they may not be), the series can be expected, according to calculations on police computers, to conclude at some point in the year 1981, if at all.

Around the rest of the country, interestingly enough, viewer habits have changed little or not at all. An emergency Nielsen poll revealed that with minor and localized exceptions, the television sets in American homes are on neither more nor less hours each day than before the national coup. And *TV Guide* magazine, after suspending publication for six weeks to meditate on the matter, examine its conscience and appear before a Congressional subcommittee, has finally announced definite plans to resume publication with regional editions and listings for all channels, no matter what the new formats. "The only thing we're worried about," said editor Merrill Pannitt, "is that some of the smart-aleck hippies running these stations now may just write us off as a lot of old fogies and try to discredit us by submitting false programming charts."

—Front-page item in the Los Angeles *Times,* May 23, 1976

That's all still a fantasy now, of course, but where d'ya think all the great revolutions begin if not in fantasies? Like Marx toking down in the third toilet stall of the British Museum men's room, like Chairman Mao's De Millean opium pipe dream of millions of militant Chinese peasants looming down the hills to tromp tyranny into fertilizer for vast fields of Five Year Plan grain, like John Sinclair vibrant with notions of a whole *nation* of rabidly alive pubescents bashing in the windows of record stores and A&Ps to get the goods they needed and deserved with the MC5 driving them on like an Internationale out of the book of Revelation—like all these forebears, I have a video vision of infinitely exhilarating pluralism.

They used to talk about how when UHF got in really strong we'd have something like eighty-six channels, so you could watch "Green Acres" on Channel 2, the Bolshoi Ballet on 34 and reruns of old Miss America pageants on 63—what a piddling peon's dream! Come the Revolution, we'll have *thousands* of channels where you can watch anything the human mind can conceive, from "I Love Lucy" to beatniks jacking off at campaign glossies of Eisenhower to Sun Ra jamming with Iggy and an old Geritol-stewed yodeler from "Ted Mack's Amateur Hour"! Plus movies, *movies*, MOVIES! All of 'em and often. All power to the People's TV!, and get up off your big fat rusty dusty and man them barricades with me! *This is a conspiracy.*

Taste varies all over the ballpark, but when it comes to the classy flicks of years past, like *Treasure of the Sierra Madre* or *I Am a Fugitive from a Chain Gang*, we can generally achieve some kind of consensus not only with the jerkoffs that pick the flicks to be televised but even with our parents, who probably saw the things at the nabes when they first came out and get all alert and sanguine at this chance to slap a bridge across that old generational chasm and buddy up with us over Bogey or W. C.

Big deal! What about all the truly great movies comprised of unreconstituted trash, which are important not only because nothing else is deranged in quite the way they are, but also because they demonstrate that occasionally intersecting tastes don't in any way prove the sharing of Good Taste cross twenty or thirty years? Nobody likes movies like *Teenagers from Outer Space* or *Wrestling Women vs. the Aztec Mummy* save any loon sane enough to realize that the whole concept of Good Taste is concocted to keep people from having a good time, from reveling in a crassness that passeth all understanding.

I recall reading an item on the entertainment page of the daily paper after *Teenagers from Outer Space* came out to the effect that responsible people all over were so turned off by this pic that the financial angels and bureaucratic bosses of the studio that sponsored and released it ganged up on the poor guy that made the film, and gave him a good talking-to about devoting his talents to such a piece of trash, and even if it was his first film he should think of the public interest, etc. The item ended by saying that the guy had actually *apologized,* and promised to do better with the money that was given him for his second film.

The whole thing was probably a bunch of bullshit dreamed up by PR to make people go see the flick, but it still is revelatory, just like the afternoon a few years ago I saw *Teenagers from Outer Space* on TV, and every commercial break the Dialing for Dollars host would snicker and practically apologize about "this, uh, movie we've got today. Boy, I sure don't know where they got this one."

But fuck those people who'd rather be watching *The Best Years of Our Lives* or *David and Lisa.* We got our own good tastes, like when you see the bizarro lushed-up Irish scrubwoman Kitty McShane, a manic crone looking for all the world like Samuel Beckett in drag, intimidating Bela Lugosi with epileptic spasms in *Mother Riley Meets the Vampire;* or the Blob oozing in a movie house which was itself showing a horror film to an audience of young dudes straining with elbow pangs to grope their sweatered dates just like the kids watching it when it originally came out—and the Blob sluices through the air vents, gets the projectionist, the projector tilts and the film goes haywire along with the lights, and then the Blob starts oozing through the projection window down to the theatre while the audience writhes, falling all over each other in hysteria. . . .

That would be a great moment in the history of the cinema even if the Blob *hadn't* proceeded to engorge not only everybody in the audience but the entire theatre as well. And that's just one of many masterpieces of a long and venerable tradition.

It becomes a bit presumptuous to start talking about standards when we've already admitted that all this stuff is trash, but I think I've seen one movie that must rank at the very top of the heap. I mean, this flick doesn't just rebel against, or even disregard, standards of taste and art. In the universe inhabited by *The Incredibly Strange Creatures Who Stopped Living and Became Mixed-Up Zombies,* such things as standards and responsibility have never been heard of. It is this lunar purity which largely imparts to the film its classic stature. Like *Beyond the Valley of the Dolls* and a very few others, it will remain as an artifact in years to come to which scholars and searchers for truth can turn and say, *"This* was trash!"

I sat up half the night waiting, and it finally came on at 2:45 A.M. First, though, came a commercial with Bing Crosby spieling in Spanish and then saying: "I was just telling my amigos about United States Savings Bonds." Perfect! And now the credits. Will they be serious about it? Heh heh heh, you bet they will. But what's this credit headed "The Entertainers" and "Dancing Girls," with a roster of names under each? Hmmm. Curiouser and curiouser.

Montage shots of sleazy fairgrounds, probably shot in the amusement park at Long Beach. Loud soundtrack of erratic, staccato saxophone rock 'n' roll, melody a bit like Chuck Berry's "Too Pooped to Pop." Rock 'n' roll or music at least related to it will be heard all the way through the movie, all of it thoroughly mediocre. But whaddaya want, *Woodstock?*

Now we're inside the gypsy fortune teller's tent. A sultry, cat-like wench with eyes like flaming agates, she is unaccountably giving the unmistakable come-on to a shabby old bald-headed fart who sits snorting up a fifth of rye and sez: "You couldn't buy enough booze to make me want you. Whyncha go out and find one o' them freaks."

What's going on here? Never mind, no time to cogitate; she becomes so incensed at the codger's insults she shrieks: "Now I will put you with the rest of my little pets!," throws acid in his face and drags him screaming behind the curtain!

Cut to nightclub scene: pas de deux with bony cat in tux and chick wearing less than you expect to see on TV. (She bears an uncanny resemblance to the gypsy fortune teller.) Cut to dressing room: dancer now soaking up rotgut like a sponge. A black cat crosses her path and she explodes into screaming, kicking hysterics.

Cut to Jerry and Harold (played by two actors named Cash Flagg and Atlas King), heroes of this thing, lounging around their pad ruminating about the meaning of life. Harold just resembles your typical fifties punk who combs his hair a lot, but Jerry looks like a cross between Pete Townshend and Alice the Goon's brother. Jerry leans back and sez: "Wonder what it's like to hold a job?"

Cut to home of Jerry's cutie, Angie. She goes through a row with her mother, who doesn't approve of Jerry at all. Jerry and Harold arrive to pick her up and take her to the carnival—Jerry beeps the horn, climbs out on the roof of the car and swings the door open with his foot! Cool cat!

Cut to montage of Jerry, Angie and Harold at the carnival, walking in on the beach, riding the rides and especially the roller-coaster in clips reminiscent of *This Is Cinerama,* interspersed with distorting mirrors and garish dolls moving back and forth in strange fun-house laughter.

Cut to girl dancer drinking in dressing room again. Her partner lectures her, they go on, she's so lushed she trips over her own feet, falls across the floor, runs offstage. The manager storms back ("I can't run a nightclub with a drunken star!"), then splits, leaving her guzzling and reading a paperback about astrology.

Cut to Jerry and Angie and Harold, still on the roller coaster, screaming in the night. Back to dancer visiting the gypsy fortune teller, who lays out the Tarot. First thing up is the Death Card. "I knew it," the dancer screams and runs out. But she runs the wrong way, behind the curtain where the gypsy dragged the old drunk. A monster hand reaches through the bars.

Jerry, Angie and Harold approach the fortune-telling tent. They go in and Angie's fortune is told. She takes it seriously, but Jerry says it's a bunch of bullshit. In fact, he scoffs so much he gets the gypsy's dander up, an action he'll regret.

An eerily wobbly organ tape begins as Jerry, Angie and Harold cruise out on the midway and stop to watch the hoochiekoo dancer, whose name is Carmelita and may or may not be the same dancer who drinks all the time and just visited the gypsy. One problem with this movie is that most of the people in it look like some other character; the club manager who bawled the dancer out for boozing, for instance, looked more than a little like the unknown and unnamed coot who got the acid thrown in his face at the beginning. So what's going on? Well, I ain't so sure. I'm not even sure it makes a difference.

Meanwhile, Angie is burning up about the way Jerry's gawking at that near-nekkid hoofer lady, so she leaves with Harold in a huff. Jerry buys a ticket and goes inside to watch the show, and there follows a feather dance like you never seen in prime time, brother. Rendered in its entirety, it consists of a bevy of bountiful babes prancing around, running from one side of the stage to the other and writhing and kneeling all arty and balletlike, meanwhile shedding more and more feathers till all they got left is a little ducky down o'er bush and nipples! And one even looks like Mary Tyler Moore!

Next up is a girl who looks exactly like Angie, singing an original rock 'n' roll ballad: "I was pretending that our ending was one of those things." Followed by the incomparable Carmelita: "Now we give you our exotic beautiful gypsy dancer!" She sings a song, too: "I'm the Pied Piper of love / Follow me. . . ."

While Jerry is slavering in the fourth row, Ortega, the gypsy's one-eyed hunchback servant with Fagin nose, taps him on the shoulder and hands him a note from Carmelita, telling him to meet her in the dressing room after the show. And he does, only he bumbles into the wrong dressing room and gets run out by a bunch of irate half-dressed dancing girls: "Thought he could get some real fast action before the show."

Stumbling down the hall, he sees her suddenly, framed in the shadows of a doorway, distant, mysterious. "Carmelita? You sent for me?"

Here comes that eerie organ music again. "Follow me."

Suddenly, the whole screen is filled by a spinning psychedelic vortex . . . down, down into it we whirl . . . the gypsy is here, hypnotizing Jerry . . . his eyes get wild, the light burns into them . . . his face snaps forward and back and his eyeballs roll to odd electronic gurgles . . . Ortega stands behind the gypsy, laughing monstrously . . . Carmelita in Garboesque hat and coat enters dressing room alone . . . the camera spins crazily around her face as she stares at it hypnotically . . . lens careens off every cranny of the dressing room, always homing back into those burning eyes. . . .

Cut to nightclub floor and a stand-up comic: "I come from a large iron and steel family—Mom irons and Dad steals. . . ." Followed by the emcee: "And now, the Hungry Mouth is proud to present a bright new singer—Don McLean!" and another dull song in full.

Back to Carmelita in the dressing room. Up comes her dancing partner: "What's wrong, Marge?" WHAT? Are Carmelita and Marge the same person? Or is it just that they look exactly alike? Or that everybody in this movie looks alike? I'm thoroughly confused but I am taking notes.

Suddenly, though, it all comes clear when Marge and her partner mount the stage, commence the pas de deux, and Jerry barges in dressed in monk's cowl with chalky face looking for all the world like the Devil in Bergman's *Seventh Seal,* if they'd let Max von Sydow play him. He stabs both dancers, cackling like a henbane fiend and runs out. I see! Right! Marge isn't Carmelita, Carmelita's in cahoots with the gypsy to kill all the other entertainers on the midway. Eliminating the competition. Okay.

Except that it isn't okay, nothing is. We're sucked just as abruptly back into another one of those nightmare montages . . . as in many other films when they wanna go Surreal and Way Out, we see a modern-jazz ballet . . . a girl who looks like Angie in a blond wig calls dreamily: "Jerry . . . Jerry . . . [*looks at camera*] Oh, there you are!" and breaks into hysterical laughter . . . Jerry writhing in bed . . . superimposition of flames, the gypsy, Ortega, endless images of women one of whom is doing the twist . . . King Kong roaring . . . the laughing midway clown marionette seen earlier . . . Jerry wakes up moaning and splashes water in his face.

The next morning Harold is out working on his car, and Jerry comes out of the house and says: "Boy, did I have a restless night last night!" Next he hightails to Angie's to apologize for being pigheaded last night. "All right," she says. "But I sure would like to know what happened after I left!"

And with that, coquettishly, she turns her parasol his way and starts twirling it! Oh no! It's turning to the psychedelic vortex! His eyes get wild! She looks out from behind the parasol and she's Carmelita! Lightning cuts back and forth between Jerry choking her and choking Carmelita. Her dad tears him away just in time. Jerry runs wildly away, goes for a walk by the railroad tracks and by gum here comes another song! Sounds something like the Sons of the Pioneers. . . .

Night. The midway. In the Hungry Mouth another song-and-dance number commences, with about twelve Gold-Diggers doing the twist and singing "Gramma's got shook outa shape from doing the twist!" Next we see a dancer holding a paper headlined DANCERS MURDERED going to the fortune teller, who snaps: "If you're looking for my sister Carmelita, she's not here." AHA! So they're sisters! This little puzzle is falling into place right nifty.

Back at the Hungry Mouth the man is bringing on "the girl with golden voice—Miss Terry Randall!" (Who *are* all these people?) Terry sings another original that goes, "Choo Choo Cha Boochie, you thrill me with the slightest touch" accompanied by odd rhythmic punctuation of strangled screams. And who wrote all these songs? Were they written especially for this movie? Or was the movie written for *them?*

Jerry goes to see the gypsy: "I've been having a nightmare, and I think you know about it!" Since half the people in this movie are lushes, the gypsy always has a handy comeback: "You been drinking?" But Jerry is not about to be put off, and asks her what goes on behind the curtain. She leers, "Why don't you go back and see?"

The sap does . . . oh no! . . . it's the vortex again! . . . the gypsy's staring eyes . . . and now she is joined by the dancer who just left . . . I start hoping for a lesbian scene, but no such luck.

Cut to family conference at Angie's house with Angie and Harold begging her parents to let them go back to the carnival. "All right, Angela, you can go, as long as Madison goes with you." WHO IS MADISON? *Harold* Madison? I sure as fuck hope so.

Meanwhile the dancer who left the gypsy's tent a few minutes back is at home with a bottle of wine and soft radio. Cuddly smiles, obviously waiting for her boyfriend. Instead she finds J. Zombie all cowled and white again, he chases her around the room, blade flashes in the light and he stabs her with a quick cut to her boyfriend's finger pressing the doorbell. When she don't answer he lets himself in and gets stabbed as well.

Jerry, somewhat recovered, pays another visit to the gypsy. She leers again: "It's too bad you know so much—now you leave me no choice." Throws acid in his face! "Take him back and put him with the rest of the little pets." But suddenly Ortega fucks up and the Zombies are all loose! Three or four of 'em! They strangle Ortega and the gypsy, whose name has been Estrella all along but wasn't revealed until Ortega speaks her name just before her death. And now here comes Carmelita, slinky gown flapping open and wotta body! But the Zombies are unimpressed and strangle her too. Now the two dead sisters are sprawled across the floor and the camera lingers with loving morbidity over Estrella's tits which brim up out of her shift and Carmelita's whole bod, which is even more naked in death than it's been the rest of the flick. What a perverted movie! Drool, drool. Finally the camera gets tired of necrophilia and rises up to watch the Zombies as they beat it out the door in search of more trouble to make, then pans back for a closeup of Estrella's staring eyes. . . .

"Howdy friends this is Guy Fletcher and I hope you're enjoying our movie." More used cars. Thanks, podner, sure am. Return after commercial to midway, night, cutting to another exotic dance number while the Zombies lurk in hallways between dressing rooms and stage. They run out onto the floor and start chasing the dancers while the audience sits impassively thinking it's part of the show until one Zombie pushes a dancer to the floor and starts strangling her. Audience screams and people start running out. Closeup of Zombie faces: they look like a cross between Kabuki and Polynesian masks, heavy on the papier-mâché. A cop runs in and shoots one Zombie dead. Cops chase the other two down the hall, shoot 'em both. Angie and Harold come in, and Angie screams. Jerry stumbles in the side door, and he really doesn't look as bad as the other Zombies, face just a little pockmarked. Of course, he just joined the team. Angie screams again. Jerry runs away and jumps out the window! The film must be approaching the climax, because a big chase scene is obviously shaping up. And indeed we cut to Jerry running up the road, Angie chasing him, the cops and the others chasing them both. They all run out to the beach and Jerry tears madly out into the rough surf around the shoals, hopping from stone to stone for about five minutes while Angie screams his name from the shore. Finally Jerry climbs atop a huge rock, one of the cops shoots him, he falls into the surf . . . is washed up on the sand . . . struggles to stand up and dies strenuously . . . they all rush up and bend over him . . . the camera backs away into the sky . . . "THE END." Followed by "Made in Hollywood, USA," as if anyone could have any doubts, and a cast list telling who played whom. Harold's last name wasn't Madison, but there was an actor in the film named Madison Clarke. Which could have solved everything: one of the players slipped momentarily and called "Harold" by his real name instead of that of the character he was playing. The only trouble is that Madison Clarke didn't play Harold. Oh, well: I'm sure he was at the carnival somewhere.

—*Creem*, March 1973

Jethro Tull in Vietnam

An awful lot of kids cut school last November when it was announced that Jethro Tull would play two shows at Detroit's Cobo Arena. The lines, longer than Cobo management had ever seen before, started forming at seven A.M. By the time the ticket office opened—three hours later—there were four thousand kids milling around outside. One observer described it as looking like "the third day of a three-day rock festival." People were buying fifty and a hundred tickets at a time, and the first show sold out in three hours. The second was sold out the next day: in the meantime, a riot had been narrowly averted, the TAC squad called in and barricades erected. All this in spite of the fact that ticket prices had gone up a dollar over the $5.50 rate of the previous May's tour, when only a thousand people were turned away and four doors to Cobo were smashed by irate Jethro fans.

The violence may not have been typical of Tull tours—yet—but the numbers were indicative of a new fever. Jethro Tull's following has grown until it has become vast enough to qualify as one of the success stories of our time. The band itself has evolved quickly from their early blues derivations into artier, more melodic and complex stuff, and by their fourth album they were getting into grand conceptual suites on a scale unmatched this side of the Moody Blues. *Aqualung* was two LP sides of unmitigated social moralizing, weighty lyrics in musical settings so heterogeneous (rock, Rock, a bit of rock 'n' roll, a lot of mostly borrowed jazz, and folk strains both British and American, as well as the odd "classical" gambit) as to have become a recognizable style.

Jethro Tull have still never had an AM hit single in this country, and are one of the prototype cases in which an "underground" group has become an international sensation strictly on the basis of their albums. By *Aqualung* they almost had to, because by that time (1970) the band's musical scenarios had inflated to a point that left no room for the traditional two or three minute whambam thank you ma'am single. You had to take the whole pie at once or not at all.

Meanwhile, Jethro Tull consolidated their position by tightening up their stage act. Their drawing power increased by geometric leaps every time they toured the States, and it wasn't only the music. The crucial element, the focal point, was Ian Anderson, wild-eyed waistcoat-tail-whipping dervish who played long, violent, echo-chambered flute solos as if he were boxing with the instrument—the Eric Clapton of wind.

Anderson has always trotted out old Roland Kirk riffs: flute vocalisms, overblowing, even the histrionics which became the eye of his stage business. Roland Kirk never to my knowledge stuck his flute between his legs in the crudest sort of phallic stage ploy, as Anderson does. But Roland Kirk was the original Wild Man of the concert flute, and Anderson should admit the debt he owes him.

I doubt if he would. I was unable to talk to him, but I spoke to Jethro drummer Barrie Barlow in the hotel bar after a gig last spring, and he scoffed at the idea of Ian being influenced by Kirk or anyone else. Their music, he went on, came totally out of the minds and experience of Jethro Tull, had no precedents, fit into no tradition, and was completely original. Which probably represents the general sentiments within the band.

In any case, they've earned the right to be arrogant. *Aqualung* was a giant and the follow-up, *Thick as a Brick,* was over a year in the making and even bigger. Bigger in every way: the only time in rock history previous to this that a single song had covered two sides of an LP was Canned Heat's "Refried Boogie" on *Livin' the Blues,* and that was just an extended jam. *Brick* was a moose of a whole other hue: a series of variations (though they really didn't vary enough to sustain forty minutes) on a single, simple theme, which began as a sort of wistful English folk melody and wound through march tempos, high energy guitar, glockenspiels, dramatic staccato outbursts like something from a movie soundtrack and plenty of soloing by Anderson, all the way from the top of side one to the end of the album.

The whole thing was built around a longish poem by Anderson, which itself set new records in the Tull canon of lofty sentiments and Biblically righteous denunciations of contemporary mores. The very first line was "I really don't mind if you sit this one out," a classic hook which set the tone for the entire piece, which was crammed with couplets like

The sandcastle virtues are all swept away
In the tidal destruction of the moral melee

Where was this stuff coming from, anyway, and what did it say about the way not only Anderson and Tull but perhaps most of their audience related to the world around them? Did they really feel that self-righteous about things in general? Or was it, like "American Pie," just a bunch of words that could have as much meaning as you wanted to invest or none at all, and happened to fit the music nicely? Ask a Tull freak and you'll get a blank look; most of them, it seems, have never stopped to analyze it. They just know what they like, which is fine.

They like it enough, in fact, that *Thick as a Brick* rocketed straight to Number One on the charts, and so far the band has done two sellout tours on the strength of it. On the second tour they sold out Madison Square Garden for a straight week. All this on the basis of an album—and a style—which on the surface would seem to tax anybody's attention span. Tull concerts now are a real experience, and a unique one, for better or worse.

Make no mistake: in terms of sheer professionalism, Jethro Tull are without peer. They stand out by never failing to deliver a fullscale *show*, complete with everything they know any kid would gladly pay his money to see: music, volume, costumes, theatrics, flashy solos, long sets, two encores. Jethro Tull are slick and disciplined; they work hard and they deliver.

What they deliver is one of the most curious melanges on any stage. If their lyrics generally take a moralistic bent, the band themselves come on like total goofballs, and the contrast works nicely. All of them dress to the teeth, usually in Victorian waistcoats and tight pants, and from the instant Ian Anderson hits the stage he works the audience with all the masterful puppeteer mojo of the Merlin he often poses as. He whirls and whips in total spastic grace, creating a maelstrom around himself, flinging his fingers in the air as if hurling arcane incantations at the balcony. His eyes take on a satyr's gleam, get wild and pop from his head. He very effectively passes himself off as a madman reeling in riptide gales from unimaginable places. He exploits his flute exhaustively: baton, wand, sword, gun, phallus, club, virtuoso's magic axe. He twirls it like a cheerleader and stirs the audience to frothing frenzies with it, then raises the ladle to his chops and puts the audience in a trance with an extended melodramatic solo.

Jethro Tull are such solid entertainers that even if you can't stand the music, they're usually providing something for you to gawk at. A lot of it is real vaudeville: Barlow walks up to the mike during a pause, holds up a toy cymbal, raises a drumstick and hits it with an extravagant flourish. As he does so he rises on left tiptoes and arches his right leg out behind him like a cartoon Nureyev, rolling his eyes at the audience and mugging shamelessly. He gets cheers and an echoing cymbal shot which seems to come from nowhere and puts him into similarly exaggerated perplexity. He looks around, scratches his head and hits the cymbals again. Again the echo. Getting really worked up, he hits the cymbal again and again, faster and faster, the echoes coming at the same pace, and suddenly the rest of the band converges on him, each of them holding identical cymbal and stick and wildly bashing away. The audience eats it up.

Costumes are utilized too, in a manner that's too calculated and too successful to be off the cuff. But what would you think if you saw a band stop an extended song in the middle to:

Read a bogus "weather report."

Run through a bit where a band member walks to the microphone and begins to gesticulate and address the audience, while another member dressed as a gorilla stands behind him aping his every move.

Hop around the stage dressed as bunny rabbits.

Stop the music again, the silence broken by the ringing of a prop phone onstage which one bandmember answers: "Hello? Oh yes, I'll see if he's here." Then he turns to the audience: "There's a call here for a Mr. Mike Nelson."

So a roadie or somebody, dressed in full skindiving gear complete with fins, mask and aqualung, flaps on from stage left, picks up the phone, wordlessly mimics a brief conversation, then flaps back as the band tears into a particularly wild passage from *Brick* to wild cheers from the gallery.

If that's your idea of entertainment, scarf up a ticket the next time Jethro Tull hit town. If you can get one, that is. It's a long way from my idea of rock 'n' roll, but then maybe that idea is dated. Or maybe this isn't rock 'n' roll, and doesn't need to apologize for being something else either. Jethro Tull are going to be around for a while, will undoubtedly get even bigger than they are now, and their musical productions will become even more inflated—it's hard to imagine them pulling a Beatles "white album" type switchback. And perhaps there is a lesson in their triumph for all of us.

If you're a band or band manager and you want to make a lot of money, you should follow the methods laid down for the Seventies by groups like Alice Cooper and Jethro Tull. You should find a style of music for which you have a certain affinity, develop that style till it's honed to a fine edge, then wrap it in whatever current social or cultural readymades seem to fit best (sexual indeterminacy in Alice's case, pompous wrath at social shibboleths and breakdown in Jethro's).

Then you want to work up some elaborate stage business. You can be pretty random about it at this point, because most bands haven't begun to think in these terms yet. Besides, the more random you are the most people are likely to call you "dada" or something equally impressive. Anyway, all that matters is that you give people some color and motion to look at so they won't fidget while they're listening to you.

The final stage is to discipline yourself rigorously, rehearsing the whole shebang till it's airtight, till you can go on and deliver one punch right after another all the way through your set without ever losing your balance. Polish the whole thing up and market it. It works.

You can reach a point in the creation of something when the trappings and the tinsel and the construction become so important that it doesn't really matter at all what's inside. The show can be a total contrivance: ultra-formulaic music, jive bits of business for punctuation, cabooses loaded with props, choreographed postures and preenings, even the audience enlisted to give it right back on cue, educated in the process through past concerts and festival movies. The whole thing can be just that vacuous, and because someone has taken the trouble to entertain them, everybody still goes away happy. Show biz is funny that way.

POSTLUDE: AFTER THE FALL

So I hassled and I hustled and I still couldn't scope it out. What wall were those Tulls coming off of anyhoo? No comprende. Till one day, quite by accident, I happened to play this album that had been mouldering in my collection called *Music of Vietnam.* It was one of those things on Folkways, you know, arcane chants from the outback, and I had it because some liberal had loaned it to me once and then disappeared from sights forever. So I put it on because I was totally danced out anyway, and IT SOUNDED JUST LIKE JETHRO TULL! Folk music from the jungles of Vietnam, some of it thousands of years old, and damned if them ole tonal clusters weren't congregating in clots highly consonant with what Ian and the boys were laying down. The rhythms were similar, though not as stiff and marchlike, and the reed cats on their bamboo flutes had Ian A. down to a T.

So I knew that there was only one thing to do. I got Warner Brothers

Records to fly me to Saigon, just to get this whole thing sorted out, scooped straight from the horse's mouth. So to speak. When I got there I strutted up to the Presidential Palace, bold as a buffalo, marched right in and planted myself square in front of President Thieu's desk. Thank God for Mo Ostin's Washington connections. History was being made here and now.

I wasted no time. "Look," I said, "I got this here album by this bunch of Limey creeps called Jethro Tull," and I hand him a copy of *Thick as a Brick*. Thieu is cool as a cod: he opens the album, leafs through a few pages of the insert with a half-smile, reads some of the lyrics, then turns to an elaborate Garrard component system behind the right side of his desk and puts the record on. Soon that same goddamn song is booming out of the giant Marshall amps in the East and West (natch) corners of the room. Directly to my right in front of the President's desk sits the Ambassador from Uganda, who had been conferring with the President when I barged in and is now obviously nonplussed, perhaps slightly offended. Breach of diplomatic protocol? Big shit! We gotta get this Tull trash sorted out for the good of America!

So while Pop Thieu is listening to the first five or ten minutes of *Thick as a Brick,* I run down the whole story to him. How Jethro Tull are so far off the wall they ain't even in the room. How I sprained my brain trying to get over or around 'em and always found 'em inescapable, so it was do or die and I was at the terminal. How I'd found the Folkways Vietnam album—then I shove that at him. Thieu looks it over with a chuckle, then hands it back. The Ugandan Ambassador is beginning to look interested. Thieu leans back in his swivel chair, puts all ten fingers together, and listens to a few more bars of Jethro Tull. Then he takes it off, turns around and hands me the most patronizing smile I've ever seen in my life.

"It has always amazed me," he says, "how you Americans can feed yourselves the worst kind of garbage and still survive, but now at last I think I understand. I don't like Jethro Tull either—I never have, not even when all my friends were bending my ear with *This Was*—but not, perhaps, for the same reasons which have driven you to such extremes.

"I don't like them because you are right. They do sound like Vietnamese folk music, and *I'm no folkie!* I despise that jerky, over-rhythmic, open-ended clatter. Give me progressive jazz anytime—Peanuts Hucko, 'Big' Tiny Little—and I am happy. A man must move with the times, and the times demand bop: how can a man in my position say that bop is wrong? I didn't get here by swimming against the tide. I see the American GIs walking by the Palace every day with those bop records in their hands, and every once in a while I go down and ask them to show them to me. I speak to them in the language that they understand: 'What's the word, Thunderbird?' And they reply that the word is 'rebop.' All these records they show me, all of these people, Chuck Berry, Elvis Presley, the Rolling Stones, I have understood through my communication with your people, are rebop, be it good or bad.

"But, as anyone can see, Vietnamese music is not rebop. It's not even bop. It's just something frozen and awkward, but insistent for all of that. These old cultures die hard. Which is why they still play that wretched noise in the rice paddies, and why something like Jethro Tull is popular with your people. Because some people, you know, just can't take rebop. And the reason for which I do not like Jethro Tull and, I would suspect, you do not like Jethro Tull is that they *have no rebop!*"

He leaned back again, point made, and smiled. I was still puzzling this one out when the Ugandan Ambassador leaned over and tapped me on the knee. "Say," he said, "what is all this obsession with 'rebop,' anyway?"

—*Creem,* May 1973

Screwing the System with Dick Clark

I was flabbergasted. You would be too. I met a great man, a statesman, one of the fathers of the counterculture. Dick Clark has been dishing up a leggily acceptable euphemism of the teenage experience on ABC-TV's "American Bandstand" for twenty years now, and recently celebrated that achievement by airing a twentieth anniversary show featuring everything from dredged regulars out of the show's acne heydays (now looking very staid indeed) to Cheech and Chong rating records (they gave one a nothing, and broke it). The show managed to poll a 42 share of the viewing audience, unprecedented for the time it was aired, and now Buddah has marketed a companion album, *20 Years of Rock 'n' Roll*, a perfect assemblage including Dick's mug up front, a twenty-four-page souvenir yearbook, a cardboard bonus record of Dick's "inside stories," and thirty original hits running all the way from "Cryin' in the Chapel" by the Orioles to Gallery's "Nice to Be with You" (a hefty portion of it old Buddah-owned noise, of course).

So in spite of hipcult accusations of galloping obsolescence, Dick Clark is currently riding higher than ever, and obviously deserves to be heard in these sargasso times of youthful post-unrest nebbishhood which some have even sworn are like the fifties all over again. They're not, of course, but Dick Clark may well have come full circle.

It was a quick walk from the offices of Buddah Records on 7th Avenue to the Ed Sullivan Theatre, where Dick was busy taping the next several months of "The $10,000 Pyramid," the weekday-morning game show he now hosts as well as holding down his institutional spot on the Saturday afternoon "American Bandstand." He's a busy institution, taping a week's worth of "Pyramid"s every day, but we'll be able to squeeze in an interview over lunch in the Chinese restaurant next door. I've got plenty of Mandrax and cigars, and I'm ready.

We watch the monitors as the credits roll on a just-finished "Pyramid" and guests Jack Klugman and Tony Randall engage in some last-minute horseplay for the cameras. Then they're off, and I'm shaking hands with Dick, momentarily distracted by the sight of an even greater celebrity, Tony Randall, bustling off with three little old ladies in tow. He holds hands with them, bills and coos. *Jeezus,* I think, *he's Felix Unger offstage too. Wodda froot.* Then we go up to the virtual broom closet that is Dick's dressing room, he gets into his civvies and I observe the antediluvian thickness of Dick's pancake makeup. Remarkably well-preserved, this boyo is—you'd have to go to Pat Boone, I think, to find a comparable case. You can see the wrinkles under the makeup, but he don't wear no toupee—*he really has hair that he combs like that.* Also, he speaks to you in a public sort of voice that's very similar to the one heard on TV. Not without a sense of humor, he nevertheless is very serious in his comments on the music business—and all his references to it are geared to a dollars-and-sense level of somehow homespun entrepreneurial pragmatism. He pronounces words like "sociological" with a careful precision that lends them a tone of solemn import and suggests he may feel obliged by his generational daddy role to come on more oracular than is his natural inclination. Nevertheless, he's a pro, and while occasionally embarrassingly pat his answers come tumbling out in a magnificently organized torrent of anecdotes, Clarkian aphorisms, and the odd ironic "frank" admission.

How wired would *you* have to get, for instance, to compete with this natural life stylin' poppa's rap: "There was a lady the other day that gave a fascinating speech in acceptance of an honorary degree she got at some college somewhere . . . Dolly Cole, she's the wife of the chairman of the board of General Motors, so you know obviously where her politics lie and where her thinking goes, but she came up with a great line, she's a self-educated lady and very charming, I did five television shows with her once, I got to know her reasonably well—she said to the graduating class, she apologized for her truck-driver language in front, she said, 'All of you here attending this school who are complaining of the materialistic world can be assured that there are a couple of parents home working their ass off to keep you here.' Which is an interesting thought. The other great line I read, and this is fabulous, is that in this generation of young people who all wanta be individualistic, the line is 'Look, I wanna be *different,* just like everybody else!,' we are really coming into a carbon-copy generation. It's really unique. As a student of young people, I've never seen such a one-dimensional group of people in all my life—in thinking, in dress, even in music habits."

I mean, did you ever! What I wouldn't give to talk, hell, *write* like that—what incredible organization, what lucidity. But I suspected the facile flash of the superficial, generalized savant, so I lammed into him: Just why *are* you so interested in young people, Dick?

"Sheer unadulterated greed. That's a facetious answer; it's mostly true. It's been a very good livelihood secondarily, and I would appreciate it if you wouldn't excerpt it and just publish that part. I enjoy it. If I didn't, there's no amount of money in the world could make me do what I do. And let's face it, it's a hell of an interesting way to make a living. You never know from day to day what young people are gonna do next."

That reminds me, Dick: Whadda you think of fag-rock?

He gets a worried look. "Do you think this is going to be widespread?"

Sure! David Bowie, Lou Reed, all those guys at the top of the charts, the queers are taking over the country!

He chews on that one a minute, and comes back typically unruffled, reflective: "Anything that's new takes a while before it gets disseminated across the country. You get the J. C. Penney versions of fashions of what the style leaders are wearing. There's an interesting premise in all of this, in the youth world, you take the lunatic fringe, the avant-garde, the style leaders, the *nuts*. And if you are careful enough to determine what they come up with that's a legitimate trend, then you'll be able to figure out eventually what the people in the middle, I don't mean necessarily geographically but in the case of our country it is pretty much the middle, will be doing in the next number of months.

"Bisexual . . . what's the other word, AC/DC? I think it's partially fad and partially goldfish swallowing, as protest was. A lot of kids got into protest because it was 'the thing.' It was not popular to criticize legitimate protest at the time, but I used to make the joke about the kid who had the sign in the bedroom closet that said 'SHAME,' and would at any given moment take the sign and go out and march. The sign was apropos to anything. That may be what's happening with the fag-drag crazy transsexual rock scene. I think that's a quickie. I think more importantly that's an indication of the desire to have show business return to music. That's why you have an Elton John, a Liberace, an Alice Cooper. That's show biz. We all know Alice is a put-on, a shuck. But what's funny is when you read the sociological commentators and how torn up the whole straight world is over this craziness. I can't attach any significance to that."

Does he then see the hope of rock's future in relatively wholesome groups like Slade, or the bubblegum androgyny of Marc Bolan? Nope. "I don't think Slade will make it in the States for the same reason T. Rex didn't make it: he thought he was Mick Jagger. He was Donny Osmond. Print it. The shmuck. I went over there at the time that there was a necessity to fill our subteen gap of idols, to try to convince [Bolan's] people that it would be a good time to move on the American market in that area. The trouble was, the poor fellow believed his own publicity, when you had Ringo Starr running around taking pictures of him with an 8-millimeter camera. He believed he was going to be Mick Jagger, which he is not. He's been so many things in his career I don't guess he knows who he is. And he has been so ill advised—this happens with so many artistic people—a man of obviously great talents, but no business acumen. And so therefore never the twain shall cross and he went into the sewer.

"I'm always distressed by the supposedly bright people who don't know what they are. Take the Monkees, who thought they were the Beatles. They could have had a very nice thing going in their area for another couple of years, despite the fact that it was a shuck. It was a commercially built commodity for which there was an audience from which they could have made a great deal of money and retired and passed it on to their children. Instead Mickey Dolenz thought he was Paul McCartney. He went up to Monterey and they laughed at him.

"Again statistically, look at the record books and you'll see that every ten years in the middle of the decade some sort of freak superstar arises. You can take it back to Rudy Vallee and Bing Crosby, through Frank Sinatra and Perry Como, then you had Bill Haley and Elvis, the Rolling Stones and the Beatles, so now you're upon it again. Sometime in the next two years there'll be an individual who will be a white, male, single performing artist. Probably American. . . ."

Changing the subject to his show, I wondered if he consciously strived to put forth a certain image of American youth in the kids that appeared on "American Bandstand."

"Well, I dunno. They're kind of middle-of-the-road kids, I guess. It wouldn't be a typical concert audience because they're dressed differently. The only dress requirements we have are that the girls can't wear pants suits. It's only because of the visual thing, because it's a hell of a lot more interesting to watch a girl in a skirt. And with long hair in closeups it's very difficult to distinguish male from female, and so you use that attractive element. That's only a matter of practicality," he adds. "It's not a prejudice on my part; I'm not a big leg man or anything."

For some reason, Dick, hippies and counterculturites seem to think you're stodgy. I asked him if he had a clue and he came back with both barrels. "That was very predominant about three or four years ago, but it's become passé now. It was a good institution to play games off of. Then it suddenly dawned on a lot of them that I'd been around for twenty years and was carrying the ball for them and that's the reason they were in business. I'm very cynical toward the underground press, of which you are one. I'll be here longer than you will, is my attitude. I will be very happy to have you make fun of me or do whatever you want, I really don't care.

"They have found now that there must be some semblance of order to stay alive. That's why FM underground freeform radio died. Because you can't turn seven crazy freaky guys loose on the air to do whatever they wanta do whenever they wanta do it, play the same cut seventeen times or play some obtuse album, 'cause who cares?

"A lot of the whole world that kids don't understand is politics and money. When you learn politics, money, the advertising world, where the skeletons are buried, you have then matured enough to stay alive. It's part of the game. And a lot of kids don't learn until they're out wandering around saying, 'Hey, I wonder why the place I was working at went out of business.' They told too many people to shove it. That's what happened to the Smothers Brothers. What a wonderful tool they had, except they painted one of the three major networks into a corner and said, 'There's no way for you to get out and we'll win.' They're winning minor dollars, but it won't amount to much by the time they pay the lawyers. So one must learn to screw the system from within."

Okay Dick, but just for the record, what did you do when you were a kid? "I was a student of the black arts. I was a hypnotist at thirteen. I lived all the way through that, my whole life I had bookshelves full of this stuff. And then when it got to be very big in the late sixties I said I better get out of this, I can't stand listening to all of this again. I was a big hit at all the parties, reading palms, putting people out. . . ."

So now how do you see yourself, the adult Dick Clark? As a moral leader for youth?

"I'm just the storekeeper. The shelves are empty, I put the stock on. Make no comment pro or con. Irving Berlin said, 'Popular music is popular because a lot of people like it.' That doesn't mean it's good or it's bad— that's the equivalent of arguing the merits of hot dogs versus hamburgers. What the hell difference does it make?"

—*Creem*, November 1973

Slade:
Sladest

I picked this album up at a dinner in the Trader Vic's trough of the local Hilton, thrown by Warner Bruhs to announce they'd nabbed these skinheads. We all sat there whomping back the Mai Tais, and midway in the no-menu like-it-or-else coolie-catered exotique entree somebody started throwing the kantoneez slop on our plates around the table. I think it was a Warner's PR jason that initiated it, but pretty soon there were mango pits and blowfish fillets flying everywhere. The meal ended in total chaos, then this truly outstanding and well-met Warnoid suggested we go up and harass the Masons, who were holding a convention on the third floor. So we elevated to the mezzanine, where cherubic hosts of baldpated sexagenarians in tuxes were escorting their quiet wives this way and that. So I just started going up to the oldie couples at random and, reaching out to gladhand them with unctuous smile on my face I would in tones of absolute Avon Calling mannerliness beam: "Eat a bowl of fuck!" Or, alternately, "Slit yer mudder's tit, sir!" And then maybe give the gerry's gleaming dome a friendly skweeze, as if to dust it off.

It was all great fun, and the next day the Warner stalwart called up to apologize for his "obnoxious" behavior. We told him we wouldn't hear of an apology, because in the face of all protocols and proprieties he had behaved in the true Slade spirit. These is rowdy lads, and right in the middle of the deadly dinner not twenty seconds before he started tossing pineapple puds around Slader Numbah One Noddy Holder, sitting just my left, sighed: "Why can't we get in a *fight* for a change?"

Cuz that's what Slade's all about. Ripping up the joint for real for once, tapdancing on the doorman's spats, stuffing a bulbous gherkin up ya sainted mudda's snooker. You wouldn't sport so rude if you was out with Dionne Warwick or even Elton John, but Slade are holler and ham hock, dumped chunk-rumple into big stompingly anthemic hard rockin trojan horses from the most classic bins of rock armory. It kinda leads nowhere but into more closed-system hysteria, and it's more than a little manufactured mania, but it hits fine and true. It'll gallop you headfirst into sweetkooze and sproing you outa yer jadofado wheelchair like a lucky stiff reprieved at last from endless iceman-cometh miasmas. Been a long burning rage in Angleterre, but's yet to really spliv U.S. cherry, so if you jump on the bandwagon with me and the rest of these reprobates mebbe it'll come to pass yet and save these fine lads from dying the Stateside death à la Marc Bolan which shouldn't happen to a Silas Marner constipatee much less a pack o' Limey louts who threw down shopwage just to dance like dinwiddies in the streets.

It's almost Slade's last chance to win us, and this album should do it if nuttin else because it's the summun bukmun umyun culling of their flashest stompers that've brickbatted straight to Numb One on them Auld Sod charts lo these last years. White-heat killers like "Gudbuy t' Jane," "Skweeze Me Pleeze Me," "Look Wot You Dun," and the suprema "Mama Weer All Crazee Now" are self-explanatory and will make you feel it even in 1973. They're gonna have a new one out pretty soon but specs dark whether these skabs or any band predicated so formulaic can long endure or top the tumescent rum-running track flayers here gathered. *Racing Form* backs them all the way, so do I, so should you. And then you can tear up your own colonial banquets like the only true beggars left.

—*Creem,* December 1973

My Night of Ecstasy with the J. Geils Band

You may think it's more kicks than pricks being a hotshot jivescamming rock magazinero, but contrary to conventional wisdom it ain't all glitz and gravy. Sure, you get the free albums, junkets, punkettes and tee-shirts, but you also have to exercise a modicum of creativity now and then—i.e., thinking up new story ideas—which sometimes necessitates engaging in actual *work*.

Case in point: We were all sitting around the office trying to figure out what in hell to do with J. Geils this time. We'd handled 'em from the Beantown Getdown history-of-the-band dryasdust angle, we'd described their stage flash in minutest detail, we'd even gone so far as to say they were better than Alice Cooper. So now we were up against the wall, Mother Howdy. Should we wimp out with a *Circus*-type spread: "The Hemorrhoids That Almost Ended Peter Wolf's Career"? Or maybe opt for the *Rolling Stone* approach: "J. Geils Discuss the Political Future of G. Gordon Liddy's Grandchildren." Or sleaze down all-out crass à la *Rock Scene*: "J. Geils Attend a Party Thrown by Mickey Ruskin, Jackie Curtis, Steve Paul's Chauffeur and Thirteen New Drag Queens."

No, newt, nada. Having the high journalistic standards we do, we engaged in a marathon thirty-eight-hour valiumosis encounter group whilst sitting around the office waiting for Buddy Miles to trash us, and came up with a concept of unparalleled brilliance: "J. Geils Explain Greaser Culture."

That's right, we intended to have Peter Wolf explaining how to hotwire a car, Seth Justman demonstrating the technique for uncapping a beer bottle with your teeth, and plenty more stuff even more revelatory to sequestered suburbanites (i.e., chickenshits) amongst our readership. So we went down to their hotel when they hit town and slapped 'em with it, and the total band response was galvanic:

"You've gotta be kidding."

So there we were, taking pictures of 'em slopping up the Boy Howdy beer, while I'm fumbling through the seeming only alternative: a "straight" interview, soberly discussing the state of rock today and the crises that we, ussens as a youth culture, have passed through in the last few years. It was so sober it was sombre, it was dreary, it was death. It wasn't working, even I was nodding out, they were all staring at me, and finally J. Geils said: "Lester, did anyone ever tell you you look like Rob Reiner?"

I leaped out of my chair at his throat: "Bullshit! Don't tell me that! I do not!" It had happened too many times before and they all started to laugh: "So that's what it takes to get him to react," said Peter Wolf, between pulling homo riffs on Danny Klein, who wears pink jackets.

So now we were on realer ground and started jiving around, and at length I said: "Hell, the only difference between you musicians and us rock writers is that people can *see* you doing what you do. I can't go up in the street and say: 'Hey, honey, dig my far-out John Lennon review,' because she can say, 'Kiss my ass, Jack, how I know you wrote that?' "

"All right," says Wolf, putting both our coins on the line, "then why don't you come onstage with us tonight and *do* your thing and let's see what happens?"

I was floored. I could see myself up there, flexing my Cheerios at last in the lights I had deserved for so long, the roar of the greasepaint, the smell of the fans, *my* fans. For is not every rock writer a frustrated rock star, and didn't I *deserve* my fifteen minutes of instant celebrityhood? Damn straight, mother. I took 'em up on it, and went home in a blear of ecstatic anticipation.

At home I tried to cool out with a little transcendental meditation, but it was all too much. I was hot to trot my dots and dashes, so I plowed through a baloney sandwich and scoured the house till I found an old beat-up typewriter left there by one of our former boarders. A useless item, really, except for such an act of theatre as I was about to perpetrate. I hadda take a sound check, so I set it up on the dining room table and plugged it in, pecked a few keys—it would barely write, but made sufficient impression on the paper that I was sure that I would emerge from this escapade not only with all the glory and groupies rightfully mine, but a masterpiece as well. My date arrived wearing a wig and I didn't even notice, that's how excited I was. I could barely concentrate on "All in the Family," that's how excited I was.

When we arrived at Cobo Hall the place was buzzing with anticipation. I lugged my axe—Smith-Corona, Mr. Advertiser!—into the dressing room and set it in a corner. A few of the women around looked at me strangely, but Peter Wolf came up and inquired if I was ready to roll:

"Everything set? Got your typewriter?"

"All *right!*"

"All right!"

Ah, at last shouldering it among my peers, the great stars of this generation! I got paranoid about leaving it in the locked dressing room while the Geils band did the first part of their set (I was coming on for the encore), so I took it out and hid it in a corner by the backstage shadows. Then I went and told second-liners Brownsville Station what I was going to do, and they laughed at me! Well, bite the bag, peons! I was in the majors now! So sure of my stardom I even dressed for the occasion: denim jacket, blue and white shirt, sweater vest. It would not do to come on trendy, I decided; wake up mama and tell Lisa Robinson the news, the next big rock 'n' roll fashion trend is gonna be the college-boy look, or my name is Carlos Santana.

I ran into Robbie, celebrated local limousine driver about fifty years old whom all the girls love because he's suaver than ten Rod Stewarts, and shaking his hand I beamed: "Wait'll you see what I'm gonna do out there tonight! I'm gonna blister 'em!"

The set seemed interminable, and when the encore came and I heard my name I strutted up and onto the boards, Smith-Corona in my hand, no trace of stage fright. I set the machine down and clenched my hands over my head like a boxer, the better to bask in the adoration of the mawsome throng, two of whom applauded, one of whom was Leslie Brown, whose desk sits to the right of mine. I grabbed the mike and hollered "Thankyouthankyou," just like on *Kick Out the Jams;* I figured to include the whole riff—"I wanta see a sea of hands out there"—would be less than subtle. As it was nobody got it, but tough shit, the same thing has happened to Yoko Ono dozens of times. So I commenced to yell at the roadies just like a true superstar: "Plug the sonofabitch in! Let's get down!"

They did so, setting it on a bench at stage right for me, and I kneeled down and with a consummate sense of theatre took my sunglasses out of my jacket pocket and put them on. Then I held up one of the two sheets of lined notebook paper I'd brought along, just for the crowd to ogle, and slipped it in the machine. I looked over at the band, who were waiting for this cue, and J. Geils cued me right back—brother! slap me five!—as we broke into the opening bars of "Give It to Me."

It was at this point that I realized the absolute ludicrousness of what I was now doing before a packed house of umpteen thousand sneering peers. The first decision I had to make was whether to treat it as a total joke and just peck at the thing desultorily, or really get into the funky bloozy woozies and try to peck along in rhythm. Hell, they had it miked, I started trying to play on the beat, grinning and nodding at the rest of the group who grinned and nodded back as the peanut galleries gawked, hawked and kfweed. The writing was coming out great too: "VDKHEOQSNCHSH-NELXIEN (+&H—SXN+ (E@JN?." I heard one of the roadies, kneeling a few feet to my right, laconically drawl: "Yer doin' great, man." Vengeful bastard.

I even threw in a bit of Townshend/Alice Cooper destructo theatre: for the song's climax I stood up and kicked over the typewriter, bench and all. Then I jumped up and down on it till I smashed it to bits, or two of them at least. It felt good, purging somehow.

Finally my moment of triumph was over, and I went out to take my bow with the rest of the band. Like Murray the K with the Stones, I was now the sixth J. Geils. The members of the group hugged me, I grimaced at the audience, we ran off the stage and that was it. Plunging into the backstage mill, I clamped my arms tightly around Leslie and my date. I felt half like Mick Jagger and half like the president of the Stooges Fan Club, and Robbie, who had joined in the encore on cowbell the night before, came forward to congratulate me. I shook his hand again: "When we gonna start our band, man?"

He just laughed, drifting away as the girls began to swarm around him again.

—*Creem*, August 1974

Johnny Ray's Better Whirlpool

It wasn't exactly the premiere of *Le Sacre du Printemps*.

Nor was it as opulent as Sly's wedding. More like the opening of a moderately high-energy new discotheque.

What it was was David Bowie's return to the boards in Afro-Anglican drag. Now, as we all know, white hippies and beatniks before them would never have existed had there not been a whole generational subculture with a gnawing yearning to be nothing less than the downest baddest *niggers* they could possibly be. And of course it was only exploding plastic inevitable that the profound and undeniably seductive ramalama of negritude should ultimately penetrate the kingdom of glitter. Everybody knows that faggots don't like music like David Bowie and the Dolls—that's for teenagers and pathophiles. Faggots like musical comedies and soul music. No gay bars have "Rebel Rebel" on the jukebox; it's all Barry White and that big discotheque beat booming out while everybody dances his or her ass off. I'm not saying that black and gay cultures have any special mysterious affinity for each other—I'll leave that for profounder explicators, Dr. David Reuben, say—what I'm saying is that everybody has been walking around for the last year or so acting like faggots ruled the world, when in actuality it's the *niggers* who control and direct everything just as it always has been and properly should be. If you don't believe it, just go ask respected social commentator Lou Reed, who wrote and recorded a song for *Sally Can't Dance* called "I Wanna Be Black" which unfortunately eventually became an outtake (probably realized he'd revealed too much).

So it was only natural that Bowie would catch on sooner or later. After all, he's no dummy.

But he is pretty weird. That's what the kid standing behind us in line was saying as the rioters who got a fin apiece from manager Tony De Fries came storming across the street at the door for the third time: "I like Bowie's music, but I don't like his personality. He's too weird." He went on to say that he wanted to buy a copy of the New York Dolls album but didn't because he was afraid somebody would see the cover lying around the house and get the wrong idea. He, like most of this audience, leaned much farther to denims than glitter. In fact, they were downright shabby. In the traditional sense.

Which is something you certainly couldn't say about Bowie. What would *you* think of a guy who came onstage in blackface with white gloves, top hat and tails over Isaac Hayes chains and a dildo with Josephine Baker's face on the head, singing "Old Folks at Home" and "Darktown Strutters' Ball" in a trilling Limey warble masquerading as a down-home bullfrog belch as he waved his hands in the air and twirled his cane while sixty or seventy Michael Jackson–lookalike pickaninnies chanted "Hi-de-ho! Hi-de-ho!" behind him, all massed afront a backdrop of magnolias and sharecropper shacks?

You would think the man had some imagination in his tack, but you can't because he doesn't. At least when it comes to spadedelia. Because he did none of the above. What he did instead was hire himself a tightly professional backup for a weird and utterly incongruous melange of glitter sentiment, negritudinal trappings, cocaine ecstasy, and Vegas schmaltz.

We walked in to a scene right out of *God's Trombones* as rendered by the Ohio Players. The stage was covered with black people—two percussionists (Emir Ksasan, Pablo Rosario), bass (Dennis Davis), the florid Mike Garson on piano, two guitarists (Carlos Alomar and Earl Slick), the ubiquitous Dave Sanborn on sax, and a clutch of "dancer/singers," as my informant at MainMan put it: Guy Andressano, Geoffrey MacCormack, Luther Vandross, Anthony Hinton, Ava Cherry, Robin Clark, and Diana Sumler. In fairness, not all of these people are black, but they all of course are artists, and they sho' is funky. Opening with "Love Train," they funkified the sweet bejesus out of that audience, who talked all the way through their set.

After the opening ensemble whoop-up, Garson plunged into a typically grandiose piano solo, which as always reminded me of the progeny of an unholy shtup between Liberace and Cecil Taylor. There was a loud drum solo which mildly roused the crowd, whose mean age was 17, although the girl in front of me just kept giggling breathily: "Daaaaaay-vid! Daaaaaayvid! Ooh, when he comes out I'm just gonna . . . *touch* him!" Ava Cherry, a curvaceous black girl with butch blond hair, sang soul torch, followed by Luther Vandross (who is fat and much given to Stepin Fetchit rolling and popping of eyes) and one of the other black girls crooning and making eyes at each other like April Stevens and Nino Tempo playing the Apollo in blackface. Ava and Geoffrey MacCormack, a slender white with black curly hair and black silk shirt who gives off the kind of gay showbiz vibes which insist on shouting from the housetops that he is just *rhapsodically* thrilled over this whole affair (I later thought he was going to stoop to kiss Bowie's toe as part of handing him an acoustic guitar), ran through a sort of Lambert, Hendricks and Ross/Pointer Sisters scat-jazz quicktalk routine. There were two solo vocals: Vandross sang something which I believe was entitled "Funky Music," and MacCormack actually sat on the piano with one knee raised and sang "Stormy Monday" to the band. Strange change that a lounge act should open for such a self-made anomaly as Bowie? Depends on your perspective, kid.

At this point in my concert scrawlings there is the notation "fat ass in face," referring to the concert patron who happened to be moving past me at that moment. It seemed as germane as the rest of the action.

Bowie's entrance was hardly as fraught with magisterial pomp as Elvis's 2001 routine: Garson played something that sounded like the theme from "The Edge of Night," Sanborn cut loose with a fine King Curtis–styled sax solo, and the singer/dancers, now mutated into gospel choir, began booming something to the effect that the "star machine is coming down / We're gonna have a party."

And here he came spindling, crackling out: white gleaming face, brilliantined hair cut short and combed back for definite early-fifties effect, grey jacket cut at the waist, blue shirt, tie slightly loosened. It was not quite stunning, although he did manage to radiate tides of nervous energy, accent the nervous, along with enough sweat to float a fleet of gondolas. I peered and peered, trying to catch the ultimate vibe . . . *Johnny Ray.* Johnny Ray on cocaine singing about 1984. Except that his opener was "John, I'm Only Dancing," transformed into a driving new arrangement in the most surging PAAAAAARTY style. It worked, which was more than you could say for David's attempts at dancing, which were stiff, jerky—at times he actually began to resemble Jobriath. A parody of a parody, except that Bowie could never really sink to self-parody because he was a parody at his inception.

Still, he worked the crowd in the finest tradition, slapping hands all night, accepting first a glass and then a whole bottle of wine from somebody ("Hope it's got LSD in it," said a seatmate), running back and forth from one end of the stage to the other, falling to his knees, kneeling down and rocking back and forth in "Rock and Roll with Me," indulging varying brands of mikestand english including at one point a definite parody of a biker stance.

Mugging, grimacing, moving his hands in arcs that might have been sensual if you couldn't *see* him thinking how sensual they were, he had definite flash but there was something brittle about it, as there was something hollow when I saw him two years ago on his first post-*Ziggy* tour, padding around lightly while Ronson served up all the moves, just as without all the gauche props and stage business the recent live album is a dismal flatulence. Bowie has always made a point of being distant on every level, from the way he treated his audience to the strong-arm tactics used by his goons on photographers. Now he is posing as a getdown dude, as if he had just decided that we won't get fooled again, that there is a we after all, which may or may not be true but is irrelevant to him in any case.

This was particularly apparent in the segment of the show where he sang his new songs, from the upcoming album which he has claimed is the "most personal" thing he's ever done, blah, blah, and you can see where he's coming from with this one just like you could read those "I've traveled, I've seen who rules the world, and I'm frightened" pronunciamentos. Bowie's new material seems to be comprised mainly of "love songs," melodramatic ballads about apparently wholesome teenage boys and girls and David's search for sincerity on this bathetic bitch of an earth. The most memorable, because most characteristic, was "Young Americans," and of course you couldn't miss the line "Ain't there one damn song that can make me break down and cry?" Touching, touching, like Johnny Ray coming on as Frankie Laine, except when he would stick one hand in front of his crotch and touch the mike delicately, mutating for himself at least into Tina Turner. He also utilized that stool that Perry Como used to fall off of on the Steve Allen show for one particularly poignant vignette. I prefer Charles Aznavour myself.

Mike Garson kept looking around as if in wonderment, bluefaced with delicate five o'clock shadow and carrying definite Richard Carpenter vibes, gazing reverently at Bowie and rolling his eyes at the band while playing piano so turgid it was downright bouncy. And the singer/dancers all massed like the Mormon Tabernacle Choir in the background, snapping their fingers, jutting their arms and shaking their butts around in perfervid Stoneground/Mad Dogs & Englishmen pep rally.

This show is going to wow them in Vegas, and it certainly didn't do badly in Detroit. But don't be fooled: Bowie is as cold as ever, and if you get off on his particular brand of lunar antibody you may well be disappointed in his latest incarnation, because he's doubling back on himself and it fits about as well as those boxing gloves he had last time out. You don't set yourself up as Mr. Sleaze and then come on like Jerry Lewis at the palsy telethon, unless you realize that you are just about as full of ersatz sincerity as Jerry Lewis and might as well ooze it from every pore because your audience doesn't care, they just want you to hit them hard and fast and then come back and hit them again, slightly altered, a little to the right this time. As far as the PAAAAAARTY goes, Bowie has just changed his props: last tour it was boxing gloves, skulls and giant hands, this tour it's black folk. As far as I'm concerned, if that pastyfaced snaggletoothed little jitterbug doesn't give me an interview pretty soon, I'm going to stop doing him all these favors.

—*Creem,* January 1975

Barry White: Just Another Way to Say I Love You

I was converted. I went down to see this molasses-voiced monument to unashamed bulbosity at Olympia Stadium right here in my Motor City, plunged myself into the middle of an audience that looked like Africa in a sportin' hat with sprinkle seasoning of gays and white folk who were just plain *weird*—old moms and dads, nut and bolt joiners off the factory line, lonely pubescent girls. . . . The only reason I went, of course, was that the tickets were free, and I wanted to take out this girl who was real big on Mr. B. She turned out to be a dud (refused to kiss me at midnight on New Year's Eve, said something about "you've got bad breath"—I'd like to see Barry write a song about *that*), but somehow in the process of trying to feel her leg and getting weird looks back while almost being put to sleep by the Ohio Players and then staring in a minor league, scaled down version of something approximating awe (don't wanna get carried away with the superlatives here, that's how us critics lose our credibility) at The Barry White Show in all its opulent glory . . . somehow, some way, somewhere just this side of the rainbow there's a place for us, all of us, and Barry White is mapping out this so to speak virgin turf.

See, first of all this massive orchestra comes out, all dressed in tuxedos and black ties (even the women), and starts sawing away (even the harpist was sawing) at "Love's Theme," which the first five thousand times I heard it on the radio I did find truly pleasant. They ocean on like this for a bit, then Barry makes his first *Grand Appearance*, and damn my fillings if he ain't a stunner, nineteen hundred pounds of pure lumbering animal, makes Leslie West look like Steve Tyler, wrapped in a coal-red cape fit to put your eyes out. But this is only a preliminary sort of preview; what he's doing is leading out the Love Unlimited Singers. By hand. What a gentleman, transcends the debonair he do, really lives up to his image maybe better'n Lou Reed even; he's yanking the pore li'l things out under his humongous red wing just to see to it that their sweet-kooze don't get hassled by any rampaging perverts who might be lurking in an audience of otherwise stolid, simple, upstanding, *loving* Barry White fans. Then the L.U. Singers do a straight Supremes imitation lounge act that's quite boring actually, and after twenty or thirty minutes of that The Man returns, Himself, In The Flesh, magisterially resplendent as he takes the stage, the orchestra lurching into one after another of his hits while all he does (*all* he does) is walk around the stage (which is in the center of the arena) in a circle, moaning the word *love* over and over in a stupefyingly insinuating basso, while he bestows his big loving eyes on various sweetbuns in the audience, and every once in a while he'll reach out to take a rose from or merely squeeze the hands of these panting lovelies for one tremulous second which they'll carry with them, unlike certain communicable diseases, for the rest of their lives.

The old boob does this for a half hour or so, then wanders off to his dressing room. *"Loooove . . . looove . . . looove . . ." And that's it! What an easy gig!* I have never been so jealous since I missed the chance to produce *Four-Way Street.* The crowd, of course, eats it up.

I never saw anything quite so immaculately vacant, and after an experience like that (the best part was seeing a guy get murdered a few feet from our car while waiting to get out of the post-concert traffic jam) my whole attitude toward the Big B underwent a radical change. I actually left his songs on when they came on the radio. I was diggin' where the cat was comin' from and where he was goin', as a matter of fact the sooner he gets there the better, but in the meantime I'm gonna wallow in each new B.W. single like a vat of cocoa butter even if I still can't tell 'em apart. As an even more special bonus, I've got a whole new *album* of Barry White masterpieces, and you can bet I play it all the time. You gotta do something when you get tired of the Dictators 'cause you've played 'em thirteen times in a row.

I don't have to tell you what kind of a treat you're in for if you fork over your hard-earned for *Just Another Way to Say I Love You*—Barry White's one artiste you can *trust.* But there is a special surprise herein for his fans and those of us, that special elite cadre who have come to consider him not just another globulous crossover act but something more akin to a *god;* Barry has mouthed *looove* so many different ways you'd think the man would be hard pressed by now to come up with a new one, but he's succeeded. His technique: slide ever-so-gently, like a palm going down a shoulder to a tit in a movie house, from simple declarations of undying devotion into the realm of prurient interest and ultimately to outright HOT DRIPPING KOOZEDELIC BUTTERED SOUL, er . . . anyway, *It* happens on "Love Serenade (Part I)": starting out as a typically tropical B.W. instrumental deck, the big fella trots out his tonsils and slides them up some truly titillational stuff: "Take it off . . . Baby, take it *all* off . . . I want you the way you came into the world . . . I don' wanna feel no clothes . . . I don' wanna see no panties . . . Take off that *brassiere,* my dear . . . Everybody's gone . . . We're gonna take the receiver off the phone . . . because baby, you and me, *heh* . . . this *night,* we're gonna get it on. . . ."

Jesus, is this ever volatile stuff! If you look at it one way, just reading those words cold, it could be interpreted as a rape scene. Listening to Barry's unctuous, pooze-ooze voice, it is conceivable that this man is dangerous; at any rate, there is absolutely no question that he's gonna get what he's after.

—*Creem,* August 1975

▌Kraftwerkfeature

Some skeezix from one of the local dailies was up here the other day to do a "human interest" story on the phenomenon you're holding in your hands, and naturally our beneficent publisher hauled me into his office to answer this fish's edition of the perennial: "Where is rock going?"

"It's being taken over by the Germans and the machines," I unhesitatingly answered. And this I believe to my funky soul. Everybody has been hearing about kraut-rock, and the stupnagling success of Kraftwerk's "Autobahn" is more than just the latest evidence in support of the case for Teutonic raillery, more than just a record, it is an *indictment*. An indictment of all those who would resist the bloodless iron will and order of the ineluctable dawn of the Machine Age. Just consider:

They used to call Chuck Berry a "guitar mechanic" (at least I heard a Moody Blues fan say that once). Why? Because any idiot could play his lines. Which, as we have all known since the prehistory of punk rock, is the very beauty of them. But think: if any idiot can play them, why not eliminate such genetic mistakes altogether, punch "Johnny B. Goode" into a computer printout and let the *machines* do it in total passive acquiescence to the Cybernetic Inevitable? A quantum leap towards this noble goal was accomplished with the advent of a crude sonic Model T called Alvin Lee, who could not only reproduce Berry licks by the bushel, but play them at 78 rpm as well. As is well known, it was the Germans who invented methamphetamine, which of all accessible tools has brought human beings within the closest twitch of machinehood, and without methamphetamine we would never have had such high plasma marks of the counterculture as

Lenny Bruce, Bob Dylan, Lou Reed and the Velvet Underground, Neal Cassady, Jack Kerouac, Allen Ginsberg's "Howl," Blue Cheer, Cream, and *Creem*, as well as all of the fine performances in Andy Warhol movies not inspired by heroin. So it can easily be seen that it was in reality the *Germans* who were responsible for *Blonde on Blonde* and *On the Road;* the Reich never died, it just reincarnated in American archetypes ground out by holloweyed jerkyfingered mannikins locked into their typewriters and guitars like rhinoceroses copulating.

Of course, just as very few speedfreaks will cop to their vice, so it took a while before due credit was rendered to the factor of machinehood as a source of our finest cultural artifacts. Nowadays, everybody is jumping on the bandwagon. People used to complain about groups like the Monkees and the Archies like voters complain about "political machines," and just recently a friend of mine recoiled in revulsion at his first exposure to Kiss, whom he termed "everything that has left me disgusted with rock 'n' roll nowadays—they're automatons!"

What he failed to suss was that sometimes automatons deliver the very finest specimens of a mass-produced, disposable commodity like rock. But history will have its way, and it was only inevitable that groups like Blue Oyster Cult would come along, singing in jive-chic about dehumanization while unconsciously fulfilling their own prophecy albeit muddled by performing as nothing more than robots whose buttons were pushed by their producers. By now the machines had clattered VU meter first out of the closet for good, and we have most recently been treated to the spectacle of such fine harbingers of the larger revolution to come as Magma's "Ork Alarm" ("The people are made of indescribable matter which to the machines is what the machines are to man . . .") and of course Lou Reed's *Metal Machine Music*, a quick-buck exploitation number assessed elsewhere in this issue.

But there is more to the Cybernetic Inevitable than this sort of methanasia. There are, in the words of the poet, "machines of loving grace." There is, hovering clean far from the burnt metal reek of exploded stars, the intricate balm of Kraftwerk.

Perhaps you are wondering how I can connect the amped-up hysteria of compulsive pathogens such as Bruce, Dylan and Reed with the clean, cool lines of Kraftwerk. This is simple. The Germans invented "speed" for the Americans (and the English—leave us not forget Rick Wakeman and Emerson, Lake & Palmer) to destroy themselves with, thus leaving the world of pop music open for ultimate conquest. A friend once asked me how I could bear to listen to Love Sculpture's version of "Sabre Dance," knowing that the producers had sped up the tape; I replied: "Anything a hand can do a machine can do better." An addendum would seem to be that anything a hand can do nervously, a machine can do effortlessly. When was the last time you heard a German band go galloping off at 965 mph hot on the heels of oblivion? No, they realize that the ultimate power is exercised *calmly,* whether it's Can with their endless rotary connections, Tangerine Dream plumbing the sargassan depths, or Kraftwerk sailing airlocked down the Autobahn.

In the beginning there was feedback: the machines speaking on their own, answering their supposed masters with shrieks of misalliance. Gradually the humans learned to control the feedback, or thought they did, and the next step was the introduction of more highly refined forms of distortion and artificial sound, in the form of the synthesizer, which the human beings sought also to control. In the music of Kraftwerk, and bands like them present and to come, we see at last the fitting culmination of this revolution, as the machines not merely overpower and play the human beings but *absorb* them, until the scientist and his technology, having developed a higher consciousness of its own, are one and the same.

Kraftwerk, whose name means "power plant," have a word for this ecstatic congress: *Menschmaschine,* which translates as "man-machine." I am conversing with Ralf Hutter and Florian Schneider, co-leaders of Kraftwerk, which they insist is not a band but a you-guessed-it. We have just returned to their hotel from a concert, where Kraftwerk executed their Top Ten hit, "Autobahn," as well as other galactic standards such as "Kometenmelodie" ("Comet Melody"), "Mitternacht" ("Midnight"), "Morgenspaziergang" ("Morning Walk," complete with chirping birds on tape), and the perfect synthesized imitation of a choo-choo train which must certainly be the programmatic follow-up to "Autobahn," to a small but rapt audience mesmerized unto somnolence. (At least half the people I took, in fact, fell asleep. But that's all right.) Now the tapes have stopped rolling and the computers have been packed up until the next gig, and the Werk's two percussionists, Wolfgang Flur and Karl Bartos, who play wired pads about the size of Ouija boards instead of standard acoustic drums, have been dispatched to their respective rooms, barred from the interview because their English is not so hot. (I have heard of members of bands playing on the same bills as Kraftwerk approaching these gentlemen with the words "So ya liked blowin' all our roadies. . . ." The Germans smiled and clapped them on the shoulders: *"Ja, ja . . ."*) Now Ralf and Florian are facing me, very sober in their black suits, narrow ties and close-cropped hair, quietly explaining behavior modification through technology.

"I think the synthesizer is very responsive to a person," says Ralf, whose boyish visage is somewhat less severe than that of Florian, who looks, as a friend put it, "like he could build a computer or push a button and blow up half the world with the same amount of emotion." "It's referred to as cold machinery," Ralf continues, "but as soon as you put a different person in the synthesizer, it's very responsive to the different vibrations. I think it's much more sensitive than a traditional instrument like a guitar."

This may be why, just before their first American tour, Kraftwerk purged themselves of guitarist/violinist Klaus Roeder, inserting Bartos in his slot. One must, at any rate, mind one's P's and Q's—I asked Hutter if a synthesizer could tell what kind of person you are and he replied: "Yes. It's like an acoustic mirror." I remarked that the next logical step would be for the machines to play *you.* He nodded: "Yes. We do this. It's like a robot thing, when it gets up to a certain stage. *It* starts playing . . . it's no longer you and I, it's *It.* Not all machines have this consciousness, however. Some machines are just limited to one *piece* of work, but complex machines . . ."

"The whole complex we use," continues Florian, referring to their equipment and headquarters in their native Dusseldorf, "can be regarded as one machine, even though it is divided into different pieces." Including, of course, the human beings within. "The Menschmaschine is our acoustic concept, and Kraftwerk is power plant—if you plug in the electricity, then it starts to work. It's feedback. You can jam with an automatic machine, sometimes just you and it alone in the studio."

They also referred to their studio as their "laboratory," and I wondered aloud if they didn't encounter certain dangers in their experiments. What's to stop the machines, I asked, from eventually taking over, or at least putting them out of work? "It's like a car," explained Florian. "You have the control, but it's your decision how much you want to control it. If you let the wheel go, the car will drive somewhere, maybe off the road. We have done electronic accidents. And it is also possible to damage your mind. But this is the risk one takes. We have power. It just depends on what you do with it."

I wondered if they could see some ramifications of what they could do with it. "Yes," said Ralf, "it's our music, we are manipulating the audience. That's what it's all about. When you play electronic music, you have the control of the imagination of the people in the room, and it can get to an extent where it's almost physical."

I mentioned the theories of William Burroughs, who says that you can start a riot with two tape recorders, and asked them if they could create a sound which would cause a riot, wreck the hall, would they like to do it? "I agree with Burroughs," said Ralf. "We would not like to do that, but we are aware of it."

"It would be very dangerous," cautioned Florian. "It could be like a boomerang."

"It would be great publicity," I nudged.

"It could be the end," said Florian, calm, unblinking. "A person doing experimental music must be responsible for the results of the experiments. They could be very dangerous emotionally."

I told them that I considered their music rather anti-emotional, and Florian quietly and patiently explained that " 'emotion' is a strange word. There is a cold emotion and other emotion, both equally valid. It's not body emotion, it's mental emotion. We like to ignore the audience while we play, and take all our concentration into the music. We are very much interested in origin of music, the source of music. The pure sound is something we would very much like to achieve."

They have been chasing the p.s.'s tail for quite a while. Setting out to be electronic classical composers in the Stockhausen tradition, they grew up listening on the one hand to late-night broadcasts of electronic music, on the other to the American pop music imported via radio and TV— especially the Beach Boys, who were a heavy influence, as is obvious from "Autobahn," although "we are not aiming so much for the music; it's the psychological structure of someone like the Beach Boys." They met at a musical academy, began in 1970 to set up their own studio, "and started working on the music, building equipment," for the eventual rearmament of their fatherland.

"After the war," explains Ralf, "German entertainment was destroyed. The German people were robbed of their culture, putting an American head on it. I think we are the first generation born after the war to shake this off, and know where to feel American music and where to feel ourselves. We are the first German group to record in our own language, use our electronic background, and create a Central European identity for ourselves. So you see another group like Tangerine Dream, although they are German they have an English name, so they create onstage an Anglo-American identity, which we completely deny. We want the whole world to know our background. We cannot deny we are from Germany, because the German mentality, which is more advanced, will always be part of our behavior. We create out of the German language, the mother language, which is very mechanical, we use as the basic structure of our music. Also the machines, from the industries of Germany."

As for the machines taking over, all the better. "We use tapes, pre-recorded, and we play tapes, also in our performance. When we recorded on TV we were not allowed to play the tape as a part of the performance, because the musicians' union felt that they would be put out of work. But I think just the opposite: with better machines, you will be able to do better work, and you will be able to spend your time and energies on a higher level."

"We don't need a choir," adds Florian. "We just turn this key, and there's the choir."

I wondered aloud if they would like to see it get to the point of electrodes in the brain so that whatever they thought would come through a loudspeaker. "Yes," enthused Ralf, "this would be fantastic."

The final solution to the music problem, I suggested.

"No, not the solution. The next step."

They then confided that they were going to spend all of the money from this tour on bigger and better equipment, that they work in their lab/studio for recreation, and that their Wernher von Braun sartorial aspect was "part of the German scientific approach."

"When the rocket was going to the moon," said Ralf, "I was so emotionally excited. . . . When I saw this on television, I thought it was one of the best performances I had ever seen."

Speaking of performances, and bearing their general appearance and demeanor in mind, I asked them what sort of groupies they got. "None," snapped Florian. "There is no such thing. This is totally an invention of the media."

All right then, what's your opinion of American or British bands utilizing either synthesizers or Germanic/swastikan overtones? Do you feel a debt to Pink Floyd? "No. It's vice versa. They draw from French classicism and German electronic music. And such performance as Rick Wakeman has nothing to do with our music," stressed Ralf. "He is something else . . . distraction. It's not electronic music, it's circus tricks on the synthesizer. I think it is paranoid. I don't want to put anybody down, but I cannot listen to it. I get nervous. It is traditional."

Not surprisingly, their taste in American acts runs to those seduced (and enervated) by adrenaline: "The MC5, and the heavy metal music of Detroit. I think Iggy and the Stooges are concerned with energy, and the Velvet Underground had a heavy Germanic influence—Nico was from Cologne, close where we live. They have this German dada influence from the twenties and thirties. I very much like 'European Son.' Nico and John Cale had this Teutonic attitude about their music which I very much like. I think Lou Reed in his *Berlin* is projecting the situation of a spy film, the spy standing in the fog smoking a cigarette. I have also been told of the program 'Hogan's Heroes,' though I have not seen it. We think that no matter what happens Americans cannot relate it. It's still American pop-corn chewing gum. It's part of history. I think the Blue Oyster Cult is funny."

They did not, however, think it was funny when I wound up the interview asking them if they would pose for pix the next morning by the Detroit freeway. "No," said Ralf, emphatically. "We do not pose. We have our own pictures."

Why? "Because," flatly, "we are paranoid."

He was just beginning to explain the ramifications of German paranoia when Florian abruptly stood up, opened the window to let the smoke out, then walked to the door and opened it, explaining with curious polite curtness that "we had also an interview with *Rolling Stone,* but it was not so long as this one. Now it is time to retire. You must excuse us."

He ushered us into the hall, quietly swung the door shut with a muffled click, and we blinked at each other in mild shock. Still, it was somehow comforting to know that they did, apparently, sleep.

—*Creem,* September 1975

David Bowie:
Station to Station

It's tough having heroes. It's the hardest thing in the world. It's harder than being a hero. Heroes are generally expected to produce something or other to reconfirm their mandarin-fingered clinch on the hot buns of the bitch muse, which sometimes comes closer to resembling a set of clawmarks running down and off the edge of a shale precipice. At sunset, even. And that's no office party, kiddo.

But hero-worshippers (fans) must live with the continually confirmed dread of hero-slippage and humiliating personal compromises in your standards and plain good sense about, oh, two to three weeks after the new elpee masterwork first hits our turntables.

A very great man (I think it was the Isley Brothers) once said that the real bottom line truism re life on this planet is that it is merely a process of sequential disappointments. So there's no reason even to romanticize your betrayals. Just paying dues, kid. I get burned, therefore I exist. No words in the history of the rock poetic genre, from Dylan to Bernie Taupin, ever said it better than Sandy Posey's pithy catalog in "Born a Woman": "Born to be stepped on, lied to, cheated and treated like dirt." And are we not all in some sense women, the niggers of the world according to contemporary social commentators (I tried to get a call through to Toynbee to confirm this like a good journalist but the bastard had the nerve to fucking *die* in the same week, *my* week!)?

Yes, we are. A great many David Bowie fans felt burned, turned into veritable women (de-virilized, as Pope Paul would have it) when David released *Young Americans*. Why? Because, interestingly enough, they thought David was trying to turn *himself* into a nigger. I was not, however, one of these people.

Now, as any faithful reader of this magazine is probably aware, David Bowie has never been my hero. I always thought all that Ziggy Stardust homo-from-Adelbaran business was a crock of shit, especially coming from a guy who wouldn't even get in a goddam airplane. I thought he wrote the absolute worst lyrics I had ever heard from a major pop figure with the exception of Bernie Taupin; lines like "Time takes a cigarette and puts it in your mouth" delivered with a face so straight it seemed like it would crack at a spontaneous word or gesture, seemed to me merely gauche. As for his music, he was as accomplished an eclectician (a.k.a. thief) as Elton John, which means that though occasionally deposited onstage after seemingly being dipped in vats of green slime and pursued by Venusian crab boys, he had Showbiz Pro written all over him. A facade as brittle as it was icy, which I guess means that it was bound to crack or thaw, and whatever real artistic potency lay beneath would have to stand or evaporate.

Crack Bowie did, in the last year or so, and the result was *Young Americans.* It was not an album beloved of trad Bowiephiles, but for somebody like your reviewer, who never put any chips on the old chicken-head anyway, it was a perfectly acceptable piece of highly listenable product. More than that, in fact—it was a highly personal musical statement disguised as a shameless fling at the disco market, the drag perhaps utilized as an emotional red herring: *Young Americans* wasn't Bowie dilettanting around with soul music, it was the bridge between melancholy and outright depression, an honest statement from a deeply troubled, mentally shattered individual who even managed, for the most part, to skirt self-pity. Like many of his peers, Bowie has cracked—and for him it was good, because it made him cut the bullshit. *Young Americans* was his first human album since *Hunky Dory,* and in my opinion the best record he ever put out.

Till now. The first things to be said about *Station to Station* are that it sounds like he's got a real live band again (even if star guitarist Earl Slick reportedly split between the sessions and the new tour), and that this is not a disco album either (though that's what the trades, and doubtless a lot of other people, are going to write it off as) but an honest attempt by a talented artist to take elements of rock, soul music, and his own idiosyncratic and occasionally pompous showtune/camp predilections and rework this seemingly contradictory melange of styles into something new and powerful that doesn't have to cop either futuristic attitudes or licks from Anthony Newley and the Velvet Underground because he's found his own voice at last.

This is the first Bowie album without a lyric sheet, and I'm glad, because aside from reservations voiced above I've always agreed with Fats Domino that it's more fun to figure them out for yourself. The first line on the album is the worst: "The return of the thin white duke / Throwing darts in lovers' eyes." Somehow, back in Rock Critics' Training School, when they told me about "pop poetry," I didn't and still don't think that they were talking about this, which is not only pretentious and mildly unpleasant, but I am currently wrestling with a terrible paranoia that this is Bowie talking about himself. I have a nightmare vision in my mind of him opening the set in his new tour by striding out onstage slowly, with a pained look in his eyes and one spotlight following him, mouthing these words. And, quite frankly, that idea terrifies me. Because if it's true, it means he's still as big an idiot as he used to be and needs a little more cocaine to straighten him out.

But I'm really not worried. Because you can always ignore the lyrics if you want, since this is one of the best *guitar* albums since *Rock 'n' Roll Animal,* it has a wail and throb that won't let up and rolls roughshod over the words. So who gives a shit what "TVC 15" means, it's a great piece of rock 'n' roll. And when words do appear out of the instrumental propulsion like swimmers caught in a rip tide not sure whether they wanna call for the lifeguard or just enjoy it, well, at those moments, dear reader, I know you're not gonna believe this but *those words usually make sense!* In fact, in (for Bowie) relatively simple, unconvoluted language, they bespeak a transition from the deep depression of the best of *Young Americans* (and here's a case of scientific proof that depression should never be knocked or avoided, it's a means to an end of division from self, a.k.a. remission) to a beautiful, swelling, intensely romantic melancholy in which the divided consciousness may not only have kissed and made up with itself but even managed to begin the leap towards *recognizing that other human beings actually exist!* And can be loved for something besides the extent to which they feed themselves to the artist's narcissism.

Specific examples of this remission are not hard to come by: lines like "Don't have to question everything in heaven or hell," along with the melodic mood that is their context, can be intensely moving according to *your* mood, and it doesn't even matter that "Wild Is the Wind" is an old Dmitri Tiomkin movie theme—even if Bowie did it for camp reasons and to indulge a personal idiosyncrasy, it doesn't sound like he did, it sounds right with the rest of the album.

Which is so impressive, such a great rocker and so promising of durability even exceeding *Young Americans,* that I'm going to go out on a limb and say that I think that Bowie has finally produced his (first) masterpiece. To hell with *Ziggy Stardust,* which amounted to starring Judy Garland in *The Reluctant Astronaut,* fuck trying to be George Orwell and William Burroughs when you've only read half of *Nova Express*—this and *Young Americans* are the first albums he's made which don't sound like scams. Bowie has dropped his pretensions, or most of them at any rate, and in doing that I believe he's finally become an artist instead of a poseur, style collector and (admittedly always great, excepting *Raw Power*) producer. He'll still never have a shot at becoming my hero, because he's neither funny nor black enough, but I can hardly wait to hear what he's going to have to say next.

—*Creem,* April 1976

PART FOUR

Slaying the
Father

from
Untitled Notes on
Lou Reed, 1980

Last spring I was going out with a girl who road-managed a rock band. When she told them she was seeing me they said, "Aw, all Lester wants to do is suck Lou Reed's cock."

I would suck Lou Reed's cock, because I would also kiss the feet of them that drafted the Magna Carta. I leave you to judge that statement as you will, because it is not to Lou Reed but to you that I surrender myself, you who read this. I care about almost nothing, but I know I'm always in good hands with you.

I'm a realist. That's why I listen to Lou Reed. And that's why I idolize him. Because the things he wrote and sang and played in the Velvet Underground were for me part of the beginning of a real revolution in the whole scheme between men and women, men and men, women and women, humans and humans. And I don't mean clones. I mean a diversity that extends to the stars.

Everybody assumes that mind and body are opposed. Why? (Leaving aside six thousand years of history.) The trog vs. the cerebrite. How boring. But we still buy it, all of us. The Velvet Underground were the greatest band that ever existed because they began to suggest that such was not so, in the very actfact of the tragic recognition of such opposition at the most groundfloor extreme angles. Angles? Ha! What is the difference between the curve of a breast on a sex goddess and the bones in the thighs of a stud and the fins on a '57 Chevy? The introduction of the Chevy into the comparison was America's idea, which Andy Warhol later perfected, which is why he is the prophet of our doom. Lou realized early on that all you need to do is touch the other's cheek and just give them some small recognition and then let them be and maybe record it and thereby perhaps justify their tragedy through art. And all art is an act of love towards the whole human race. Aw, Lou, it's the best music ever made, the instrumental intro to "All Tomorrow's Parties" is like watching dawn break over a bank of buildings through the windows of these elegantly hermetic cages, which feels too well spoken, which I suspect is the other knife that cuts through your guts, the continents that divide literature and music and don't care about either.

Two nights ago my friend John Morthland was over and we talked about Iran and the future of this embassy we live in. We ended up agreeing that we were expatriates in our own homeland, and where did that leave us? Exiles on main street. Which is exactly where you always were, Lou, which is not a bad place to be. If you *felt at home* there, you'd really be psychotic. But you knew that a long time ago.

We will end up there in one way or another, probably sharing bar beers with our parents at our side, and they will know what no one else must know, that the unspeakable sin, the love that dare not speak its name, the dope addict, finally came home to roost.

Let Us Now Praise Famous Death Dwarves,

or, How I Slugged It Out with Lou Reed
and Stayed Awake

Ego? It may not be the greatest word of the twentieth century, but it's sure the driving poison in the vitals of every popstar.

Who else but Lou Reed would get himself fat as a pig, then hire the most cretinous band of teenage cortical cavities he could find to tote around the country on an all-time death drag tour?

Who else would doze his way back over the pond in a giant secobarbital capsule and labor for months with people like Bob Ezrin, Steve Winwood and Jack Bruce to puke up *Berlin*, a gargantuan slab of maggoty rancor that may well be the most depressed album ever made?

Who else would then poke his arm so full of vigorating vitamins that he lost all that fat overnight, then cartwheel onstage in spastic epic(ene) colitic fits when everybody expected him to bloat up and die? Who else would make this gig looking like some bizarre crossbreed of Jerry Lewis of idiot movies fame and a monkey on cantharides? Who else but Lou Reed could have survived making a public embarrassment of himself for so long that he actually managed to lasso a great rock 'n' roll band to back up his monkeyshines?

Name me somebody who would come back from the quagmire that was *Berlin* to make *Sally Can't Dance*, an album that broke its own ankles going out of every seasoned Reed fan's way to make all possible concessions to commercialism on the lowest level of palatable pap, and get that crappy platter in the Top Ten?

Who else would write whole new volumes in tonsorial culture: shaving his traditionally kinky locks to the skull for the simian charm; then topping even his own act by carving Iron Crosses in that mangy patch of stubble (a whim which put him in Rona Barrett's column: "Well, they said it couldn't be done, but somebody's finally managed to invent a totally new hairstyle . . ."); then redo his dome Hitler Youth blond so he resembled a bubblegum Kenneth Anger, which is obviously one damn cool way for a popstar to look, especially if he's been looking like sulking shit for as long as Lou had?

Who but Lou Reed could add a whole new entry to the annals of onstage tastelessness by tying off during the middle of "Heroin" and pretending to shoot up with an actual syringe which, on at least one gig, he then handed to a member of the audience as a souvenir?

What other rock artist would put up with an interview by the author of this article, read the resultant vicious vitriol-spew with approval, and then invite me back for a second round because of course he's such a masochist he loved the hatchet in his back?

Not a living soul, that's who.

Why is this guy, who has made a career out of terminal twitches ever since the Velvet Underground surfaced dead on arrival in 1966, still here? Well, for one thing, the Velvets emerged from under one of the many entrepreneurial wings of Andy Warhol, who has managed to accomplish more in this culture while acting (in public at least) like a total autistic null-node than almost any other figure of the sixties. Lou learned a lot from Andy, mainly about becoming a successful public personality by selling your own private quirks to an audience greedy for more and more geeks. The prime lesson he learned was that to succeed as this kind of mass-consumed nonentity you must expertly erect walls upon walls to reinforce the walls that your own quirky vulnerability has already put there.

In other words, Lou Reed is a completely depraved pervert and pathetic death dwarf and everything else you want to think he is. On top of that he's a liar, a wasted talent, an artist continually in flux, and a huckster selling pounds of his own flesh. A panderer living off the dumbbell nihilism of a seventies generation that doesn't have the energy to commit suicide. Lou Reed is the guy that gave dignity and poetry and rock 'n' roll to smack, speed, homosexuality, sadomasochism, murder, misogyny, stumblebum passivity, and suicide, and then proceeded to belie all his achievements and return to the mire by turning the whole thing into a monumental bad joke with himself as the woozily insistent Henny Youngman in the center ring, mumbling punch lines that kept losing their punch.

Lou Reed's enjoyed a solo career renaissance primarily by passing himself off as the most burnt-out reprobate around; and it wasn't all show by a long shot. People kept expecting him to die, so perversely he came back not to haunt them, as he perhaps would like to think (although I think he'd rather have another hit record even if he had to sing about it never raining in California to get it), but to clean up. In the sense of the marketplace. A friend of mine who works in a record store in Cambridge Mass told me about the people who buy Lou Reed records: "You get like these twenty-eight-year-old straight divorcee types, asking for *Transformer* and the Velvet Underground . . . but the amazing thing is that suddenly there's all these *fourteen-year-olds*, coming in all wide-eyed: 'Hey, uh . . . do you have any *Lou Reed* records?' "

Right. That spooky man, booga booga. Meanwhile, his chronic multiple abuses of the mind and body rise and fall according to the weather. He had the shakes all the way through his fat-man tour in spite of massive Valium ingestion. Blue Weaver on the recording of *Berlin:* "We went in and laid down all the instrumental tracks, the whole thing was done and sounded great. Then they brought Lou in. He can't do it straight, he's got to go down to the bar and then have a snort of this and that, and then they'd prop him up in a chair and let him start singing. It was supposed to be great, but something went wrong somewhere."

I had a friend working as a busboy in Max's Kansas City when Lou was in transit from blubber to his present emaciation, and the guy called me up one day: *"Your boy* was in again last night. . . . Jesus, *he looks like an insect* . . . or like something that belongs in an intensive care ward . . . almost no flesh on the bones, all the flesh that's there sort of dead and sallow and hanging, his eyes are always darting all over the place, his skull is shaved and you can see the pallor under the bristles, it looks like he's got iron plates implanted in his head. . . . Everybody agreed that they'd never seen anything as bad as this. Plus all the waitresses hate him because he never tips."

Lou Reed is my own hero principally because he stands for all the most fucked up things that I could ever possibly conceive of. Which probably only shows the limits of my imagination.

The central heroic myth of the sixties was the burnout. Live fast, be bad, get messy, die young. More than just "hope I die before I get old," it was a whole cool stalk we had down or tried to get. Partially it has to do with the absolute nonexistence of real, objective, straight-arrow, head-held-high, noble, achieving heroes. Myself, I always wanted to emulate the most self-destructive bastard I could see, as long as he moved with some sense of style. Thus Lou Reed. Getting off vicariously on various forms of deviant experience compensated somehow for the emptiness of our own drearily "normal" lives. It's like you never want to see the reality; it's too clammy watching someone shoot up junk and turn blue. It ain't like listening to the records.

That's why Lou Reed was necessary. And what may be even more important is that he had the good sense (or maybe just brain rot, hard to tell) to realize that the whole concept of sleaze, "decadence," degeneracy, was a joke, and turned himself into a clown, the Pit into a puddle. Any numbskull can be a degenerate, but not everybody realizes that even now; like Jim Morrison, Lou realized the implicit absurdity of the rock 'n' roll bête-noire badass pose and parodied, deglamorized it. Though that may be giving him too much credit. Most probably he had no idea what he was doing, which was half the mystique. Anyway, he made a great bozo, a sort of Eric Burdon of sleaze. The persistent conceit of Lou's recent press releases—that he's the "street poet of rock 'n' roll"—just may be true in an unintended way. The street, after all, is not the most intellectual place in the world. In fact, it's littered with dopey jerkoffs and putzes of every stripe. Dunceville. Rubbery befuddlement. And Lou is the king of 'em all, y'all.

Yep, the Champ was coming to town, and I was ready for battle. I guzzled Scotch by the case and chewed Valiums like Jujubes. Tried to shoot speed but the quack doctor who services every freako and housewife on Woodward Ave. threw me out of his offices. Mostly I just listened to my Velvets records and what I could stand of *Sally Can't Dance*, and boned up on my insults. Word had filtered back to me that the Original Miscreant had gotten a good hoot out of the last slash job I did on him. People were speaking in hushed tones of "a love-hate relationship . . . it's incredible," stammered Dennis Katz, Lou's manager, whose brother Steve graduated from Blood, Sweat & Tears to producing Lou Reed albums, which should give you some indication of what happened to a functioning Underground Movement in America.

Now, I'll admit that I'm flattered by the fact that one of my heroes has become one of my fans (several of them have, in fact; in fact, this usually coincides with my conclusion that said hero is dogshit) (and please don't infer hubris from this; I'm amazed that I can get away with this shit), but I must flatly dismiss all this "love-hate" folderol as pure hype. The promoters rigged it up. The fact is that Lou, like all heroes, is there for the beating up. They wouldn't be heroes if they were infallible, in fact they wouldn't be heroes if they weren't miserable wretched dogs, the pariahs of the earth, besides which the only reason to build up an idol is to tear it down again, just like anything else. A hero is a goddam stupid thing to have in the first place and a general block to anything you might wanta accomplish on your own. Plus part of the whole exhilaration of admiring somebody for their artistic accomplishments is *resenting* 'em 'cause they never live up to your expectations. Plus which they all love the abuse, they're worse than academics, so the only thing left to do is go whole hog nihilistic and tear everybody you ever respected to shreds. Fuck 'em!

So I was gnashing ready to pound Lou to a sniveling pulp the minute he hit town. THIS WAS IT! THE BIG DAY! THE ONLY OLD HERO, MUCH LESS ROCK MUSICIAN, LEFT WORTH DOING BATTLE WITH!

I went into the Hilton and found Lou's party in the restaurant and sat down at a table adjacent. Then I got up and walked over. He's sitting there vibing away in his black T-shirt and shades, scowling like a house whose fire has just been put out, muttering to himself as he picked desultorily at indistinct clots of food on his plate: "Goddam fucking place . . . what a shithole . . . dump . . . fucking nerve . . . assholes. . . ." Turned out he'd been refused entrance to Trader Vic's because of the way he was dressed, and he was fuming about it. I walk up, shake hands: "Hi Lou . . . I believe you remember me."

Dead cold fish handshake. "Unfortunately." Just sat there. Didn't move. Didn't smile. Didn't even sneer. Concrete scowl. Solid veneer, with cement behind that. My party had just finished sitting down and ordering when suddenly Lou bolted up from his table and stalked out of the room, muttering something about going to get a newspaper. By the time we finished eating and had another drink he still hadn't returned. It was getting perilously close to, uh, showtime, and his road manager Barbara Fulk was getting nervous: "Where in god's name could he have gone?" Turned out later he'd gone for a walk around the block and gotten lost. An old song was ricocheting through my head, some faint memory of a time in 1968 when I told my nephew about this kid who was hero-worshipping me because I'd turned him on to Velvet Underground albums, speed, etc. "I don't wanna be anybody's fuckin' *hero*," I snarled at the time.

My nephew made up a two-line song on the spot:

Don't wanna be a hero
Just wanna be a zero.

The show was great. To hell with it. Later we're back at the hotel and Barbara is telling me that Lou is finally ready, so we walk down the hall to the Great Man's (at least temporal) sanctum sanctorum.

There he was, sprawled out on his bed, surrounded by his cohorts, roadies and sycophants, as well as a strange somewhat female thing which had been at the table with him at dinner, which I had in fact at first mistaken for Barbara, and which I now got a closer look at.

You simultaneously wanted to look away and sort of surreptitiously gawk. At first glance I'd thought it was some big dark swarthy European woman with long rank thick hair falling about her shoulders. Then I noticed that it had a beard, and I figured, well, cool, the bearded lady, with Lou Reed, that fits. But now I was up closer and it was almost unmistakably a guy. Except that behind its see-thru blouse, it seemed to have tits. Or something. It was beyond the bizarre, between light and shade. It was grotesque. Not only grotesque, it was abject, like something that might have grovelingly scampered in when Lou opened the door to get the milk and papers in the morning, and just stayed around. Like a dog that you could beat or pat on the head, either way didn't matter because any kind of attention was recognition of its very existence. Purely strange, a mother lode of unholy awe. If the album *Berlin* was melted down in a vat and reshaped into human form, it would be this creature. It was like the physical externalization of all that fat and mung Lou must have lost when he shot those vitamins last winter. Strange as a yeti from the cozy brown snow of the East. Later I noticed it, midway in the interview, turning the pages of a book. But from the way it did it, it was obvious that it was not reading, it was merely turning pages, quivering uncertainty frozen incarnate. At one point I yelled at Lou, "Fuck you, I ain't gonna talk to *you*, I'm gonna interview *her!*"

"She's a he," Lou said, "and you ain't int'rv'wing 'm, man." His tone was the same even, sullen, occasionally venally darting mutter he maintained all night.

Later I was told that this creature, whose name was Rachel but whom the people in my party referred to next day as Thing, was introduced to the concert-hall people as "Lou's babysitter." Hmmm, seemingly a long way down from Betty, the blond wife he brought on the last tour, who was rather wholesome looking as she gulped coffee and kept track of things Lou lost. Still, you never know. What's really interesting is that here's Lou Reed, the cat's gay, he's a celeb, he's traveling, he's got lots of money, it stands to reason he could have beautiful boys or whatever he wanted around him. So you gotta conclude he wanted this strange, large, frightened being that never talked and barely ever lifted its head. There was a sense of permanency, even protectiveness, about the relationship.

Me, I was drunk. I glugged about a half-quart of Johnnie Walker Black while waiting for Lou to get ready to argue, and what the hell, last time Lou was in town *he* was drinking double Johnnie Walkers while I sat there nursing my Bloody Mary, trying to think of questions while he rambled on woozily saying things like "Will Yoko leave Paul?" and "I admire Burt Reynolds a lot."

Now we were back in the fray, and he just sat there, too goddam cool even though I was almost positive he was speeding or coking his brain pan shiny. He obviously considered me a total bumpkin and I played it to the hilt, demanding more Scotch (which he refused to give me: "Enough of your drinking. Stop. You can't handle it. I don't want you to get wasted"), doing jive spade routines and hollering (to me hilariously funny) things like "Oh pardon me *suh*, it's furthest from my mind, I'm just lookin' for HAW HAW HAW!"

Lou started off with a backhanded compliment that turned into a kudoferous insult midway. "You know that I basically like you in spite of myself. Common sense leads me to believe that you're an idiot, but somehow the epistemological things that you come out with sometimes betray the fact that you're kind of onomatopoetic in a subterranean reptilian way."

"Goddam, Lou," I enthused, "you sound just like Allen Ginsberg!"

"You sound like his father. You should do like Peter Orlovsky and go have shock. You don't know any more than when you started. You just kind of chase your tail."

Damn, beat me to the first good left hook. "That's what I was gonna say to *you!* Do you ever feel like a self-parody?"

"No. If I listened to you assholes I would. You're comic strips."

"That's okay," I hoohawed, losing ground steadily, "I don't mind being a comic strip. *Transformer* was a comic strip that transcended itself."

He told me to shut up, and we sat there and stared at each other like two old geezers at the spittoon.

"Okay," I summoned my bluster, "now let's decide whether we're gonna talk about me or you."

"You."

"All right. You start."

"Okay . . . ummm . . . who's gonna win the pennant?"

I don't know shit about sports. "I saw Bowie the other night," I said.

"Lucky you. I think it's very sad."

"He ripped off all your riffs, obviously." I intended this as a big contention, although I really meant more than what I said. Just look in your copy of *Rock Dreams* and you'll see it right there, the Myth: Lou Reed looking younger, innocent, fingering his lip wide-eyed in a Quaalude haze, as Bowie lurks behind him, pure Lugosi, eyes glittering, ready to strike.

Lou wouldn't go for it. "Everybody steals riffs. You steal yours. David wrote some really great songs."

"Aw c'mon," I shouted at the top of my lungs, "anybody can write great songs! Sam the Sham wrote great *songs!* Did David ever write anything better than 'Wooly Bully'?"

"You ever listen to 'The Bewlay Brothers,' shithead?"

"Yeah, *fucker,* I listened to those fuckin' lyrics, motherfucker!"

"Name one lyric from that song."

"I didn't lis— I've heard it . . . but what I and millions of fans all over the world wanna know about Bowie is: first you, then Jagger, then Iggy. What in the hell's he got?"

"Jagger and Iggy?"

"Yeah, you know he fucks everybody in the rock 'n' roll circuit. He's a bigger groupie than Jann Wenner!"

Deadpan. "He's the one who's getting fucked."

"Didja fuck 'im?" All bravado. But like bullfighting on a handball court.

"He's fucking himself. He doesn't know it, though." Even. Level. Vibrating soundless hum.

I figured I'd better change the subject. Behind Lou's bed was a cassette deck emanating an endless stream of the kind of funky synthesizer Muzak that Herbie Hancock snores up. "Hey, Lou, why doncha turn off all that jazz shit?"

"That's not jazz shit, and you wouldn't know the difference anyway."

"I'm telling you that—"

"You don't know, you've never listened."

"—that Bowie"—and here I began to sing in loud Ezio Pinza baritone—"ripped off all his shit that's decent from you, you and Iggy!"

"What does Iggy have to do with it?"

"You were the originals!"

"The original what?"

I went on about Iggy and Bowie, and he surprised me with a totally unexpected blast at the Pop: "David tried to help the cat. David's brilliant and Iggy is . . . stupid. Very sweet but very stupid. If he'd listened to David or me, if he'd asked questions every once in a while . . . I'd say, 'Man, just make a one-five change, and I'll put it together for you. You can take all the credit. It's so simple, but the way you're doin' it now you're just making a fool out of yourself. And it's just gonna get worse and worse.' He's not even a good imitation of a bad Jim Morrison, and he was never any good anyway. . . ."

Iggy a fool. This from the man who provoked mass snickers on two continents two years running with *Transformer* ("You hit me with a flower") and *Berlin*. I decided that I'd had enough of this horseshit, so I bulldozed on: "Did you shoot speed tonight before you went on?"

He acted genuinely surprised. "Did I shoot *speed?* No, I didn't. Speed kills. I'm not a speedfreak." This started out as essentially the same rap Lou gave me one time when I went to see the Velvets at the Whisky in 1969, as he sat there in a dressing room drinking honey from a jar and talking a mile a minute, about all the "energy in the streets of New York," and lecturing me about the evils of drugs. All speedfreaks are liars; anybody that keeps their mouth open that much can't tell the truth all the time or they'd run out of things to say. But now he got downright clinical. "You better define your terms. What kind of speed do you do—hydrochloride meth, hydrochloride amphetamine, how many milligrams . . . ?"

The pharmacological lecture was in full swing, and all I could do was giggle derisively. "I used to shoot Obetrols, shit, man!"

"Bullshit you used to shoot Obetrols." Lou was warming to his subject now, revving up. Closing in for the kill. Show you up, punk. "You'd be dead, you'd kill yourself. You were probably stupid and didn't even put 'em through cotton. You could have gotten gangrene that way. . . ."

Then he's pressing me again, playing dirty: "What's an Obetrol?"

I got mad again. "It's in the neighborhood of Desoxyn. You know what an Obetrol is, you lyin' sack of shit! This is the *fourth* time I've interviewed you and you lied every time! The first time—"

"What's Desoxyn?" He had just said this, in the same dead monotone, for the fifteenth time. Interrupting me every second word in the tirade above, coldly insistent, sure of himself, all the clammy finality of a technician who knows every inch of his lab with both eyes put out.

But I was cool. "It's a Methedrine derivative."

The kill: "It's fifteen milligrams of pure methamphetamine hydrochloride with some cake paste to keep it together." Like an old green iron file slamming shut. "If you do take speed," he continued, "you're a good example of why speed freaks have bad names. There's A-heads and there's speedfreaks. . . . Desoxyn's fifteen milligrams of methamphetamine hydrochloride held together with cake paste, Obetrol is fifteen milligrams of—"

"Hey, Lou, you got anything to drink?"

"No . . . You don't know what you're doing, you haven't done any research. You make it good for the rest of us by taking the crap off the market. Plus you're poor. [I told you he'd stop at nothing. It's this kind of thing that may well be Lou Reed's last tenuous hold on herodom. And I don't mean heroism.] And even if you weren't poor you wouldn't know what you were buying anyway. You wouldn't know how to weigh it, you don't know your metabolism, you don't know your sleeping quotient, you don't know when to eat and not to eat, you don't know about electricity . . ."

"The main thing is money, power and ego," I said, quoting an old Ralph J. Gleason column for some reason. I was getting a little dazed.

"No, it has to do with electricity and the cell structure. . . ."

I decided to change my tack again. "Lou, we're gonna have to do it straight. I'll take off my sunglasses [ludicrously macho Silva-Thin wraparounds parodying the ones he sported on the first Velvets album, which I had been wearing all evening] if you'll take off yours." He did. I did. Focus in on shriveled body sprawled on the bed facing me with Thing behind him staring at beehives on the moon, Lou's sallow skin almost as whitish yellow as his hair, whole face and frame so transcendently emaciated he had indeed become insectival. His eyes were rusty, like two copper coins lying in desert sands under the sun all day with telephone wires humming overhead, but he looked straight at me. Maybe through me. Then again, maybe it was a good day for him. Last time I saw him his left eyeball kept rolling off to the side, and it was no parlor trick. Anyway, I was ready to ask my Big Question, the one I'd pondered over for months.

"Do you ever resent people for the way that you have lived out what they might think of as the dark side of their lives for them, vicariously, in your music or your life?"

He didn't seem to have the slightest idea what I was talking about; shook his head.

"Like," I pressed on, "I listen to your records: shootin' smack, shootin' speed, committing suicide—"

"That's three percent out of a hundred songs."

"Like with all this decadence and glitter shit—none of it would have happened if not for you, and yet I wonder if you—"

"I didn't have anything to do with it."

"Bullshit, you *started* it, singing about smack, drag queens, etc."

"What's decadent about that?"

"Okay, let's define decadence. You tell me what you think is decadence."

"You. Because you used to be able to write and now you're just fulla shit. You don't keep track of music, you're not on top of what's happening, you don't know the players or who's doin' what. It's all jive, you're getting very egocentric."

I let it pass. The true artist does not stoop to respond in kind to jibes from an old con. Besides, he was half right. But I simply could not believe that he could so blithely disclaim everything that he had disseminated, no, *stood for and exploited,* for so many years. It was like seeing a dinosaur retreating into an ice cave. He'd done the same thing before. Last interview he merely disclaimed association with the gay movement, which he really doesn't have anything to do with. But now, post–*Sally Can't Dance* and apparently ready to clean up as much of his act's exoskeleton as it took to hit the bigger time *(But you shoot up onstage. But it's only a rock 'n' roll show. This ain't Altamont. Or the Exploding Plastic Inevitable),* he was brushing it all away like dandruff off his black street-punk T-shirt. "I dismissed decadence when I did 'The Murder Mystery.' " Grand sweeping statements like this are the kind of bullshit to which this pop star is particularly prone. Like all the rest of them, I guess.

"Bullshit, man, when you did *Transformer* you were playing to pseudo-decadence, to an audience that wanted to buy a reprocessed form of decadence. . . . "

Barbara interrupted. "Lou . . . it's getting late."

Suddenly the tone of the whole scene changed. He was a petulant kid, up past bedtime, not exactly whiny, still insectival, but also blatantly pampered, cajoled, looked after, leashed, nursed, checked unless he chose to make a scene and possibly blow his cool. "Oh, it's fun arguing with Lester."

"But you have to get up in the morning," she insisted, "and go to Dayton."

"Oh," replied Lou, hardy old buzzard, blow winds blow and all that, "I'll live through it." Besides, other things were on his mind. He wanted to play me some records. The Artist actually wanted to submit something to me, the Critic, for my consideration and verdict! I felt honored. So what did he wanna submit? The Ron Wood solo album.

Jesus. If there's one thing I hate to hear out of musicians it's music talk. Most boring thing on the face of the earth. Especially since the only album I could think of that could conceivably be more nothing than that Herbie Hancock shit he was playing before was this Ron Wood set. Blandest of the bland. I yelled at him to shut it off—"I've heard that crap!"—but he was off again, into another subject that interested *him*, the selfish sonofabitch, and not listening to me at all.

"This guy George Benson, years ago, he was a bass player, invented the Benson amplifier, absolutely no distortion, totally clean, totally pure sound. It's interesting what Hancock's doing with the Arp."

It was getting worse. He had been patient with me, but I was beginning to have visions of future Lou Reed albums: stalwart Andy Newmark and Willie Weeks, who have appeared on every album made by every hasbeen popstar in the world recently, playing with Lou Reed, so the follow-up to *Sally Can't Dance* sounds like the Ron Wood album like George Harrison's *Dark Horse* like all those other faceless LPs involving this floating crap game of technically impeccable hacks. And on top of that a funky Herbie Hancock Moog spider jiving around, while on top of *that* Lou drones his usuals in that slurred and basically arrhythmic voice: "You're allll fucked . . . I can do anything I want . . . putdown, putdown . . . speed, speed, New York, New York . . ."

"I hate Herbie Hancock," I said.

"I've got something here," he said, "that is the stuff I want to do, that I meant by heavy metal. I had to wait a couple of years so I could get the equipment, now I've got it and it's done. I could have sold it as electronic classical music, except the one I've got that I've finished now is heavy metal, no kidding around."

I was too drunk to be ready to hear it, but it didn't matter because he turned on the tape again and it was—*the Ron Wood album!* I made him shut it off and he continued: "I could take Hendrix. Hendrix was one of the great guitar players, but I was better. But that's only because I wanted to do a certain thing and the thing I wanted to do that blew his mind is the thing I've finally got done that I'll stick on RCA when the rock 'n' roll shit gets taken care of. Now most people can take maybe five minutes of it—"

Sounds promising, but I was more interested in talking attitudes than music, and besides Lou has been such a bullshit liar for so long that I cut in: "I think most people think you're dead. Because you've encouraged them to." He wasn't interested. Remembering the first night I owned *Berlin* (I took it to a friend's birthday party, where every new arrival wanted to hear it, so we got to listen to its entirety about twenty-five times in one night. The party ended up with a room full of total strangers making vicious verbal slashes at each other. But we had laughed at the record, so), I asked him: "When you recorded *Berlin,* did you think people would laugh at it?"

Lou took his snoot and grabbed a coconut. "I couldn't care less."

"You know, Lou, one thing that I kinda resent about *Berlin* is that you never give her point of view. It was a very selfish album: 'I'm beating you up, bitch.' 'You're dead, bitch.' "

"She was making it with a dealer."

Hoping to pry a little autobiographical dirt (which is what a good portion of *Berlin* amounts to) out of Lou, I asked him about Betty, his ex-wife, and got a typically effusive answer: "She was a secretary when one was needed at the time."

She was a nursemaid, but then many people close to Lou seem to fall into that role. We argued a bit about the autobiographic content of his songs, and Lou asserted, predictably, that his songs were not autobiographical but existed in a zone of their own, and moreover could only be truly understood by a certain distinct elite audience. I told him that in my estimation the majority of his solo work suffered principally by its obviousness, all the subtlety left ages ago and he's just an old ham cradling the asp; I asked him if all his songs had elite meanings to please explain to me the secret meaning of *Sally*'s "Animal Language," otherwise known as the Bow Wow Song (dead dog meets cat, they try to fuck, fail, shoot up fat man's sweat) (really a specimen of mind rot at its finest).

" 'Animal Language' isn't obvious. Who do you think the animals are? You think it's a dog and a cat? Who's the dog, who's the cat, who are the animals that are so fucked up they gotta shoot up somebody's sweat to get off?"

I dunno, Lou, you tell me. There are eight million stories in the Naked City. . . . "One thing I like about you," I interjected, "is that you're not afraid to lower yourself. For instance, 'New York Stars.' I thought you were lowering yourself by splattering all these people like the Dolls and dumb little bands with your freelance spleen, but then I realized that you've been lowering yourself for years."

His riposte: "You really are an asshole. You went past assholism into some kinda urinary tract. The next time you come up with a phrase as good as 'curtains laced with diamonds dear for you,' instead of all this Dee-troit bullshit, let me know."

"Obviously," I said, "what you're selling under your name now is pasteurized decadence. In the old days you were really a badass, Lou, but now it's all pasteurized."

He told me that I was jaded. "You've made a career out of being a degenerate," I said, "and I think you should fess up to that. You have not primarily distinguished yourself as a musician; although you have come up with some great riffs, and I don't know why you keep trying to play me all this high-tech music crap, because basically you're a lit. In your worst moments you could be considered like a bad imitation of Tennessee Williams."

"That's like saying in your worst moments you could be considered a bad imitation of you."

"Don't you ever feel like a victim of yourself?"

"No."

Barbara is whispering to me: "Do you really think it's going to get any better?"

"Sure," I said, and turned to Lou. "What do you think that the sense of guilt manifested in most of your songs has to do with being Jewish?"

"I don't know anyone Jewish."

Barbara starts to put the pressure on in earnest: "It's three-thirty, Lou."

"Well, that's true, it's three-thirty. So . . . what? What would you like me to do, lock the door, hang my feet from the ceiling and listen to half a channel of my stereo?"

"Yes," she said.

"Cat wants to talk," Lou mumbled. "I think you're wrong. Dennis said if I wanted to, I could. I said sure. Directions from the higher up. Go ahead and call him. Call him up."

She just grunted no. I could not believe that this man was actually asking this woman to call his manager and wake him up at three-thirty in the morning to ask whether or not he could stay up a little bit later to talk to me. And of course it didn't really have anything to do with me. It was a cranky child, but then a large part of Lou's mythic appeal has always been his total infantilism. Now he was ready to talk all night, even though neither one of us had been listening to the other at all: "I think it's being made very hard on the cat, personally. I'm telling you, no, I'm interested in some of the things he has to say, even though I think he's an idiot."

"We think the same thing of each other," I offered. I was getting tired.

"He's trashy," continued Lou, "and I think you oughta get a kick out of trash while you can."

"But you *have been,*" insisted Barbara, "for almost *two hours!*"

"Well, I feel like getting some more. There's some shit I wanna play him, against his will." He turned back to me. "This guy George Benson, invented the hollowbody electric bass with absolutely no distortion . . . "

"Uh, lissen, Lou," I said. "Barbara's right. We gotta go too. This could go on forever." I gathered up my stuff and started for the door. As I was going out I could hear his voice behind me, dull basso, stale bitchy badinage fluttering off into dust: "You Seattle boys are all the same . . . A-200 . . . corn flakes . . . "

I never met a hero I didn't like. But then, I never met a hero. But then, maybe I wasn't looking for one.

—*Creem*, March 1975

How to
Succeed in
Torture Without
Really Trying,

or, Louie Come Home, All Is Forgiven

This is not Round Three.

By now I am sure there are many of you out there who may have grown a bit weary of this Lou Reed subject. To tell the truth, I'm almost getting bored with Lou myself, and he is certainly not my hero anymore. My new hero is President Amin of Uganda.

You may, however, wonder how such an album as *Metal Machine Music* could be sold, first by the artist to his record company, then by said record company to the "hard rock" consumers of America.

In case you just got here or think *Metal Machine Music* refers to something in the neighborhood of Bad Company, let me briefly explain that what we have here is a one-hour two-record set of nothing, absolutely nothing but screaming feedback noise recorded at various frequencies, played back against various other noise layers, split down the middle into two totally separate channels of utterly inhuman shrieks and hisses, and sold to an audience that was, to put it as mildly as possible, unprepared for it. Because sentient humans simply find it impossible not to vacate any room where it is playing. With certain isolated exceptions: mutants, mental patients, shriek freaks, masochists, sadists, amphetamine addicts, hate buffs, drug-numbed weirdos too walled off by chemicals to feel anything, other people whose nervous systems are already so bent out of shape that it sounds perfectly acceptable, the last category possibly including the author of this article, who likes *Metal Machine Music* so much that he acquired (did not buy) an 8-track RCA cartridge (on which are imprinted the words "SPECIAL VALUE!") so that he can listen to it in his car.

The release of *Metal Machine Music* is nothing if not an event in the history of the recording industry, and we at *Creem* are proud to celebrate it. Not since the halcyon days of Bruce Springsteen has there been a public so divided. (That 98% of them are on one side glowering and spitting at the other 2 percent means nothing; we at *Creem* will always stand up for the rights of minority groups, and you won't find many groups smaller, nor more fervent, than *MMM* fans.) As of this writing, it looks like *MMM* is gonna be a heavyweight contender in our *Creem* Readers' Poll categories both of "Disappointment of the Year" and "Ripoff of the Year." Then again, every once in a while a ballot rolls in like that from one Carole Pressler of Rocky River, Ohio, who not only voted *MMM* as all three of the Top Albums of 1975, but voted for sides A and D as Top Two Singles of the year, and side B as Best Rhythm & Blues Single.

Yes, these people actually exist, and it would be unfair both to them and to Lou to star *Metal Machine Music* in a snuff film. Which is exactly what RCA is doing right now. But let's not jump the groove, we gots to hear it *all*. This postmortem begins when I get a call from a lovely agent named after a British hypnotic sedative who says she is doing free-lance publicity for Lou. She tells me that Lou feels bad about the "misunderstandings" involved in the release of *Metal Machine Music*, wants to clear them up and apologize to all the fans who may have been taken unaware. (But that's just the *point!* spits the Imp of the Perverse.) She then tells me Lou is preparing a new album, the long-awaited *Coney Island Baby*, whose song titles alone should give sufficient indication of its content and tone: "Glory of Love," "A Gift to the Women of the World," "Crazy Feeling," "She's My Best Friend," "Charley's Girl" (single), "Nobody's Business," "Born to Be Loved," "Oo-ee Baby," "You Don't Know What It's Like," and "A Sheltered Life," which, she informs me with tongue so far in cheek it's lapping the Jersey shoreline, is "reggae."

Okay. I'm nobody's dummy. I'm everybody's dummy. I believe everything I read, see, and hear. If minions close to the cell say Lou is gonna make an album of sensitive songs for friends and lovers, I say it's right on that the dude should make so as to release concomitant with Valentine's Day. So I call the old geezer up at the latest hotel he's holed up in, Room 605 in the Gramercy Park. Above-mentioned agent told me to call him "three-ish," so I called three-ish, and the operator told me the line was busy. So I waited a few minutes and tried again. Same results. And again. And same still. Meanwhile Louie's girl is calling me on the other line telling me he just rang her up to ask where the fuck is the interviewer. So I call the hotel back, all of this red tape long distance, mind you, and still busy, so I tell the bitch at the desk to buzz in on the creep and tell him Bangs wants to talk to him. I get dead air. So call back yet *again*, buzz, click, chrk, clack, and there he is: "Boy, do you *believe* the operators in this fucking place?"

"Sure," I tell him. "I figured anybody that would put out an album like *Metal Machine Music* was the same kind of person as would tell somebody to call 'em up at a specified time and then give out with a busy signal."

I meant it as a Boy Howdy, but he squared off to fight straightaway: "Fuck you," etc., etc., etc. I told him poppa don't take no mess, this is halftime, so cessation of hostilities. He relaxes his guard, unzips his Frankenstein jumpsuit, and out steps: Jimmy Stewart! A sincere, friendly, helpful, likeable fellow. *This* is the real Lou Reed: a downhome Long Islander who lies through his teeth so good we might as well run the pone poacher for president. "*Metal Machine Music* is probably one of the best things I ever did," he beams, "and I've been thinking about doing it ever since I've been listening to LaMonte [Young, whose name Lou couldn't even remember to spell right on the back of the album]. I had also been listening to Xenakis a lot. You know the drone thing? Well, doing it with a band, you always hadda depend on other people. And inevitably you find that one person is stronger than another."

Note the tone of humility. Still, I had to demur in the direction of this particular piece of music having no direction. Like, each side is sixteen minutes and one second, ending as abruptly as they begin, with tape slice.

"I did it like that because I wanted to cut it hot," said Lou. "And since you're dealing in certain types of distortion up to a certain level of harmonics, I had to have the grooves as wide as possible, because the closer they are, the lower your gain."

"Then why didn't you make it eight minutes on a side," I said, "like an old Elvis album?"

"That would have been a ripoff. It was marketed wrong as it was. There was an information breakdown. They wanted to put it out on Red Seal, and I said no, because that would have been pretentious. I wasn't going to put it out at all. But a friend of mine at another record company asked to hear it, and said why don't you play it for [appellation deleted]. He was the head of classical music at RCA. I think *Metal Machine Music* got him fired. I played it for him and he loved it. I thought he must be mad, but he said we really must put it out. He bypassed the A&R people there and went right to Glancy, said 'We have to have it out on Red Seal.'

I said no way. He said why. I said 'Because it seems dilettantish and hypocritical, like saying "The really smart, complicated stuff is over here, in the classical bin, meanwhile the shit rock 'n' roll goes over here where the shmucks are." ' I said 'Fuck you, if you want it out you put it out on the regular label with all the other stuff. All you do is put on a disclaimer.' Which didn't happen, unfortunately. In other words if a kid saw the cover where I'm standin' with a microphone and said, 'Wow, a live album!' they'd say 'What a ripoff!' What they shoulda had was a disclaimer that said before you buy it listen to it for two minutes, because you're not gonna like it, and I said in the liner notes you're not gonna like it."

Breathes there a fan with soul so jade he'd not grant Lou the mantle of an Honest Man. A Patrician, even. Yet vexatious vanity hath wrought a whoozis azzole tryina fool. He may not be a knickerbocker but he shore do can lie. And quoth high sware in frae. Gibberish is as gibberish does, and gibberish stands and beats its monkey footpalms 'pon the strand at 6th Ave. and 44th St. When you try to ask people at RCA about *Metal Machine Music,* they get uptight. They ask not to be quoted, then they launch a fusillade of styrofoam to the effect that Lou is an artist and an intellectual they respect greatly, thus subclause respecting his right to "experiment." Then they fervently assert that I would be doing Lou and everybody else a favor if I would just let *Metal Machine Music* die a quiet death and slip away forgotten, because, of course, his next album is "the best thing he's ever done" and everybody's gonna love it.

I tell them that I think that sort of attitude is unfair to Lou and his fans. They sit there on the long-distance lam telling me that if I really care about Lou as much as they suspect I do, I won't want to hurt him by digging this *thing* up *now.* Get the picture? "An act of necrophilia," one of the anonymous RCA execs called my labors here. He also concurred, albeit under his breath, when I pronounced *MMM* a sort of schizophrenic ultimatum. He made strange noises when I brandished this album as prima facie evidence in the case against this curious practice known as "Artist Control." Only one RCA employee stonewalled. Ernie Gilbert, new A&R director of Red Seal: "I profess total and complete ignorance."

But a picture begins to emerge. Lou took this thing to the very top of the corp. The guy who headed Red Seal when he first walked in with his machine tapes now works for another company, was not fired as Lou had said, and while demanding that his identity be held in strict secrecy is not afraid of speaking the truth on this caper: "Well, as soon as he came walking into my office I could see this guy was not too well connected with reality. If he was a person walking in off the street with this shit I woulda threw him out. But I hadda handle him with kid gloves, because he was an artist in whom the company had a long-term commitment. He's not my artist, I couldn't get his hackles up, I couldn't tell him it was just a buncha shit. So I told him it was a 'violent assault on the senses.' Jesus Christ, it was fuckin' torture music! There were a few interesting cadences, but he was ready to read anything into anything I said. I led him to believe it was not too bad a work, because I couldn't commit myself. I said I'm not gonna put it out on the Red Seal label, and then I gave him a lotta classical records in the hope that he'd write better stuff next time. All I heard of it after that was that he was supposed to write a very strong disclaimer, which I guess he never did."

So now we have our scenario. Just imagine that wired little weasel, marching through the offices of one of the biggest media conglomerates in the world with his machine music tapes in his hand, not just confident but downright *cocky* that what he had here was the greatest (had to be, since most unbearable) masterpiece in musical history. Lou took *Metal Machine Music* straight to the top, to Kenneth Glancy, president of RCA Records, and worked his way down from there. Office to office, and every one he goes into he just presses the button and out comes ZZZZZZZRRRRRRRRR EEEEEEEEGGGGGGGGGGRRRRRAAAAARRRRRRRRGGGGG GGGGHHHHHHNNNNNNNNNNNNNNNIIIIIIIIIIEEEEEEEEERRRRR RRRRRRRRR . . . all down the line ebrey one-a-dem egg-zecks past de bucks. "Sure, anything, just get it outta my office!" Right! And into the STREET! From whence it came. Kinda reminds you of Melville, don't it?

Well, I told Lou that I thought *Metal Machine Music* was a *rock 'n' roll* album. "I think so too," he mutters in that peculiar geriatric code of his which passes for speech (perish conversation). "I realized at a certain point that to really do stuff like 'Sister Ray' and 'I Heard Her Call My Name' right, one, it hadda be recorded right, and two, you hadda have certain machines to do it."

"Except it misses certain things," I said. "Like the beat, the lyrics . . ."

"That's not true. If you had a small mind, you'd miss it, but the beat is about like—" and here he verbally mimicked a hammering heart. A *Chorus Line* of hammering hearts. "Very, very fast. And on each side there's a harmonic buildup, whether people believe it or not I don't really give a fuck anymore. It had to be very carefully mastered, because if it was mastered wrong it would all go down the drain because it would go into distortion. It's using distortion but it's not distorted.

"Whether people know it or not, there is a difference between each side, there is a reason why it's 16:01 because I hadda keep it under seventeen. What people don't seem to realize is that you don't listen to it on speakers, because if you do you miss half the fun," he says delightedly. "It should be listened to on headphones because there's left and right but there's no center. It's constantly changing and sometimes one channel goes out entirely. There's infinite ways of listening to it.

"Sometimes I lift the left channel a lot and the right a little and then jack up the left and drop the right almost entirely and it's as though you got whacked in the head! But if you're listening without earphones, you won't get the effect. Each time around there's more harmonics that are added on bass and on treble, and I went as far as you can go without making the needle hop on the record, which is why I kept it at that time. I made it 16:01 to try to get the fact across that I was trying to be as accurate as possible with the stupid thing."

I outlined my feelings re *MetMachMus* to Lou: that as classical music it added nothing to a genre that may well be depleted. As rock 'n' roll it's interesting garage electronic rock 'n' roll. As a statement it's great, as a giant FUCK YOU it shows integrity—a sick, twisted, dunced-out, malevolent, perverted, psychopathic integrity, but integrity nevertheless, to say this is what I think of you and this is how I feel right now and if you don't like it too bad. "Of course," I added, "that's also commercial suicide. Which I suppose is the reason for this phone call."

"It was a giant fuck you, but not precisely the way you're saying it. [The former head of Red Seal] got me curious to see how it would hold up against LaMonte, Xenakis, etc. And I think it held up well against them all, in fact is far better. But I'm not interested in anybody's opinion except my own. When you say 'garage music,' well, that's true to an untrained ear maybe, but there's all kinds of symphonic ripoffs in there, running all through it, little pastoral parts, but they go by like—bap! in five seconds. Like Beethoven's Third, or Mozart . . . ."

"Yeah, but that's all by accident."

"You wanna bet? You don't do a note-for-note symphonic thing by accident. No way."

"Well then, how did you get those in there? With a pair of tweezers?"

"No, I had the machines do it. It's very simple for anybody that knows what I'm talking about. Bach and Beethoven both wrote pieces that weren't supposed to be played by people. Now people play them, and I'm sure if they were around now they'd be amazed but they'd also be playing with machines, because nobody can play that thing. But you don't accidentally have part of *The Glass Harp* in there. You don't accidentally have part of *Eroica*."

"Where are these?"

"Well, they keep building up. The thing is, you have to listen for it. But most people get stopped by the initial thing they hear, which is fine by me."

"Well, the initial thing they hear is really not that extreme. It's not so far from, say, 'L.A. Blues' by the Stooges. And that came out in 1970."

"When I was in Japan they liked it. There are about seven thousand different melodies going on at one time or another, and each time around there's more. Like harmonics increase, and melodies increase, in a different combination again. I don't expect anybody with no musical background to get it. I took classical piano for fifteen fucking years, theory, composition, the whole thing, and I'm getting so fucking tired of people saying, 'Oh, it's a rock 'n' roll guy fucking around with electronic music.' That's bullshit. One of these days I'm gonna pull my degrees out and say, 'Does that make me legitimate?' But I don't wanna do that because that's horseshit too. So Neil Sedaka went to Juilliard, so what else is new? But like I told some of the ad people at RCA, they said it's freaky. I said right, and Stravinsky's *Firebird* is freaky.

"As far as taking it seriously, that's an individual thing, but when people start saying 'I have the background,' they're getting in a little over their head, and it's very bad to get in over your head with me when it comes to that because . . . I never pulled a Cale and started talking about studying in a conservatory, but if I ever said what really is my background, a lot of people would have to take their thumbs out of their ass and say, 'He's putting us on!' Well, don't be too sure. I just happen to like rock 'n' roll. But all I'm saying now is that I'm sorry about a kid shelling out that kind of bread for that kind of music when I know they wouldn't like it. But when people start landing on me about their background versus mine, well, I didn't go to college just to beat the draft."

Pomp and circumstance. Fine. What about *Coney Island Baby*?

"They're not what people think of as archetypal Lou Reed songs, but they forgot like on the first Velvets album, 'I'll Be Your Mirror,' 'Femme Fatale.' I've always liked that kind of stuff, and now you're going to have a whole album full of it."

Lou Reed, the Moonlight & You.

"Right. 'The Many Moods of Lou Reed,' just like Johnny Mathis, and if they don't like it they can shove it."

"Are you serious? Is this an album of sensitive songs of love and friendship?"

"Absolutely. What it is, it's gonna be the kinda stuff you'd play if you were in a bar and you didn't wanna hear about it. It's the Brooklyn–Long

Island axis at work. Like you know the Harptones' 'Glory of Love,' doo wop, I wanted to rip that off them but not use the song, do my own."

I observed that Lou did seem to keep rewriting himself, *Metal Machine Music* to the contrary. "Oh, I've been rewriting the same song for a long time. Except my bullshit is worth most people's diamonds. And diamonds are a girl's best friend. *Sally Can't Dance* is cheap and tedious. Had it been done right . . . "

I noted that the production was very slick. "It was produced in the slimiest way possible. I think that's shit. I like leakage. I wish all the Dolbys were just ripped outa the studio. I've spent more time getting rid of all that fucking shit. I like all the old Velvets records; I don't like Lou Reed records. I like *Berlin* and I positively LOVE *Metal Machine Music*, because that's the idea I had years ago but I didn't have the money or machines to do it. I wasn't gonna put it out except that Clive [*Clive???*] had sent me over to see [appellation deleted], and [ditto, it's Mr. ex–Red Seal again] was outasight. Because he caught all those things and said, 'Ah, what are you doing putting in Beethoven's *Pastoral*,' and it blew my mind that he knew about it. Because like there's tons of those things in there, but if you don't know them you wouldn't catch it. Just sit down and you can hear Beethoven right in the opening part of it. It's down here in, like, you know, about the fifteenth harmonic. But it's not the only one there, there's about seventeen more going at the same time. It just depends which one you catch. And when I say Beethoven, y'know, there are other people in there. Vivaldi . . . I used pretty obvious ones. . . . "

"Sometime we'll have to sit down," I said, "with a tape or the record and you can point these out to me."

"Un-uh. Why?"

"Because I'm not convinced."

"Well, I don't care. Why should I sit down with you and show it to you? It's hard to do, because they occur at the same time. They overlay and depending on your mood which one you hear. I mean like you'll have Vivaldi on top of one of the other ones and that's on top of another one and meantime you've got the drone harmonic building."

Curious image, all those old dead composers stacked atop each other carcass on rotted postpustulant dusty carcass, in layers, strata really, prone yet aligned on a stairway to the stars right there in that old warehouse, the Harmonic Building, next door to the Brill Building. Or do I misinterpret? One must be careful when treading through the rice paddies of the avant-garde, lest a full chute of napalm come slag-screaming down your backbone. R.I.P., John Rockwell.

"There's also some frequencies on there that are dangerous. What I'm talking about is like in France they have a sound gun. It's a weapon. It puts out frequencies which kill people, just like they do operations with sound. It's a very delicate brain operation, they have surgical instruments that are sound. They've had this weapon since 1945. Hitler didn't have it, the French did of all people. Maybe that's why they play such bad rock 'n' roll."

"They like you over there."

"The only one they liked was 'Heroin,' that's because it's the center of it. But anyway, if you check out the rules of the FCC, there's certain frequencies that it's illegal to put on a record. The masterer can't put them on, and they won't, and you can't record it. But I got those frequencies on this record. I tested the thing out at shows during intermission. We played it very softly to see what would happen. Which was exactly what I thought would happen: fights, a lot of irritation," he began to laugh, "it was fabulous, I loved it. People getting very uptight and not knowing why, because we played it very low."

He rambled on for a while after that, mostly about his former manager, Dennis Katz, from whom Lou recently departed rather acrimoniously. ("I've got that kike by the balls," said Lou, who is Jewish himself. "If you ever wondered why they have noses like pigs, now you know. Just like the operators in this hotel—they're niggers, whattaya expect?") Finally we rang off. The highlight for me of this particular conversation with Lou was having JoAnn, a seventeen-year-old friend who positively idolizes the old fraud, listen in for the first ten minutes and ask later: "Lester, why was Lou so *boring?*"

"It's not his fault," I said. "It's just he's like Instant Douse. Like having B.O. or something."

She understood, and I got ready to write my article, when not two days later the phone rang, hot wires straight from RCA-NYC to these plains, it was my faverave publicitous agent, and after we spoke briefly of John Denver he said, "I've got somebody here that wants to talk to you."

Sure enough. And in fine fettle too. "I'm not gonna apologize to anybody for *Metal Machine Music,*" the New Old Lou snarled, "and I don't think any disclaimer shoulda been put on the cover. Just because some kid paid $7.98 for it, I don't care if they pay $59.98 or $75 for it, they should be *grateful* I put that fucking thing out, and if they don't like it they can go eat ratshit. I make records for me. Same goes for this new album. I listened to those songs last night, and they're fucking great songs."

"You mean you changed the lineup, and we can expect more sleaze and vituperation?"

"Yeah. The new song titles are 'Kicks,' 'Dirt,' 'Glory of Love,' 'I

Wanna Be Black,' 'Leave Me Alone (Street Hasslin'),' and 'Nowhere at All.' Fuck this Dennis Katz bullshit of 'Oh yeah, sorry kids, the next album'll be songs you'll like.' "

"What about all that stuff you said yesterday, then?"

"Oh, you know, twenty minutes' sleep and a glass of carrot juice and I'm fine. I've never made any bones about the fact that I take amphetamines. Any sane person would every chance they get. But I'm not in favor of legalization, because I don't want all those idiots running around grinding their teeth at me. I only take Methedrine, which most people don't realize is a vitamin. Vitamin M. If people don't realize how much fun it is listening to *Metal Machine Music,* let 'em go smoke their fucking marijuana, which is just bad acid anyway, and we've already been through that and forgotten it. I don't make records for fucking flower children."

I was beginning to feel like Johnny Carson. "Speaking of fucking, Lou—do you ever fuck to *Metal Machine Music?*"

"I never fuck. I haven't had it up in so long I can't remember when the last time was."

"But listen, I was cruising in my car with *Metal Machine Music* blaring the other day, when this beautiful girl crossing at a light smiled and winked at me!" (A true story.)

He cackled. "Are you sure it was a girl?"

Well, yeah, reasonably as you can be these days. And I'm also reasonably sure about some other things having to do with this whole sequence of alleged events. The way I see it, *Metal Machine Music* is the logical follow-up to *Sally Can't Dance,* rather than any kind of divergence. Depersonalization in action: first you make an album that you did not produce (though you got half-credit), played guitar on only one track, used for material either old shit outa your bottom drawers or dreck you coulda scribbled in the cab on the way to the sessions, and do all but a couple of the vocals in one take. The only way you can possibly remove yourself more from what you are purveying after that is to walk into a room, switch on some tape recorders, push some buttons, adjust some mikes, let the static fly, and cut it off an hour later. And the reason for all this is that it simply hurts to feel, anything, so the more distance the better. Also indicative of an artist with total contempt for his audience (and thus, by all the laws of symbiosis *and* parasitism, himself). Note that if we can believe Lou when he says he doesn't like any of his solo albums except *Berlin* and *Metal Machine Music,* he is beginning to let his audience in on the nature of his relationship to them, which is, to put it mildly, slightly askew. Every time he does something *he* really likes or cares about, it bombs; every time he slings out some cheap trough of chintz dimestore decadence, the little scads eat it up. And never the twain shall meet.

Which, actually, is in his favor. Because now, and only now, when everybody in the Western world has written him off as either a bad joke or a drug casualty, is he free to finally *make* a record that feels, that hurts, that might be real and not just more jokes. Because he's kicked up such a dirt storm that everybody's blinded anyway, they're just waiting for the old lunatic to speed himself to death and they positively *would not notice* if he made a record with the depth and sensitivity of his best work for the late Velvet Underground. Now, I hope that *Coney Island Baby*, which as of this writing he has realigned again back into the Valentine's Day package originally promoted, might be that record. Of course, I don't believe it will be, or that Lou will write anything but loony toons ever again, because a few too many brain cells have took it on the lam from that organism that treated them so hatefully. But all that's okay too, because I live for laughs, which is why I love Lou. As far as *Metal Machine Music* goes, I listen to it all the time, but I'll never forget what Howard Kaylan told me Lou said to him after unsuccessfully trying to sell the layers-and-layers-of-sonic-frequencies concept (which was only a speed trip in the first place) to Flo and Eddie: "Well, anybody who gets to side four is dumber than I am." So, slimy critter that he is, we're right back where we started from. The joke's on you, kid. And if I were you, I'd take advantage of it.

—*Creem*, February 1976

The Greatest
Album Ever Made

It has been suggested that in my annual regress report to the stockholders, published here last month, I neglected in all five thousand words to ever once mention why *Metal Machine Music* is a *good* album. So here, especially in the light of *Coney Island Baby,* are the reasons:

1. If you ever thought feedback was the best thing that ever happened to the guitar, well, Lou just got rid of the guitars.

2. I realize that any idiot with the equipment could have made this album, including me, you or Lou. That's one of the main reasons I like it so much. As with the Godz and Tangerine Dream, not only does it bring you closer to the artist, but someday, god willing, I may get to do my *own Metal Machine Music.* It's all folk music, anyway.

3. When you wake up in the morning with the worst hangover of your life, *Metal Machine Music* is the best medicine. Because when you first arise you're probably so fucked (i.e., still drunk) that it doesn't even really hurt yet (not like it's going to), so you should put this album on immediately, not only to clear all the crap out of your head, but to prepare you for what's in store the rest of the day.

4. Speaking of clearing out crap, I once had this friend who would say, "I take acid at least every two months & JUST BLOW ALL THE BAD SHIT OUTA MY BRAIN!" So I say the same thing about *MMM.* Except that I take it about once a day, like vitamins.

5. In his excellent liner notes, Lou asserts that he and the other speedfreaks did not start World Wars I, II, "or the Bay of Pigs, for that matter." And he's right. If everybody took amphetamines, all the time,

everybody would understand each other. Either that or never listen or bother with the other son of a bitch, because they'd all be too busy spending three days drawing psychedelic lines around a piece of steno paper until it's totally black, writing eighty-page letters about meaningless occurrences to their mothers, or creating *MMM.* There would be no more wars, and peace and harmony would reign. Just imagine Gerald Ford on speed—he might manifest some glimmer of personality. Or Ronald Reagan—a blood vessel in his snapping-turtle lips would immediately burst, perhaps ridding us of *that* cocksucker. As is well known by now, JFK enjoyed regular injections of Meth and vitamins from happy croakers. 'Nuff said. He may not have actually *accomplished* anything (except the Bay of Pigs—wait a minute, Lou hasn't been doing his homework), but he had style and a winning smile.

6. I have heard this record characterized as "anti-human" and "anti-emotional." That it is, in a sense, since it is music made more by tape recorders, amps, speakers, microphones and ring modulators than any set of human hands and emotions. But so what? Almost *all* music today is anti-emotional and made by machines too. From Elton John to disco to *Sally Can't Dance* (which Lou doesn't realize is one of his best albums, precisely because it's so cold) it's computerized formula production line shit into which the human heart enters very rarely if at all. At least Lou is upfront about it, which makes him *more* human than the rest of those MOR dicknoses. Besides which, any record that sends listeners fleeing the room screaming for surcease of aural flagellation or, alternately, getting physical and disturbing your medications to the point of *breaking* the damn thing, can hardly be accused, at least in results if not original creative man-hours, of lacking emotional content.

Why do people go to see movies like *Jaws, The Exorcist,* or *Ilsa, She Wolf of the SS?* So they can get beaten over the head with baseball bats, have their nerves wrenched while electrodes are being stapled to their spines, and be generally brutalized at least once every fifteen minutes or so (the time between the face falling out of the bottom of the sunk boat and the guy's bit-off leg hitting the bottom of the ocean). This is what, today, is commonly understood as entertainment, as *fun,* as *art* even! So they've got a lot of nerve landing on Lou for *MMM.* At least here there's no fifteen minutes of bullshit padding between brutalizations. Anybody who got off on *The Exorcist* should like this record. It's certainly far more moral a product.

7. Charisma. Lou's been slipping of late, but for those who remember and understand the Myth, the Legend—i.e., he was an emblem of absolute

negativism—*MMM* has more charisma than a cage full of porcupines has quills.

8. All landlords are mealymouthed bastards who would let the ruins of Pompeii fall on your four-poster before they'd lift a finger. They deserve whatever they get, and *MMM* is the all-time guaranteed lease breaker. Every tenant in America should own a copy of this album. *Forearmed!*

9. My pet land hermit crab, Spud, who sometimes goes for days at a time curled up inside his shell in a corner of the cage so you gotta check to see if he's dead, likes *MMM* a lot. Every time I put it on, he comes out of his shell and starts crawling happily around the sand and climbing the bars. It is, in fact, the only time I ever see him get any exercise. Either that or he's dancing.

10. I have been told that Lou's recordings, but most specifically this item, have become a kind of secret cult among teenage mental institution inmates all across the nation. I have been told further that those adolescents who have been subjected to electroshock therapy enjoy a particular affinity for *MMM*, that it reportedly "soothes their nerves," and is ultimately a kind of anthem. If anyone out there reading this knows any more about this phenomenon, please get in touch with me immediately.

11. I played it for President Idi "Big Daddy" Amin of Uganda when he flew me and Lisa Robinson over there to interview him for upcoming cover articles in *Creem* and *Hit Parader,* and he absolutely loved it. I gave him a copy, and now by special edict he has it piped through the Muzak vents of every supermarket (all thirty-five of them) and doctor's waiting room (all eight) in his great nation, so that the citizens there may be inspired to ever fiercer heights of patriotism for his regime and all that it stands for. He wanted to declare it the Ugandan national anthem, but I told him that I would have to check with the American teenage shock vets first, and being a wise, fair, graciously diplomatic politician, he of course immediately assented, and then, genial host that he is, whisked us off to see a live multiple snuff film done sans cameras and celluloid. "We can't afford them," he explained. "And besides, the next time you have a dangling conversation with Paul Simon, you can inform him that the theatre is not really dead."

12. I think that, in this time of recession/depression and with the whole music business tightening its belt, it is truly thoughtful of Lou to cut recording costs as much as *MMM* must have, especially when you consider the stupefying self-indulgence of so many of today's rock "masterpieces" with their overproductions so baroquely lavish it all turns to tinsel. Only James Brown, I think, approaches Lou's achievement here in terms of sheer

economy and minimal booking of expensive studio time. *MMM* is actually, far from some nihilist rampage, one giant WIN button. Or, more precisely, two, since it is a two record set.

13. And *why* is this, of all Lou Reed albums (and the man's songwriting prolifigacy is indeed astounding. "Just lock Lou in a room for an hour," Dennis Katz told me once, "and when you let him out he's got fifteen new songs!" The reason why he keeps on recording old Velvet Underground outtakes he wrote upwards of a decade ago is that he's saving all of his best new stuff for 863 LPs to be released, one every two months, after he dies, assuming that he ever does. "I'm not gonna let those bloodsuckers rip me off and tarnish my memory like happened to poor Jimi," he confided to me once over two Schaefer's drafts at McSorley's. "My fans will never get less than A+ quality, as my friend Bob Christgau would put it, and besides it's quite likely that I will live forever, because me and some doctor friends I hang out with just discovered that there's a secret, heretofore unknown ingredient in methamphetamine which retards the aging process. So theoretically if you can get and just keep shooting this stuff, you could live for the rest of human history, which is why we're doing some resynthesizing experiments to see if we can bring this certain ingredient a little more into the foreground of the compound. I think it's called atropine. It's been around a long time, the Indians knew about it but recognized in the face of their dog-race inferiority it would be more moral to forget about it and submit themselves to extermination by white Europeans, who were the only ones with the technological knowhow to extract the raw chemical and refine it into a form you can cook up and shoot. But anyway that's where you got that Ponce de León business, and his only problem was the fucker, being a dumb spic, naturally had no idea how to prepare it in any potent form. So everybody concluded it was a myth and forgot about it until I came along, and potency is my middle name. So now you can let your readers in on the little secret that not only am I the toughest, baddest, most well-hung stud in show business, which actually is only because in 1973 I went to Sweden and had a transplant so now instead of a cock I got a horse doctor's syringe, not only that but there's a damn good chance I'm even gonna cut that punk Cagliostro at his own riffs and live forever. Of course, you never can discount unforeseen circumstances, plane crashes and the like, which is why I got these eight hundred albums in the can just in case. There's all sorts of stuff, like one is I rewrote my own version of *Rigoletto*, you know that opera by Scriabin, except it's set in this Puerto Rican leather bar where all the customers are amputated at the thigh and rolling around on these little carts on wheels. They keep trying to have punchouts, except

the carts keep bumping and they can't reach each other. So they get very frustrated. I sang all the parts myself, and I stole all the lyrics off old 'Lucas Tanner' dialogue, but nobody will notice the difference because I made the music *salsa* and it's so fucking loud you can't hear any of the words. But I'm not gonna put that out just yet. They'll have to wait a while for that. What my next album is gonna be is the follow-up to *Metal Machine Music*, which sounds exactly the same except it's gonna be a concept album about all this stuff I was telling you about before about aging and a five-record set in a gold embossed box with a booklet inside featuring blown-up Polaroid SX-70s of me tying off, hitting up, sterilizing my works with alcohol and then going out Christmas shopping for Andy and all the kids at Bloomingdale's and the Pleasure Chest, where the last pic is me modeling a cock ring on my horse geezer. I predict by that time the general public will have grown ears and gotten hip enough to appreciate *Metal Machine Music*, so this follow-up, which I'm gonna call *Triumph of the Will*, will be the best-selling LP of all time and those ratfucks in Chicago can suck my asshole along with that little blob Elton John who could use some speed almost as bad as Leslie West but can't have any of mine, because as I think it was Pat Ast said in that *fabulous* review of *Coney Island Baby* in the *Soho Weekly News*, 'I have seen rock's future and its name is Lou Reed' "), a double album, you ask? Simple—the two discs are, according to Lou, symbolic of two tits ("There's never more than two," he explained), to signify that this is, albeit mechanized, a very *sexy* album designed to cut in heavily on the hot Barry White market.

14. Everybody knows that drugs come in sexes. Downs are feminine, speed is masculine. Downs make you all nice and sweet and pliant and tenderized like with E-Z Bake, whereas speed makes you aggressive and visceral and forthright and a real take-charge kind of guy/gal. (Makes no difference, because all humans are the same sex, except albinos. It is the drugs that, obviously, determine the gender of the being.) So which one you take when you get up in the morning just involves whether you wanna be Donna Mills or Joe Don Baker that day. It's totally your prerogative.

Similarly, *Coney Island Baby*, fine and indeed heartfelt as it is, is a downs LP. No putdown involved—Lou's favorite old Velvet songs were always the ballads, and he's got a right to get sweet on himself. Love is silt. Anybody who has ever taken Quaaludes and wound up loving the rest of the human race so much they ended up in bed with a human turnip knows that. The lyrics are better than any Lou-*née* Tunes in a while, but note that not since *Transformer* have so many of them been explicitly preoccupied with the, er, ah . . . "gay" scene. Which certainly can't be said of *CIB*'s immediate predecessor. Me, I like sex with vegetables, but I nurse this lingering paranoia that someday, some drunken night, I may get a radish between the sheets and discover it's homosexual. Thus I feel threatened by *Coney Island Baby,* just as I feel threatened by Valiums, Tuinals, Seconals, Quaaludes and Compoz. *Metal Machine Music,* on the contrary, reinforces my sense of myself as a man. With it I can kill, even Puerto Ricans, which is the ultimate bar mitzvah. Under my blacklight presidential campaign poster of Hunter Thompson, I bolt upright in repose, my rifle casually draped cross my lap, listening to *MMM* and dreaming of My Lai as starring Fritz the Cat. So fuck downs, avoid *Coney Island Baby* like guys who wear green on Thursdays, and keep it (your fist) up tight.

15. *MMM* is Lou's soul. If there is one thing he would like to see buried in a time capsule, this is it.

16. It sounds better on Romilar than any other record I have ever heard.

17. It is the greatest record ever made in the history of the human eardrum. Number Two: *Kiss Alive!*

—*Creem,* March 1976

Lou, I understand you wanna be "dominant." Okay, dominate me. Go ahead, beat me to a pulp, worse, rule my life, do whatever your mind conceives whatever your heart and sinews rush to . . . is it me that can't accept it or you? Who would you really like to kill? Not yourself, because you wouldn't have made all those albums if that was it. Other people, too many, specific people, too limited, too silly. You know your hatred is just like anybody else's. The real question is what to live for. And I can't answer it. Except another one of your records. And another chance for me to write. Art for art's sake, corny as that. And I bet Andy believes it too. Otherwise he woulda killed himself a long time ago.

PART FIVE

Slaying the Children, Burying the Dead, Signs of Life

Iggy Pop:
Blowtorch in Bondage

By any normal standards, Iggy Pop's gig at the Palladium last Friday night was a triumph. Iggy himself was in ferociously fine form, and the crowd was ravenously enthusiastic—he could have had as many encores as he wanted. But normal standards have never seemed relevant to Iggy—from the earliest days, when the Stooges went onstage not even knowing how to play their instruments, to the present, when he finally seems to be on the verge of becoming one of the strangest stars we've ever seen. What kind of person tries, for his third and most crucial attempt, to make it in big-time rock 'n' roll with an album called *The Idiot?* The kind, I suppose, who at one time regularly made a practice of literally diving headfirst from the lip of the stage into the middle of his audience and who on Friday night repeatedly twisted his face and body up into masks and gestures symbolic of "idiocy," torment, and, most of all, bondage.

More than anyone else in the seemingly endless parade of professionally anomic rockers, Iggy really is isolated, and this isolation manifests itself in lightning-stricken desperation. He's the most intense performer *I've* ever seen, and that intensity comes from a murderous drivenness that has in the past also made him the most dangerous performer alive: the plunges into the third row, cutting himself and rolling in broken glass onstage, getting into verbal and occasionally physical brawls with his audiences. When Iggy sang, "I'm losing all my feelings / And I'm runnin' out of friends" in "I Need Somebody" on *Raw Power,* he was describing, succinctly, as usual, the problem, the anomie. That there is no solution but death is why all the rest of it happens. This is a person who feels profoundly unalive, or, conversely, so rawly alive, and so imprisoned by it, that all feeling is perceived as pain. But feeling is still courted, in the most apocalyptic terms, which are really the only terms the performer can even understand, and the performance begins to look more and more like a seizure every time he hurls himself across the stage.

It's not minimizing all this to say that what it means for Iggy is ambivalence. "I'm dying in a story / I'm only living to sing this song," another line from "I Need Somebody," conveys the powerful ambivalence he feels towards his audience, his art itself. An apocalypse isn't supposed to be manageable, and when the carnage is done it ain't the audience that's gonna be bleeding. But manage the apocalypse is exactly what Iggy is now trying to do, because this idiot is no fool, and he knows the lie of a manageable Armageddon is the only way to make it in the rock 'n' roll end of showbiz and survive. That's why David Bowie is twerping around, trimming the dementia here and there with neat little clips, and that's why *The Idiot*, Iggy's new album (produced and influenced in every respect by Bowie, who also plays piano in Iggy's current touring band), rings so false.

A far more powerful documentation of the Iggy holocaust at its most nihilistically out of control is available on *Metallic K.O.*, a bootleg import (on Skydog) of the last concert the Stooges ever played, at the Michigan Palace in Detroit in January of 1974. I was at the gig immediately preceding it, at a little club in Warren, Michigan, two nights before, where the love-hate affair the Stooges had been carrying on with their audience for so long finally careened to its inevitable consequences. The audience, which consisted largely of bikers, was unusually hostile, and Iggy, as usual, fed on that hostility, soaked it up and gave it back and absorbed it all over again in an eerie, frightening symbiosis. "All right," he finally said, stopping a song in the middle, "you assholes wanta hear 'Louie, Louie,' we'll give you 'Louie, Louie.'" So the Stooges played a forty-five-minute version of "Louie, Louie," including new lyrics improvised by the Pop on the spot consisting of "You can suck my ass / You biker faggot sissies," etc.

By now the hatred in the room is one huge livid wave, and Iggy singles out one heckler who has been particularly abusive: "Listen, asshole, you heckle me one more time and I'm gonna come down there and kick your ass." "Fuck you, you little punk," responds the biker. So Iggy jumps off the stage, runs through the middle of the crowd, and the guy beats the shit out of him, ending the evening's musical festivities by sending the lead singer back to his motel room and a doctor. I walk into the dressing room, where I encounter the manager of the club offering to punch out anybody in the band who will take him on. The next day the bike gang, who call themselves the Scorpions, will phone WABX-FM and promise to kill Iggy and the Stooges if they play the Michigan Palace on Thursday night. They do (play, that is), and nobody gets killed, but *Metallic K.O.* is the only rock album I know where you can actually hear hurled beer bottles breaking against guitar strings.

On one level I suppose all of this is very funny, but if you look past the surface violence and simple abusiveness to the person at the center it's not funny at all. The reason it's not is the aforementioned ambivalence. Jungle war with bike gangs is one thing, but it gets a little more complicated when those of us who love being around that war (at least vicariously) have to stop to consider why and what we're loving. Because one of the things we're loving is self-hate, and another may well be a human being committing suicide. Here's a quote from a review of Iggy's new live show in the British rock weekly *Sounds:* "Iggy's a dancer and more, a hyper-active packet of muscle and sinew straight out of Michelangelo's wet dreams . . . who leaps and claws at air, audience and mike stand in an unsurpassable display that spells one thing—MEAT." Ignoring the florid prose, I'd like to ask the guy who wrote that how he would like to be thought of as a piece of meat, how he thinks the meat feels. Or if he thinks it feels at all. Yeah, Iggy's got a fantastic body; it's so fantastic he's crying in every nerve to explode out of it into some unimaginable freedom. It's as if someone writhing in torment has made that writhing into a kind of poetry, and we watch in awe of such beautiful writhing, so impressed that we perhaps forget what inspired it in the first place.

As for the performer himself, he carries that hurt like spikes in his heart, but there is simultaneously a strong element of unconsciousness in his art, which is one of the main reasons why it's so beautiful and so intense. During Iggy's second encore Friday night, as he sang a song called "China Girl" with a stagehand holding a light under him for dramatic Fu Manchu effect, he pulled his face taut with his hands to make slits of his eyes and began to hop in a bizarre imitation of some bound coolie. It was at once grotesque and lovely, conveying in a few simple gestures a pathos so immense that I'm sure if Iggy himself could have seen what he looked like at that moment he would have been mortified. Because there was a vulnerability so naked it wrenched the heart. At that moment I realized that this man did not know what he was doing, and maybe precisely because of that it was one of the most *alive* things I've ever witnessed, just as the performance on *Metallic K.O.* is wrigglingly, obscenely alive, and the person singing on *The Idiot* sounds like a dead man. Iggy may finally become the superstar we always knew he could be, and he's already transcended the punk-rock he almost singlehandedly birthed, but there are questions unanswered, and a life hanging on the answers, and I'm not even sure that those answers exist.

—*Village Voice*, 28 March 1977

I Saw God and/or Tangerine Dream

I decided it would be a real fun idea to get fucked up on drugs and go see Tangerine Dream with Laserium. So I drank two bottles of cough syrup and subwayed up to Avery Fisher Hall for a night I'll never forget. For one thing, emerging from the subways into this slick esthete's Elysium is like crawling out of a ditch into Jackie Onassis's iris—a mind-expanding experience in itself. A woman there told me that the management had quite soured on rock clientele, and it was easy to see why: here's this cornersteel of cultural corporations, and what staggers into it but the zit-pocked lumpen of Madison Square Garden. And when worlds collide, someone has to take the slide.

What kind of person goes to a Tangerine Dream concert? Here's a group with three or maybe even four synthesizers, no vocals, no rhythm section; they sound like silt seeping on the ocean floor—and this place is sold out. Freebies are rife, yet I don't think that kid in front of me wiped out in his seat got in for nothing. So I ask some of the Tangs' fans what they find in their music, and get a lot of cosmic, Todd Rundgren mulchmouth. I tell one guy I think they're just a bunch of shit, a poor man's Fripp and Eno, and he looks me over and says: "Well, you gotta have *imagination*. . . ."

Everyone is stoned. Some converse re the comparative merits of various items in the Tangs' oeuvre—one guy declares the double album *Zeit* a masterpiece, another is an *Alpha Centauri* man. Three times as many males as females at least. A thirtyish guy sitting next to me in ratty beard and ratty sweater reminisces about 1968 forerunner Tonto's Expanding

Head Band, and tells me about the time the Tangs played the Rheims Cathedral in France. ("6000 people cram the ancient building with a 2000 capacity," boast the program notes.) "They didn't have any bathrooms in the cathedral," he laughs, "so the kids pissed all over it. After it was over the high fathers, monsignors or whatever, said it was the devil and asked for an exorcism of the church."

DJ Alison Steele comes out, a fashion-modelish silhouette in the dimmed green light, and says that the management does not allow smoking in the theatre. As soon as she says her name, people around me scream out, "Eat shit!" and, "You're a prune!" The microphone she spoke through will stand there unused for the rest of the evening, a thin, black line cutting into the psychemodal otherness of Laserium.

The music begins. Three technological monoliths emitting urps and hissings and pings and swooshings in the dark, little rows of lights flickering futuristically as the three men at the keyboards, who never say a word, send out sonar blips through the congealing air. Yeah, let's swim all the way out, through the Jell-O into the limestone. I close my eyes and settle back into the ooze of my seat, feeling the power of the cough syrup building inside me as the marijuana fumes sift through the cracks in the air, trying to conjure up some inner-eyelid secret movie. Oh lawd, I got the blues so bad I feel just like a cask of Amontillado. Yes, there it is, the swirls under the surface of my life are reconfiguring into: Daniel Patrick Moynihan, caricatured by Ronald Searle. He dissolves like a specter on a window shade, and is replaced by neon tubing writhing slowly into lines and forms until I think it is going to spell out a word, but no, it doesn't quite make it. Goddamn it, I guess I'll have to try harder. On the other hand, maybe no news is good news.

I open my eyes again. Now the Laserium, which I had forgotten all about in my druggy meanderings, has begun to arise from the deep and do its shtick on the screen above the synthesizers. First, a bunch of varicolored clots slowly sludging around each other; they could be anything from badly seeded clouds to cotton-candy cobwebs to decomposing bodies. Then two pristine laser circles appear afront the muck, one red and one blue, expanding and contracting and puckering at each other. They get larger and larger until they are gyrating and rubberbanding all over the place with a curiously restful freneticism. The synthesizers whisper to them as they bounce. The music goes on for a long time, seems to ebb rather than end.

Intermission. Many audience members seem uncertain whether it actually *is* intermission or if they should just pick up their stethoscopes and walk.

Back for more of the same, but more aggressive this time, if that's a way to describe quicksand. The Laserium begins to flash more violently, exploding in dots and points and lines that needle your retinae as the synthesizers suck you off and down and the towering mirrors at the sides of the stage turn slowly, reflecting beams of white light that are palpably irritating but by and gone and by again in a flash. I close my eyes to check into home control, to see if any little twisted-wax visions might be coagulating. Nothing. Blank grey. I open them and offer myself up totally to the Laserium. Flash, flash, flash—the intensity grows until I am totally flattened; I feel like an eight-track cartridge that has just been jammed home. After that, I become slightly bored and restless, although the other bodies around me are rapt. I have seen God, and the advantage of having seen God is that you can always look away. God don't care.

So, finally, picking up my coat and lugging my clanking cough-syrup bottles, I push my way through the slack and sprawling bodies—out, out, out into the aisle. As I am walking up it, I am struck by an odd figure doddering ahead of me, doubled over under raggedy cloth and drained hair. I don't trust my Dextromethorphaned eyes, so I move closer until I can see her, unmistakably, almost crawling out the door . . . *a shopping bag lady!*

What's *she* doing at a Tangerine Dream concert? Did someone at CBS give her a ticket, or did she find one cast off by a jaded rock critic in some 14th Street garbage can? Never mind—there will be a place for her in the wiring of this brave, new world. I myself had earlier considered giving one of my extra tickets to a wino so he could get a little sleep in a comfortable chair. Look, there's got to be some place to send these whipped dogs so we don't have to look at them, and where better than Avery Fisher Hall? Let them paw through the refuse of a better world, listening to the bleeps and blips and hisses and amusing their faded eyes with the test patterns and static that our great communications combines have no better use for anyway. Just before I left, I turned around for one last taste of the Tangs and Laserium, and by gum, I had my first real hallucination since drinking the Romilar that afternoon: I saw a whole audience of shopping-bag ladies.

—*Village Voice*, 18 April 1977

Where Were You When Elvis Died?

Where were *you* when Elvis died? What were you doing, and what did it give you an excuse to do with the rest of your day? That's what we'll be talking about in the future when we remember this grand occasion. Like Pearl Harbor or JFK's assassination, it boiled down to individual reminiscences, which is perhaps as it should be, because in spite of his greatness, etc., etc., Elvis had left us each as alone as he was; I mean, he wasn't exactly a Man of the People anymore, if you get my drift. If you don't I will drift even further, away from Elvis into the contemplation of why all our public heroes seem to reinforce our own solitude.

The ultimate sin of any performer is contempt for the audience. Those who indulge in it will ultimately reap the scorn of those they've dumped on, whether they live forever like Andy Paleface Warhol or die fashionably early like Lenny Bruce, Jimi Hendrix, Janis Joplin, Jim Morrison, Charlie Parker, Billie Holiday. The two things that distinguish those deaths from Elvis's (he and they having drug habits vaguely in common) were that all of them died on the outside looking in and none of them took their audience for granted. Which is why it's just a little bit harder for me to see Elvis as a tragic figure; I see him as being more like the Pentagon, a giant armored institution nobody knows anything about except that its power is legendary.

Obviously we all liked Elvis better than the Pentagon, but look at what a paltry statement that is. In the end, Elvis's scorn for his fans as manifested in "new" albums full of previously released material and one new song to make sure all us suckers would buy it was mirrored in the scorn we all secretly or not so secretly felt for a man who came closer to godhood than Carlos Castaneda until military conscription tamed and revealed him for the dumb lackey he always was in the first place. And ever since, for almost two decades now, we've been waiting for him to get wild again, fools that we are, and he probably knew better than any of us in his heart of hearts that it was never gonna happen, his heart of hearts so obviously not being our collective heart of hearts, he being so obviously just some poor dumb Southern boy with a Big Daddy manager to screen the world for him and filter out anything which might erode his status as big strapping baby bringing home the bucks, and finally being sort of perversely celebrated at least by rock critics for his utter contempt for whoever cared about him.

And Elvis was perverse; only a true pervert could put out something like *Having Fun with Elvis On Stage,* that album released three or so years back which consisted *entirely* of between-song onstage patter so redundant it would make both Willy Burroughs and Gert Stein blush. Elvis was into marketing boredom when Andy Warhol was still doing shoe ads, but Elvis's sin was his failure to realize that his fans were not perverse—they loved him without qualification, no matter what he dumped on them they loyally lapped it up, and that's why I feel a hell of a lot sorrier for all those poor jerks than for Elvis himself. I mean, who's left they can stand all night in the rain for? Nobody, and the true tragedy is the tragedy of an entire generation which refuses to give up its adolescence even as it feels its menopausal paunch begin to blossom and its hair recede over the horizon— along with Elvis and everything else they once thought they believed in. Will they care in five years what he's been doing for the last twenty?

Sure Elvis's death is a relatively minor ironic variant on the future-shock mazurka, and perhaps the most significant thing about Elvis's exit is that the entire history of the seventies has been retreads and brutal demystification; three of Elvis's ex-bodyguards recently got together with this hacker from the New York *Post* and whipped up a book which dosed us with all the dirt we'd yearned for for so long. Elvis was the last of our sacred cows to be publicly mutilated; everybody knows Keith Richard likes his junk, but when Elvis went onstage in a stupor nobody breathed a hint of "Quaalude. . . . " In a way, this was both good and bad, good because Elvis wasn't encouraging other people to think it was cool to be a walking *Physicians' Desk Reference,* bad because Elvis stood for that Nixonian Secrecy-as-Virtue which was passed off as the essence of Americanism for a few years there. In a sense he could be seen not only as a phenomenon that exploded in the fifties to help shape the psychic jailbreak of the sixties but ultimately as a perfect cultural expression of what the Nixon years were all about. Not that he prospered more then, but that his passion for the privacy of potentates allowed him to get away with almost literal murder, certainly with the symbolic rape of his fans, meaning that we might all do better to think about waving good-bye with one upraised finger.

I got the news of Elvis's death while drinking beer with a friend and fellow music journalist on his fire escape on 21st Street in Chelsea. Chelsea is a good neighborhood; in spite of the fact that the insane woman who lives upstairs keeps him awake all night every night with her rants at no one, my friend stays there because he likes the sense of community within diversity in that neighborhood: old-time card-carrying Communists live in his building alongside people of every persuasion popularly lumped as "ethnic." When we heard about Elvis we knew a wake was in order, so I went out to the deli for a case of beer. As I left the building I passed some Latin guys hanging out by the front door. "Heard the news? Elvis is dead!" I told them. They looked at me with contemptuous indifference. *So what.* Maybe if I had told them Donna Summer was dead I might have gotten a reaction; I do recall walking in this neighborhood wearing a T-shirt that said "Disco Sucks" with a vast unamused muttering in my wake, which only goes to show that not for everyone was Elvis the still-reigning King of Rock 'n' Roll, in fact not for everyone is rock 'n' roll the still-reigning music. By now, each citizen has found his own little obsessive corner to blast his brains in: as the sixties were supremely narcissistic, solipsism's what the seventies have been about, and nowhere is this better demonstrated than in the world of "pop" music. And Elvis may have been the greatest solipsist of all.

I asked for two six-packs at the deli and told the guy behind the counter the news. He looked fifty years old, greying, big belly, life still in his eyes, and he said: "Shit, that's too bad. I guess our only hope now is if the Beatles get back together."

Fifty years old.

I told him I thought that would be the biggest anticlimax in history and that the best thing the Stones could do now would be to break up and spare us all further embarrassments.

He laughed, and gave me directions to a meat market down the street. There I asked the counterman the same question I had been asking everyone. He was in his fifties too, and he said, "You know what? I don't *care* that bastard's dead. I took my wife to see him in Vegas in '73, we paid fourteen dollars a ticket, and he came out and sang for twenty minutes. Then he fell down. Then he stood up and sang a couple more songs, then he fell down again. Finally he said, 'Well, shit, I might as well sing sitting as standing.' So he squatted on the stage and asked the band what song they wanted to do next, but before they could answer he was complaining about the lights. 'They're too bright,' he says. 'They hurt my eyes. Put 'em out or I don't sing a note.' So they do. So me and my wife are sitting in total blackness listening to this guy sing songs we knew and loved, and I ain't just talking about his old goddam songs, but he totally *butchered* all of 'em. Fuck him. I'm not saying I'm glad he's dead, but I know one thing: I got taken when I went to see Elvis Presley."

I got taken too the one time I saw Elvis, but in a totally different way. It was the autumn of 1971, and two tickets to an Elvis show turned up at the offices of *Creem* magazine, where I was then employed. It was decided that those staff members who had never had the privilege of witnessing Elvis should get the tickets, which was how me and art director Charlie Auringer ended up in nearly the front row of the biggest arena in Detroit. Earlier Charlie had said, "Do you realize how much we could get if we sold these fucking things?" I didn't, but how precious they were became totally clear the instant Elvis sauntered onto the stage. He was the only male performer I have ever seen to whom I responded sexually; it wasn't real arousal, rather an erection of the heart, when I looked at him I went mad with desire and envy and worship and self-projection. I mean, Mick Jagger, whom I saw as far back as 1964 and twice in '65, never even came close.

There was Elvis, dressed up in this ridiculous white suit which looked like some studded Arthurian castle, and he was too fat, and the buckle on his belt was as big as your head except that your head is not made of solid gold, and any lesser man would have been the spittin' image of a Neil Diamond damfool in such a getup, but on Elvis it fit. What didn't? No matter how lousy his records ever got, no matter how intently he pursued mediocrity, there was still some hint, some flash left over from the days when . . . well, I wasn't there, so I won't presume to comment. But I will say this: Elvis Presley was the man who brought overt blatant vulgar sexual frenzy to the popular arts in America (and thereby to the nation itself, since putting "popular arts" and "America" in the same sentence seems almost redundant). It has been said that he was the first white to sing like a black person, which is untrue in terms of hard facts but totally true in terms of cultural impact. But what's more crucial is that when Elvis started wiggling his hips and Ed Sullivan refused to show it, the entire country went into a paroxysm of sexual frustration leading to abiding discontent which culminated in the explosion of psychedelic-militant folklore which was the sixties.

I mean, don't tell me about Lenny Bruce, man—Lenny Bruce said dirty words in public and obtained a kind of consensual martyrdom. Plus which Lenny Bruce was hip, too goddam hip if you ask me, which was his undoing, whereas Elvis was not hip at all, Elvis was a goddam truck driver who worshipped his mother and would never say shit or fuck around her, and Elvis alerted America to the fact that it had a groin with imperatives that had been stifled. Lenny Bruce demonstrated how far you could push a society as repressed as ours and how much you could get away with, but Elvis kicked "How Much Is That Doggie in the Window" *out* the window and replaced it with "Let's fuck." The rest of us are still reeling from the impact. Sexual chaos reigns currently, but out of chaos may flow true understanding and harmony, and either way Elvis almost singlehandedly opened the floodgates. That night in Detroit, a night I will never forget, he had but to ever so slightly move one shoulder muscle, not even a shrug, and the girls in the gallery hit by its ray screamed, fainted, howled in heat. Literally, every time this man moved any part of his body the slightest centimeter, tens or tens of thousands of people went berserk. Not Sinatra, not Jagger, not the Beatles, nobody you can come up with ever elicited such hysteria among so many. And this after a decade and a half of crappy records, of making a point of not trying.

If love truly is going out of fashion forever, which I do not believe, then along with our nurtured indifference to each other will be an even more contemptuous indifference to each others' objects of reverence. I thought it was Iggy Stooge, you thought it was Joni Mitchell or whoever else seemed to speak for your own private, entirely circumscribed situation's many pains and few ecstasies. We will continue to fragment in this manner, because solipsism holds all the cards at present; it is a king whose domain engulfs even Elvis's. But I can guarantee you one thing: we will never again agree on anything as we agreed on Elvis. So I won't bother saying good-bye to his corpse. I will say good-bye to you.

—*Village Voice,* 29 August 1977

Peter Laughner

Peter Laughner is dead.

    Perhaps the name means nothing to you. If it doesn't I would hope that you would read this anyway, because one of the reasons I am writing it is that there is more than a little of what killed Peter in me, as there may well be in you. This is a magazine created by rock writers about rock musicians for rock fans, and Peter was all three. Before dying on June 22nd at the age of twenty-four of acute pancreatitis, he founded Cleveland, Ohio's original legendary underground rock band, Rocket from the Tombs. They played an amphetamine-driven blend of Velvets-Stooges, and Peter dashed off lyrics on the order of "I can't think / I need a drink / Life stinks." Later they more or less mutated into Pere Ubu, who can be heard (including guitar solos by Peter) on the first *Max's Kansas City* album. I found it interesting that when they were interviewed in a recent issue of this magazine, they didn't mention their deposed founder once.

    But then, perhaps they were being kind. Peter was a great writer as well as being a gifted musician. You can get some idea of his style from what was probably the best thing he ever had published, his review of Lou Reed's *Coney Island Baby* in the March 1976 issue of *Creem:*

        This album made me so morose and depressed when I got the advance copy that I stayed drunk for three days. I didn't go to work. I had a horrible physical fight with my wife over a stupid bottle of 10 mg Valiums. (She threw an ashtray, a brick, and a five foot candelabra at me, but I got her down and beat her head on the wooden floor.) I called up the editor of this magazine (on my bill) and did virtually nothing but cough up phlegm in an alcoholic stupor for three hours, wishing somewhere in the back of my deadened brain that he could give me a clue as to why I should like this record. I came on to my sister-in-law: "C'mon over and gimme head while I'm passed out." I cadged drinks off anyone who would come near me or let me into their apartments. I ended up the whole debacle passing out stone cold after puking and pissing myself at a band rehearsal, had to be kicked awake by my lead singer . . . before dropping six Valiums (and three vitamin B complexes, so I must've figured to wake up, or at least that the autopsy would say my liver was OK).

That is more than just the braggadocio of a post-teen druggie. I believe that the key to Peter's life and death, at least insofar as they apply to us, can be found in that autobiographical review. Later on he reminisces about his college days: "All my papers were manic droolings about the parallels between Lou Reed's lyrics and whatever academia we were supposed to be analyzing in preparation for our passage into the halls of higher learning. 'Sweet Jane' I compared with Alexander Pope, 'Some Kinda Love' lined right up with T. S. Eliot's 'The Hollow Men' . . . plus I had a rock band and we played all these songs, fueled pharmaceutically. . . . In this way I cleverly avoided all intellectual and creative responsibilities at the cleavage of the decades. . . . Who needed the promise of college and career? Lou Reed was my Woody Guthrie, and with enough amphetamine I would be the new Lou Reed!"

I originally met Peter via what was to be the first of many three A.M. phone calls. I had been listening to *White Light/White Heat* at the time; he told me he was listening to *Berlin.* It was the kind of thing of which long friendships were born. Later he visited me often in Detroit, and it never seemed odd to me that absolutely every time we got together we wound up blitzed out of our skulls on booze or speed or both; nor did it occur to me to wonder exactly what sort of friendship it might be in which both parties had to be totally numbed to be around one another. At the end of one of our all-night sorties Peter ended up back in the hospital in Cleveland, and even wrote about it in a Rory Gallagher story for *Creem.*

Peter was in the hospital a lot during the last two years of his life, in fact. Around the time I moved to New York from Detroit (last fall), he called me up and told me that the doctors had informed him that he was going to die if he didn't stop all drinking and the use of drugs. "It's gonna hafta be Valium and grass from here on out," he said. "Shit, you gotta have *somethin'*."

But it was also around this time that his midnight phone calls began to take on a creepy tinge. Sometimes he would be mushmouthed on morphine or pain pills, sometimes hoarse from a few days' bout with speed and cognac and beer. On one visit in the fall, he no sooner walked in the door than he plunked himself down in the middle of the living room floor, pulled a pint of Courvoisier from his pocket, asked for a can of Rheingold from the refrigerator, and began chasing one with the other as fast as he possibly could. It was at this point that our macho buddy drink and drug rituals began to me to seem a little formularized.

We ended the night with me speeding my brains out dashing off inferior reviews of records I barely began to listen to, Peter on the couch in a drink-and-Valium coma. The next time he came to town the first thing he did was ask for my *PDR*—he had a pill he wanted to look up. He didn't even know what it was, but he wanted to shoot it. I advised him to slow down a little, so he settled for another coma from orally ingested liquor and codeine and Valium.

By this time I was beginning to have reservations about a lot of aspects of our friendship, so before he hit town the next and last time, I laid it on the line: I told him that I thought he was committing suicide, and that I couldn't subsidize it by getting high with him any longer. I said that I would see him but wouldn't drink with him and that he couldn't stay here. I didn't say that I was afraid of him dropping dead on my floor. He promised to abide by my wishes.

He didn't. The next and last time Peter hit town he had his father (almost literally) in tow. I walked into my apartment and there they were: father and son, business suit and black leather, both drunk, both smiling in their horror. It was a tableau worth more words than I have. He told me his father was Sgt. something of the New York police force, and I believed him, and asked Sgt. something what the hell he was doing in my house. Things got a little hostile, then things got confused, then he left almost as soon as I realized who he really was, though I may be ascribing to him furtiveness he did not really possess, leaving me alone once again with Peter. I was getting ready to form my own band at the time, so we spent an afternoon trying to work up arrangements to go with lyrics I'd written. The music came quick and fast, because Peter was brilliant, but he had a little bottle of wine he kept taking nips off of. I did not have the guts to say anything about it. Jamming the next day we got totally shitfaced, and he gave me some Dalmanes, which are approximate to Librium, before rushing out the door, where he met my then girlfriend on the way in. "I just gave Lester some Dalmanes," he breathlessly told her, "so you better go up and check up on him because he may be dead! I gotta go see Patti Smith."

That night was the occasion of the *Punk* magazine benefit at CBGB's, at which the well-known incident of Peter trying to push his way onstage to jam with Patti's group and getting kicked off by Lenny Kaye and her brother occurred. J. D. Daugherty said that for the rest of the night Peter just stood around the club seething in wounded rage, glaring at everyone with splintered red eyes. He came by my place to drop off something he'd borrowed (every time he visited me he borrowed something, always an album or a book or a pair of sunglasses to take away as some kind of memento or fetish . . .) next day, and when I saw him down in the street (because I wouldn't let him up here) he looked terrible: dressed in his usual Lou Reed uniform of black leather jacket and gloves, he also had on a red T-shirt with holes cut into it by scissors, and a really corny imitation black leather plastic hat that I hadn't known he'd taken the night before (Lester's dead but I'm wearing his hat), which he begged me to let him wear back to Cleveland. I said no, and told him that he could buy one just like it for five dollars at Korvette's. He thought I was making fun of him; his state had been and was such that he couldn't tell the difference between the real thing and a piece of apparel that got me laughed at when I wore it to CBGB's. He looked at once ghastly and pathetic, the T-shirt and askew cap creating a nightmare Little Rascals effect of some horribly diseased eight-year-old. I got really angry and lit into him: "You're *killing* yourself just so you can be like Lou Reed and Tom Verlaine [who doesn't even take drugs, but was Peter's idol], two people who everybody in this town knows are complete assholes!"

It was the last time I ever saw him. It would have been the last time anyway, because had he called again I was planning to tell him that my own will-power was too flimsy: I could not trust myself to be around him and not get drunk or take drugs, so I had no choice but to never be around him. To tell the truth, being his friend at all had gotten so harrowing and ugly that I was looking for an out anyway.

When he went back to Cleveland he checked immediately into the hospital. I saw Patti a couple of days later and asked her about the incident at CBGB's, and she said: "It's nothin'. Peter's all right, everybody gets thrown off our stage." I called up his mother and told her to relay the message that Patti was not mad at him; she later wrote me that when she did, it was the only time she saw him smile.

Now he is dead, and I hope you don't take this as mere sentiment or another antidrug lecture. I would just like to try to preserve some of the meaning of Peter's life and death for those of us both in and out of the scene he immolated himself to emulate. I especially would like to direct it at a certain little Cleveland asshole who laughed when I went to CBGB's the night of Peter's death and told everyone about it. Because this kid's death was not meaningless, he wasn't just some fool who took too many drugs and so what because we all knew it was coming. Peter Laughner had his private pains and compulsions, but at least in part he died because he wanted to be Lou Reed. That certainly was not Lou's fault; it was Peter's. Though he was a casualty of the times, he brought it all upon himself.

In a sense Peter reminded me of a character in an old Terry Southern story, "You're Too Hip, Baby." It was about a guy in the bohemian scene in Paris around 1960, who followed all the jazz musicians, poets, and hipsters around, took all the right drugs, did and said all the right things. Eventually he became so rigidly correct that another hipster dismissed him with, "You're too hip, baby. I just can't carry you anymore." And there is something of that aspect of Peter in myself and almost everyone I know. Inasmuch as today I would not walk across the street to spit on Lou Reed, not because of Peter but because Peter's death was the end of an era for me—an era of the most intense worship of nihilism and deathtripping in all marketable forms. (And perhaps just one more signal that the twin concepts of nihilism and the antihero have had it. What began with *The Wild One* and James "nobody understands me" Dean, ran with increasingly vehement negativism up through the Stones and Velvets and Iggy has finally culminated in the ersatz jive of groups like Suicide, who are not just oppressive and offensive but so *boring* that they lead you to think it may be time, in spite of all indications to the contrary from the exterior society, to begin thinking in terms of heroes again, of love instead of hate, of energy instead of violence, of strength instead of cruelty, of action instead of reaction.)

But I suspect it's also the beginning of an era—the "new wave" can boast its first casualty, and given the predilection of this scene for drugs and general destructiveness you can bet there'll be plenty more. It seems just too corny to say that you might prefer to give yourself over to life and the pursuit of positive energies. I recall sitting around my mother's parlor with one of my old speed-shooting buddies in 1971, telling him I was going to try to give up drugs (of course I didn't) and haltingly explaining: "Well . . . it's just . . . I kinda wanna devote myself to *life*. . . ." I was embarrassed. He laughed for fifteen minutes. Three months later he was dead. But if

Peter Laughner died in part for my sins I tell you now that I will never take amphetamines again (all they ever make me write anymore is crap anyway) and if you wanna kill yourself you can too but stay away from me because it's just too sad, besides which *I haven't got the time.* Perhaps the best epitaph I could offer Peter comes from the conclusion of his own *Coney Island Baby* review: "Here I sit, sober and perhaps even lucid, on the sort of winter's day that makes you realize a New Year is just around the corner and you've got very little to show for it, but if you are going to get anything done on this planet, you better pick it up with both hands and DO IT YOURSELF." Good-bye baby and amen.

You know what? I don't care that he's dead. That's what I wrote in a letter to his sister-in-law after finishing the above, and then I went out and mailed it to her, but walking down Sixth Avenue something in the sunlight struck me, a glint in the leaves made me dizzy, the sounds and the feel of breath and being lifted me above myself right into the middle of the street, and I don't know if Peter was looking down on me then but the sky was crying warm blood, and it may have been only that pounding in my veins at the ecstasy of being alive. See, because when all is said and done I don't care that he is dead, though I feel a certain complicity, because other than that there would be only anger left, anger at life and anger at our blood that spills out of our weakness into troughs of uncaring. If I let myself get started I will only begin to rant and threaten those who glamorize death, but there is a death in the balance and you better look long and hard at it you stupid fuckheads, you who treat life as a camp joke, you who have lost your sense of wonder about the state of being alive itself, I AM OUT FOR YOU, I know who you are and I'll shoot you down with the weapons at my command and I don't mean guns.

And ultimately this lance of blame must turn back upon myself, whom I have nothing to say in defense of, any more than I can honestly say I will never take drugs again because of Peter Laughner, which would only be a terrible insult to his memory. Realizing life is precious the natural tendency is to trample on it, like laughing at a funeral. But there are voluntary reactions. I volunteer not to feel anything about him from this day out, but I will not forget that this kid killed himself for something torn T-shirts represented in the battle fires of his ripped emotions, and that does not make your T-shirts profound, on the contrary, it makes you a bunch of assholes if you espouse what he latched onto in support of his long death agony, and if I have run out of feeling for the dead I can also truly say that from here on out I am only interested in true feeling, and the pursuit of some ultimate escape from that was what killed Peter, which is all I truly know of his life, except that the hardest thing in this living world is to confront your own pain and go through it, but somehow life is not a paltry thing after all next to this child's inheritance of eternal black. So don't anybody try to wave good-bye.

—*New York Rocker,* September–October 1977

The Clash

PART ONE

The Empire may be terminally stagnant, but every time I come to England it feels like massive changes are underway.

First time was 1972 for Slade, who had the punters hooting; but your music scene in general was in such miserable shape that most of the hits on the radio were resurrected oldies. Second time was for David Essex (haw haw haw) and Mott (sigh) almost exactly two years ago; I didn't even bother listening to the radio, and though I had a good time the closest thing to a musical highlight of my trip was attending an Edgar Froese (entropy incarnate) press party. I never gave much of a damn about pub rock, which was about the only thing you guys had going at the time, and I had just about written you off for dead when punk rock came along.

So here I am back again through the corporate graces of CBS International to see the Clash, to hear new wave bands on the radio (a treat for American ears), and find the Empire jumping again at last.

About time, too. I don't know about you, but as far as I was concerned things started going downhill for rock around 1968; I'd date it from the ascendance of Cream, who were the first fake superstar band, the first sign of strain in what had crested in 1967. Ever since then things have just gotten worse, through Grand Funk and James Taylor and wonderful years like 1974, when the only thing interesting going on was Roxy Music, finally culminating last year in the ascendance of things like disco and jazz-rock, which are dead enough to suggest the end of popular music as anything more than room spray.

I was thinking of giving up writing about music altogether last year when all of a sudden I started getting phone calls from all these slick magazine journalists who wanted to know about this new phenomenon called "punk rock." I was a little bit confused at first, because as far as I was concerned punk rock was something which had first raised its grimy snout around 1966 in groups like the Seeds and Count Five and was dead and buried after the Stooges broke up and the Dictators' first LP bombed.

I mean, it's easy to forget that just a little over a year ago there was *only one thing:* the first Ramones album.

But who could have predicted that that record would have such an impact—all it took was that and the ferocious *edge* of the Sex Pistols' "Anarchy in the U.K.," and suddenly it was as if someone had unleashed the floodgates as ten million little groups all over the world came storming in, mashing up the residents with their guitars and yammering discontented non sequiturs about how bored and fed up they were with everything.

I was too, and so were you—that's why we went out and bought all those shitty singles last spring and summer by the likes of the Users and Cortinas and Slaughter and the Dogs, because better Slaughter and the Dogs at what price wretchedness than *one more* mewly-mouthed simper-whimper from Linda Ronstadt. Buying records became fun again, and one reason it did was that all these groups embodied the who-gives-a-damn-let's-just-slam-it-at-'em spirit of great rock 'n' roll. Unfortunately many of these wonderful slices of vinyl didn't possess any of the other components of same, with the result that (for me, round about *Live at the Roxy*) many people simply got FED UP. Meaning that it's just too goddam easy to slap on a dog collar and black leather jacket and start puking all over the room about how you're gonna sniff some glue and stab some backs.

Punk had repeated the very attitudes it copped (BOREDOM and INDIFFERENCE), and we were all waiting for a group to come along who at least went through the motions of GIVING A DAMN about SOME-THING.

Ergo, the Clash.

You see, dear reader, so much of what's (doled) out as punk merely amounts to saying I suck, you suck, the world sucks, and who gives a damn—which is, er, ah, somehow *insufficient.*

Don't ask *me* why; I'm just an observer, really. But any observer could tell that, to put it in terms of Us vs. Them, saying the above is exactly what They want you to do, because it amounts to capitulation. It *is* unutterably boring and disheartening to try to find some fun or meaning while shoveling through all the shit we've been handed the last few years, but merely puking on yourself is not gonna change anything. (I know, 'cause I tried it.) I guess what it all boils down to is:

(a) You can't like people who don't like themselves; and

(b) You gotta like people who stand up for what they believe in, as long as what they believe in is

(c) Righteous.

A precious and elusive quantity, this righteousness. Needless to say, most punk rock is not exactly OD'ing on it. In fact, most punk rockers probably think it's the purview of hippies, unless you happen to be black and Rastafarian, in which case righteousness shall cover the land, presumably when punks have attained No Future.

It's kinda hard to put into mere mortal words, but I guess I should say that being righteous means you're more or less on the side of the angels, waging Armageddon for the ultimate victory of the forces of Good over the Kingdom of Death (see how perilously we skirt hippiedom here?), working to enlighten others as to their own possibilities rather than merely sprawling in the muck yodeling about what a drag everything is.

The righteous minstrel may be rife with lamentations and criticisms of the existing order, but even if he doesn't have a coherent program for social change he is informed of hope. The MC5 were righteous where the Stooges were not. The third and fourth Velvet Underground albums were righteous, the first and second weren't. (Needless to say, Lou Reed is not righteous.) Patti Smith has been righteous. The Stones have flirted with righteousness (e.g., "Salt of the Earth"), but when they were good the Beatles were all-righteous. The Sex Pistols are not righteous, but, perhaps more than any other new wave band, the Clash are.

The reason they are is that beneath their wired harsh soundscape lurks a persistent humanism. It's hard to put your finger on in the actual lyrics, which are mostly pretty despairing, but it's in the kind of thing that could make somebody like Mark P. write that their debut album was his life. To appreciate it in the Clash's music you might have to be the sort of person who could see Joe Strummer crying out for a riot of his own as someone making a positive statement. You perceive that as much as this music seethes with rage and pain, it also champs at the bit of the present system of things, lunging after some glimpse of a new and better world.

I know it's easy to be cynical about all this; in fact, one of the most uncool things you can do these days is to be committed about anything. The Clash are so committed they're downright militant. Because of that, they speak to dole-queue British youth today of their immediate concerns with an authority that nobody else has quite mustered. Because they do, I doubt if they will make much sense to most American listeners.

But more about that later. Right now, while we're on the subject of politics, I would like to make a couple of things perfectly clear:

1. I do not know shit about the English class system.
2. I do not care shit about the English class system.

I've *heard* about it, understand. I've heard it has something to do with why Rod Stewart now makes music for housewives, and why Pete Townshend is so screwed up. I guess it also has something to do with another *NME* writer sneering to me, "Joe Strummer has a fucking middle-class education, man!" I surmise further that this is supposed to indicate that he isn't worth a shit, and that his songs are all fake street-graffiti. Which is fine by me: Joe Strummer is a fake. That only puts him in there with Dylan and Jagger and Townshend and most of the other great rock songwriters, because almost all of them in one way or another were fakes. Townshend had a middle-class education. Lou Reed went to Syracuse University before matriculating to the sidewalks of New York. Dylan faked his whole career; the only difference was that he used to be good at it and now he sucks.

The point is that, like Richard Hell says, rock 'n' roll is an arena in which you recreate yourself, and all this blathering about authenticity is just a bunch of crap. The Clash are authentic because their music carries such brutal conviction, not because they're Noble Savages.

Here's a note to CBS International: you can relax because I liked the Clash as people better than any other band I have ever met with the possible exception of Talking Heads, and their music it goes without saying is great. (I mean *you* think so, don't you? Good, then release their album in the U.S. So what if it gets zero radio play; *Clive* knew how to subsidize the arts.)

Here's a superlative for ads: "Best band in the UK!"—Lester Bangs. Here's another one: "Thanks for the wonderful vacation!"—Lester Bangs. (You know I love you, Ellie.) Okay, now that all that's out of the way, here we go. . . .

I was sitting in the British Airways terminal in New York City on the eve of my departure, reading *The War Against the Jews, 1933–1945* when I looked up just in time to see a crippled woman in a wheelchair a few feet away from me. My eyes snapped back down to my book in that shameful nervous reflex we know so well, but a moment later she had wheeled over to a couple of feet from where I was sitting, and when I could fight off the awareness of my embarrassment of her presence no longer I looked up again and we said hello to each other.

She was a very small person about thirty years old with a pretty face, blond hair and blazing blue eyes. She said that she had been on vacation in the States for three months and was now, ever so reluctantly, returning to England.

"I like the people in America so much better," she said. "Christ, it's so nice to be someplace where people recognize that you *exist*. In England, if you're handicapped no one will look at or speak to you except old people. And they just pat you on the head."

It is four days later, and I've driven from London to Derby with Ellie Smith from CBS and Clash manager Bernard Rhodes for the first of my projected three nights and two days with the band. I am not in the best of shape, since I've still got jet lag, have been averaging two or three hours' sleep a night since I got here, and the previous night was stranded in Aylesbury by the Stiff's Greatest Hits tour, hitching a ride back to London with a roadie in the course of which we were stopped by provincial police in search of dope and forced to empty all our pockets, something which had not happened to me since the hippie heydaze of 1967.

This morning when I went by Mick Farren's flat to pick up my bags he had told me, "You look like *Night of the Living Dead.*"

Nevertheless, I make sure after checking into the Derby Post House to hit the first night's gig, whatever my condition, in my most thoughtful camouflage. You see, the kind of reports we get over in the States about your punk rock scene had led me to expect seething audiences of rabid little miscreants out for blood at all costs, and naturally I figured the chances of getting a great story were better if I happened to get cannibalized. So I took off my black leather jacket and dressed as straight as I possibly could, the coup de grace (I thought) being a blue promotional sweater that said "Capitol Records" on the chest, by which I fantasized picking up some residual EMI-hostility from battle-feral Pistols fans. I should mention that I also decided not to get a haircut which I desperately needed before leaving the States, on the not-so-off chance of being mistaken for a hippie. When I came out of my room and Ellie and photographer Pennie Smith saw me, they laughed.

When I got to the gig I pushed my way down through the pogoing masses, right into the belly of the beast, and stood there through openers the Lous' and Richard Hell and the Voidoids' sets, waiting for the dog soldiers of anarch-apocalypse to slam my skull into my ankles under a new wave riptide.

Need I mention that nothing of the kind transpired?

Listen: if I were you I would take up arms and march on the media centers of Merrie Olde, *NME* included, and trash them beyond recognition. Because what I experienced, this first night and all subsequent on this tour, was so far from what we Americans've read in the papers and seen on TV that it amounts to a mass defamation of character, if not cultural genocide. Nobody gave a damn about my long hair, or could have cared less about some stupid sweater. Sure there was gob and beercups flung at/ the bands, and the mob was pushing sideways first right and then left, but I hate to disappoint anybody who hasn't been there but this scene is neither *Clockwork Orange* nor *Lord of the Flies*. When I got tired of the back-and-forth group shove I simply stuck my elbows out and a space formed around me.

What I am saying is that I have been at outdoor rock festivals in the hippie era in America where the vibes and violence were ten times worse than at any of the gigs I saw on this Clash tour, and the bands said later that this Derby engagement was the worst they had seen. What I am saying is that contrary to almost all reports published everywhere, I found British punks everywhere I went to be basically if not manifestly *gentle* people. *They are a bunch of nice boys and girls and don't let anybody (them included) tell you different.*

Yeah, they like to pogo. On the subject of this odd tribal rug-cut, of course the first thing I saw when I entered the hall was a couple of hundred little heads near the lip of the stage all bobbing up and down like anthropomorphized pistons in some Max Fleischer cartoon on the Industrial Revolution.

When I'd heard about pogoing before I thought it was the stupidest thing anybody'd ever told me about, but as soon as I saw it in living *sproing* it made perfect sense. I mean, it's obviously no more stupid than the Seconal idiot-dance popularized five years ago by Grand Funk audiences. In fact, it's sheer logic (if not poetry) in motion: when you're packed into a standing sweatshop with ten thousand other little bodies all mashed together, it stands to reason you can't dance in the traditional manner (i.e., sideways sway).

No, obviously if you wanna do the boogaloo to what the new breed say you gotta by dint of sheer population explosion shake your booty and your body in a *vertical* trajectory. Which won't be strictly rigid anyway, because this necessarily involves losing your footing every two seconds, the next step is falling earthward slightly sideways and becoming entangled with your neighbors, which is as good a way as any of making new friends if not copping a graze of tit.

There is, however, one other aspect of audience appreciation which ain't nearly so cute: gobbing. For some reason this qualifies as news to everybody, so I'm gonna serve notice right here and now: LISTEN YA LITTLE PINHEADS, IT'S NAUSEATING AND MORONIC, AND I DON'T MEAN GOOD MORONIC, I MEAN JERKED OFF, THE BANDS ALL HATE IT (the ones I talked to, anyway) AND WOULD ALL PLAY BETTER AND BE MUCH HAPPIER IF YOU FIGURED OUT SOME MORE ORIGINAL WAY OF SHOWING YOUR AP-PRECIATION.

(After the second night I asked Mick Jones about it and he looked like he was going to puke.

"But doesn't it add to the general atmosphere of chaos and anarchy?" I wondered.

"No," he said. "It's fucking disgusting.")

End of moral lecture. The Clash were a bit of a disappointment the first night. They played well, everything was in the right place, but the show seemed to lack energy somehow. A colleague who saw them a year ago had come back to the States telling me that they were the only group he'd ever seen onstage who were truly *wired*. It was this I was looking for and what I got in its place was mere professionalism, and hell, I could go let the Rolling Stones put me to sleep again if that was all I cared about.

Back up in the dressing room I cracked, "Duff gig, eh fellas?" and they laughed, but you could tell they didn't think it was funny. Later I found out that Joe Strummer had an abscessed tooth which had turned into glandular fever, and since the rest of the band draw their energy off him they were all suffering. By rights he should have taken a week off and headed straight for the nearest hospital, but he refused to cancel any gigs, no mere gesture of integrity.

A process of escalating admiration for this band had begun for me which was to continue until it broached something like awe. See, because it's easy to *sing* about your righteous politics, but as we all know actions speak louder than words, and the Clash are one of the very few examples

I've seen where they would rather set an example by their personal conduct than *talk* about it all day.

Case in point. When we got back to their hotel I had a couple of interesting lessons to learn. First thing was they went up to their rooms while Ellie, Pennie, a bunch of fans and I sat in the lobby. I began to make with the grouch squawks because if there's one thing I have learned to detest over the years it's sitting around some goddamn hotel lobby like a soggy douchebag parasite waiting for some lousy high-and-mighty rock 'n' roll band to *maybe deign* to put in an imperial appearance.

But then a few minutes later the Clash came down and joined us and I realized that unlike most of the bands I'd ever met they weren't stuck up, weren't on a star trip, were in fact genuinely interested in meeting and getting acquainted with their fans on a one-to-one, noncondescending level.

Mick Jones was especially sociable, so I moved in on him and commenced my second misinformed balls-up of the evening. A day or two earlier I'd asked a friend what sort of questions he thought might be appropriate for the Clash, and he'd said, "Oh, you might do what you did with Richard Hell and ask 'em just exactly what their political *program* is, what they intend to *do* once they get past all the bullshit rhetoric. Mind you, it's liable to get you thrown off the tour."

So, vainglorious as ever, I zeroed in on Mick and started drunkenly needling him with what I thought were devastating barbs. He just laughed at me and parried every one with a joke, while the fans chortled at the spectacle of this oafish American with all his dumbass sallies. Finally he looked me right in the eye and said, "Hey Lester: why are you asking *me* all these fucking questions?"

In a flash I realized that he was right. Here was I, a grown man, traveling all the way across the Atlantic Ocean and motoring up into the provinces of England, just to ask a goddamn rock 'n' roll band for the meaning of life! Some people never learn. I certainly didn't, because I immediately started in on him with my standard cultural-genocide rap: "Blah blah blah depersonalization blab blab blab solipsism blah blah yip yap etc. . . . "

"What in the fuck are you talking about?"

"Blah blab no one wants to have any emotions anymore blab blip human heart an endangered species blah blare cultural fascism blab blurb etc. etc. etc. . . . "

"Well," says Mick, "don't look at *me*. If it bothers you so much why don't *you* do something about it?"

"Yeah," says one of the fans, a young black punk girl sweet as could be, "you're depressing us *all!*"

Seventeen punk fan spike heads nod in agreement. Mick just keeps laughing at me.

Having bummed out almost the entire population of one room, I took my show into another: the bar, where I sat down at a table with Ellie and Paul Simonon and started in on them. Paul gets up and walks out. Ellie says, "Lester, you look a little tired. Are you sure you want another lager . . . ?"

Later I am out in the lobby with the rest of them again, in a state not far from walking coma, when Mick gestured at a teenage fan sitting there and said, "Lester, my room is full tonight; can Adrian stay with you?"

I finally freaked. Here I was, stuck in the middle of a dying nation with all these funny looking *children* who didn't even realize the world was coming to an end, and now on top of everything else they expected me to turn my room into a hippie crash pad! I surmised through all my confusion that some monstrous joke was being played on me, so I got testy about it, Mick repeated the request and finally I said that Adrian could *maybe* stay but he would have to go to the house phone, call my hotel and see if there was room. So the poor humiliated kid did just that while an embarrassed if not downright creepy silence fell over the room and Mick stared at me in shock, as if he had never seen this particular species of so-called human before.

Poor Adrian came back saying there was indeed room, so I grudgingly assented, and back to the hotel we went. The next morning when I was in a more sober if still jet-lagged frame of mind, he showed me a copy of his Clash fanzine, *48 Thrills,* which I bought for 20p, and in the course of breakfast conversation I learned that the Clash make a regular practice of inviting their fans back from the gigs with them, and then go so far as to let them sleep on the floors of their rooms.

Now, dear reader, I don't know how much time you may have actually spent around bigtime rock 'n' roll bands—you may not think so, but the less the luckier you are in most cases—but let me assure you that the way the Clash treat their fans falls so far outside the normal run of these things as to be outright revolutionary. I'm going to say it and I'm going to say it slow: most rockstars are goddamn pigs who have the usual burly corps of hired thugs to keep the fans away from them at all costs, excepting the usual select contingent of lucky (?) nubiles who they'll maybe deign to allow up to their rooms for the privilege of sucking on their coveted wangers, after which often as not they get pitched out into the streets to find their way home without even cabfare. The whole thing is sick to the marrow, and I simply could not believe that any band, especially one as *musically* brutal as the Clash, could depart so far from this fetid norm.

I mentioned it to Mick in the van that day en route to Cardiff, also by way of making some kind of amends for my own behavior: "Listen, man, I've just got to say that I really *respect* you . . . I mean, I had no idea that any group could be as good to its fans as this. . . . "

He just laughed. "Oh, so is that gonna be the hook for your story, then?"

And that for me is the essence of the Clash's greatness, over and beyond their music, why I fell in love with them, why it wasn't necessary to do any boring interviews with them about politics or the class system or any of that: because here at last is a band which not only preaches something good but practices it as well, that instead of talking about changes in social behavior puts the model of a truly egalitarian society into practice in their own conduct.

The fact that Mick would make a joke out of it only shows how far they're going towards the realization of all the hopes we ever had about rock 'n' roll as utopian dream—because if rock 'n' roll *is* truly the democratic artform, then the democracy has got to begin at home; that is, the everlasting and totally disgusting walls between artists and audience must come down, elitism must perish, the "stars" have got to be humanized, demythologized, and the audience has got to be treated with more respect. Otherwise it's all a shuck, a ripoff, and the music is as dead as the Stones' and Led Zep's has become.

It's no news by now that the reason most of rock's establishment have dried up creatively is that they've cut themselves off from the real world of everyday experience as exemplified by their fans. The ultimate question is how long a group like the Clash can continue to practice total egalitarianism in the face of mushrooming popularity. *Must* the walls go up inevitably, eventually, and if so when? Groups like the Grateful Dead have practiced this free-access principle at least in the past, but the Dead never had glamour which, whether they like it or not (and I'd bet money they do) the Clash are saddled with—I mean, not for nothing does Mick Jones resemble a young and already slightly dissipated Keith Richard—beside which the Dead aren't really a rock 'n' roll band and the Clash are nothing else but. And just like Mick said to me the first night, don't ask me why I obsessively look to rock 'n' roll bands for some kind of model for a better society . . . I guess it's just that I glimpsed something beautiful in a flashbulb moment once, and perhaps mistaking it for a prophecy have been seeking its fulfillment ever since. And perhaps that nothing else in the world ever seemed to hold even this much promise.

It may look like I make too much of all this. We could leave all significance at the picture of Mick Jones just a hot guitarist in a white jumpsuit and a rock 'n' roll kid on the road obviously having the time of his life and all political pretensions be damned, but still there is a mood around the Clash, call it whatever you want, that is positive in a way I've never sensed around almost any other band, and I've been around most of them. Something unpretentiously moral, and something both self-affirming and life-affirming—as opposed, say, to the simple ruthless hedonism and avarice of so many superstars, or the grim tautlipped monomaniacal ambition of most of the pretenders to their thrones.

But enough of all that. The highlight of the first day's bus ride occurred when I casually mentioned that I had a tape of the new Ramones album. The whole band practically leaped at my throat: "Why didn't you say so before? Shit, put it on *right now!*" So I did and in a moment they were bouncing all over the van to the strains of "Cretin Hop." *Rocket to Russia* thereafter became the soundtrack to the rest of my leg of the tour.

I am also glad to be able to tell everybody that the Clash are solid Muppets fans. (They even asked me if I had connections to get them on the show.) Their fave rave is Kermit, a pretty conventional choice if y'ask me—I'm a Fozzie Bear man myself. That night as we were walking into the hall for the gig in Cardiff, Paul said, "Hey, Lester, I just figured out why you like Fozzie Bear—the two of you look a lot alike!" And then he slaps me on the back.

All right, at this point I would like to say a few words about this Simonon fellow. Namely that HE LOOKS LIKE A MUPPET. I'm not sure which one, some kinda composite, but don't let that brooding visage in the photos fool you—this guy is a real clown. (Takes one to know one, after all.) He smokes a lot, and when he gets really out there on it makes with cartoon non sequiturs that nobody else can fathom (often having to do with manager Bernie), but stoned or not when he's talking to you and you're looking in that face you're staring right into a red-spiked big-eyed beaming cartoon, of whom it would probably not be amiss to say he lives for pranks. Onstage he's different; bouncing in and out of crouch, rarely smiling but in fact brooding over his fretboard ever in ominous motion, he takes on a distinctly simian aspect: the missing link, Cro-Magnon, Piltdown man, Cardiff giant.

It is undoubtedly this combination of mischievous boychild and Paleo-lithic primate which has sent swoonblips quavering through feminine hearts as disparate as Patti Smith and Caroline Coon—no doubt about it, Paul is the ladies' man of the group without half trying, and I doubt if there are very many gigs where he doesn't end up pogoing his pronger in some sweet honey's hive. Watch out, though, Paul—remember, clap doth not a Muppet befit.

The gig in Cardiff presents quite a contrast to Derby. It's at a college, and anybody who has ever served time in one of those dreary institutions of lower pedantry will know what manner of douse that portends. Once again the band delivers maybe 60% of what I know they're capable of, but with an audience like this there's no blaming them. I'm not saying that all college students are subhuman—I'm just saying that if you aim to spend a few years mastering the art of pomposity, these are places where you can be taught by undisputed experts.

Here at Cardiff about five people are pogoing, all male, while the rest of the student bodies stand around looking at them with practiced expressions of aloof amusement plastered on their mugs. After it's all over some cat goes back to interview Mick, and the most intelligent question he can think of is "What do you think of David Bowie?"

Meanwhile I got acquainted with the lead singer of the Lous, a good all-woman band from Paris. She says that she resents being thought of as a "woman musician," instead of a musician pure and simple, echoing a sentiment previously voiced to me by Talking Heads' Tina Weymouth. "It's a lot of bullshit," she says. I agree; what I don't say is that I am developing a definite carnal interest which I will be too shy to broach. I invite her back to our hotel; she says yes, then disappears.

When we get there it's the usual scene in the lobby, except that this time the management has thoughtfully set out sandwiches and beer. The beer goes down our gullets, and I'm just about to start putting the sand-wiches to the same purpose when I discover somebody has other ideas: a clot of bread and egg salad goes whizzing to *splat* right in the back of my head! I look around and confront a solid wall of innocent faces. So I take a bite and *wham!* another one.

In a minute sandwiches are flying everywhere, everybody's getting pelted, I'm wearing a slice of cabbage on my head and have just about accepted this level of chaos when I smell something burning.

"Hey, Lester," somebody says, "you shouldn't smoke so much!" I reach around to pat the back of my head and—some joker has set my hair on fire! I pivot in my seat and Paul is looking at me, giggling. "Simonon you fuckhead—" I begin, only to smell more smoke, look under my chair where there's a piece of eight-by-ten paper curling up in flames. Cursing at the top of my lungs, I leap up and get a chair on the other side of the table where my back's to no one and I can keep an eye on the red-domed Muppet. Only trouble is that I'll find out a day or so hence that it wasn't him set the fires at all: it was Bernie, the group's manager. Eventually the beer runs out, and Mick says he's hungry. Bernie refuses to let him take the van out hunting for open eateries, which we probably wouldn't be able to find at four A.M. in Cardiff anyway, and we all go to bed wearing egg salad.

Next morning sees us driving to Bristol, a large industrial city where we put up in a Holiday Inn, much to everyone's delight. By this time the mood around the band has combined with my tenacious jet-lag and liberal amounts of alcohol to put me into a kind of ecstasy state the like of which I have never known on the road before.

Past all the glory and the gigs themselves, touring in any form is a pretty drab and tiresome business, but with the Clash I feel that I have reapprehended that aforementioned glimpse of some Better World of infinite possibilities, and so, inspired and a little delirious, I forgo my usual nap between vantrip and showtime by which I'd hoped to eventually whip the jet-lag, spending the afternoon drinking cognac and writing.

By now I'm ready to go with the flow, with anything, as it has begun to seem to me, delusory or not, that there is some state of grace overlaying this whole project, something right in the soul that makes all the headache-inducing day-to-day pain-in-the-ass practical logistics run as smoothly as the tempers of the people involved, the whole enterprise sailing along in perfect harmony and in such dazzling contrast to the brutal logistics of Led Zep–type tours albeit on a much smaller level . . . somehow, whether it really is so or a simple basic healthiness on the part of all involved heightened by my mental state, I have begun to see this trip as somehow symbolic pilgrimage to that Promised Land that rock 'n' roll has cynically sneered at since the collapse of the sixties.

At this point, in my hotel room in Bristol, if six white horses and a chariot of gold had materialized in the hallway, I would have been no more surprised than at room service, would've just climbed right in and settled back for that long-promised ascent to endless astral weeks in the heavenly land.

What I got instead around six P.M. was a call from Joe Strummer saying meet him in the lobby in five minutes if I wanted to go to the sound check. So I floated down the elevators and when I got there I saw a sheepish group of little not-quite punks all huddled around one couch. They were dressed in half-committal punk regalia, a safety pin here and there, a couple of little slogans chalked on their school blazers, their hair greased and twisted up into a cosmetic weekend approximation of spikes. "Hey," I said, "you guys Clash fans?"

"Well," they mumbled, "sorta . . . "

"Well, whattaya mean? You're punks, aren't ya?"

"Well, we'd like to be . . . but we're *scared* . . . "

When Joe came down I took him aside and, indicating the poor little things, told him what they'd said, also asking if he wanted to get them into the gig with us and thus offer a little encouragement for them to take that next, last, crucial step out into full-fledged punk pariahdom and thus sorely needed self-respect.

"Forget it," he said. "If they haven't got the courage to do it on their own, I'm bloody well not gonna lead 'em on by the hand."

On the way to the sound check I mentioned that I thought the band hadn't been as good as I knew they could be the previous two nights, adding that I hadn't wanted to say anything about it.

"Why not?" he said.

I realized that I didn't have an answer. I tell this story to point out something about the Clash, and Joe Strummer in particular, that both impressed and showed me up for the sometimes hypocritical "diplomat" I can be. I mean their simple, straightforward honesty, their undogmatic insistence on the truth and why worry about stepping on people's toes because if we're not straight with each other we're never going to get anything accomplished anyway.

It seems like such a simple thing, and I suppose it is, but it runs contrary to almost everything the music business runs on: the hype, the grease, the glad-handing. And it goes a long way towards creating that aforementioned mood of positive clarity and unpeachy morality. Strummer himself, at once the "leader" of the group (though he'd deny it) and the least voluble (though his sickness might have had a lot to do with it), conveys an immediate physical and personal impact of ground-level directness and honesty, a no-bullshit concern with cutting straight to the heart of the matter in a way that is not brusque or impatient but concise and distinctly nonfrivolous.

Serious without being solemn, quiet without being remote or haughty,

Strummer offers a distinct contrast to Mick's voluble wit and twinkle of eye and Paul's loony toon playfulness. He is almost certainly the group's soul, and I wish I could say I had gotten to know him better.

From the instant we hit the hall for the sound check we all sense that tonight's gig is going to be a hot one. The place itself looks like an abandoned meatpacking room—large and empty with cold stone floors and stark white walls. It's plain dire, and in one of the most common of rock 'n' roll ironies the atmosphere is perfect and the acoustics great.

While the Clash are warming up at their sound check, they play something very funky which I later discover is a Booker T. number, thus implanting an idea in my mind which later grows into a conviction that in spite of the brilliance manifested in things like "White Riot," they actually play better and certainly more interestingly when they *slow down* and get, well, funky. You can hear it in the live if not studio version of "Police and Thieves," as well as in "(White Man) In Hammersmith Palais," probably the best thing they've written.

Somewhere in their assimilation of reggae is the closest thing yet to the lost chord, the missing link between black music and white noise, rock capable of making a bow to black forms without smearing on the blackface. It's there in Mick's intro to "Police and Thieves" and unstatedly in the band's whole onstage attitude. I understand why all these groups thought they had to play 120 miles per hour these last couple of years—to get us out of the bog created by everything that preceded them this decade—but the point has been made, and I for one could use a little funk, especially from somebody as good at it as the Clash. Why should any great rock 'n' roll band do what's *expected* of 'em anyhow? The Clash are a certain idea in many people's minds, which is only all the more reason why they should *break* that idea and broach something else. Just one critic's opinion y'understand but that's what god put us here for.

In any case, tonight is the payload. The band is taut terror from the instant they hit the stage, everything they're supposed to be and more. I reflect for the first time that I have never seen a band that *moved* like this: with most of 'em you can see the rockinroll steps choreographed five minutes in advance, but the Clash hop around each other in all configurations totally non-selfconsciously, galvanized by their music alone, Jones and Simonon changing places at the whims of the whams coming out of their guitars, springs in the soles of their tennies.

Strummer, obviously driven to make up to this audience the loss of energy suffered by the last two nights' crowds, is an angry live wire whipping around the middle of the front stage, divesting himself of guitar to fall on one knee in no Elvis parody but pure outside-of-self frenzy, snarling through his shattered dental bombsite with face screwed up in all the rage you'd ever need to convince you of the Clash's authenticity, a desperation uncontrived, unstaged, a fury unleashed on the stage and writhing in upon itself in real pain that connects with the nerves of the audience like summer thunderbolts, and at this time pogoing reveals itself as such a pitifully insufficient response to a man by all appearances trapped and screaming, and it's not your class system, it's not Britain-on-the-wane, it's not even glandular fever, it's the cage of life itself and all the anguish to break through which sometimes translates as flash or something equally petty but in any case is rock 'n' roll's burning marrow.

It was one of those performances for which all the serviceable critical terms like "electrifying" are so pathetically inadequate, and after it was over I realized the futility of hitting Strummer for that interview I kept putting off on the "politics" of the situation. The politics of rock 'n' roll, in England or America or anywhere else, is that a whole lot of kids want to be fried out of their skins by the most scalding propulsion they can find, for a night they can pretend is the rest of their lives, and whether the next day they go back to work in shops or boredom on the dole or American TV doldrums in Mom 'n' Daddy's living room nothing can cancel the reality of that night in the revivifying flames when for once if only then in your life you were blasted outside of yourself and the monotony which defines most life anywhere at any time, when you supped on lightning and nothing else in the realms of the living or dead mattered at all.

PART TWO

Back at the hotel everybody decides to reconvene in the Holiday Inn's bar to celebrate this back-in-form gig. I stop off by my room and while sitting on the john start reading an article in *Newsweek* called "Is America Turning Right?" (Ans: yes.) It's so strange to be out here in the middle of a foreign land, reading about your own country and realizing how at home you feel where you have come, how much your homeland is the foreign, alien realm.

This feeling weighed on me more and more heavily the longer I stayed in England—on previous visits I'd always been anxious to get back to the States, and New York homesickness has become a congenital disease whenever I travel. But I have felt for so long that there is something dead, rotten and cold in American culture, not just in the music but in the society at every level down to formularized stasis and entropy, and the supreme irony is that all I ever read in *NME* is how fucked up life is for you guys, when to me your desperation seems like health and my country's pabulum complacency seems like death.

I mean, at least you got some stakes to play for. *Our* National Front has already won, insidiously invisible as a wall socket. The difference is that for you No Future means being thrown on the slagheap of economic refuse, for me it means an infinity of television mirrors that tell the most hideous lies lapped up by my nation of technocratic Trilbys. A little taste of death in every mass inoculation against the bacteria of doubt.

But then I peeked behind the shower curtain: Marisa Berenson was there. "I've got films of you shitting," I said.

"So what?" she said. "I just sold the negatives to WPLJ for their next TV ad. They're gonna have it in neon laserium. I'll be *immortal.*"

I mean, would you wanna be a ball bearing? That's how all the television families feel and that's how I feel when I go to discos, places where people *cultivate* their ballbearingness. In America, that is. So what did I go down into now but the Bristol (remember Bristol?) Holiday Inn's idea of a real swinging disco where vacationing Americanskis could feel at home. I felt like climbing right up the walls, but there were girls there, and the band seemed amused and unfeared of venturing within the witches' cauldron of disco ionization which is genocide in my book, buddy, but then us Americans do have a tendency to take things a bit far.

This club reminded me of everything I was hosannah-glad to escape when I left New York: flashing dance floors, machine music at ballpeen volumes, lights aflash that it's all whole bulb orgone bolloxed FUN FUN FUN blinker city kids till daddy takes the console away. I begin to evince overt hostility: grinding of teeth, hissing of breath, balling and banging of fists off fake naugahyde. Fat lot of good it'll do ya, kid. Discotheques are concentration camps, like Pleasure Island in Walt Disney's *Pinocchio.* You play that goddam Baccara record one more time, Dad, your nose is gonna grow and we're gonna saw it off into toothpicks.

I'm seething in barely suppressed rage when Glen Matlock, a puckish pup with more than a hint of wry in his eye, leans across the lucite teentall flashlight piña colada table and says, "Hey, wanna hear an advance tape of the Rich Kids album?"

"Sure!" You can see immediately why Glen got kicked out of the Pistols: I wouldn't trust one of these cleanpop whiz kids with a hot lead pole. But I would tell 'em to say hello. I don't give a shit for the Raspberries and Glen looks an awful lot like Eric Carmen—except I can't help gotta say it not such a *sissy*—and it's all Paul McCartney's fault anyway, and I mean McCartney ca. Beatles wonderwaxings we all waned and wuvved so well, but in spite of all gurgling bloody messes we're just gonna have to keep on dealing with these emissaries from the land of Bide-a-Wee and His Imperial Pop the Magic Dragon, besides which I'd just danced to James Brown and needed some Coppertone oil and Band-Aids.

Let's see, how else can I insult this guy, shamepug rippin' off the galvanic force of our PUNK flotilla with his courtly gestures in the lateral of melody, harmonies, Hollies, all those lies? So he puts it on his tape deck and it's the old Neil Diamond–penned Monkees toon, "I'm a Believer."

"Hey!" I said. "That's fuckin' *good!* That's *great!* You gotta helluva band there! Better than the original!"

Ol' Puck he just keeps sitting back sipping his drink, laughing at me through lighthouse teeth. Has this tad heard "Muskrat Love"?

"Whattaya *laughin'* at?" I quack. "I'm *serious.* Glen, anybody that can cut the Monkees at their own riffs is okay in my book!"

Then the next song comes on. It's also a Monkees toon. "Hey, what is this—you gonna make your first album 'The Monkees' Greatest Hits'?"

Well, I know I'm not the world's fastest human . . . from the time it was released until about six months ago I thought Brian Wilson was singing "She's giving me *citations*" (instead of the factual "excitations") in "Good Vibrations," I thought the song was about a policewoman he fell in love with or something. So far as I'm concerned the Rich Kids SHOULD make their first album (call it this too, beats *Never Mind the Bollocks* by miles) "The Monkees' Greatest Hits." *I'd* buy it. *Everybody'd* buy it. Not only that, you could count on all the rock critics in *NME* to write lengthy analyses of the conceptual quagmire behind this whole helpful heaping scamful—I mean, let's see Malcolm top that one. Come to think of it, the coolest thing the Pistols could have done when they finally got around to releasing their album would be to've called it "Eric Clapton." Who cares how much it helps sales, think of the *important* part: the *insult.* Plus a nice surprise for subscribers to *Guitar Player* magazine, would-be closet hearthside Holmstrummed Djangos, etc. *They* don't want a baby that looks like that, even if its last name is Gibson. Les Paul, where are you? Gone skateboarding, I guess.

With Dick Dale.

Oh yeah, the Clash. Well, closing time came along as it always has a habit of doing at obscenely punescent hours in England—I mean, what is this eleven o'clock shit anyway? Anarchy for me means the bars stay open twenty-four hours a day. Hmmm, guess that makes Vegas the model of Anarchic Society. Okay, Malcolm, Bernie, whoever else manages all those like snorkers and droners all over the place, it's uproots lock stock and barrel time, drop the whole mess right in the middle of Caesar's Palace, and since Johnny Rotten is obviously a hell of a lot smarter than Hunter S. Thompson we got ourselves a whole new American Dream here. No, guess it wouldn't work, bands on the dole can't afford anything past the slot machines, cancel that one. We go up to Mick's room for beer and talk instead.

He's elated and funny though somewhat subdued. I remark that I haven't seen any groupies on this tour and ask him if he ever hies any of the little local honeys up to bed and if so why not tonite?

Mick looks more tired, more wasted than he actually is (contrary to his git-pikkin hero, he eschews most all forms of drugs most all of the time) (whole damn healthy bunch, this—not a bent-spoon man or parlous freaksche in the lot). "We don't get into all of that much. You saw those girls out there—most of 'em are too young." (Quite true, more later.) "But groupies . . . I dunno, just never see that many I guess. I've got a girlfriend I get to see about once a month, but other than that . . . " he shrugs, "when you're playin' this much, you don't need it so much. Sometimes I feel like I'm losin' interest in sex entirely.

"Don't get me wrong. We're a band of regular blokes. It's just that a lot of that stuff you're talking about doesn't seem to . . . apply."

See, didn't I tell you it was the Heavenly Land? The Clash are not only not sexist, they are so healthy they don't even have to *tell* you how unsexist they are; no sanctimony, no phonies, just ponies and miles and miles of green Welsh grass with balls bouncing. . . .

Now I will repeat myself from part one that THIS is exactly and precisely what I mean by Clash = model for New Society: a society of *normal* people, by which I mean that we are surrounded by queers, and I am not talking about gay people. I'm talking about . . . well, when lambs draw breathin Albion with Sesame Street Crayolas, we won't see no lovers runnin' each other's bodies down, get me. I mean fuck this and fuck that, but make love when the tides are right and I *do* want a baby that looks like that. And so, secretly smiling across the rain, does William Blake.

Next day was a long drive southwest. Actually this being Sunday and my three days *assignment* up I'm sposed to go back to London, but previous eventide when I'd told Mick this he'd asked me to stick around and damned if I didn't—a first for me. Usually you just wanna get home, get the story out and head beerward.

But as y'all can see my feelings about the Clash had long ago gotten way beyond all the professional malarkey, we liked hanging out together. Besides which I still kept a spyglass out for that Promised Land's colors so sure to come a-blowin' around every fresh hillock curve, hey there moocow say hello to James Joyce for me, gnarly carcasses of trees the day before had set to mind the voices Under Milk Wood . . . land rife with ghosts who don't come croonin' around no Post Houses way past midnite with Automatic Slim and Razor-Totin' Jim, no, the reality is you could be touring Atlantis and it'd still look like motorway::carpark::gasstop::pissbreak::souvenir shop::et deadening ectera . . .

Joe kills the dull van hours with Nazitrocity thrillers by Sven Hassel, Mick is just about to start reading Kerouac's *The Subterraneans* but borrows my copy of Charles Bukowski's new book *Love Is a Dog from Hell* instead which flips him out so next two days he keeps passing it around the van trying to get the other guys to read certain poems like the one about the poet who came onstage to read and vomited in the grand piano instead (and woulda done it again too) but they seem unimpressed, Joe wrapped up in his stormtroopers and Paul spliffing in bigeyed space monkey glee playing the new Ramones over and over and every time Joey shouts "LOBOTOMAAY!!" at the top of side two he pops a top out of somebody's head, the pogo beginning to make like spirogyra, sprintillatin' all over the place, tho it's true there's no stoppin' the cretins from hoppin' once they start they're like *germs* that jump. Meanwhile poor little Nicky Headon the drummer who I won't get to know really well this trip is bundling jacket tighter in the front seat and swigging cough mixture in unsuccessful attempt to ward off miserable bronchoid. At one point Mickey, the driver, a big thick-necked lug with a skinhead haircut, lets Nicky take the wheel and we go skittering all over the road.

Golly gee, you must get bored reading such stuff. Did you know that this toot is costing IPC (who for all I know put out not just *NME* but also a you're-still-alive monthly newsletter for retired rear admirals of the Guianan Fleet) seven and a half cents a word? An equitable deal, you might assert, until you consider that in this scheme of things, such diverse organisms as "salicylaceous" and "uh" receive equal recompense, talk about your class systems or lack of same. NOW you know why 99% of all publicly printed writers are hacks, because clichés pay as good as pearls, although there is a certain unalloyed ineluctable Ramonesquelike logic to the way these endless reams of copy just plow on thru and thru all these crappy music papers like one thickplug pencil's line piledriving from here on out to Heaven.

I mean look, face it, both reader and writer know that almost all of what's gonna pass from the latter to the former is justa buncha jizjaz anyway, so why not just give up the ghost of pretense to form and subject and just make these rags ramble fit to the trolley you prob'ly read 'em on . . . you may say that I take liberties, and you are right, but I will have done my good deed for the day if I can make you see that the whole point is YOU SHOULD BE TAKING LIBERTIES TOO. Nothing is inscribed so deep in the earth a little eyewash won't uproot it, that's the whole point of the so-called "new wave"—to REINVENT YOURSELF AND EVERYTHING AROUND YOU CONSTANTLY, especially since all of it is already the other thing anyway, the Clash a broadside a pamphlet an urgent handbill in a taut and moving fist, *NME* staff having advertised themselves a rock 'n' roll band for so many years nobody can deny 'em now, as you are writing history that I read, as you are he as I am we as weasels all together, Jesus am I turning into Steve Hillage or David Allen, over the falls in any case but at least we melted the walls leaving home plate clear for baseball in the snow.

Are you an imbecile? If so, apply today for free gardening stamp books at the tubestop of your choice. Think of the promising career that may be passing you by *at this very moment* like a Greyhound. Nobody loves a poorhouse Nazi. Dogs are more alert than most clerks.

Plan 9: In America there is such a crying need for computer operators they actually put ads on commercial TV begging people to sign up. British youth are massively unemployed. Relocate the entire under-twenty-five population of Britain to training centers in New Jersey and Massachusetts. Teach them all to tap out codes. Give them lots of speed and let them play with their computers night and day. Then put them on TV smiling with pinball eyes: "Hi! I used to be a lazy sod! But then I discovered COMPUTROCIDE DYNAMICS, INC., and it's changed my life completely! I'm happy! I'm useful! I walk, talk, dress and act normal! I'm an up and coming go getter in a happening industry! Good Christ, Mabel, I've got a *job.*" He begins to bawl maudlinly, drooling and dribbling sentimental mucus out his nose. "And to think . . . that only two months ago I was stuck back in *England* . . . unemployed, unemployable, no prospects, no respect, a worthless hunk of human shit! Thank you, Uncle Sam!"

So don't go tellin' me you're bored with the U.S.A., buddy. I've heard all that shit one too many pinko punko times. We'll just drink us these two more beers and then go find a bar where you know everybody is drinkin' beer they bought with money they owned by the sweat of their brows, from *workin'*, get me, buddy? 'Cause I got a right to work. Niggers got a right to work, too. Same as white men. When your nose is pushin' up grindstone you got no time to worry about the size of the other guy's snout. Because you know, like I know, like both the Vienna Boys Choir and the guy who sells hot watches at Sixth Avenue and 14th St. know, that we were born for one purpose and one purpose only: TO WORK. *Haul* that slag! Hog that slod! Whelp that mute and look at us: at our uncontestable NOBILITY; at our national biological PRIDE; at our stolid steroid HOPE.

Who says it's a big old complicated world? I'll tell ya what it comes down to, buddy: one word: JOB. You got one, you're okay, scot free, a prince in fact in your own hard-won domain! You don't got one, you're a miserable slug and a drag on this great nation's economically rusting drainpipes. You might just as well go drown yourself in mud. We need the water to conserve for honest upright workin' folks! Folks with the godsod sense to treat that job like GOLD. 'Cause that's just what it stands for and WHY ELSE DO YOU THINK I KEEP TELLING YOU IT'S THE MOST IMPORTANT THING IN THE UNIVERSE? Your ticket to human citizenship.

One man, one job. One dog, one stool.

The hotel has a lobby and coffeeshop which look out upon a body of water. No one can figure out whether it's the English Channel or not. Even the waitresses don't know. I'm feeling good, having slept in the afternoon, and there's a sense in the air that everybody's up for the gig. Last night consolidated energies; tonight should be the payload.

We wind through narrow streets to a small club that reminds me much of the slightly sleazy little joints where bands like the Iron Butterfly and Strawberry Alarm Clock, uh, got their *chops* together, or, uh, paid whatever *dues* were expected of them when they were coming up and I was in school. This type of place you can write the script before you get off the bus; manager a fat middle-aged brute who glowers over waitresses and rock bands equally, hates the music, hates the kids but figures there's money to be made. The decor inside is ersatz-tropicana, suggesting that this place has not so long ago been put to uses far removed from punk rock. Enrico Cadillac vibes.

I walk in the dressing room which actually is not a dressing room but a minuscule space partitioned off where three bands are supposed to set up, almost literally on top of one another. The Voidoids' Bob Quine walks in, takes a look and lays his guitar case on the floor: "Guess this is it."

Neither of the opening acts has been getting the audience response they deserve on this tour. These are Clash audiences, people who know all their songs by heart, have never heard of the Lous and maybe are vaguely familiar with Richard Hell. Richard is depressed because his band isn't getting the support he hoped for from their record company on this trek. The *Blank Generation* album hasn't been released yet—the Voidoids think it's because Sire wants to flog a few more import copies, although I hear later in the week that strikes have shut down all the record pressing plants in Britain. The result is that the kids in the audience don't know most of the songs, the lyrics, nothing but that Ork/Stiff EP to go on, so they settle for gobbing on the band, screaming for the Clash.

I tell Hell and Quine that I have never heard the band so tight, which is true—there's just no way that night-after-night playing, in no matter how degraded circumstances, can't put more gristle and fire in your music. Interestingly enough, Ivan Julian and Marc Bell, Hell's second guitarist and drummer, are both in good spirits—they've toured before, know what to expect.

Someday Quine will be recognized for the pivotal figure that he is on his instrument—he is the first guitarist to take the breakthroughs of early Lou Reed and James Williamson and work through them to a new, individual vocabulary, driven into odd places by obsessive attention to *On the Corner*–era Miles Davis. Of course I'm prejudiced, because he played on my record as well, but he is one of the few guitarists I know who can handle the supertechnology that is threatening to swallow players and instruments whole—"You gotta hear this new box I got," is how he'll usually preface his latest discovery, "it creates the most *offensive noise . . .*"—without losing contact with his musical emotions in the process. Onstage he projects the cool remote stance learned from his jazz mentors—shades, beard, expressionless face, bald head, old sportcoat—but his solos always burn, the more so because there is always something constricted in them, pent up, waiting to be released.

Tonight's crowd is good—they respond instinctively to the Voidoids though they're unfamiliar with them, and it doesn't seem at all odd to see kids pogoing to Quine's Miles Davis riffs. (He steals from *Agharta*! And makes it *work!*) Hell and the Voidoids get the only encore on my leg of the tour, and they make good use of it, bringing Glen Matlock out to play bass. The Clash's set is brisk, hot, clean—consensus among us fellow travelers is that it's solid but lacks the cutting vengeance of last night.

Even on a small stage—and this one is tiny—the group are in constant motion, snapping in and out of one another's territory with electrified sprints and lunges that have their own grace, nobody knocking knees or bumping shoulders, even as the Voidoids in certain states which they hate and I think among their best reel and spin in hair's-breadth near-collisions with each other that are totally graceless but supremely driven. You can really see why Tom Verlaine wanted Hell out of Television—he flings himself all over the stage as if battering furiously at the gates of some bolted haven, and if Ivan and Bob know when to dodge you can also see plainly why Hell would have been in a group called the Heartbreakers—because that sumbitch is hard as oak, and he's just looking for the proper axe because something inside seethes poisonously to be let out.

In the dressing room I met some fans. There was Martin, who was fourteen and had a band of his own called Crissus. I thought Martin was a girl until I heard his name (no offense, Martin), but look at it this way: here, on some remote southern shore of the old Isle, this kid who is just entering puberty, this *child,* has been so inspired by the New Wave that he is already starting to make his move. I asked him whether Crissus had recorded yet, and he laughed: "Are you kidding?"

"Why not? Everybody else is." (Not said cynically either.)

I asked Martin what he liked about the Clash in particular as opposed to other New Wave bands. His reply: "Their total physical and psychic resistance to the fascist imperialist enemies of the people at all levels, and their understanding of the distinction between art and propaganda. They know that the propaganda has to be palatable to the People if they're going to be able to (a) listen to it, (b) understand it, and (c) react to it, rising in People's War. They recognize that the form must be as revolutionary as the content—in Cuba they did it with radio and ice cream and baseball and boxing, with the understanding that sports and music are the most effective vectors for communist ideology. Rock 'n' roll as a form is anarchistic, but if we could just figure out some way to make the *content* as compelling as the form *then* we'd be getting somewhere!

"For the present, we must recognize that there is only so much revolutionary information that can be transmitted in so circumscribed a space and time, and so we must be content in the knowledge that the potency of form ensures the efficacy of content, that is, that the driving primitive African beat and boarlike guitars will keep bringing the audience back for repeated hypnotized listenings until the revolutionary message laid out plainly in the lyrics cannot help but sink in!"

Martin was bright for his age. Not quite as bright as all that, though.

Or maybe brighter. Because of course he didn't say that. I made that up. What Martin said was, "I like the Clash because of their clothes!"

And so it went with all the other fans I interviewed over the six nights I saw them. *Nobody* mentioned politics, not even the dole, and I certainly wasn't going to start giving them cues. This night, I got such typical response as: "Their sound—I dunno, it just makes you jump!" "The music, which is exciting, and the lyrics, which are heavy, and the way they look onstage!" (which is stripped down to zippers and denims for instant combat, or perhaps stage flexibility).

As we were all still wandering out, Mick in the middle of a cluster of fans as usual, not soaking up adoration but genuinely interested in getting to know them, about halfway between bandstand and door, the owner of the club began making noises about "bleeding punk rockers—try to have a decent club, they come in here and mess it up—"

Mick looked at him indifferently. "Bollocks."

"Look, you lot, clear out now, we don't want your kind hanging round here," and of course he had his little oaf militia to hustle them toward the exits. Finally I said to him, "If you dislike them so much, why don't you open a different kind of club?"

Instantly he was up against me, belly and breath and menace: "Wot're you lookin' for, some trouble, then?"

"No, I just asked you a question."

You know, it's like all the other similar scenes you've ever seen all your life—YOU REALLY DON'T WANT TO GET INTO SOME KIND OF STUPID VIOLENCE WITH THESE PEOPLE, but you finally just get tired of being herded like swine.

When we got out front a few Teds showed up—first I'd seen in England, really, and I had the impulse to go gladhanding up to them every inch the Yankee tourist gawker dodo: "Hey, you're *Teds,* aren't you? I've heard about you guys! You don't like anything after Gene Vincent! Man, you guys are one bunch of stubborn motherfuckers!"

I didn't do that, though—I looked at Mick and the fans, and they looked wary, staring at indistinct spots like you do when you scent violence in the air and don't want it. They were treading lightly. But then, outside of certain scenes with each other, almost all the punks I've *ever* seen tread lightly! They're worse than hippies! More like beatniks.

But what was really funny was that the Teds were treading lightly too—they just sort of shuffled up with their dates, in their ruffled shirts and velour jackets and started muttering generalities: "Bleedin' punks . . . shit . . . buncha bloody freaks . . . " Really, you had to strain to hear them. They seemed almost embarrassed. It was like they had to do it.

I had never seen anything quite like it in the U.S., because aside from certain ethnic urban gangs, there is nothing in the U.S. quite like the Teds-Punks thing. We've got bikers, but even bikers claim contemporaneity. The Teds seem as sad as the punks seemed touching and oddly inspiring—these people know that time has passed them by, and they are not entirely wrong when they assert that it's time's defect and not their own. They remember one fine moment in their lives when everything—music, sex, dreams—seemed to coalesce, when they could tell everybody trying to strap them to the ironing board to get fucked and know in their bones that they were right. But that moment passed, and they got scared, just like kids in the U.S. are mostly scared of New Wave, just like people I know who freak out when I put on Miles Davis records and beg me to take them off because there is something in them so emotionally huge and threatening that it's plain "depressing."

The Teds were poignant for me, even more so because their style of dress made them as absurd to us as we were to them (but in a different way—they look "quaint," a very final dismissal). They looked like people who had had a glimpse and were supping at the dry bone of that memory forever, but man, that glimpse, just *try* to take it away from me, punk motherfucker. . . . Not that the punks are trying to infringe on the Teds; just that unlike the punks, who pay socially for their stance but at least have the arrogance of their freshness, the Teds looked like people backed into a final corner by a society which simply can't accept anybody getting loose.

In America you can ease into middle age with the accoutrements of adolescence still prominent and suffer relatively minor embarrassment: okay, so the guy's still got his sideburns and rod and beer and beergut and wife and three kids and a duplex and never grew up. So what? You're not supposed to grow up in America. You're supposed to consume. But in Britain it seems there is some ideal, no, some dry river one is expected to ford, so you can enter that sedate bubble where you raise a family, contribute in your small way to your society and keep your mouth shut. Until you get old, that is, when you can become an "eccentric"—do and say outrageous things, naughty things, because it's expected of you, you've crossed to the other mirror of the telescope of childhood.

In between, it looks like quiet desperation all the way to an outsider.

All that stiff-upper-lip, carry-on shit. If Freud was right when he said that all societies are based on repression, then England must be the apex of Western civilization. There was a recently published conversation between Tennessee Williams and William Burroughs, in which Burroughs said he didn't like the English because their social graces had evolved to a point where they could be entertaining all evening for the rest of their lives but nobody ever told you anything personal, anything *real* about themselves. I think he's right. We've got the opposite problem in America right now —in New York City today there's a TV talk show host who's so narcissistic that every Wednesday he lays down on a couch and pours out his insecurities to his analyst . . . *on the air!*

You guys strike me as a whole lot of people who laugh at the wrong time, who constantly study the art of concealment. Then again, it occurs to me that it could actually be that there is something irritating me that you don't suffer from—which is certainly not meant as self-aggrandizement on my part—but that you've been around awhile, have come to wry terms with your indigenous diseases, whereas we Americans got bugs under our skin that make us all twitch in Nervous Norvusisms that must amuse you highly. But even here there is a difference—at our best we recognize our sickness, and struggle constantly to deal with it. You're real big on sweeping the dirt under the carpet. So it's no wonder that, like Johnny Rotten says, you've got "problems"—more like boils bursting, I'd say.

And now, as I get ready to close off, I feel uncomfortably pompous and smug—I'll be back with the payoff next week, the sum of what I see in this whole "punk" movement, for anybody who wants to hear it—but here I sit on what feels like a sweeping and enormously presumptuous generalization on not just the punks but your whole country.

Well, then, let the fool make a fool out of himself, but I'll tell you one thing: the Teds are a hell of a symptom of the rot in your society, much more telling in their way than the punks, because the punks, much as they go on about boredom and no future, at least offer possibilities, whereas the Teds are landlocked. You cocksuckers have effectively enclosed these people, who are only trying to not give up some of their original passion in the interests of total homogenization, in an invisible concentration camp. Your contempt stymies them, so they strike out at the only people who are more vulnerable and passive than they are: the punks.

The almost saintly thing about the punks is that for the most part they don't seem to find it necessary to strike out with that sort of viciousness against anybody—except themselves.

So to anyone who is reading this who is in a position of "status," "responsibility," "power," unlike the average *NME* reader, I say congratulations—you've created a society of cannibals and suicides.

PART THREE

> Recent history is the record of the vast conspiracy to impose one level of mechanical consciousness on mankind and exterminate all manifestations of that unique part of human sentience   which the individual shares with his Creator. The suppression of contemplative individuality is near complete.
>
> The only immediate historical data that we can know and act on are those fed to our senses through systems of mass communication.
>
> These media are exactly the places where the deepest and most personal sensitivities and confessions of reality are most prohibited, mocked, suppressed. . . .
>
> A few individuals, poets, have had the luck and courage and fate to glimpse something new through the crack in mass consciousness . . . the police and newspapers have moved in, mad movie manufacturers from Hollywood are at this moment preparing bestial stereotypes of the scene. . . .
>
> How many hypocrites are there in America? How many trembling lambs, fearful of discovery? What authority have we set up over ourselves, that we are not as we Are?
>
> —Allen Ginsberg, "Poetry, Violence, and the Trembling Lambs"

We're still standing around in front of the club, and Mick Jones and I have been talking to three fans who've hitchhiked from Dover for the gig. They're invited back to the hotel in the more or less loose way these things happen, and Mick looks at me: "Lester, can you put them up in your room tonight?"

It's two girls and a guy and my room is small but they're nice and the conversation's been good so far so I say sure if they don't mind sleeping on the floor. We all climb in the van and immediately Mickey, the driver, begins to bitch about having to carry extra people.

He's not the most sanguine guy in the world but it's been a long drive from Bristol and cats like him got no stage to let it out on. So I try to mollify him a bit, telling him he's like Neal Cassady (because on those long stretches of motorway he is).

"Yeah," he snaps. "I'm drivin' a *star!*"

When we get back to the hotel the surliness escalates. I'm wandering around the lobby trying to locate some beer, so I miss the first part of the trouble. The fans, Mickey the driver, Mick's friend and traveling companion Robin, Paul Simonon and Nicky Headon sitting there, and the sandwiches are flying as usual, so at first I don't notice what's going on. But when I sit down in my chair I realize that most of the sandwiches are being thrown by Mickey and Robin at the male fan.

I look around at the fan, who seems to be wearing bits of tomato, egg, lettuce, mayonnaise and bread all over his body, is shrinking back in his chair in the most abject humiliation. Confused, I hand him a beer and tell him it's all right.

Mickey: "It is *not* all right!" He leaps up and runs across to us, pummeling the fan with his fists. The kid tries to roll up into a ball. A moment later Robin is over; first he grinds the remainder of the sandwich glop all in the kid's hair and clothes, then he's grabbed a cushion off one of the chairs and is smothering his face in it. Finally everybody sits down, and an ugly silence falls.

I don't want to get my face punched in, but finally I've got to say something. I look at Mickey, speaking calmly. "Why are you acting like such an asshole?"

"What's an asshole?" he demands.

"There are all kinds," I say. "You just know one when you see one."

"That little fucker fucked up my jacket!"

He indicates a small stain on his windbreaker.

"So what?" I say. "If you're gonna start throwing sandwiches you've gotta expect stuff like that."

"We didn't start it—*he* did," says Mickey.

"Oh," I say, knowing full well it's a lie.

Another even nastier silence. Finally I say, "Well, I'm sorry about your jacket. You must value it a lot."

"Fucking right I do."

"Would you have punched one of them if they'd stained it?" I ask, indicating Paul and Nicky, who are still sitting there in silence.

"Yeah." Then he starts in on me, verbally, trying to incite whatever he can. I won't bore you with the details.

After a few minutes, Robin stands up and asks me if I want to go up to Mick's room. After everything that has just happened, I can sit there and say, "Yeah, that sounds pretty good." I look at Liz, one of the girl fans.

"Wanna go up and see Mick?"

"No," she says.

So the three fans and I head for the elevator to my room. Somehow, only when we get there does the full sense of the scene just past hit me. "I guess they're hypocrites, aren't they?" says the kid with food smeared all over him. The girls are incensed. It won't be until tomorrow that it occurs to me that I've been reading *The War Against the Jews*, trying to figure out how a whole nation could stand by and let atrocities happen, yet I sit there somehow *refusing to perceive* for several minutes that someone sitting right next to me was being verbally abused and physically brutalized for no reason at all.

By the time we get up to my room the kid is already making excuses for the Clash. "I'm not mad at anybody," he's saying. "It's not the band's fault."

By this time I'm seething. "What do you mean? They sat right there and let it happen! I sat right there and let it happen! What gives anybody the right to do shit like that to you?"

I curse myself again and again for not having acted. Because now I'm sitting in my room, heart pounding, nerves which I've pushed to the breaking point by not pacing myself on this tour twitching, uptight and itching to smash somebody in the face. I realize that that *goon* down there has only infected me with his own poison, but there is nothing I can do about it except try vainly to cool out.

The girls are enraged at the Clash, the kid is slowly admitting to his own anger past utter mortification, and we keep hashing it over and over until we realize that's not going to do us any good. So the conversation turns to other things. The kid works in a hotel in Torquay, a really swanky place, and regales us with stories of some of the foibles and antics of famous guests such as Henry Kissinger and Frank Sinatra. He tells us what pigs most of the big-name rock groups that have stayed there are. The only guests who are worse than the rock stars, he says, are the Arabs. When the rock stars leave, the rooms are decimated; when the Arabs leave, they're decimated and full of bullet holes. Which of course brings us right back to tonight's incident.

"What they don't realize," he says, "is that when they throw food all around like that, it's somebody like me who's got to get down on his hands and knees and clean it up."

Which means somebody like the Clash themselves. I suppose I'm going to seem very moralistic about this, and I don't mean for this incident to dominate this story, but if I close my eyes it will not go away.

I recall the first time I read about the Clash, the cover story *NME* ran last spring, being a little surprised when it was said that on their first tour they were (already?) tearing up hotel rooms. I mean even then it struck you a bit odd, coming atop all their righteous rhetoric. If somebody screws around with you, fine, smash 'em back if you want. But random destruction is so . . . *asinine*. And so redolent of self-hate.

I suppose there's no basic difference between the Clash trashing hotels and their fans leaving beermug shards all over concert-hall floors, it's all just the product of frustration and who cares. But some things you just gotta see as a package deal. Meaning that the nature of any enterprise at all levels is defined by what's coming down from the top. What's at the top with most of the big rock groups is diseased, so their whole operation reflects the sickness, down to the employment of brutal thugs to keep the fans away from them in the name of "security" (whose?). What's at the top in the Clash organization seems so basically good, moral, principled, it's no wonder that except for this incident everything has seemed to run smoothly on this tour, everybody has seemed so happy.

When Led Zeppelin or the Stones tour everybody's got to suffer to compensate for indulgence of the big babies at the top, so all kinds of minor functionaries and innocent bystanders can get ground into shit. But even Led Zeppelin don't invite their fans back to the hotel *and then* beat them up.

At about four A.M. one of the girls said to the boy fan, "Looks like you've got a shiner." You could begin to see the discoloration in his right eye. By the time they left, it would have turned into a purple lump half an inch thick and the width of a shilling.

I sat up all night with them, getting to know them in that transient, pleasant intimacy common to travelers. We exchanged addresses and warm goodbyes and they left to hitchhike back to Dover in a mild drizzle around 7:30 A.M. The scene with Mickey had left me too wound up to sleep, and we were all supposed to show in the lobby at nine for the drive to Birmingham. So I showered, dressed, packed and went down for breakfast, where I met and talked with a guy named John who was replacing Mickey for today's drive. Which was fortunate, because I would have hopped the first train to London rather than spend another few hours in a van with that shithead.

In fact I didn't say anything on the drive to Birmingham. I figured there was no point in getting into what could be a prolonged argument with anybody in a small enclosed space. But as soon as we checked into the hotel that afternoon, I called Mick's room and asked if I could come over. It had been eating at me since it happened, and I had to get it out of my system. Mick, Robin, and Paul were there, and I repeated what had happened. They didn't seem particularly concerned. When I asked Paul why he hadn't done anything, he said, "Mickey's just that kind of bloke; you don't want to get in his way. Besides, it seemed like it was all in fun—I 'ave a tussle with me mates every once in a while."

I pushed the issue, and when I was done Mick said, "Well, I feel as if I've just had a severe reprimand."

"Yeah," said Robin. "You sound like my father."

I told them I didn't mean to set myself up as judge and jury. But you could see that Mick was upset; more than anybody else in the Clash, he loves the group's fans. After a short depressed silence, he said he was going out for a walk, got up and left the room.

The mood at the Birmingham concert hall was ominous. Clash road manager Corky was handing out "I WANT COMPLETE CONTROL" buttons to the kids going in the door, and police were confiscating them as soon as they got inside. The mood of the crowd was ugly—they gobbed all over Richard Hell even more than usual, and he started gobbing back, which was a mistake.

When I walked into the dressing room Joe Strummer immediately confronted me: "Lester, what's all this shit you're raisin' then?"

"You mean about last night?"

"Yeah. That guy was a bleedin' little ligger. . . ."

Rather than tell him he was wrong and get into a hassle just before showtime, I left the dressing room. Out in the hall Mick came up to me, obviously still concerned. "I've heard four different stories about what happened last night," he said, "but the main thing is that it better not happen again."

Later there was a party in a disco above the hall, and I spoke briefly to Bernie Rhodes. I told him I loved the group, and liked Mick the best. He sighed, "Yeah, but Mick's my biggest problem. . . ."

The real problem, of course, is how to reconcile Mick's attitude towards the fans with the group's escalating popularity in some realistic manner. Meaning that eventually you have to draw the line, and who's going to decide when and where it's to be drawn? Without this one-on-one contact with their audience, the Clash would seem as likely to fall into elitist alienation as most bands preceding them, but if it gets to the point that several thousand people want into your hotel room you've got to find some way of dealing with it. I certainly don't have the answer—all I know is that total access is as unreasonable as Zep/Stones–style security can be fascistically offensive.

In spite of tension between police and audience, the band had played a great set, channeling all the frustration into a liberating mass seizure. I couldn't help comparing this, especially in the light of most of the publicity accorded punks in the dailies, to the last time I was in Birmingham, for Slade in 1972. At that show I'd been warned not to take my tape recorder into the audience because they'd surely break it; they didn't, but they did smash every seat in the house, fights broke out everywhere, and Dave Hill was injured by flying shrapnel.

Of course, that *was* your standard football audience, and what's a little authentic violence in the face of a generation five years on who would seem to prefer rebellion by clothes and hairstyles?

Speaking of which I experienced a revelation of sorts at the after-gig party. I am loath to confess it, but I must say that try as I might I have never been able to find punk girls sexy. Somehow that chopped hair will just douse you every time, never mind the thought of trying to kiss somebody with a safety pin through her mouth (by the way, I didn't see a single safety pin through the flesh the entire time I was in England)—but now, in the disco upstairs, with Don Letts manning the turntable, alternating punk and reggae at mindmelting volumes, a whole pack of punkettes got out on that dance floor and started pogoing away and . . . well . . . suddenly it all began to make real tight *sense*. . . .

In fact, it was one of the highlights of my trip. I tried dancing a little bit, but mostly I just had to stand there and stare and stare, as one girl in black leather did James Brown steps, while Ari Up of the Slits, in all sorts of rags and a fishnet shawl, hopped highfooting around the dancefloor like some mix of spider and strutting ostrich, and the drummer from the Lous first walked around the floor on her knees, then got down on all fours and walked the dog for real as my eyeballs and then brain fell out a little at a time.

I suppose all you English tots are used to this sort of thing, but for this American it was Tod Browning's *Freaks* doing the Cretin Hop in the hypnotantalizing pulsating flesh. Like, if anybody starts asking me about the *sociological significance* of all this punk stuff I'm just gonna flash back to that Lous drummer down on all fours marching in circles, recalling most vividly her face as she did so: the fact that it was serene, *blank*, unconcerned, *unselfconscious.*

Much the same sort of thing strikes me next night, when for my last night on the tour, I attend a gig in Coventry with fellow rock critic Simon Frith. Simon, his wife, Gill, and I are surrounded by these strange children, the age difference somehow even more accentuated when there are three of us instead of just me blending with the geeks.

We note things like nonfunctional zippers sewn into the middle of shirts, and I'm almost passing out on my feet after six days of three hours' sleep a night on the road when suddenly something very strange runs over me. It's a kid moving through the crowd in a jagged mechanical pivoting careen, like a robot with crossed circuits, staring fixedly at nothing I can see, certainly not seeing me as we collide and he spazzmos on. When I ask Simon what in the hell that was he says they do it all the time—"Curious, isn't it?"—and when I ask if such a gait might be the byproduct of amphetamine abuse he laughs: "This is no pill scene. Most of these kids have never had anything stronger than stout." (The Clash, contrary to reputation, are not into speed either, at least not on the road.) Then we stare for a moment at the pogoing army, and Simon says, "Very tribal, isn't it?"

That it is. Between the Voidoids' and the Clash's sets, the PA broadcasts "Anarchy in the U.K.," and the whole audience, pogoing wildly, sings the entire song. I reflect how such a sight must strike terror, or something, into the heart of a middle-aged policeman looking on; but then I recall Slade getting their audience to sing along to "You'll Never Walk Alone" in '72, and the symmetry is inescapable. I *know* about the dole, I recognize the differences, but I wonder just exactly what, in the end, we can all understand this thing to be about.

When the Clash come on in Coventry, Joe repeats a little speech he first tried out in Birmingham: "Listen—before we play anything, we'd like to ask you one favor: please don't spit on us. We're just trying to do something good up here and it throws us off our stride." I was glad to hear it, because what gobbing really represents to me, besides nausea, is *people doing what they think is expected of them rather than whatever it is they might really want to do.*

Which of course *should* be what the New Wave is against.

Or rather, the converse should be what it's all about. At its best New Wave/punk represents a fundamental and age-old Utopian dream: that if you give people the license to be as outrageous as they want in absolutely any fashion they can dream up, *they'll be creative about it,* and do something good besides. Realize their own potentials and finally start doing what they really want to do. Which also presupposes that people don't want somebody else telling them what to do. That most people are capable of a certain spontaneity, given the option.

As it is, the punks constitute a form of passive resistance to a slick social order, but the question remains as to just what alternatives they are going to come up with. Singing along to "Anarchy" and "White Riot" constitutes no more than a show of solidarity, and there are plenty of people who think this is all no more than a bunch of stupid kids on a faddist's binge. They're wrong, because at the very least all of this amounts to a gesture of faith in mass and individual unrealized possibilities, which counts for a lot in an era when there are plenty of voices who would tell you that all human behavior can be reduced to a formula.

But if anything more than fashion and what usually amount to poses is going to finally come of all this, then everybody listening is going to have to pick up the possibilities with both hands and fulfill 'em themselves. Either that or end up with a new set of surrogate mommies and daddies, just like hippies did, because in spite of whatever they set in motion that's exactly what, say, Charles Manson and John Sinclair were.

The paradox for me is that the punks, in their very gentleness behind all the sneers and attitudes copped, are lambs—and believe me, I'm with the lambs over the bullies and manipulators of this world all the way—but what are lambs without a shepherd? Rastas aside, I don't want no Jesuses in *my* Promised Land, and if I didn't find it at the end of my road with the Clash I did catch a glimpse of it, on that road, in the way they acted towards their fans, towards me, towards people who worked for them, towards women, and ultimately towards themselves, every day. Meaning that even if we don't need any more leaders, we could do with a lot more models. If that's what the punks really amount to, then perhaps we actually do have the germ of a new society, or at least a new sensibility, that cuts through things like class and race and sex.

If not, well . . . I started talking to a girl who knew Simon and Gill, who I figured was a student in one of Simon's classes. She was very fresh, very wholesome, very young in a jacket covered with buttons bearing groups' names, and very miffed that the Clash had asked the audience not to spit on them. "After all," she said, *"they* started it!"

"But look," I said, "they play better when you don't."

"I don't care! I just want to jump up and down! That's all my students want, too!"

I blinked. "Your *students?* Wait a second, how old are you?"

"Twenty-four. I'm a schoolteacher."

Honestly, I couldn't help myself.

"Then . . . but . . . what are you doing here? I mean, why do you like the Clash?"

"Because they make me jump up and down!" And she pogoed away.

—*New Musical Express* (London), 10, 17, and 24 December 1977

Richard Hell:
Death Means Never
Having to Say
You're Incomplete

Life's not worth living. . . .
—Louis-Ferdinand Céline,
*Journey to the End of the
Night*

There's nothing to win by
This sort of an outcry . . .
—Richard Hell, "Who Says
(It's Good to Be Alive)?"

Once these principles had been established, and
thanks to a series of erudite experiments, he had been
able to perform on his tongue silent melodies and mute
funeral marches. . . . He even succeeded in transferring
specific pieces of music to his palate, following the
composer step by step, rendering his intentions. . . .
But tonight Des Esseintes had no wish to listen to the
taste of music.
—Joris-Karl Huysmans,
Against Nature

Please kill me.
—Richard Hell, on a T-shirt

This being an article about Richard Hell, it seems manifestly appropriate that I begin by talking about myself:

I licked the wine droplets off her breasts, then I licked her body dry, then there was nothing left to do. She slept, I prowled my apartment just as when I'm alone, searching for reasons for being where I always found them: in books, records, magazines and media, experience in the world being something for hippies and already known and behind me. These drugs all exhausted I prowl incessantly, or else stare at the space between ferocious discontent and rationalized oppression. To strike out is what we have all dreamed of but none of the old targets will do, ergo a decade that looks like a mules' trough to me, but we all sup at it and oh how they drone in discontent, no yelps or yowls or yawps to be heard. In the time of hedonist fascism nobody dares scream or judge what is so pathetically suspended in mid-air, which is life itself—nobody till now, that is. Meaning that if you aren't mad you're crazy—we are being eaten body and soul and no one is fighting. In fact practically no one sees it, but if you listen to the poets you will hear, and vomit up your rage. Richard Hell is one of the poets.

Trying to tell you why I believe in at least part of what Richard Hell is saying might be like scraping the silence out of my heart. It will prove easier, I'm afraid, to explain why I must ultimately reject his program. I'm passionate about his music, even as I suspect that this music and all we feel for it is a displaced passion. I wanted to write a book about why nobody wants to have emotions anymore, and because he's one of the few thinkers I respect, I showed some of my writing to Richard a year or so ago. He read this Cassandriad several times with a quiet unblinking intensity, then said: "The thing is that people don't have to *try* not to feel anything anymore; they just *can't*. . . ."

I still deny that, and need look no further for evidence than the sight of Richard Hell onstage: writhing, twisting, lunging, smashing into his guitar players like some wounded dervish. There is nothing farther from blankness than his eyes, bulging like splintered beehives, screaming to be let out of here, wherever we understand here to be. And we do not understand, and that is why we cannot connect, and that is why Richard Hell is at least temporarily necessary.

The only trouble, and what limits his necessity, is that his intelligence, so awesome in possibility, is finally reduced to the torment it revels in. For that I resent him, but I must give credence to the original intelligence all the same. Richard Hell is a walking exile on main street, a wounded lover who aspires to be his own merciless judge and jury, walking out hand in hand with himself. Why do you think somebody writes a song that says, "I could live with you in another world"? It's not because he cannot function in this world—any idiot can do that—but because functioning with this world's ideas of communication is at best intolerable, at worst cause for a most extreme form of violence, which in Richard's case is implosive, where, say, the Sex Pistols' is explosive.

From an interview with Legs McNeil in *Punk* magazine, early 1976:

> R: Basically I have one feeling . . . the desire to get out of here. And any other feelings I have come from trying to analyze, you know, why I want to go away. . . . See, I always feel uncomfortable and I just want to . . . walk out of the room. It's not going to any other place or any other sensation, or anything like that, it's just to get out of "here." . . .
>
> L: Where do you feel comfortable?
>
> R: When I'm asleep . . .
>
> L: Are you glad you were born?
>
> R: I have my doubts. . . . Did you ever read Nietzsche?
>
> L: Ha ha ha.
>
> R: Legs listen to me, he said that anything that makes you laugh, anything that's funny indicates an emotion that's died. Every time you laugh that's an emotion, a serious emotion that doesn't exist with you any more . . . and that's why I think you and everything else is so funny.
>
> L: Yeah I do too, but that's not funny.
>
> R: That's 'cause you don't have any emotions [hysterical laughter].

That was my first real exposure to Richard Hell, although I had heard good things about him previously. Naturally I was interested, because it seemed to me then, as it does now, that the only questions worth asking today are whether humans are going to have any emotions tomorrow, and what the quality of life will be if the answer is no. If the seventies are really going to be remembered as the decade when, like a character in Margaret Drabble's *The Ice Age,* people actually welcomed depression as a relief from anxiety, then the seething anxiety of Richard's music and his disturbing pessimism about the ultimate value of life itself are crucially important. Yeah, he used to be in a couple of groups called Television and the

Heartbreakers who have gone on to New Wave prominence, and yes, he was the first person to wear a torn T-shirt onstage, but all that is irrelevant in the face of the fundamental questions he raises, and the ominousness of his answers to them.

I had been looking forward to interviewing Richard for a long time. Through hanging out at CBGB's I'd become fairly close friends with him and everybody in his band, close enough to be gratified that when their album, *Blank Generation,* finally appeared, it turned out to be one of the wildest rock 'n' roll onslaughts of the year. But there were also things in his music and his persona that bothered me: the feeling that when he was onstage he was singing not so much for the sake of communicating with his audience but somehow almost totally for himself, and the unsettling sense that he didn't have to cut his flesh like Iggy or the Dead Boys' Stiv Bators to give off an aura of pain or simple unpleasantness. It's the same thing that comes across on his album's terrible cover, where he intentionally reduces the most fanatically penetrating eyes in rock 'n' roll to the level of a drugged toad. On a perhaps less immediate level, I'd sampled some of his favorite books, like Lautréamont's *Maldoror,* a frighteningly powerful celebration of the principle of pure evil, which Richard used to re-read regularly during a period when he thought he was a vampire; and Huysmans's *Against Nature,* a novel about a man who, having sampled all the decadent pleasures of the world, cloistered himself away to steep his body and mind in every synthetic sensation he could possibly find, eventually resulting in a debilitation that brought him to the edge of death. *Against Nature* is Richard's favorite book; when I asked him why, he spoke in admiring terms of the protagonist's independence and individualism. A fellow writer told me that Richard once told her that the best thing about being a rock 'n' roll star would be the option of constructing his environment so that he would never have to be around anyone he didn't want to know from, which not only sounds like building your own concentration camp but is just exactly what most of the declining rockstars of the sixties have done to themselves.

I called and left a message about the interview at two o'clock in the afternoon. That night around twelve he phoned me back, and when I asked him how tomorrow would be he said, "Well, what are you doing right now?"

Somehow it seemed appropriate to be slogging my tape recorder over to the Lower East Side in the wee hours of the morning to do an interview with Richard Hell, as appropriate as his insistence that we leave the TV on at a low drone while we talked, spooling out gang war with John Garfield, Elvis memorial record ads, and a movie called *The Monster and the Girl* which took us almost up to dawn. His apartment is a somehow orderly welter of the artifacts of his private passions: a few records, lots of film and poetry books in lines and stacks, a mess of tattered rock magazines and pictures of Richard and the Voidoids across the floor, pictures tacked up on the walls of Sissy Spacek in *Carrie,* Orson Welles, the poet Theresa Stern, Brigitte Bardot, and a blow-up of an old snapshot which turned out to be Richard's father, who died when he was seven.

We had been watching TV and talking awhile when the subject got around to a recent and very complimentary review, in which the writer had implied that Richard's tonsorial and sartorial manifestations and adoption of the name "Hell" constituted a pose. This infuriated him: "Part of the form of rock 'n' roll is having the courage of your convictions as a teenager, and doing stuff that would be outrageous and embarrassing to a lot of people, but constitutes a lot of your appeal to your audience because they like to see people who have the courage to turn themselves inside out in public. And for me, this whole style of dress and the way you look is a means, just like the combination of colors you use in a painting, for communicating. And it's only people who are scared and shy and threatened who find it necessary to perceive that as a pose."

I asked Richard whether he didn't feel scared, shy and threatened himself. (I know *I* do.)

"I don't feel threatened by anything rock 'n' roll bands do. I'm very much an outsider, shy and lonely, but the essence of being a rock 'n' roller is that you can create your own world there in spite of what everybody else thinks. And then, hopefully, it creates a world that other people are just as relieved and pleased to become a part of. And putting a hole in your shirt takes courage; it's saying, 'I don't give a fuck if somebody says I'm a jerk; I'm deliberately removing myself from them.' "

"But isn't that a retreat?"

"It's the opposite, it's a process of aggression. If you don't do it you're retreating. It's showing that not only do you not accept the status quo but you're asserting the fact that whatever you do is of equal importance. And the extent to which you assert your own importance in the face of all the people who would deny it will create a movement. And that's what happened."

"Yeah, but isn't so much of the punk movement involved with self-hatred?"

"I think there's a lot of basis for self-hatred. To transcend something you've first got to fully accept the fact that it exists. I would much rather listen to the music of somebody that hates themself and says it, than to listen to the music of Barry Manilow. There's an initial thrill of being able to release all this stuff that would have led you to just tear yourself apart inside before. Most punk rockers are very young, and I'm sure there's a certain number of them that will grasp the significance of what they're saying and will demand enough of themselves as human beings to go on to finding something else they can affirm. Or else they'll die. That's the dilemma I'm facing right now: whether I'll die or whether I'll find something I can affirm. It's gotta be one or the other. This has been tormenting me now since the release of the record. That was the moment when it all coalesced: I don't have anything to live for. For me rock 'n' roll is the frontier of consciousness, the place where you face the unsentimental question of whether the struggle to remain alive is greater than what you derive by being alive. Which is a struggle by definition, but I'm questioning what's the inherent good in that? I don't like to talk about it because it sounds sentimental and self-pitying, but for me it's not. I look at it, like, very clinically."

I look at it so differently that I was at a loss for words. I asked him how he saw love fitting into this picture, and he reiterated the message of "Love Comes in Spurts," that in general the concept was a lie. So I asked him if this wouldn't possibly lead to a certain narcissism.

"I have no way of knowing because I have nothing to compare it to; I can't know anybody else as well as I know myself. It's the artist's job to be narcissistic, constantly analyzing and paying attention to yourself to see how things affect you. One thing I wanted to bring back to rock 'n' roll was the knowledge that you invent yourself. That's why I changed my name, why I did all the clothing style things, haircut, everything. So naturally, if you invent yourself, you love yourself. The idea of inventing yourself is creating the most ideal image that you could imagine. So that's totally positive. Nobody would have ever called me handsome until I got into rock 'n' roll. That is the ultimate message of the New Wave: if you just amass the courage that is necessary, you can completely invent yourself. You can be your own hero, and once everybody is their own hero, then everybody is gonna be able to communicate with each other on a real basis rather than a hand-me-down set of societal standards. And it's much healthier for you and the world if you do it.

"People misread what I meant by 'Blank Generation.' To me, 'blank' is a line where you can fill in anything. It's positive. It's the idea that you have the option of making yourself anything you want, filling in the blank. And that's something that provides a uniquely powerful sense to this generation. It's saying, 'I entirely reject your standards for judging my behavior.' And I support that entirely. It can be used politically as powerfully as it can be used artistically or emotionally, in the sense of saying, 'I have been classified null by the society that I live in,' and it can be accepted as a self-description in that way. They have been completely rejected. It's like Ralph Ellison's book *Invisible Man*—punks are niggers. If I go on the street, I can't get a cab, I get nothin' but abuse in restaurants, in New York City or anywhere else in the country. The treatment that you would classify as being prejudicial to minority races is precisely the same accorded to people who go around dressed like me. It's a very rare day that I don't get some kinda shit walking down my own block where I've lived for two years."

I asked him why, as he'd told me once before, he thought adolescence was the best part of a person's life.

"Adolescence is the point in your life where you are inevitably forced by circumstances to face the most crucial questions about life, period. And the extent to which you maintain the attitude that you had as a teenager is the extent to which you remain alive, as far as I'm concerned. You increase your ability to operate efficiently in the face of the environment you perceive as you get older, but that doesn't mean that the turmoil inside you is lessened any. I can't speak for anybody but myself, but I know that I haven't resolved any of those things."

"You don't feel that you've made more of a peace with yourself than when you were sixteen years old?"

"I'm worse. I could never have had any respect for myself and thought for a minute about deliberately dying at the age of sixteen. Now I can very dispassionately and confidently imagine myself sticking a pistol into my mouth and pulling the trigger."

"What would stop you?"

"Habit. Just habit. You're so used to being alive. The power of habit is so overwhelming. Gertrude Stein wrote a thesis about it in college. Eating is an addiction. You gotta go out and get yourself food if you're gonna live, just like you gotta go out and get yourself junk if you're a junkie; there's no difference. Anything that's necessary for maintaining yourself in a condition of health is an addiction. There are similarities between addiction to a drug and being alive, which is what I was saying in 'Who Says?': 'Once born you're addicted / And so you depict it / As good, but who kicked it?' "

"But the difference between that and drug addiction is that there's no *alternative* to food or life!"

"There's death. I have no idea what it would be like, I just know that it would remove me . . . it would render void a lot of things that are horrifying and painful and disgusting to me."

Just for the record, I would like it known by anybody who cares that I don't think life is a perpetual dive. And even though it's genuinely frightening, I don't think Richard Hell's fascination with death is anything else but stupid. *I* suspect almost every day that I'm living for nothing, I get depressed and I feel self-destructive and a lot of the time I don't like myself. What's more, the proximity of other humans often fills me with overwhelming anxiety, but I also feel that this precarious sentience is all we've got and, simplistic as it may seem, it's a person's duty to the potentials of his own soul to make the best of it. We're all stuck on this often miserable earth where life is essentially tragic, but there are glints of beauty and bedrock joy that come shining through from time to precious time to remind anybody who cares to see that there is something higher and larger than ourselves. And I am not talking about your putrefying gods, I am talking about a sense of wonder about life itself and the feeling that there is some redemptive factor you must at least *search* for until you drop dead of natural causes. And all the Richard Hells are chickenshits who trash the precious gift too blithely, and they deserve to be given no credence, but shocked awake in some violent manner.

Either that or spanked and put to bed.

Look, I started out this thing saying how much I *respected* this guy's mind and perceptions. I still do, in a curious way—it's just that he paints half the picture of total reality with consummate brilliance, and the other half is Crayola slashes across a field of Silly Putty and Green Slime. In other words, he's got a great grasp of the *problems* of being alive in the seventies, but his solutions suck. And, just like Eldridge Cleaver said, there comes a time when we all must choose.

By his own terms, he doesn't transcend his self-hate; in fact, it would seem that transcendence is not what he is looking for. His whole picture is a self-fulfilling prophecy—he has designed his world in such a way that things ought to work out every bit as miserably as he expects, a Pyrrhic gratification at best.

But the purpose of art is to transcend—which reminds me, Richard, why not live for your art if nothing else? And the greatest art is not narcissistic, as you claim, but transcends the morass of self to reach out and profoundly reflect that world which will move on irrespective of whether you pull the trigger or not. Did Dostoyevsky sit around mewling about I, I, I? Or Huysmans, for that matter? You may say that Des Esseintes was a projection of Huysmans himself, but there was an essential distance there, just as there is in all the greatest writers, because the ultimate art is created not out of navel-gazing one's personal pain but out of a clear perception of the unsentimental fact that, though we all die sooner or later, not all life foreshadows that assignation.

In other words, life is not an addiction; you've got it ass-backwards. Addiction is slavery, and I don't feel in bondage just because I have to keep breathing and eating a cup of yogurt once in a while to go on writing these words. Furthermore, adolescence is one of the *worst* parts of life, it's the cloud of unknowing and a state of total awkwardness when the fun you have always seems to be tempered by some kind of stupid bullshit like parents or zits or what-have-you. Most importantly, it seems to me that there is a war on today which goes far beyond rest-of-society vs. punks; it's the war for the preservation of the heart against all those forces which conspire to murder it, which you know about because you pinned some of them in "Liars Beware." But you are not waging that war. You can call me self-righteous for saying that, and condescending for what I will finish this off with, but I don't care because it is out of nothing but love that I tell you that, in spite of being one of the greatest rock 'n' rollers I have ever heard, you are full of shit. So if you do choose to go down, I promise to dig up that crypt and kick your ass.

Your fan,
Lester

—*Gig*, January 1978

Growing Up True
Is Hard to Do

In 1971, Bob Seger released a single on Capitol which I guess was only a regional hit but was also one of the most powerful things I have ever heard. It was called "Lookin' Back," the music was smoky funky powerchords that didn't have to tell you they were, and the words went like this: "They hit the street / You feel 'em starin' / You know they hate you, you can feel their eyes a-glarin' / Because you're different / Because you're free / Because you're everything deep down they wish they could be / They're lookin' back / They're lookin' back / Too many people lookin' back."

Bob Seger has a new album out called *Stranger in Town* which will probably go platinum. This album is mostly songs even more soul-searching than the ones on *Night Moves*, which I guess makes it better because they search the soul of his present instead of his adolescence, but musically it's just a "hard rock" version of an awful lot of what schlumps around the airwaves these days. Which I guess I gotta say makes it not free, and if I want shackles round my foot pedals I'll go to Jamaica.

On the other hand, nobody has more of a right to sell out than Bob Seger. I lived in Detroit from 1971 to 1976, and it was downright sad the way you'd see him opening year after year for every lousy band in the world; in 1972 he was even reduced (well, there was no gun at his head, true) to going onstage in a Leon Russell top hat, with lame girl-singer backup. I mean we're in real Ted Nugent territory here, a guy that breaks his ass and balls and whatever else he's got for a solid fucking decade on the worst grind circuit in the world, and not just because he wants to be a star—the guy actually has something he wants to share with people. Which is just one of the things that separates him from Ted Nugent. It's been said that Bob Seger is a moralist, and I don't think you'd have to read the lyrics quoted above to know that's true. But how about this: "I take my card and I stand in line / To make a buck I work overtime / Dear Sir letters keep coming in the mail / I work my back till it's wracked with pain / The boss can't even recall my name / . . . To workers I'm just another drone / To Ma Bell I'm just another phone / I'm just another statistic on a sheet / I'm just another consensus on the street / . . . Hey it's me / And I feel like a number / Feel like a stranger / . . . in this land / I'm not a number / I'm not a number / Dammit I'm a man."

If it seems like we're getting close to Rastafarian or especially Clash territory here it's because we are, although it must be understood that it's parallelism and not influence—hell, Bob grew up in *Detroit*, and I wouldn't be surprised if he never even heard of the Clash. The song I just quoted is on *Stranger in Town*. After his success with *Night Moves* he could have just kept grinding out a proven formula: nothing is more salable today than people's reminiscences of a backseat make-out adolescence a lot of them—cf. Meat Loaf—never had. He nixed that sellout album for the same reason that in 1971 he wrote a song as topical as the one I just quoted: innate integrity.

The difference between "Lookin' Back" and "Feel Like a Number" is seven years: from hippie alienation and paranoia to the feeling that we're dwarfed by institutions we don't really understand, except that somebody somewhere wants us to believe that human beings don't matter much anymore. It would be condescending to say, Gee, isn't it amazing that this long-haired midwestern journeyman rock sharecropper thinks about such high-flown concepts, because everybody's freaked out by them these days. The average purchaser of current Seger albums is probably a male kid who works on some shit job and has never even considered dropping out, is in fact a stranger to the concept, so he'll understand "Feel Like a Number" in a second. But it's no accident that the album is called *Stranger in Town*. Bob Seger feels like a stranger in this society, especially the rock superstar version of interlocking corporations. And that doesn't mean he's some old-fashioned "relic," even though he's embarrassed enough to use the word himself; it means he's a man of sanity and insight. I respect Bob Seger as much as almost anybody I can think of in the music business today.

But the music business today still must be recognized as *by definition* an enemy, if not the most crucial enemy, of music and the people who try to perform it honestly. And that's where this album goes limp. Because while Bob is singing with candor or maybe the word should be "guts" about his alienation, the aging process vis-à-vis his line of work, etc., this album cops out musically just like *Night Moves.* It's homogenized. Seger knows he needs that radio play, and he also knows that in 1978 "Looking Back" (musically, let alone lyrically) won't get it. So in a sense he's bowing before the Beast. I don't know whether I blame him or not, and I'm certainly not saying he should replace the Muscle Shoals Rhythm Section with the Voidoids Minus Richard Hell. But the reason that the lyrics of the Clash and the Rastafarians carry all the wallop they should is that the music is as tough as the words.

There's a popular idea that the flirtation with chaos is something you must grow out of, but I believe that while you shouldn't hang on to your adolescence like it was a state of grace, you should leave yourself the latitude to go berserk from time to time. What this has to do with Bob Seger should be obvious. He writes all these songs about the tension between wanting to keep rocking when you're pushing forty, kinda like Ian Hunter. But Hunter always wanted to be Dylan, whereas Bob just wants to make sure that some kid has something decent to put on the eight-track while he cruises down Woodward—with ideas about life and identity and all that also there if and when you want 'em. Now Seger knows that to get his insights onto the radio so the kid will buy his records in the first place, he's gotta make records that just kinda sound like everybody who has sold out. And that may be pragmatic, but it's still fucked. Like I say, I don't know if I blame him, since he is dues-paying incarnate, but I also think that he of all people knows life is short, that it really is true that you only get one chance to speak your real piece despite the wisdom of all the people who would tell you only fools even try. Right now he's got a chance to do something that only about four or five people have had a shot at: both to make records that deal honestly with aging in rock 'n' roll (or aging period) *and* to make music that would be as challenging now as his "East Side Story" was in 1966, or "Lookin' Back" was in 1971. And I think that if he snubs this opportunity I'm gonna end up feeling like he flat-out betrayed the gift.

—*Village Voice,* 5 June 1978

The White
Noise Supremacists

The other day I was talking on the phone with a friend who hangs out on the CBGB's scene a lot. She was regaling me with examples of the delights available to females in the New York subway system. "So the train came to a sudden halt and I fell on my ass in the middle of the car, and not only did nobody offer to help me up but all these boons just sat there laughing at me."

"Boons?" I said. "What's boons?"

"You know," she said. "Black guys."

"Why do you call them that?"

"I dunno. From 'baboons,' I guess."

I didn't say anything.

"Look, I know it's not cool," she finally said. "But neither is being a woman in this city. Every fucking place you go you get these cats hassling you, and sometimes they try to pimp you. And a lot of the times when they hassle you they're black, and when they try to pimp me they're always black. Eventually you can't help it, you just end up reacting."

Sometimes I think nothing is simple but the feeling of pain.

When I was first asked to write this article, I said sure, because the racism (not to mention the sexism, which is even more pervasive and a whole other piece) on the American New Wave scene had been something that I'd been bothered by for a long time. When I told the guys in my own band that I was doing this, they just laughed. "Well, I guess the money's good," said one. "What makes you think the racism in punk has anything special about it that separates it from the rest of the society?" asked another.

"Because the rest of society doesn't go around acting like racism is real hip and cool," I answered heatedly.

"Oh yeah," he sneered. "Just walk into a factory sometime. Or jail."

All right. Power is what we're talking about, or the feeling that you don't have any, or how much ostensible power you can rip outta some other poor sucker's hide. It works the same everywhere, of course, but one of the things that makes the punk stance unique is how it seems to assume substance or at least style by the *abdication* of power: *Look at me! I'm a cretinous little wretch! And proud of it!* So many of the people around the CBGB's and Max's scene have always seemed emotionally if not outright physically crippled—you see speech impediments, hunchbacks, limps, but most of all an overwhelming spiritual flatness. You take parental indifference, a crappy educational system, lots of drugs, media overload, a society with no values left except the hysterical emphasis on physical perfection, and you end up with these little nubbins: the only rebellion around, as *Life* magazine once labeled the Beats. Richard Hell gave us the catchphrase "Blank Generation," although he insists that he didn't mean a crowd with all the dynamism of a static-furry TV screen but rather a bunch of people finally freed by the collapse of all values to reinvent themselves, to make art statements of their whole lives. Unfortunately, such a great utopian dream, which certainly is not on its first go-round here, remains just that, because most people would rather follow. What you're left with, aside from the argument that it beats singles bars, is compassion. When the Ramones bring that sign onstage that says "GABBA GABBA HEY," what it really stands for is "We accept you." Once you get past the armor of dog collars, black leather, and S&M affectations, you've got some of the gentlest or at least most harmless people in the world: Sid Vicious legends aside, almost all their violence is self-directed.

So if they're all such a bunch of little white lambs, why do some of them have it in for little black lambs? Richard Pinkston, a black friend I've known since my Detroit days, tells me, "When I go to CBGB's I feel like I'm in East Berlin. It's like, I don't mind liberal guilt if it gets me in the restaurant, even if I know the guy still hates me in his mind. But it's like down there they're *striving* to be offensive however they can, so it's more vocal and they're freer. It's semi–mob thinking."

Richard Hell and the Voidoids are one of the few integrated bands on the scene ("integrated"—what a stupid word). I heard that when he first formed the band, Richard got flak from certain quarters about Ivan Julian, a black rhythm guitarist from Washington, D.C., who once played with the Foundations of "Build Me Up Buttercup" fame. I think it says something about what sort of person Richard is that he told all those people to get fucked then and doesn't much want to talk about it now. "I don't remember anything special. I just think that most people that say stuff like what you're talking about are so far beneath contempt that it has no effect that's really powerful. Among musicians there's more professional jealousy than any kind of racial thing; there's so much backbiting in any scene, it's like girls talking about shoes. All musicians are such scum anyway that it couldn't possibly make any difference because you expect 'em to say the worst shit in the world about you."

I called up Ivan, who was the guy having trouble at the pinhead lunch counter in the first place. "Well, I was first drawn to this scene by the simple fact of a lot of people with musical and social attitudes more or less in common. No one's ever said anything to my face, but I overheard shit. A lot of people are just ignorant assholes. I don't think there's any more racism at CBGB's, where I went every night for about the first year I lived here, than anywhere else in New York City. Maybe a little bit less, because I find New York City a million times more racist than D.C., or Maryland and Virginia where I grew up. There's racism there, outright killings around where I lived, but here it's a lot more insidious. You get four or five different extremes, so many cultures that can't stand each other. It's like, when we toured Europe I was amazed at the bigotry between people from two parts of the same country. They'd accept me, but to each other they were niggers, man. And at CBGB's it's sorta the same way, sometimes. Mutants can learn to hate each other and have prejudices too. Like Mingus said in *Beneath the Underdog:* forty or fifty years ago, in the ghetto, the lighter you were the better you were. Then you'd turn another corner and if you were somewhat light, like Mingus, there'd be a buncha guys saying 'Shit-colored mutha' ready to trash your ass. My point is, regardless of how much people might have in common they still draw away. There are certain people on the scene, like say this girl in one band who's nothing but a loudmouthed racist bitch—it's obvious we want nothing to do with each other, so I stay away from her and vice versa.

"I'll tell you one thing: the entrepreneurs, record company people and shit are a hell of a lot worse. People like Richard Gottehrer, who produced our album, and Seymour Stein and a lot of the other people up at Sire Records. They were *totally* condescending, they'd talk to you differently, like you were a child or something. I heard a lot of clichés on the level of being invited over to somebody's house for fried chicken."

I was reminded instantly of the day I was in the office of a white woman of some intelligence, education, and influence in the music business, and the subject of race came up. "Oh," she said, "I liked them so much better when they were just *Negroes.* When they became *blacks . . ."* She wrinkled her nose irritably.

"Race hate?" says Voidoids lead guitarist Bob Quine. "Sure, it gives me 'n' Ivan something to do onstage: *The Defiant Ones."*

But the ease and insight of the Voidoids are somewhat anomalous on the New York scene. This scene and the punk stance in general are riddled with self-hate, which is always reflexive, and anytime you conclude that life stinks and the human race mostly amounts to a pile of shit, you've got the perfect breeding ground for fascism. A lot of outsiders, in fact, think punk *is* fascist, but that's only because they can't see beyond certain buzzwords, symbols, and pieces of regalia that (I *think*) really aren't that significant: Ron Asheton of the Stooges used to wear swastikas, Iron Crosses, and jackboots onstage, but I don't remember any right-wing rants ever popping up in the music he did with Iggy or his own later band, which many people were not exactly thrilled to hear was called the New Order.

In the past three years Ron's sartorial legacy has given us an international subculture whose members might easily be mistaken at first glance for little brownshirts. They aren't, for the most part. Only someone as dumb as the Ramones are always accused of being could be offended when they sing "I'm a Nazi schatze," or tell us that the first rule is to obey the laws of Germany and then follow it with "Eat kosher salami." I've hung out with the Ramones, and they treat everybody of any race or sex the same—who *they* hate isn't Jews or blacks or gays or anybody but certain spike-conk assholes who just last week graduated from *The Rocky Horror Picture Show* lines to skag-dabblings and now stumble around Max's busting their nuts trying to be decadent.

Whereas you don't have to try at all to be a racist. It's a little coiled clot of venom lurking there in all of us, white and black, goy and Jew, ready to strike out when we feel embattled, belittled, brutalized. Which is why it has to be monitored, made taboo and restrained, by society and the individual. But there's a difference between hate and a little of the old *épater* gob at authority: swastikas in punk are basically another way for kids to get a rise out of their parents and maybe the press, both of whom deserve the irritation. To the extent that most of these spikedomes ever had a clue on what that stuff originally meant, it only went so far as their intent to shock. "It's like a stance," as Ivan says. "A real immature way of being dangerous."

Maybe. Except that after a while this casual, even ironic embrace of the totems of bigotry crosses over into the real poison. Around 1970 there was a carbuncle named Wayne McGuire who kept contributing installments of something he called "An Aquarian Journal" to *Fusion* magazine, wherein he suggested between burblings of regurgitated Nietzsche and bad Céline ellipses that the Velvet Underground represented some kind of mystical milestone in the destiny of the Aryan race, and even tried to link their music with the ideas of Mel Lyman, who was one of the prototypes for the current crop of mindnapping cult-daddies.

On a less systematic level, we had little outcroppings like Iggy hollering, "Our next selection tonight for all you Hebrew ladies in the audience is entitled 'Rich Bitch'!" on the 1974 recorded-live bootleg *Metallic K.O.*, and my old home turf *Creem* magazine, where around the same time I was actually rather proud of myself for writing things like (in an article on David Bowie's "soul" phase): "Now, as we all know, white hippies and beatniks before them would never have existed had there not been a whole generational subculture with a gnawing yearning to be nothing less than the downest baddest *niggers*. . . . Everybody has been walking around for the last year or so acting like faggots ruled the world, when in actuality it's the *niggers* who control and direct everything just as it always has been and properly should be."

I figured all this was in the Lenny Bruce spirit of let's-defuse-them-epithets-by-slinging-'em-out—in Detroit I thought absolutely nothing of going to parties with people like David Ruffin and Bobby Womack where I'd get drunk, maul the women, and improvise blues songs along the lines of "Sho' wish ah wuz a nigger / Then mah dick'd be bigger," and of course they all laughed. It took years before I realized what an asshole I'd been, not to mention how lucky I was to get out of there with my white hide intact.

I'm sure a lot of those guys were very happy to see this white kid drunk on his ass making a complete fool if not a human TV set out of himself, but to this day I wonder how many of them hated my guts right then. Because Lenny Bruce was wrong—maybe in a better world than this such parlor games would amount to cleansing jet offtakes, and between friends, where a certain bond of mutual trust has been firmly established, good natured racial tradeoffs can be part of the vocabulary of understood affections. But beyond that trouble begins—when you fail to realize that no matter how harmless your intentions are, there is no reason to think that any shit that comes out of your mouth is going to be understood or happily received. Took me a long time to find it out, but those words are *lethal*, man, and you shouldn't just go slinging them around for effect. This seems almost too simple and obvious to say, but maybe it's good to have something simple and obvious stated once in a while, especially in this citadel of journalistic overthink. If you're black or Jewish or Latin or gay those little vernacular epithets are bullets that riddle your guts and then fester and burn there, like torture-flak hailing on you wherever you go. Ivan Julian told me that whenever he hears the word "nigger," no matter who says it, black or white, he wants to kill. Once when I was drunk I told Hell that the only reason hippies ever existed in the first place was because of niggers, and when I mentioned it to Ivan while doing this article I said, "You probably don't even remember—" "Oh yeah, I remember," he cut me off. And that was two years ago, one ostensibly harmless little slip. You take a lifetime of that, and you've got grounds for trying in any way possible, even if it's only by convincing one individual at a time, to remove those words from the face of the earth. Just like Hitler and Idi Amin and all other enemies of the human race.

Another reason for getting rid of all those little verbal barbs is that no matter how *you* intend them, you can't say them without risking misinterpretation by some other bigoted asshole; your irony just might be his cup of hate. Things like the *Creem* articles and partydown exhibitionism represented a reaction against the hippie counterculture and what a lot of us regarded as its pious pussyfooting around questions of racial and sexual identity, questions we were quite prepared to drive over with bulldozers. We believed nothing could be worse, more pretentious and hypocritical, than the hippies and the liberal masochism in whose sidecar they toked along, so we embraced an indiscriminate, half-joking and half-hostile mindlessness which seemed to represent, as Mark Jacobson pointed out in his *Voice* piece on Legs McNeil, a new kind of cool. "I don't discriminate," I used to laugh, "I'm prejudiced against *everybody!*" I thought it made for a nicely charismatic mix of Lenny Bruce freespleen and W. C. Fields misanthropy, conveniently ignoring Lenny's delirious, nigh-psychopathic inability to resolve the contradictions between his idealism and his infantile, scatological exhibitionism, as well as the fact that W. C. Fields's racism was as real and vile as—or more real and vile than—anybody else's. But when I got to New York in 1976 I discovered that some kind of bridge had been crossed by a lot of the people I thought were my peers in this emergent Cretins' Lib generation.

This was stuff even I had to recognize as utterly repellent. I first noticed it the first time I threw a party. The staff of *Punk* magazine came, as well as members of several of the hottest CBGB's bands, and when I did what we always used to do at parties in Detroit—put on soul records so everybody could dance—I began to hear this: "What're you playing all that nigger disco shit for, Lester?"

"That's not nigger disco shit," I snarled, "that's *Otis Redding,* you assholes!" But they didn't want to hear about it, and now I wonder if in any way I hadn't dug my own grave, or at least helped contribute to their ugliness and the new schism between us. The music editor of this paper has theorized that one of the most important things about New Wave is how much of it is almost purely white music, and what a massive departure that represents from the almost universally blues-derived rock of the past. I don't necessarily agree with that—it ignores the reggae influence running through music as diverse as that of the Clash, Pere Ubu, Public Image Ltd., and the Police, not to mention the Chuck Berry licks at the core of Steve Jones's attack. But there is at least a grain of truth there—the Contortions' James Brown/Albert Ayler spasms aside, most of the SoHo bands are as white as John Cage, and there's an evolution of sound, rhythm, and stance running from the Velvets through the Stooges to the Ramones and their children that takes us farther and farther from the black-stud postures of Mick Jagger that Lou Reed and Iggy partake in but that Joey Ramone certainly doesn't. I respect Joey for that, for having the courage to be himself, especially at the sacrifice of a whole passel of macho defenses. Joey is a white American kid from Forest Hills, and as such his cultural inputs have been white, from "The Jetsons" through Alice Cooper. But none of this cancels out the fact that most of the greatest, deepest music America has produced has been, when not entirely black, the product of miscegenation. "You can't appreciate rock 'n' roll without appreciating where it comes from," as Pinkston put it.

Musical questions, however, can be passed off as matters of taste. Something harder to pass off entered the air in 1977, when I started encountering little zaps like this: I opened up a copy of a Florida punk fanzine called *New Order* and read an article by Miriam Linna of the Cramps, Nervus Rex, and now Zantees: "I love the Ramones [because] this is the celebration of everything American—everything teenaged and wonderful and white and urban. . . ." You could say the "white" jumping out of that sentence was just like Ornette Coleman declaring *This Is Our Music,* except that the same issue featured a full-page shot of Miriam and one of her little friends posing proudly with their leathers and shades and a pistol in front of the headquarters of the United White People's Party, under a sign bearing three flags: "GOD" (cross), "COUNTRY" (stars and stripes), "RACE" (swastika).

Sorry, Miriam, I can go just so far with affectations of kneejerk cretinism before I puke. I remember the guy in the American Nazi Party being asked, "What about the six million?" in PBS's *California Reich,* and answering "Well, the way I heard it it was only really four-and-a-half million, but I wish it was six," and I imagine you'd find that pretty hilarious too. I probably would have at one time. If that makes me a wimp now, good, that means you and anybody else who wants to get their random vicarious kicks off White Power can stay the fuck away from me.

More recently, I've heard occasional stories like the one about one of the members of Teenage Jesus and the Jerks yelling "Hey, you bunch of fucking niggers" at a crowd of black kids in front of Hurrah one night and I am not sorry to report getting the shit kicked out of him for it. When I told this to Richard Hell, he dismissed it: "He thinks he's being part of something by doing that—joining a club that'll welcome him with open arms, trying to get accepted. It's not real. Maybe I'm naive, but I think that's what all racism is—not really directed at the target but designed to impress some other moron."

He may be right, but so what? James Chance of the Contortions used to come up to Bob Quine pleading for Bob to play him his Charlie Parker records. Now, in a *New York Rocker* interview, James dismisses the magical qualities of black music as "just a bunch of nigger bullshit." Why? Because James wants to be famous, and ripping off Albert Ayler isn't enough. My, isn't he *outrageous?* ("He's got the shtick down," said Danny Fields, stifling a yawn, when they put James on the cover of *Soho Weekly News.*) And congrats to Andy Shernoff of the Dictators, who did so well they're now called the Rhythm Dukes, for winning the *Punk* magazine Drunk as a Skunk contest by describing "Camp Runamuck" as "where Puerto Ricans are kept until they learn to be human."

Mind you, I like a cheap laugh at somebody else's expense as well as the next person. So I got mine off Nico, who did "Deutschland Über Alles" at CBGB's last month and was just naive enough to explain to Mary Harron, in a recent interview in *New Wave Rock,* why she was dropped by Island Records: "I made a mistake. I said in *Melody Maker* to some interviewer that I didn't like negroes. That's all. They took it so *personally* . . . although it's a whole different race. I mean, Bob Marley doesn't resemble a *negro,* does he? . . . He's an archetype of Jamaican . . . but with the features like white people. I don't like the features. They're so much like animals. . . . it's cannibals, no?"

Haw haw haw, doncha just love them dumb kraut cunts? And speaking of dumbness and krauts, my old pal Legs McNeil has this band called Shrapnel, who are busy refighting World War II onstage in dogtags, army surplus clothes, and helmets that fall over their eyes like cowlicks, while they sing songs with titles like "Combat Love." Personally I think it's not offensive (well, about as offensive as "Hogan's Heroes") that they're too young to remember Vietnam—it's funny. The whole show is a cartoon (it's no accident that they open their set with the "Underdog" theme) and a damn good one. Musically they're up there too—tight dragstrip guitar wranglings that could put them on a par with the MC5 someday, combined with a stage act that could make them as popular as Kiss. The only problem, which has left me with such mixed feelings I hardly know what to say to them, is that the lyrics of some of the songs are nothing but racist swill. The other night I sat in the front row at CBGB's and watched them deliver one of the hottest sets I've seen from any band this year while a kid in the seat right next to me kept yelling out requests for " 'Hey Little Gook!' 'Hey Little Gook!' " the whole time. Christgau, who considers them "proto-fascist" and hates them, told me they also had lyrics on the order of "Send all the spics back to Cuba." I mentioned this to Legs and he seemed genuinely upset: "No," he swore, "it's 'Send all the *spies* back to Cuba.' "

"Okay," I said (Christgau still doesn't believe him), "what about 'Hey Little Gook'?"

"Aw c'mon," he said, "that's just like in a World War II movie where they say 'kraut' and 'slants' and stuff like that!"

I told him I thought there was a difference between using words in dramatic context and just to draw a cheap laugh in a song. But the truth is that by now I was becoming more confused than ever. All I knew was that when you added all this sort of stuff up you realized a line had been crossed by certain people we thought we knew, even believed in, while we weren't looking. Either that or they were always across that line and we never bothered to look until we tripped over it. And sometimes you even find that you yourself have drifted across that line. I was in Bleecker Bob's the other night, drunk and stoned, when a black couple walked in. They asked for some disco record, Bob didn't have it of course, a few minutes went by, and reverting in the haze to my Detroit days I said something about such and such band or music having to do with "niggers." A couple more minutes went by. Then Bob said, "You know what, Lester? When you said that, those two people were standing right behind you."

I looked around and they were out on the sidewalk, looking at the display in his front window. Stricken, I rushed out and began to burble: "Listen . . . somebody just told me what I said in there . . . and I know it doesn't mean anything to you, I'm not asking for some kind of absolution, but I just want you to know that . . . I have some idea . . . how utterly, utterly *awful* it was. . . ."

I stared at them helplessly. The guy just smiled, dripping contempt.

"Oh, that's okay, man . . . it's just your head. . . ." *I've run up against a million assholes like you before, and I'll meet a million after you—so fucking what?*

I stumbled back into the store, feeling like total garbage, like the compleat hypocrite, like I had suddenly glimpsed myself as everything I claimed to despise. Bob said, "Look, Lester, don't worry about it, forget it, it happens to everybody," and, the final irony, sold me a reggae album I wondered how I was going to listen to.

If there's nothing more poisonous than bigotry, there's nothing more pathetic than liberal guilt. I feel like an asshole even retelling the story here, as if I expected some sort of expiation for what cannot be undone, or as if such a tale would be news to anybody. In a way Bob was right: I put a dollop more pain in the world, and that was that. There is certainly something almost emetically self-serving about the unreeling of such confessions in the pages of papers like the *Voice*—it's the sort of thing that contributed to the punk reaction in the first place. But it illustrates one primal fact: how easily and suddenly you may find yourself imprisoned and suffocated by the very liberation from cant, dogma, and hypocrisy you thought you'd achieved. That sometimes—usually?—you'll find that you don't know where to draw the line until you're miles across it in a field of land mines. Like wanting the celebration of violent disorder that was the Sex Pistols, ending up with Sid and Nancy instead, yet realizing the next day that you still want to hear Sid sing "Somethin' Else" and see *The Great Rock 'n' Roll Swindle,* and not just because you want to understand this whole episode better but to get your kicks. These are contradictions that refuse to be resolved, which maybe is what most of life eventually amounts to.

But that's begging the question again. Most people, I guess, don't even think about drawing the lines: they just seem to go through life reacting at random, like the cabdriver who told me that the report we were listening to on the radio about Three Mile Island was just a bunch of bullshit dreamed up by the press to sell papers or keep us tuned in. And maybe if you go on like that (assuming, of course, that we all *don't* melt), nothing will blow up in your face. But you may end up imploding instead. A lot of people around CBGB's are already mad at me about this article, and the arguments seem mostly to run along the lines of Why don't you can it because there's not really that much racism down here and all you're gonna do is create more problems for our scene just when this Sid Vicious thing had blown over. I mentioned Pinkston's experience and was told he was paranoid. Like the people at Harrisburg who didn't wanna leave their jobs and actually believed it would be safe to stick around after the pregnant women and children were evacuated, these kids are not gonna believe this stuff exists until it happens to them. Hell, a lot of them are Jewish and still don't believe it even though they know about the neighborhoods their parents can't get into.

When I started writing this, I was worried I might trigger incidents of punk-bashing by black gangs. Now I realize that nobody cares. Most white people think the whole subject of racism is boring, and anybody looking for somebody to stomp is gonna find them irrespective of magazine articles. Because nothing could make the rage of the underclass greater than it is already, and nothing short of a hydrogen bomb on their own heads or a sudden brutal bigoted slap in the face will make almost anybody think about anybody else's problems but their own. And that's where you cross over the line. At least when you allow the poison in you to erupt, that can be dealt with; maybe the greater evil occurs when you refuse to recognize that the poison even exists. In other words, when you assent by passivity or indifference. Hell, most people *live* on the other side of that line.

There is something called Rock Against Racism (and now Rock Against Sexism) in England, an attempt at simple decency by a lot of people whom one would think too young and naive to begin to appreciate the contradictions. Yippie bullshit aside, it could never happen in New York, which is deeply saddening, not because you want to think that rock 'n' roll can save the world but because since rock 'n' roll is bound to stay in your life you would hope to see it reach some point where it might not add to the cruelty and exploitation already in the world. In a place where people are as walled off from one another as we are in America now, all you can do is try to make some sort of simple, humble, and finally private beginning. You feel like things like this should not need to be said, articles like this should perhaps not even be written. You may think, as I do of the sexism in the Stranglers' and Dead Boys' lyrics, that the people and things I've talked about here are so stupid as to be beneath serious consideration. But would you say the same thing to the black disco artist who was refused admittance to Studio 54 even though he had a Top Ten crossover hit which they were probably playing inside the damn place at the time, the doorman/bouncer explaining to a white friend of the artist, "I'm not letting this guy in—he just looks like another street nigger to me"? Or would you rather argue the difference between Racist Chic and Racist Cool? If you would, just make sure you do it in the nearest factory. Or jail.

—*Village Voice*, 30 April 1979

Sham 69
Is Innocent!

This is the truth! There was only one Sex Pistols! There is only one Ramones! Sometimes we go out to clubs that call themselves rock discos! We get pissed off! It costs money! We have to be among people! Several sexes in black leather jackets shove us! They are scum! What have we got! Fuckall! We don't even push back!

In England they do! That's why Sham 69's having trouble over there! Half their fans are punks and half are skinhead neo-Nazis! They shove each other! Then they punch each other's faces in! It's disgusting! It makes the dailies! The group broke up once because of it! Then they reformed! Their leader Jimmy Pursey had the nerve to bill himself Joe Public! Everysouse! Fuck him! I like him! All his interviews in *New Musical Express* he comes across sincere! So what! Kiss was as good as this group! First Sham album on Sire sounded like Ramones outtakes with some pubkid football-chanting over 'em! It was great! I guess! Sorta! Better than nondescripts like the Members! At least Jimmy Pursey has a personality! He sings lead for the group! He takes off his shirt! When he jumps around the stage and screams there's a big vein or muscle that stands out on the left side of his neck! Wow! His eyes bulge! He's pissed off! So am I! Who isn't! But piss stinks different here! We've all got our causes! He's never been to 14th Street! He speaks! "Anyway who gives a damn? / I'm doin' the best I can!" So what! Lotsa bored Anglophiles in that audience! They got two encores anyway! Everybody gets two encores these days! Fuck all encores! Who pays for this shit! Who is Everyman! Me and You! Fuck all! Even Halston 'n' Andy are Everyman!

Recall summer of '77 NY media freaks tryin' to outdo each other blabbin' "Punk is dead," well ha ha ha IT'S THE HIPPEST HAPPENIN GOIN YOU TRANKS! Course all the good bands died two years ago or are lonely struggling to break middle America inch by inch like Patti and the Ramones! Maybe they will! Everybody else is a big fish in a little pond! No guts! Fuck 'em! Jim Purse's got a new song called "The Hostages Are Innocent"! What hostages! Tell us the clear truth! Tattoo on *Fantasy Island* looks like a hostage to me! Or maybe he means the Wilmington Ten! Who the fuck are they! Who gives a shit! George Davis is innocent! So was Slade! They never sussed that English football shouts wouldn't level American concert halls! This group is just that stupid! And even more arrogant! More blab from staged Jim Wednesday night! "It's about time that sixteen-year-olds had somebody sixteen years old to speak for them! You don't have somebody like that! That's why we're here! Bruce Springsteen is okay but he's thirty years old!" Yeah Jim he's lost his innocence! Not like you! He has no lyrics like "What's it all about? / Money, work it out!"

Right! That's why Alice Cooper was the father of seventies rock 'n' roll! He knew! That's also why Sham 69's new album *The Adventures of Hersham Boys* sounds like Alice circa "Under My Wheels"! Jimmy got scared of his own power! Just like Alice! What men they were! There were giants in those days! So now they've both ended up making overproduced the-boys-are-united albums that blare and blare! I'd buy this one like I bought *Killer*! Except it's not as good! But so what! It's nine years later and no one cares! Except Alice because he's washed up! Now! And Jimmy! Because just like Alice he's got scared of himself or his audience and settled for a cartoon instead! So this is hot wank! Better no doubt than the next Kiss album! But Kiss were a better group when they were smokin'! And they had nothin' to say! And these guys don't either! So don't let them kid you! Buy their album! It's exciting! Buy all albums by new angry British groups! They stink too! If you pay you won't care! If you care you'll defect from both the Sham and Kiss Armies! But you don't care! Neither do I! So let's buy!

—*Village Voice,* 17 December 1979

New
Year's
Eve

Lately every time you turn around somebody's saying: "The eighties are coming!" Like at the stroke of midnite on New Year's it's all gonna be *different!* And when you tell 'em, "Come on, you know everything's just gonna keep on slowly sinking," they get downright *mad!* Spoilsports! No sense of social duty! It's true that I am antisocial! But so is my whole crowd. When our fave bar the Bells of Hell closed down a few months back we all stayed in our apartments instead of seeking out a new watering hole. (Perhaps suggesting that, like the buffalo, we are soon to disappear.) I told my shrink this and he said: "You're all pathetic."

Another time when I complained I was getting weirded out around other people because I never saw 'em because all I did was lay in bed with the covers over my head because I truly believed as the mighty Ramones quoth that there was "nothin' to do and nowhere to go" so I just wanted to be sedated, my shrink suggested I call up all my friends in all their separate little cells and see if we couldn't figure out some way to repatriate ourselves in the human race and enjoy it. So I conducted this plebiscite, and when I came back he said: "So what's the consensus?" I said, "The consensus is, 'Whaddaya wanna be around people for? Most of 'em suck anyway!'"

I suppose you think I'm being negative. All right, if I'm negative you go tell *Mother* there's something wrong with the womb! Ha, gotcha! Besides which, as the eighties loom I suspect that my antisocial minority will soon be a majority, and we'll have an antisociety! Imagine that! Will Rogers the ultimate outlaw! And what better time to inaugurate this ghost town than New Year's Eve! Ring out the old, ring in the old! And older and older. I ask you, have you *ever* had a New Year's Eve you enjoyed? Of course not! Why? Because you've persisted in this insane delusion that somehow things are supposed to keep getting better, or that the cyclical nature of the ying-yang means that the earth is supposed to replenish itself or some such horseshit! Horseshit doesn't even replenish itself. Do these sidewalks? This peeling paint, crumbling plaster, backed-up plumbing? A replenishable landlord? Fuck no!

There are two directions in which extants can go: (a) stasis or (b) decay. And New Year's Eve is the biggest bummer yet, because we all go out with these expectations and get totally soused just so we can stand to be around each other because we've spent the late fall and winter's first blush sinking deeper into *TV Guide,* and now we're expected to positively revel in proximity to these globs of hideous humanity. So OF COURSE horrible scenes ensue.

The first New Year's I have a clear memory of was probably the first one I was old enough to get drunk for: I got stoned on nutmeg instead. All my friends did get drunk tho and exiting this teenclub full of depressed zit-lumpen reduced to flat colas we drove aimlessly around El Cajon, inevitably ending in the line at Jack in the Box where, as people vomited all over the inside of my car, I said "Welcome to 1967." We shoulda known right away Hippie wouldn't work.

1968: I went to a party where everybody drank too much vodka too fast and pawed each other or tried to while Donovan trilled of fat angels. Only saw one person vomit: my girlfriend, all over her brand-new white hiphuggers. (Earlier in the evening I had told her, re said fem-trousers: "You look like a Tijuana whore." A downy lad I was and twee.) I was on Marezine and kept seeing little men with axes and hammers chopping naked gabbling pigmy demons to death in other people's lapels. When I got home I hallucinated all kinds of people coming into my room and reached out to them screaming, "Don't dissolve! Don't dissolve!" But sure enough they did. Then I thought I saw a friend of mine silhouetted behind the windowshade whispering from the garden: "Lester! Lester!" I leaped out of bed and yanked up the shade, pathetically grateful for some human companionship. There was nothing there but the empty street with leaves blowing.

I went into the bathroom to take a piss and hallucinated that my mother was ogling my dick with one huge roc eyeball through a crack in the door. Then I went back to bed and dreamed that narcs in steelgrey suits were stationed at strategic points all over my school watching me through slowly swiveling Silva-Thin shades. For the first two months of 1968 I couldn't look anybody in the eye.

1969: Me 'n' a buncha buddies went cruisin' in some dude's jalopy. We beered awhile to no avail. One pal who later joined the navy where he majored in underwater demolition (exhorting me to enlist by his bonded side: "It's real fun blowin' up stuff!") said, "Let's go out 'n' git us sum *scrunt.*" Nobody else said anything. Eventually we all went home too depressed even to feel drunk and fell asleep. The whole evening shoulda been written by (or inflicted on) Robbe-Grillet.

1970: New Year's Eve I spent getting drunk on beer watching TV at my girlfriend's parents' house, periodically ducking out to drive by the motel bungalow of some needle-freak friends because I wanted to buy some heroin, which I had never tried. Finally they were home and sold me some. When I got back to my girlfriend's house I ran in the bathroom and tried to snort it. Not yet hep to rolled-up bills, I dumped the stuff onto a mirror held at a precarious angle over the sink, balanced it an inch from my nose, and honked amighty. Nothing happened except later I drank some Country Club Malt Liquor, went home, and wrote a review for *Rolling Stone* (which never got printed) of a Bob Dylan bootleg. Next day I bragged to all my friends: "I wrote a record review on *heroin* last night!" Being too lame to ingest the shit was the only time I ever got lucky on a New Year's Eve.

1971: I stayed home and read the Bible. No, that's a lie. What I did was go to the drive-in with my girlfriend—all hopped up (me, that is) on vodka and her mother's thyroid pills, totally unable to concentrate on the double feature of *I Drink Your Blood* (starring Ronda Fultz, Jadine Wong, and somebody merely billed "Bhaskar") and *I Eat Your Skin* (William Joyce, Heather Hewitt) which would have been impossible under any circumstances anyway, thinking all night how next morning I was gonna do like Jack Kerouac and just jump in my car eating speed with one hand while flicking the starter with the other and drive drive drive till I plashed through Blakean breakers of light on the golden prows of the Rocky Mountain Shield. Of course I didn't, woke up with a muzzy hangover instead, which is probably just as well: I coulda ended up being John Denver.

1972: New Year's I spent dead drunk and gutpit-depressed at my mother's house in California. Called up my friend Nick in NYC and miserably groaned through several leagues of whiskey, "I think I'm becoming an alcoholic." He didn't wanna hear that because he was just about to spend New Year's Day making his way down Broadway from 99th Street having one drink in every bar along the way until he ended at Broadway and Third, the very last bar, St. Adrian Co., also known as the Broadway Central Bar, being an adjunct of the Broadway Central Hotel, a flophouse. He called back the next day: "Sorry Les, I'm too depressed to talk."

1973: Went to a party with my ex-puppylove-girlfriend (she of the greened hiphuggers) and her sis and brother-in-law. Most everybody else there was a swinging single, or trying to be. I danced dirty with the hostess. It was right out of *Doctors' Wives*. My ex-galf'd got mad at me for rubbing up agin said hussy and huffed a bit. I bet Gore Vidal never came out with anything as deft as, "Whattayou care? *You* won't fuck me!" She cried. Later in the car in savage ugly liquored sexual frustration I dug one of my nails into her wrist until it bled. She told me I was a sissy. I was.

1974: Back in California again, staying at my old girlfriend's deserted tho furnished apartment, as, unbeknownst to Mom, she's off livin' with some forty-five-year-old businessman who when he stands next to ya drinkin' at the bar always keeps a fistful of dollars taut-gripped so he can shoot 'em out as he snoots it up. That kinda guy. So there I am enjoying her empty apartment, lying around listening to *Raw Power* and *Berlin* all the time, when I get this bright idea: I'll take all these sleaze-rock LPs to this night's singles/married/whatever-they-think-they-are party, and *blast 'em*. Ey-pa-TAY, MUTHAFUCKA! So I scoop up all the discs 'n' off we go 'n' all nite long I keep slipping 'em on the record player bumming everybody out tho they was also kinda fascinated, like this room got kinda *quiet* at times, waxen even, p'raps understandable this being California suburbs everybody's dressed to the fillings in all kinda *chains* and whatnot, taco tanktopping it with frappe de la Yardley on the side, big hoop earrings, all the guys got sideburns so sharp they smoke, when Lou wafts thru: "Caroline says . . . as she gets up off the floor . . . 'Why is it that you beat me? . . . It isn't any fun. . . .'"

Meanwhile all these folks is loungin' around 'bout to broach a dolce vita thru the looking glass. Frozen moments, all of them bad. Icy lips and frigid sunglasses.

"It's not me that's frigid it's my Foster Grants!"

"It's not me that's impotent it's my English Leather!"

"Well let's swap!"

"Wow! Okay!"

"Hey, this decadence stuff up my butt is fun!"

Sadly, it never happened that way. I can't remember this New Year's Eve and hadda make something up. But the stories you make up the next day are always better than what actually happened.

1975: Sensible for once. I dropped some speed and Valium, went to the office, which was deserted, and stayed up all night writing a story for the February issue of *Creem*. Devotion to duty? No. Retreat from Gehenna.

1976: I had been going out with this girl for a couple of months kinda scene-makin photog-lolligagin around Detroit. She'd decided I was a fag since one nite in Oct/Nov thereabouts at a Barry White concert when we'z sittin behind Ohio Players, the world's worst opening act, and she sez, re the bass player, "He's got a nice ass" and I sat up a bit to look and she gave me a weird stare and that was that. So anyway me and this snope-lobe keep a-datin', but no sex. I was clumsy and shy and she, well, I guess her cameras woulda got in the way. Anyhow here come New Year's Eve, the biggun, and lord if fuckin *Creem* magazine don't rent a whole suite in this post-rundowntown hotel just to, ah, *entertain* all the important folk't might just happen to turn up like, say, local disc jockeys or Martin Mull who'd done his shtick downstairs and did it upstairs too. For some dumb reason I kinda liked this girl. I dunno, well actually I do know: in front she looked like somebody I used to love named Judy, and in back she looked like somebody I did love but wouldn't see me at the time named Nancy. So MEA CULPA MUHFUH, etc. Anyhoo, come to find out that the only reason she even went to dis bash wid me was that I jus' happenda work at the *same magazine* as this guy name Charlie Auringer who ALL the broads there-abouts were hot for cause'n he jes set back so indifferent all the time, eyeball-to-snowboot, that kinda thing. When I saw her blatantly USING me to get to Charlie I got pissed. And did what any other righteously upstandin Rasta woulda done: slunk downstairs 'n' drunk muhsef tuh null-hood. But I was not alone in this endeavor, and long about midnite her 'n' me miraculously ended up side by side, right there stageside table in the lounge downstairs, balloons enuff to snuff Steve Martin agozzlin thru the air, treacle paper everywhere, Flo and Eddie runnin' around grabbin' all the asses they could JUST EXACTLY like in that Fugs song "Dirty Old Man," confetti falling, and me and Lee Anne (for that was her name) both of us in li'l tinsel tophats, socute, herecum midnite, whammo, out go the lites.

I sling my drunken arm around her shoulders and go to kiss her. She turns away tautlipped.

"Hey! I take you out all the time! I like you! We do things together! Boy and Girl! And you won't even kiss me on New Year's Eve!!!!!!??!!!!! What *is* this shit?"

"You've got bad breath," she said.

It could only get better. Having finally won the heart of the aforementioned Nancy, we moved to New York where we starved Barefoot in the Park and huddled together against this city watching Donny and Marie every single Friday nite. New Year's Eve we watched Jimmy and Rosalynn instead. Their preinaugural ball. We teardropped together when Loretta Lynn sang "One's on the Way." We felt hope for society. We were young and idealistic and in love. We were walking sugar comas too stunned to find our way to a diabetic ward should all that glop we ate back up into our lymph ducts. Six months later she left me to listen to the Sex Pistols in peace.

I went through a couple of minor affairs after that whilst mostly staying drunk and practically taking up residence at CBGB's where I played the role of Bukowskian bohemian/artiste in ze big sitcom. It got me some real great women—the kind that sit crosslegged on your floor after you've both been up all night on bad drugs and won't fuck you but are perfectly amenable to describing in linoleum detail their various suicide attempts and highly complex postexistential *Weltanschauung* derived from Richard Hell and countless auditions of dear Sidney warbling "My Way," a philosophical stance reducible to Life is not worth living and everything stinks but killing yourself is too much effort so what the fuck you got anything else to drink?

It sooner or later became apparent that any women who shared my tastes in music might be predicted miles ahead as burnt-out hunchbacked mutes, half-retarded drug repositories given to heavy facial tic action. It was not that I sought something out of *Fascinating Womanhood.* I can whip up a Stouffer's Spinach Soufflé deft as Régine herself, but I did feel there might be some slight possibility that something existed somewhere in between these two outposts of you're-right-gimme-the-gun-I-wanna-blow-my-brains-out-first. In fact I was ripe as Li'l Abner in full flushblush, and fell in love Xmas '77 with the first of what would turn out to be a succession of women who, like myself, were gainfully employed in various aspects of media and were not about to end up aborting a broken vodka bottle on the steps of CBGB's. These were to be women of refinement and urbane cachet. Some of them took cabs everywhere they went! I also noticed a propensity toward the employment of what they laughingly referred to as "my faggot houseboy," making little jokes about how handy his imagined infantile-fixated compulsions were when it came to scrubbing the bathroom. The first one I engaged even had a doorman, who thought I was a hoodlum and hated my guts because no thirty-year-old man walks around jobless in a black leather jacket alla time, and who knows but what he may have been right.

As for my new love, hardly had we finished giggling fantasies about "honeymooning" in that heartshaped bathtub in the Poconos when that bastard Reality (who oughta be terminated with extreme prejudice) set in. It took exactly one week for it to become clear though thick with silence that we had absolutely nothing in common, were in fact the mindlessly magnetic attraction of plupolar opposites. I was still into nothing but platters of shrieking anomic noise while her favorite form of leisuretime wowzow was watching endless made-for-TV movies about occultists bending sinister in obscure New England hamlets. It was nobody's fault and nothing we could do about it but spend the next months torturing each other. Our New Year's Eve: We awoke to find ourselves sitting on her couch in the deepening silence watching Guy Lombardo's Royal Canadians play "Auld Lang Syne" without even a nod to Jimi's revolutionary interpolations. And then the big ball dropped on all those cheering idiots slow as a senile meteorite. It was the only time in my life I have ever observed this I am told quite popular ritual (though I am a definite Yule Log fan), and it certainly will be the last, inasmuch as it was one of the possibly four or five dreariest experiences I have known. We didn't even have any drinks, though we had money. Guess we were so gone we forgot to drink, marijuana would needless to say have been much more deadly than usual. I felt like an E string adrift somewhere in the nether gulfs of the second Dire Straits album.

Next day I went to a dinner party with five of my oldest and dearest friends where absolutely nobody could think of a single word to say. Best line of the afternoon: "Does anybody know any good jokes?" (Delivered at dinner table, quantifying silence to brink of catatonia.)

1979: New Year's things seemed to be looking up. I had plenty of money, got wired up on beer and bennies and showed up at a friend's party at the exact instant I'd been informed the jumpin punkins'd be lifting off. Only trouble was nobody else was there yet but the host and his girlfriend/ roommate and a cousin from Buffalo or somewhere and we all sat nursing tepid beers, our massed alpha-waves bouncing off Randy Mantooth's forehead on "Emergency One!" An hour or so of such terror and the bennies itched me right outa my chair and down to the since-shut fave bar the Bells of Hell where I made a pretty good job of picking up this woman I'd never met before till the bartender Phil walked over and said to me, "Do you realize that for the last half hour every other thing you've said has had something to do with homosexuality? What's your problem, Lester?" *She* much less I hadn't seemed to notice if such were fact but I was just drunk enough for liberal guilt so I blurted out this real vitreous solution about how I'd had a deadly relationship the previous summer with *another* media maiden who was a self-declared faghag so gee whiz I didn't mean to be prejudiced against anybody but maybe I really *did* harbor some previously unsussed resentment. . . . Naturally this had a real salutary effect on the nascent whoknows mebbe truelove beside me. I took her number and split.

Later I went to a party where I met a British socialist-type girl who gave me her number as well as wrote at the bottom of the scrap "I liked you." Of course I called her and we saw each other for about three months, earnestly discussing the Clash vs. *The Guardian* over Japanese dinners. The full extent of our physicals was a peck g'nite on the cheek as she departed at her subway stop headed for Iceland or Brooklyn I forget which. I soon grew to hate her, and we parted in ash-curdling acrimony. But later on that same New Year's Eve nite I *really* lucked out by going back to the Bells where this totally comatose thirty-year-old stranger who worked for UPI hung all over me to my manifest indifference and the embarrassment of everyone else at our table. I could have told her to go foist her slumbrous blandishments elsewhere, but I was too much of a wimp. Finally I got up to leave. I was just a ways past the door when I heard these steps following me down the sidewalk.

"Wait . . ."

I waited, stood gallantly propping the creep up till I could hail her a cab. Meanwhile I lectured her in my best Bill Cosby voice. "Listen: you are truly foolish. You don't know me. I could be David Berkowitz, the Boston Strangler, Richard Speck with a new set of contacts. You really oughta be more careful." I swear, sometimes I wonder if I'm not Jewish, and a Jewish mother at that.

When I went to put her in the cab, she asked, "Aren't you going to take me home?"

All right, that's it, I said to myself like Richard Burton looking at his paycheck for *The Medusa Touch,* and got into the cab. All the ride to her Upper East Side Laura Mars swankpad she kept prattling about the black leather jacket I was wearing.

"Are you a member of a *motorcycle club* or something?"

I laughed. "Hell no—I'm a media hack, just like you!"

She didn't get the joke. When we got out at her corner (where believe me I had *no thought* in ten purgatories of paying), she kept up this leather routine, persisted at this spume of dogs till finally in a rage I tore the jacket off and flung it at her.

"*Here, take* the damn thing if that's all you're interested in!"

"NO, no . . ."

Up in her digs the footlights was boss. She had Grand Marnier nightcapwise while I opted for the more proletarian Pinch-with-water. I commenced the usual routine and she pushed me away, blubbering incoherently about some guy she loved who's stationed with Reuters in Bangkok. She tried to call him. He wasn't home. We hung out in her kitchen awhile and somehow, suddenly, from the way she was acting towards me and my clothes I got the creepy feeling for the first time in my life that just maybe this one wanted me to slap her around a little bit or maybe a lot or who knows what beyond that. This was some time after having been flashed back to the scene in *City of Night* where the customer throws the hustler out of his house in a rage because this supposed steerhunk truck driver committed the unpardonable gaffe of letting drop that he too had read D. H. Lawrence. I'd had the feeling that something was expected of me, but up till now hadn't a clue what and doubted she did either. She kept baiting me verbally, weird little zingers from the twilight zone bouncing off the fact that I was about as butch as a college professor who has been sedentary for thirty years. This talk alternated with zonkout google slurs.

It got boring in spite of all freak appeal after a while so I went over and looked through her record collection. The only album she owned that I could remotely relate to was *Surrealistic Pillow.* I put it on. It sounded nice. We ended up on the couch again where she recommenced to drool aloud. I seem to remember at one point telling her that it really didn't make any difference to me whether we had sex or not, especially considering the deadening effects of all the speed and booze inside me. Later I grabbed her head between my palms and forced her waxen eyes to look straight into mine sorta and I said in measured dramatic tones, "Do you know what I see when I look into your eyes? Stark, naked terror." What an asshole I was. A bit later I snapped, "You got any *drugs?*" By now I was actually beginning to enjoy playing the role. She brought out this vial of pain pills left over from previous misadventure, asked me what use I could possibly have for them. I said that when I had a real bad combination hangover this stuff was the only thing that eased it. Then she decided maybe she'd better hold on to them after all, giving me two and stuffing the vial down her purse, which was interesting. About five minutes after that she passed out curled sitting up in a foetal ball on the couch as the sun came up through the curtains. What the fuck, I said, I'll give the bitch the B production she wants: I robbed her. I dug in the purse for the vial, actually found myself looking for a moment at her wallet, either couldn't go that far or realized how silly this whole charade was, grabbed the fifth of Pinch on the way out the door, stomping down just a little meaner in my badass Frye boots. Still as tough and mature obviously as the '73 night of the famous fingernail-dig.

I wished I could call up Dotson Rader for a Merit Badge. Out in the street I hailed a cab; the driver was a middle-aged black guy. I said, "Jesus, man, I'm so glad to be around another human being at last! Can I tell you a story?"

Sure, he says, so I belched up the mess, capping it with the declaration that when I got home I was gonna call her and tell her that she was a sicko weirdo Goodbar so-'n'-so and yeh baby I stole your pills 'n' booze but you stole a li'l bit o' my *soul*.

When I finished my story, the driver, who had laughed uproariously throughout, turned and said: "Aw, hell, man, why go to all that fuckin' trouble? Look, here's whatcha do. Wait till 'bout two o'clock in the afternoon when you know she's up, then phone her and real calm and polite say, 'I just called to see if you were all right.' Then after she answers tell her to go fuck herself an' hang up!"

I realized immediately that he was right and I was still halfway up a horse on some backlot in Hollywood. I thanked him profusely. When I got home I drank her Pinch, took more speed, listened to the Clash through headphones feeling the righteous wrath of all us boots-in-the-alley working class minorities. Then I dialed her number. She wasn't home. When I told a friend of mine about it a couple days later he just laughed and said: "So you let some barfly take you home, so what?" So I got to be Rough Trade for a Night, something I can tell my apple-eyed grandchildren about around the hearth, so fuck you, you're just jealous because you never got mistaken for Sonny Barger. I did learn one valuable lesson, though, which convinced me that what all those hippies called karma actually does exist. That very next New Year's Night, twenty-four hours later, somebody stole my black leather jacket out of the cloakroom at the Bells.

So here I sit, contemplating a coming New Year's Eve which is gonna usher in a whole new decade doubtless brimming with little surprises beyond the usual roster of economic/spiritual depression, romantic wrongways unto entropy, comforting lapses into autism, etc. I guess I could ring up one of those wayout punk philosopher girls and ask her if she wants to drop by with a couple razor blades, dutch treat. Or enlist in the New Army and ask to be stationed in upper Greenland. Or even move back to Detroit and ask Lee Anne to marry me while I returned to work at *Creem*, in the mailroom. The possibilities are endless. Don't guess this piece is gonna help my standing with the ladies much New Year's or any other night. But that's cool too; I could marry my mother. If she would have me. Go ahead and feel distaste for my antics with the lush, call me misogynous, misanthrope, Mr. Rogers. Just don't call me late for my Zoom 'n' Locker Room! Every single one of you has acted every bit as oafishly base some New Year's or other or several or all of them. And you're gonna do it again this year. The occasion just seems to bring out the worst in us: hatred of ourselves, probably deriving from repression of the clear knowledge that we're another year older and deeper in debt but ain't accomplished hackshit and in fact are likely backpedaling; hatred of the rest of the human race because they've got our number in this department, especially including women if you're a man or vice-versa, 'cause that's just like neighborhood gang war, "beating up the kids from Spain" every weekend like the Dictators said. Whoever's on the other side of the wall gives you something to do in the form of mashing their skulls, don't really matter a damn which special-interested group they belong to, all interchangeable when you get right down to it. There's a lot of free-floating rage in the air these days and New Year's Eve is just one better excuse to vent it. 'Course that means you're gonna wind up rendered a crawling slavering subhuman dog yourself, but that's half the fun. The only alternatives re this "human dignity" stuff are that old saw about crossing the International Dateline, total isolation (always a good move anyway), or perhaps most sensibly JUST GIVING INTO THE THING AND ACTING LIKE TOTAL WRETCHED DISGUSTING BEASTS. And maybe if we all get drunk enough we'll all have blackouts so trackless and remarkably sustained that we'll never remember all the reprehensible things we said and did to each other, hence no guilt. Either that or we'll all wind up killing each other at last. Though that may be the dream of a blind optimist. If so, an alternate experiment in participatory democracy might be arranged whereby we'd all agree to stockpile beforehand so when we wake up on New Year's Day we've made sure there's a thousand whiskey bottles around the bed, and then we can start over again immediately, quick as a Wheaties Olympian, before a single one o' them ghastly memories sifts back in. And what's more, don't anybody get up, from sea to shining sea, don't get up ever but just keep on like that under or over the covers, your option, en masse till New Year's 1990. We've worked hard at wrecking after degrading everything we ever cared about, and deserve a good Puritan rest. Like Gore Vidal said when Tennessee Williams told him he'd slept through the sixties: "You didn't miss a thing."

—*Village Voice*, 26 December 1979

Otis Rush
Mugged by an
Iceberg

It's weird. Sometimes you just have to get so fed up with everything around you, down to the terminal, and *especially* all the wretched excess that's being marketed disguised as its diametrical opposite, before you can get back to the thing you felt in the first place. Lately I've begun to think it's not so much a question of all current music being worthless swill as that, let's face it, *entertainment,* in whatever form, nine times outta ten just ain't that entertaining anymore. So this friend of mine calls me up, knowing that as usual I hate everything, and says, "Listen, if I was you I'd really skip the next two six-packs and go over to Record City and buy this Otis Rush album. It's truly brutal."

Otis Rush. Who the fuck is Otis Rush? Otis Spann, Otis Rush, the blues the schmooz, same old three-chord bullshit and some sorry fucker whining about the poozwack that absconded. I got a whole damn apartment fulla blues records, PLUS I *got* the blues my own damn self, life is obviously not worth living, even that's a cliché, music stinks, people are concave units at best, but every time I talked to my friend on the phone that Otis Rush album was playing in the background. Finally I got some money, enough to pretend I had the latitude to be adventurous for an hour or two, there was certainly nothing else to buy, so to shut him up as much as anything else I went to Record City and bought *Groaning the Blues: Original Cobra Recordings 1956–58* by Otis Rush on the import Flyright label.

Is anybody out there awake? Well, those of you that are, *kick* everybody I just put to sleep and tell 'em lissen up, 'cause this album has not left my turntable for two weeks and if the purpose of record reviews in the first place is to enable us all to make more wise buys (in Gristede parlance), why then you all should join me in being proud owners of this basically predictable mid-fifties Chicago blues album with its hot titles like "She's a Good 'Un," "Jump Sister Bessie," "Checking On My Baby," "Sit Down Baby," "Baby Baby Baby," "Baby to Baby," "Baby Me," "Me Baby," "Love That Woman," "Keep on Loving Me Baby," "My Baby Is a Good 'Un" (no, it's not the same song, I don't think), "I Can't Quit You Baby," and many many more.

Why? Because Otis Rush, whom I understand has cut some less distinguished sides just about every time he hit a studio since (though some swear by *Cold Day in Hell*), took something, some dorsal blast of rage and love, into the studio with him this time. This album is the same old story. It is also thunder and lightning, the great creaks and groans when earth ruptures and we have no ground we can call our own. I am not kidding. This album is primal, elemental, violent, nerve-wracked, frustrated beyond all limits, and one of the great guitar (Stratocaster) LPs to be released in our time. It means nothing except that this guy had a life and it apparently was pretty unpleasant and he wants revenge on the universe and he gets it every time he assaults his instrument. And believe me, assault is the word. In 1958 Otis Rush (trading lead riffs with Ike Turner on "Double Trouble," *the* cut, no Eric Clapton jokes please) was tearing out jagged wangbar-bashing lines that would make people call Jimi Hendrix a genius when he pulled them out of a hell of a lot more technology over a decade later. The guitar cuts through erratically, viciously, seemingly at random, in coruscating blasts that collide head-on with the vocals. Rush is a down-and-out son-of-a-bitch and he doesn't like it one bit, and in one song ("Checking On My Baby") you can actually hear a saxophone laughing at his wretched plight. His singing is as fierce as any of the other Big Boys in the neighborhood, but it's that guitar work you'll keep coming back for. It's beyond blues, beyond rock, certainly into atonal propositions too lewd for a family publication such as this. It sounds like giant bloody icebergs shuddering up to crunch together in the deepest, longest night of typically endless midwestern winter, and if you don't think there's icebergs in the Midwest you've never been here. This album is a masterpiece. It has nothing to do with anything but pain and hate and exorcism and impossibility, and if I were you I'd buy it and sink into the molten futility of "Double Trouble" as soon as possible. It's better than killing yourself. How many other current records can you say that about?

Thinking the
Unthinkable
About John Lennon

You always wonder how you will react to these things, but I can't say I was all that surprised when NBC broke into "The Tonight Show" to say that John Lennon was dead. I always thought that he would be the first of the Beatles to die, because he was always the one who lived the most on the existential edge, whether by diving knees-first into left-wing adventurism or by just shutting up for five years when he decided he really didn't have anything much to say; but I had always figured it would be by his own hand. That he was merely the latest celebrity to be gunned down by a probable psychotic only underscores the banality surrounding his death.

Look: I don't think I'm insensitive or a curmudgeon. In 1965 John Lennon was one of the most important people in the world. It's just that today I feel deeply alienated from rock 'n' roll and what it has meant or could mean, alienated from my fellow men and women and their dreams or aspirations.

I don't know which is more pathetic, the people of my generation who refuse to let their 1960s adolescence die a natural death, or the younger ones who will snatch and gobble any shred, any scrap of a dream that someone declared over ten years ago. Perhaps the younger ones are sadder, because at least my peers may have some nostalgic memory of the long-cold embers they're kneeling to blow upon, whereas the kids who have to make do with things like the *Beatlemania* show are being sold a bill of goods.

I can't mourn John Lennon. I didn't know the guy. But I do know that when all is said and done, that's all he was—a guy. The refusal of his fans to ever let him just be that was finally almost as lethal as his "assassin" (and please, let's have no more talk of this being a "political" killing, and don't call him a "rock 'n' roll martyr"). Did you watch the TV specials on Tuesday night? Did you see all those people standing in the street in front of the Dakota apartment where Lennon lived singing "Hey Jude"? What do you think the *real*—cynical, sneeringly sarcastic, witheringly witty and iconoclastic—John Lennon would have said about that?

John Lennon at his best despised cheap sentiment and had to learn the hard way that once you've made your mark on history those who can't will be so grateful they'll turn it into a cage for you. Those who choose to falsify their memories—to pine for a neverland 1960s that never really happened *that* way in the first place—insult the retroactive Eden they enshrine.

So in this time of gut-curdling sanctimonies about ultimate icons, I hope you will bear with my own pontifications long enough to let me say that the Beatles were certainly far more than a group of four talented musicians who might even have been the best of their generation. The Beatles were most of all a moment. But their generation was not the only generation in history, and to keep turning the gutted lantern of those dreams this way and that in hopes the flame will somehow flicker up again in the eighties is as futile a pursuit as trying to turn Lennon's lyrics into poetry. It is for that moment—not for John Lennon the man—that you are mourning, if you are mourning. Ultimately you are mourning for yourself.

Remember that other guy, the old friend of theirs, who once said, "Don't follow leaders"? Well, he was right. But the very people who took those words and made them into banners were violating the slogan they carried. And they're still doing it today. The Beatles did lead but they led with a wink. They may have been more popular than Jesus, but I don't think they wanted to be the world's religion. That would have cheapened and rendered tawdry what was special and wonderful about them. John Lennon didn't want that, or he wouldn't have retired for the last half of the seventies. What happened Monday night was only the most extreme extension of all the forces that led him to do so in the first place.

In some of his last interviews before he died, he said, "What I realized during the five years away was that when I said the dream is over, I had made the physical break from the Beatles, but mentally there is still this big thing on my back about what people expected of me." And: "We were the hip ones of the sixties. But the world is not like the sixties. The whole world has changed." And: "Produce your own dream. It's quite possible to do anything . . . the unknown is what it is. And to be frightened of it is what sends everybody scurrying around chasing dreams, illusions."

Good-bye, baby, and amen.

—Los Angeles *Times*, 11 December 1980

A Reasonable Guide to Horrible Noise

Christgau calls it "skronk." I have always opted for the more obvious "horrible noise." Guitars and human voices are primary vectors, though just about every other musical instrument has been employed over the years, as well as smashed crockery (e.g., first Pere Ubu album, "Sentimental Journey"), scraped garbage-can lids and bongolated oil drums (early Stooges), not to mention phono cartridges, toothpicks, pipe cleaners, etc. (John Cage, *Variations II*). You probably can't stand it, but this stuff has its adherents (like me) and esthetic (if you want to call it that).

Look at it this way: there are many here among us for whom the life force is best represented by the livid twitching of one tortured nerve, or even a full-scale anxiety attack. I do not subscribe to this point of view 100%, but I understand it, have lived it. Thus the shriek, the caterwaul, the chainsaw gnarlgnashing, the yowl and the whizz that decapitates may be reheard by the adventurous or emotionally damaged as mellifluous bursts of unarguable affirmation. And one could, if so inclined, take it even further than that: in his essential book *The Tuning of the World*, under the heading "Sacred Noise and Secular Silence," composer R. Murray Schafer reports that during the Middle Ages to which we are after all now returning "a certain type of noise, which we may now call Sacred Noise, was not only absent from the lists of proscripted sounds which societies from time to time drew up, but was, in fact, quite deliberately invoked as a break from the tedium of tranquility." Or, as Han Shan also did once advise one of his Zen acolytes at Kyoto in lieu of canewhipping the whelp, "If you're feeling uptight and truly would prefer to sail into the mystic, just chuglug two quarts of coffee and throw on side one of the first Clash album (Eng. edition) at ten, full treble, no bass." Any more koans you need answered, refer 'em to Wild Man Fischer.

The point of all this, of course, is that hideous racket is *liberating:* to "go with the flow," as Jerry Brown put it in his book *Thoughts* (City Lights, 1975), is always a wiser course of action than planting oneself directly in the path of the Seventh Avenue express, itself best portrayed on record by "Sister Ray" and the first New York Dolls album. I am also firmly convinced that one reason for the popularity of rap music, like disco and punk before it, is that it's so utterly annoying to those of us whose cup of blare it isn't; more than once its fans have walked up to a doorless telephone booth I was occupying, set their mammoth radios down on the sidewalk five inches from my feet, and stood there smiling at me. They didn't want to use the phone, but I find it hard to begrudge them such gleeful rudeness; how could I, after walking all over the city with my also highly audible cassette player emitting free jazz, *Metal Machine Music*, PiL's "Theme," Miles Davis's "Rated X" and Iannis Xenakis's *Electro-Acoustic Music*, part of which the composer described as sound paintings of the bombing of Greece? So fair is fair, even given the differences in taste.

Which also extends into questions of set and setting. Once I was eating lunch with two friends near St. Mark's Place, and a familiar sound started coming out of the jukebox. It took me a few seconds to recognize it, but that voice was unmistakable: "Hey," I said, "it's Lydia and the Jerks doing 'Orphans'!" One friend laughed: "Well folks, enjoy your meals!" But she hadn't noticed it till I'd brought it to her attention, and in context it didn't sound all *that* more yakkety than the Beatles' "Helter Skelter," which immediately preceded it. Then of course there is the whole question of Muzak and whether digestion really is improved by the theme from *Dr. Zhivago.* Or whether heavy metal and punk are essentially the same sound, or disco and punk equally oppressive. But then, when Patti Smith reviewed *Velvet Underground Live 1969* in *Creem* back in '75, she said she liked it precisely because it *was* oppressive, with which I at least partially concur. Everybody has their little peculiarities, as evidenced by the fact that some people actually like to listen to the radio! So perhaps I can best bear witness to my own by listing a few of the Gehennas of wretched squawl which have made me most aware that I am alive over the years:

■ The Stooges, "L.A. Blues," *Fun House* (Elektra): After assaulting us for half an hour with six songs including the bulleted-boar tenor sax of Steve Mackay, the Ann Arbor visionaries let the whole thing explode and melt all over itself in this arrhythmic 1970 offering, replete with igneous feedback blankets, Mackay blowing his brains out and disappearing forever, and the man called Pop mewling, snarling, sighing, and licking his paws.

■ The Germs, "Forming"/"Live" (What? single): It was all downhill for Darby and Co. after this 1978 debut. They could not yet play the rather standard-issue Ramonesclone headbangisms of their album, so they had to toddle along a guitar and rhythm track that sounded like Malt-o-Meal being trailed from dining room to TV set, while Darb puled burble whose chorus you could tell he had reached whenever he repeated the words "Pull my trigger / I'm bigger than. . . ."

■ *A Taste of DNA* (American Clave EP, 1981): The lead instrument in the new, improved DNA is neither Arto Lindsay's slamming and scrapings of the electric twelve-string guitar he never plays chords on nor his laconically imploding epiglottis. It is Tim Wright's bass, which ain't even bereft of melody. And Ikue Mori cuts Sunny Murray in my book. Sure wish Ayler was alive to play with these folks (don't laugh; Ornette almost played on "Radio Ethiopia")—*he* played "skronk" (the word sounds like something straight from his bell) if anybody ever did.

■ *The Sounds of the Junkyard* (Folkways): Recorded live, of course, and quite a bit more soothing than you would expect, though with titles like "Burning Out an Old Car" you know it can't miss.

■ Yoko Ono, "Don't Worry Kyoko, Mummy's Only Looking for a Hand in the Snow" (flip of John's "Cold Turkey" single, and side two of *Live Peace in Toronto* LP, Apple, 1969–70): Interesting not only for John's churning blues-unto-feedback guitar riff and how far ahead of her time Yoko was vocally (though dig Patty Waters's "Black Is the Color" on ESP-Disk in early sixties) but for lyrical correspondence with Lydia Lunch's "Orphans," featured on

■ *Teenage Jesus and the Jerks* (Migraine EP, 1980). If, as Christgau says, "Arto is the king of skronk," then Lydia's slide guitar work certainly qualifies her as queen. Guys in my sixth-grade neighborhood used to entertain themselves by tying the head of a cat to one hot-rod fender and its tail to another and driving the cars apart slowly, which sounded a lot like part of this. Unless it's for Catholic-school beatings by nuns, nostalgia doesn't account for Lydia's passionate "Baby Doll" wailing. If you only want to try one, make it this—nothing more deathly shrill has ever been recorded.

■ Jad Fair, *The Zombies of Mora-Tau* (Armageddon EP, 1980): Jad is half of 1/2 Japanese, and with his brother David made a 1/2 J. *three-record set* that I still haven't been able to listen to all the way through. A previous EP containing such highlights as "School of Love" was great, but this might even be better for the way Jad integrates atonal air-raid guitar with sub–Jonathan Richman white-burba-infantilismus vocals that as they natter tunelessly onward actually tell little stories ("And I said, 'Dr. Frankenstein, you must die,' and I shot him" and you hear the gun KABLOO-IE!). This may be a whole new songwriting genre, or at least one terminal of the Lou Reed "I walked to the chair / Then I sat in it" school of lyrics.

■ Lou Reed: *Metal Machine Music* (RCA, 1975): Don't see this around much any more, but it sure caused a ruckus when he sprang it on *Transformer / Sally Can't Dance* rocky horror fans: a two-record, hour-long set of shrieking feedback run through various pieces of high-tech equipment. Sounded great in midwestern suburbs, but kinda unnecessary in NYC.

■ Blue Cheer, *Vincebus Eruptum* (Philips, 1968): These guys may well have been the first true heavy metal band, but what counts here is not whether Leigh Stephens birthed that macho grunt before Mark Farner (both stole it from Hendrix) but that Stephens's sub-sub-sub-sub-Hendrix guitar overdubs stumbled around each other so ineptly they verged on a truly bracing atonality.

■ *The Mars EP* (Infidelity, 1980): With Teenage Jesus, DNA, and the Contortions, this group was featured on the watershed *No New York* LP (You mean you don't own a copy? What are you, *sick* or something?). But for my money this piece of beyond-lyrics, often beyond-discernible-instrumentation psychotic noise is their absolute masterpiece—despite *John Gavanti*, their version of Mozart's *Don Giovanni*, which I have never been able to listen to all the way through. This is not "industrial" but *human* music, and so what if said humans sound like they're in a bad way? You are too. As it grinds and grieves and grovels, you cannot deny that they certainly plow what they sow. Best cut: "Scorn." Best rumor: Somebody dropped the original tapes, produced by Arto Lindsay, in water. And accidentally, at that.

—*Village Voice,* 30 September–6 October 1981

PART SIX

Unpublishable

Fragments,
1976–1982

will not listen to reason. I think, however, that I may have found a solution. I called up a local aspiring movie company, turning out American International–imitation thrill-flix from Michigan (their latest was *Attack of the Wolverines*), and we're going to star Mongo in a snuff movie, which from what I've been told will clean up at the grind house nabes even better than blaxploitation and kung fu did last year. I don't think anybody will miss him, but just in case I've hired a stand-in to reply to all queries with "No." In fact, I've even stopped answering the phone:

RING

"Lester?"

"No."

"Is he there?"

"No."

"Do you know when he will be back?"

"No."

"Can you take a leave word?"

"No."

"This isn't an answering service?"

"No."

"Well, just tell him Van Morrison called; I'm having trouble coming up with some lyrics for my next album, and I know how good Lester is with rhyming couplets, like that one he gave Ted Nugent: 'First course I bit off her left tit / Second course I shoved *Kiss Alive* up her slit / There was no way to follow that / So I shoved *Metal Machine Music* after it by way of tat.' Do you know that song?"

"No."

"Okay, well, tell Lester as soon as you see him, okay? Because I'm desperate. I haven't been able to get an album together since *Veedon Fleece* and even when it was playing that barely existed and I'm a little worried, not really uptight but just mildly apprehensive, y'dig?"

"No."

"Okay, fine, gotta run, just give my message to Lester."

"No."

"By the way, what's your name?"

"Idi Amin."

The Jewish people do not exist. They did not exist before Hitler, and were a myth created entirely by his propagandists to cover up the fact that he killed 6,000,000 Jehovah's Witnesses.

Hip hip hooray. A vote in favor of hatred. Isn't it better now that all cards are in the open than in the glorious fifties sixties when they had a million rags to wipe their jerkoffs on. I am proud to be alive. And I am young! Know enough teenage suicides! Not even wimps! Takes courage to be a wimp nowadays! I don't want no scripts. Who indeed will read this, who in fact will care, you see the existentialist equation perhaps has changed (a) I will live (b) maybe no one will see this, naw, it was always like that, women and drugs made it feel different, enough lies. Enough. But to go on! Hey boy, you only thirty years old! Dead! Burnt out! Washed up! Finished! A bit of flotsam! And in that flotsam your salvation! In one grain of that wood. In one bit of that irrelevance. If you can bring yourself to describe it, you might be a writer again. You might be a writer. Who is? I do not believe in Maldoror. Burroughs wrote Naked Lunch when almost fifty. Take them out of your hide. You are young. Yes, you. You are dead. But you choose to. It's rockin' time. In spite of all trends, fads, bits of money cleaved or flaking off the big circus, I think there's a load out there, still, say, hey say, it's rockin' time.

There was no getting around it: I was hungry, which meant I'd have to leave the apartment. The street was empty but not quite neutral: the switchings of streetlights was enough to set my nerves on edge. Some little seething bit of lidded granulate black intelligence looking out at you. The deli, on the other hand, was full of bodies: five of them. I walked in anyway. I could feel it the instant I did, and shrunk from the contact. Stopped a moment to look at the racks of dried fruits and nuts. *Why am I doing this?* I reasoned. *I have no idea if I want these or not. Better stick to whatever it is I know I want.* So I headed towards the back, dread in a glance at the soda case. There was a puffy punkette girl there. I had to pass her. I didn't say anything. My flesh crawled. Then I stared at the yogurt. *You know this is what you're going to buy,* I thought. *Pick it up.* It didn't even take me that long to pick out Peach and Piña Colada. Then, however, I had to stand near the front for an eternity while one of the two men behind the counter, a mideastern man who looked like the father of the other one, bagged the punkette's groceries. Everything she was buying contained white sugar except the cigarettes. Hershey bars. Froot Loops. I looked away. She looked at me. I looked farther away. There were two guys in their thirties standing near there. You couldn't tell if they were in line or what. I guess they were just hanging out. "Excuse me," I said. They didn't say anything. I loathed them. What kind of person hangs out in a deli smaller than my living room? I didn't want to know. While I was waiting I listened to the music blaring out of the ceiling. It sounded like skeletal remains of robots being pounded against each other while a cocaine ball bearing twangs your notochord and mewls about some woman he claims is a demon. Finally the punkette got her bag of groceries and left. "Is this all?" asked Dad Hamid. "Yes," I said. "A dollar thirty," he said. I counted thirteen dimes out of my freezing palm and handed them to him. I was waiting for him to count them but he flung them into the drawer with a crash that splattered spiderlike across my nervous system. Clutching my yogurt in its little brown bag to my chest, I huddled out the door. Once back on the almost-neutral sidewalk, I exhaled involuntarily, turning into an audible laugh as my shoulders sagged. *Good god in heaven,* I thought. *What is the matter with all those people?*

I bought *The Ice Age* by Margaret Drabble. Read it fast, too—had a better time than any book since *La Nausée.* It's all about people who actually welcome depression as a relief from anxiety. Our time! Let's face it, we cannot cooperate and we hate each other.

If we're all that separate what can we do? Well, freeze! I mean, it is a viable alternative. Have you ever had someone sit down and explain why suicide is a "viable alternative"? I have. It's hilarious. I don't believe in "viable alternatives." I believe in blind alleys.

Right next to *The Ice Age* was *Ice!,* which I bought too and read in one night. It's a Bantam thriller about how the new ice age is coming gonna swallow us all up, I guess a more crass plebe-prole version of the "alienation" Drabble is dealing in—hers comes from inside, this chill from outside, what's the difference? But last week I'm at my favorite newsstand when all of a sudden there's another one: *Ice.* Without the exclamation this time. A completely different novel by a completely different author on the same subject: how our world must inevitably and soon succumb to polar frigidities. Undoubtedly true as publication of these two books proves, but that's not what's interesting here, what's interesting is that two separate novelists wrote two separate books telling us all to forget it, and they even structured the damn tomes the same: both of 'em start off in first chapter first page and finish last chapter last page with a spate of pseudocosmic spew: "The great universe moved on" and all that. As if we needed it in the first place! It was crap when Melville did it and it's crap now! Of course the great universe moves on—why in the hell do ya think we read novels? To preserve the illusion that it doesn't!

At least 50% of the time when you call R.Q. up on the phone, he immediately says, "Can't talk sorry thanks!" in a constricted voice with a rueful little laugh and rings off.

P.N. has a Phone-Mate automatic answering machine, which he leaves on twenty-four hours a day, to screen out all calls he does not want. You dial his number, hear a ring, then the tape: "This is P—— N—— via answerphone. I'm busy right now, but if you want to leave a message wait until after the beep." The voice seems to issue from some etherous vaporous void, and there is a strange protracted lag between the last word of his message and the actual beep. Sometimes, after I hear the beep and say who it is, he immediately picks up. Often he does not. Sometimes the latter option obtains for weeks.

V.B. says never to call her before eleven P.M. Then I have to let it ring once, hang up and dial again, or let it ring twice, hang up and dial again. I can never remember which. Often she doesn't answer anyway, either because the phone has been pulled out of the wall or she can't imagine anyone calling she would want to speak to. Until very recently, she was at home almost twenty-four hours a day.

N.T. leaves his phone off the hook most of the time. The surest way to lose his friendship is to give his number to someone without asking first. Like R.Q., he is listed in the phone book under a name other than his own.

J.R. lets his girlfriend answer the phone 90% of the time, and almost never goes out of the house, especially since he bought his new thirty-inch color set and an extensive array of video games.

J.M. always answers his phone, but all his friends laugh about his habit of responding to your query of whether he'd like to come out/over with, "Nah, why don't you come over here?" He denies this.

W.G. used to get drunk and hang out on the corner round St. Mark's Place every time he left his apartment; like most of the rest of us, he found that alcohol made it easier for him to stand being around human beings other than himself. Now he is trying not to drink, so he doesn't go out much at all. We have been friends for almost nine years, and I can't remember having spoken to him on the phone more than a couple of times. I think he has once.

R.W. lives in Detroit, in a little house at the end of a bombed-out street in the ghetto. He says they finally diagnosed him: "agoraphobia." Fear of the marketplace. He has lost his phone service several times. The last time I visited him, he had let bushes in front of his house go untrimmed until they completely covered his porch.

These are my best friends in the world. I do not have a phone, and consider it a minor neurosis that I keep house so appallingly that almost no one ever wants to visit me up here. Although I have no idea why, I am more gregarious than my friends. I visit them. Then we have conversations like the following:

R.Q.: "Admit it, the human race is worthless. You know it's true!"

L.B.: "No, I think they just don't know any better. They mean well."

R.Q.: "They don't mean anything. They aren't even human beings."

Or:

N.T.: "I sure wish I could figure out some way to live without ever having to go outside of the house."

L.B.: "Why?"

N.T.: "I can't stand being around people. Don't worry, you're not one."

L.B.: "But how can you be a writer when you never have any experiences?"

N.T.: "Use your imagination!"

Unfortunately, I suspect it's starting to go the way of my emotions.

Increasingly, I feel like Tom Sawyer at his own funeral. One day I even wrote my own obituary: "He was promising. . . ." Then it occurred to me:

"Shit, I can't even commit suicide! Look what I'd have for a tombstone: *Blondie!*"

I quit! I quit! But I don't quit you (the reader)! And I am not alone! I am not the only writer who respects you! So DON'T READ ANYBODY WHO DOESN'T. Oh sorry, that means no reading. No it doesn't, read Dostoyevsky (no I'm not as good as him according to me, never will be don't think, so what who cares)—JUST STAND UP FOR YOUR-SELVES WILL YOU!!! WRITE YOUR OWN FUCKING MAGA-ZINES!

Ahhhhhh, it's useless. No, it's not. We may hate ourselves but there is enough we love, we shall be redeemed, no longer reduced. How can I believe anything but this and go on putting words on paper? The paper should stay where it is otherwise. Where it came from. You know. You don't? Well don't ask me cause I don't either. Am I turning into the male Joan Baez. Then stop reading. And please tell me. I have no answers, no Big Picture, no future, no nothing except one plea: THINK FOR YOUR-SELF. You refuse? Hmmmmmm. I'm presuming, I know. For now. I will go knock myself out and return in a more reasonable frame of mind. Perhaps tear all this up.

Buried deep in the Sex Pistols' *The Great Rock 'n' Roll Swindle*, one of
the greatest albums ever made, is Johnny Rotten singing to San Francisco:
"Belsen was a gas I heard the other day / In the open graves where the Jews
all lay / Life is fun and I wish you were here / They wrote on postcards
to those held dear." At the end of the song he begins to shriek: "We don't
mind! Belsen was a gas! Kill someone! Kill yourself! We don't mind! Please
someone! Kill someone! Kill yourself!" Then there is a moment of silence
and the crowd screams. It's one of the most frightening things I've ever
heard. You wonder exactly what they might know they were screaming for.
As you wonder exactly what you might be affirming by listening to this over
and over again. On one level Johnny Rotten/Lydon is an insect buzzing
atop the massed ruins of a civilization leveled by itself, which I suppose
justifies him right there, on another level he's just another trafficker in
cheap nihilism with all that it includes—cheap racism, sexism, etc. I'm still
not comfortable with "Bodies." But then I never was, which may be the
point. But then I wonder if he is. After which I cease to wonder at anything
beyond the power of this music.

In life things never do what they should. In rock 'n' roll things always
do what they should. That's why it's fascist.

I am surrounded by psychotics. Often I suspect I am one. Then
certain records come out and I know I am not alone.

Man on radio: "I'm not here to teach you to think."

Neither am I. What I am here for is to con you into buying anything
by PiL.

I would not presume to say the audience in San Francisco wanted to die, but dying takes no courage now. That may be why John Lydon/ Rotten quit the Sex Pistols immediately after that night. There are only so many times you can tell somebody something in plain English till you realize they don't get the irony even in that; they don't hear the words. All they see is a reflection of a spurious notion of the self and a spurious passion too, so you stop attempting to communicate. If people want to think Belsen was a cheap joke, that's their problem. So Rotten/Lydon retreated to England, where he formed Public Image Ltd., which people on both sides of the pond have not been shy telling me they think is also a joke.

But then most people don't listen to music, as the Sex Pistols proved conclusively.

I don't give a fuck about John Lydon. I suspect him to be a pompous little putz. Let him blab in *NME*. Still, I think he knows what he's doing, and PiL is the proof. Because *The Metal Box* is one of the strongest records I've heard in years. PiL's first was just a big fuck you to all the people who bought the Pistols on sight and never heard a word and this album contin- ues that tradition from its film-can packaging to its music—but even the first album contained "Theme," one of the best arguments for not commit- ting suicide I know.

The first words in this new album are "Slow motion." Like Jean Malaquais: "Please do not understand me too quickly." I think that could be Lydon's motto. This group never tours—the result is they spend all their time working in the studio on this stuff, as shown by the fact that there are three different versions of "Death Disco," their second single, and two radically different versions of "Memories," their third. One, the twelve- inch, is a fairly straightforward indictment, no, a rant against nostalgia culture. I read in *NME* that it was directed at the "Mod Revival" in England but then I don't believe anything I read in *NME* anymore. Whether or not it applies to "Happy Days," *Grease*, all the proliferating falsifications of what I and everyone I know experienced once in what it is now so convenient to call "the fifties" or "the sixties," as if life was really measured or lived in arbitrary decades, when the history books are sold like comix I for one will still be listening to Lydon: "You make me feel ashamed / Enacting attitudes / Remember ridicule? / It should be clear by now / Your words are useless, full of excuses, false confidence / Someone has used you well / Used you well."

Then, on the album version, the whole sound shifts, into a new and hotter realm. It's something I have never in my life heard anyone do in the middle of a track, and as the grooves begin to burn themselves away he resumes: "I could be wrong / It could be hate / As far as I can see clinging desperately / No personality dragging on and on and on and on / I think you're slightly late / Slightly late . . . "

There aren't many pieces of music that (his next lines: "This person's had enough of useless memories") express completely how I feel as a human citizen of this—whatever you want to call it. I don't mean to glorify such a feeling, it's just that it's lonely and there are I suppose only a few people whose alienation matches anyone else's. Maybe someone else finds it somewhere else. For me, I'll stake ten years of writing about this shit on *Blank Generation* and *The Metal Box*. And *On the Corner* and *Get Up with It* by Miles Davis, which got kudos from jazz critics who never listened to them again and were rejected by the fans. The reason is the same: this is negative music, in all cases this is bleak music, this is music from the other side of something I feel but *I* don't want to cross, but if you feel the same then perhaps at least you can affirm this music, which knows that there is nothing that can be affirmed till almost (and that's my word, not theirs) everything has been denied. Or you can laugh hysterically at it, like a friend of mine who has actually attempted suicide a couple of times. When I played him "Theme" and said "Can you relate to that" he laughed harder. "Sure," he said. "Who couldn't?"

from "All My Friends Are Hermits," 1980

I called her. Right in the middle of the conversation, she said: "What do you feel like doing right now?" I replied, automatically, same tone of voice as one might say "I could go for a tuna sandwich on rye," I said: "I wanna fuck." A second of silence. Then: "Okay," she said, just as casually. "Come on over." I got there fast. She met me at the door in a frowzy black slip, hair all a mess, no makeup, barefoot, half-asleep, emotionally neutral to the world. I thought she was the sexiest thing I'd ever seen in my life. Especially in that ratty old black slip. I couldn't believe I was about to be holding something as magnificent as this in my arms, such a hunk of *woo*-man, such a primal Earth Goddess, such a lush juicy creation of the Almighty God in Heaven or Hell I didn't care which and she had a brain besides! I had it made. Life couldn't get any better than this! Like Swamp Dogg once sang: "If I die tomorrow / I've lived tonight!" Damn straight! Who cared if Western civilization was sinking into entropy or gearing up for Armageddon, I never could decide which? All my philosophy was gibberish, and Western civilization was a bucket of shit in the first place! So who cared! I wanted to fuck this woman in the mud of a ditch while a firestorm of whitehot PLO and Israeli bullets whizzed over our heads! I wanted to take her down to the Everglades and throw her down in the swamp and do dirty things to her till she screamed like a polecat tangled up in an electrified fence for "More! More! More! Stop! Stop! Stop! No, don't! Eat me! Kill me! Break me! Fuck me!" And then I'd push her down so deep in the mud and the green slime and rotting tropical overgrowth it almost buried both of us in our faces and hair and mouths and we'd love like reptiles slither down lower than the gutter our screaming bellies pounding together in the muck from which all life sprang before we or the media or New York magazine careers or anything else amounted to shit! Alligators would come slogging over, take one look at the likes of us and turn right around and hightail it the other way! Water moccasins cowered at the bottom of the river, scared we'd bite 'em and then they'd die! Because we are death as well as life! We are jungle fever, beri-beri, Mau Maus ravenous for each other after which we'll go machete and bar-bee-cue us some missionaries! We have become one with the primordial ooze! Beats the Upper East Side for shitsure! Then I yank her up from the slime and jet nonstop to Cambodia. I want to fuck her on top of a pile of bleached bones, mountains of skulls, hundreds of rotting carcasses! I want to feel death all around me, that's how alive I feel just looking at her, and TO BE INSIDE . . . yeah I want death from sea to shining sea, mountains of it blotting out the horizon, I want to scream with wild dog joy in the pit of a smoking charnel house! In Makindye Prison, Kampala, Uganda! On top of spilled organs of the dead a foot deep! I want Idi Amin to see us! He's been around a bit, I know, but he's never seen this! Might learn something! I want to fuck death, I want death to know that it ain't shit, I can lick it, because what I am holding in my arms right now and am about to carry into the bedroom and to which I will deliver up my body and soul deep in the center of her belly, the center of *her*, I'm serving notice right now is the final and absolute inarguable rebuttal that shoots death down forever!

Review of Peter Guralnick's
Lost Highway: Journeys &
Arrivals of American Musicians

It's not often these days that anything makes you feel genuine awe, much less (non-jingoistic) patriotism. But those are two of the most pertinent words which come to mind when I think of Peter Guralnick's new book *Lost Highway*. As in his previous *Feel Like Going Home*, his subject is the fathers of American music—here, twenty-one seminal figures in the by now all but lost arts of blues, rhythm 'n' blues, country and western, and the original rock 'n' roll.

You put the book down feeling that its sweep is vast, that you have read of giants who walked among us, inspired by the truly mighty dreams and possibilities of the kind of place where any kid could grow up to become Elvis Presley. Hence the patriotism. Which feels even stranger to say than it would anyway, because this book's main theme is how these men were buried by those very dreams, Elvis being only the most obvious case in point. Ernest Tubb, Hank Snow, Bobby Bland, Waylon Jennings, Hank Williams, Jr., Howlin' Wolf, Merle Haggard, Charlie Rich and the others less famous written of here have all probably lost something of themselves in the bone-wearying life of musicians on the road—possibly best summed up by a friend of Ernest Tubb who says, "I think Ernest will die right in the back of that damn bus."

In a very real sense this is a book about a bunch of defeated men, commercial success or failure seeming to make very little difference. Like Guralnick, the reader is struck by the way in which the pursuit of success seriously, inevitably distorted the very core of their being, as well as the music itself. To paraphrase Little Richard, they all got (or didn't get) what they wanted but almost invariably lost what they had.

The amazing thing is that a book about defeat could be so beautiful. In part this is because Guralnick understands so well and expresses so eloquently the forces that grind many of America's greatest artists to dust. But it's also because he never loses sight of the dream that set them all on that highway in the first place. Thus we see Ernest Tubb, for instance, go from first hearing the Call—"The thought of being a professional musician never entered his mind," writes Guralnick, " . . . until he heard Jimmie Rodgers' first Blue Yodel, which came out on the Victor Label in 1927 when he was thirteen. From that day on he knew exactly what he wanted to be"—to being a victim of Nashville's recent "cultural schizophrenia" in which the present can no longer come to terms with a past it has always at least nominally venerated.

"Cultural schizophrenia," in fact, is a major recurrent theme of the book: urban and rural, black and white, the realities of the road vs. songs celebrating home and family life. "All of 'em were totally nuts," says an admiring insider of Elvis, Jerry Lee Lewis and the rest of the progenitors of rockabilly on Sam Phillips's Sun Records. "I think every one of them must have come in on the midnight train from nowhere. I mean, it was like they came from outer space." Years later, Johnny Cash will sing "I Wish I Was Crazy Again" with Waylon Jennings, and Jerry Lee will have a hit called "Middle Age Crazy." What getting "crazy," "real gone," being a "bopcat" was all about, though, was a historically inevitable racial confluence: "I recall one jockey telling me that Elvis Presley was so country he shouldn't be played after five A.M.," said Sam Phillips. "And others said he was too black for them." There are scenes of white and black dancers on opposite sides of cordoned-off rooms in southern jukejoints, literally dancing the barriers down; perhaps the most extreme example of American music as racial melting pot is Stoney Edwards, number-two-ranked "black" country and western singer behind Charley Pride, who says, "I grew up not knowing what I was, Negro, Indian, or white. . . . I can't see anything in my future to equal the pain I been through. . . . I was never really accepted by anyone until I started singing country music." More lucky (or willful) was Big Joe Turner, who turned down a job singing with Count Basie because he would have had to stop shouting the blues during the brass parts, and of whom Guralnick writes: "He remained a free man. When boogie woogie fell into decline, Big Joe Turner became known as a blues shouter. When rock 'n' roll came into vogue, he was a rock 'n' roller. He did it, as he explains, without ever changing his style."

And in fact the figures in the book who come off best (meaning happiest) are those with sheer indomitable will like Turner, or Howlin' Wolf who got up from a car accident which sent him flying through a windshield at the age of sixty-three, went right back on the road and toured for the rest of his life with severe kidney damage, stopping off at a hospital in every city he played for dialysis treatment. Others developed a strategy that kept 'em guessing, like Merle Haggard, of whom Guralnick writes: "His whole career, in fact, can be looked upon as a series of deliberate avoidances [walking out on "The Ed Sullivan Show," quitting a network production of *Oklahoma!*], instinctive retreats from the obvious, and restatements of his central role as an outsider. . . . Perhaps this is what has enabled him to create the astonishing body of work that represents the 'career' of Merle Haggard." For country boys who went looking for an elusive but palpable American dream and inevitably if unintentionally cut themselves off from their roots in the process, accommodation simply does not work.

Perhaps the saddest example of this in the book is Charlie Rich, who started off as one of the original Sun Records bopcats with "Lonely Weekends" in the fifties, went through years of alcoholism and obscurity, hit again in the mid-sixties with the almost-novelty "Mohair Sam," followed it up with a song he truly cared about which flopped, and has been a deeply cautious and troubled man ever since, even though he climbed out of obscurity once again in the mid-seventies with "Behind Closed Doors." Today he is, seemingly against all odds, enshrined as the Silver Fox, a veritable country music institution, with a seldom broken string of hit singles and albums.

Yet we realize his sadness (and Guralnick pulls off the nigh-impossible, making us feel for the problems of somebody richer and more "successful" than we are) when we see him going to the Village Vanguard in New York City and encountering racial hostility and a fusion-jazz group that has nothing to do with jazz as he has known and played it ("I just wanted to show you, it's not . . . the way it was," he says), and later when his wife, who has kept him together through decades of failures and successes, says,

> "I think it's almost a tragedy when you lose your enthusiasm for something that suited you. . . . It turns into a business, and it just about destroys your creativity. . . . Sometimes I wish he was just playing somewhere for free, playing piano alone or with a small group, just so he could enjoy the music."
>
> "I did that for about twenty years," Charlie protests softly. His broad, melancholy face always has a slightly hurt look about it. It is at once more mobile and more handsome in its private grief than in the countless grins and strained grimaces he has

learned to adopt for TV appearances and ads. "When I first started working those little clubs in Memphis, I could play anything I wanted to for ten or fifteen dollars a night. Then when I went to Sun Records I went with the idea that I would do just about anything, as long as I could keep close to the music. I thought I could work the studio gig, make a little bit, and play my jazz at home. . . . You know, when you have a wife and a family, you have to sacrifice a little bit. . . . But there comes a time when you've been working at something so long, trying so long and so hard, that you reach a point where you get scared. And you start thinking to yourself, what am I going to be doing when I'm sixty-five? I don't want to be playing the Nightlighter Club when I'm sixty-five years old. Which could very easily have been the end result. And still could be."

Lost Highway is a book of lives, real lives in America, that are at once larger-than-life and human and humble. Maybe you will come away saying, as Guralnick does in his introduction, "I love the music as much as I ever did, but I have a public confession to make: I don't want to be a rock 'n' roll star any more." Yet he consistently gives us scenes along the road that are so strange and haunting (Hank Williams, Jr., as a teenager, driving around in the very same car his daddy died in, after having it customized and souped-up), or touching (Stoney Edwards confessing, "I ain't never found anything that was more exciting than making corn whiskey"), that they make the whole trip worthwhile. And when it's done, you may find yourself feeling, as Elvis's producer Felton Jarvis said upon learning of Presley's death, "It's like someone just came up and told me there aren't going to be any more cheeseburgers in the world." Or you may conclude, about all these people, America, and even yourself, what Guralnick concludes of Nashville legend/madman/producer Cowboy Jack Clement: "Maybe it's the journey, not the arrival, that matters."

—Los Angeles *Herald-Examiner*, 15 April 1980

from
Notes for Review of
Peter Guralnick's
Lost Highway, 1980

Sam Phillips. Reclusive. PG's dream of meeting Sam, his 'n' his friends' fifties fantasies: like other kids dream of being President, Joe Namath, curing cancer, "my friends and I had constructed elaborate fantasies not just about Elvis but about the man who had been the first to record Elvis, Jerry Lee Lewis, Carl Perkins . . ." As he interviewed more 'n' more people who'd recorded at Sun Records with Sam Phillips, even as they complained abt royalty rates, the fantasy ballooned, "only fueled my vision of this behind-the-scenes Machiavellian genius who had discovered so many of the unique talents of a generation and seemingly gotten the very best out of them while they were still on his label." Finally gets to meet his Machiavelli. 1978 at SP's radio station, WWEE in Memphis. Promised no more than fifteen-minute interview, talks for hours . . . PG particularly struck by contrast between all pix he'd ever seen of Sam when young "a slick-haired businessman with a sly, almost foxy smile and the slit-eyed look of Jerry Lee Lewis" and shock of seeing real older Sam now: "an Old Testament prophet in tennis sneakers, his long hair and long reddish beard only matching the oracular tone and language that came out in the cadences of a southern preacher. . . . I realized as he talked that he was speaking to every fantasy I had ever had abt him," that telling the story of Sun Records in Memphis in the fifties "he was telling the story of how one man, and one group, had made history."

"My mission," Sam told PG, "was to bring out of a person what was in him, to recognize that individual's unique quality and then to find the key to unlock it."

On the list of people who could easily have said exactly the same thing: Charles Manson, Captain Beefheart, Lee Strasberg, Alfred Hitchcock, Joseph Stalin. Sam Phillips, clearly, is a shaman. Was and still is. The power of the shamanistic gift is volatile, according to the nature of the gifted one himself: if he's been abused early or has an evil streak or's just a plain psychopath, then watch out; if he's fundamentally healthy and motivated by humanitarian or loving impulses, his effects on those around him, whose own talents vary wildly, though that makes no difference here, can often produce incidents, moments, occasions, personal chemistries that are absolutely magical in the strictest sense, and if we're lucky, they get recorded.

As Sam himself will tell you: "My greatest contribution, I think, was to open up an area of freedom within the artist himself, to help him express what *he* believed his message to be. Talking about egos—these people unfortunately did not *have* an ego. They had a desire—but at the same time to deal with a person that had dreamed, and dreamed, and dreamed . . . to deal with them under conditions where they were so afraid of being denied again—it took a pure instinctive quality on the part of any person that got the revealing aspects out of these people. It took an 'umble spirit. I don't care if it was me or somebody else."

One quality I've noticed in those few true shamans it's been my good fortune to observe up close: they don't walk around bellowing how they're the Messiah—some of their students, yes—the true Masters just do their work and go. Think of Sam Phillips as a lightning rod—and recognize that what happened in those Sun studios in the mid-fifties wasn't just a case of Brilliant Producer and Talented Hillbillies hitting on the better mousetrap of stealing black music and selling it in a white-matinee-idol package, or even just a landmark in the history of rock 'n' roll. It was a landmark in the history of Western culture: that bunch of hillbillies in that shabby little room, some of them more than just half illiterate, changed the course of the history of the world. And it shocked all of them with the possible exception of Sam every bit as much as it shocked the most miscegenation-obsessive southern racist fanatic cranking out handbills six months later warning everybody that these primitive jungle rhythms were gonna wind up making virgin daughters pregnant 'n' after nine months bearing an epidemic of li'l black bucks even though most of the fathers too far gone on dope to say "I do" were putatively white.

It was June of 1951 when Phillips cut what many archivists/authorities agree was the first actual rock 'n' roll hit, "Rocket 88" by Jackie Breston (Sam leased it to Chess, it was about a hot rod) and in six months he had started the Sun label. Guralnick: "For the next two years Sun's roster was made up almost exclusively of black artists"—their first hit was by Rufus Thomas—blues singers like Joe Hill Louis, Dr. Isaiah Ross (claimed to cure the "Boogie Disease"), Howlin' Wolf, "whom Phillips remembers . . . not only as the most distinctive blues singer he ever recorded but as . . . the most unique *individual* whom he ever met in all his years in the record business."

Probably the biggest controversy in the Sun legend centers around Phillips's decision ("not without a great deal of soul-searching," assures Guralnick) in the wake of Elvis's first big breakthroughs in the summer of 1954 to largely (totally? on this Guralnick is never precise) "abandon his black constituency." Or, as reggae artist Winston "Burning Spear" Rodney had it in a song called "Days of Slavery": "They use us / Until they refuse us."

The famous pre-Elvis quote from Sam about how if only he had him a honky could sing like a darkie has been repeated so often in so many contexts—including Guralnick's—that there's gotta be some truth to it—except what? Sam explained it to Guralnick like this: "I saw what I was doing as not deserting the black man . . . but when I started out [1950] there was nobody on the scene recording black music, and by this time [1954] there was an awful lot of good black music that was being recorded by Atlantic, Specialty, Chess, Checker, and I felt that they could handle it real good. And I saw that what I was trying to do with white men was to broaden the base, to try to get more radio stations to play this kind of music, to give it more widespread exposure. I knew we had a hard trip for all of us. The Southern white man had an expression for his basic roots in country music in the Grand Ole Opry, but we didn't have that for the black man—and yet without those people there would have been no idea for us that was free of great encumbrance."

Lofty words, and I suspect a trifle disingenuous. Guralnick's interpretation, I think, isn't much more credible, though given his hero worship it's understandable: "What he was looking for from the beginning was the same unique quality he had found in Howlin' Wolf, the same *differentness* that he continues to prize to this day." Guralnick then spends the better part of a long paragraph stressing how much value Sam puts on the *individual*, how he loathes *conformity*, replete with quotes like "You can be a nonconformist and not be a rebel. And you can be a rebel and not be an outcast. Believe in what you believe in, and don't let *anybody*, I don't care who it is, get you off that path." Surely this is Sam Phillips buying his own myth, if not his own hype. It's interesting stuff, especially the part about how you can be a nonconformist without rebelling and a rebel without getting blackballed, but it's also a lot of windy rhetoric with whose basic sentiments we can all agree—pure shtick on one very real level, it goes so perfectly with the Moses mane and the beard of the prophet. I mean, fuck it, who's to say what Sam Phillips's "real" motives were? Might they not have been as confused and unplanned and even self-contradictory as anything else anybody else thought and then went and did some other time some other place? I mean, does everybody always sit down with this slide-ruled *plan* and a ten-point moral code on the wall behind 'em and then go into battle for the clear-cut Cause with all this pat as that and never deviating? I don't even know why I'm writing this many words when I'm supposed to be handing in a fifteen-hundred-word book review, so I can sort of begin to imagine how easy it must have been for Sam and everybody around him to get just a wee bit *spacy* when it became obvious that Elvis Presley was gonna be the single biggest human being to hit this planet since Jesus Christ.

But what I didn't see was that Sam was talking about Elvis: "You can be a nonconformist and not be a rebel. And you can be a rebel and not be an outcast." In another part of the book Guralnick remembers himself and his friends (a) waiting to see what Elvis was gonna be like when he got out of the army, and (b) having to watch and listen to what Elvis *was* like when he got out of the army. When they shoulda known by the attitude with which he went in. Just imagine if that'd been Chuck Berry instead: "All right, motherfuckers, you can cut my hair but you in for it now!" Or Jerry Lee: "Sure, draft me, what the hell, I kin kick ass good as the next SOB." One thinks of the famous picture from the late forties of Robert Mitchum getting busted for grass. *The army?* Big fucking deal. Life's fulla little pains in the ass, this is two years of bullshit, what the hell, I'll still be a star when I get out, oh, well, let's stay drunk till boot camp . . . Not Elvis. Elvis was a *momma's boy!* Elvis was *dutiful!* Elvis was a clod, always. But he had something, something at once physical and mystical, that put him in the realm of the beyond, automatically, far beyond any of his contemporaries, much less a Mick Jagger, who from the beginning worked so damn *hard* at being outrageous it was a little exhausting just watching him. The Beatles were four yobs, or rather three yobs and a librarian named Paul. Watch *A Hard Day's Night* on TV now and it's obvious how worthless that whole business was when removed from its immediate context of hysteria. Fuck the Beatles, fuck the songs, fuck the cute direction and Marx Brothers comparisons: it's BLATANTLY OBVIOUS that the most rock 'n' roll human being in the whole movie is the fucking grandfather! That wily old slime of Paul's! He had more energy than the four moptops put together! Plus the *spirit!* He was a true anarchist!

The Beatles were nothing. The Stones were something, still are I think, Dylan, well, but rock in the sixties in general was just plain overrated. In fact, the sixties were overrated. The Sex Pistols were a hundred times more of a kick in the ass of a sagging culture than the Beatles. But *Elvis*— the only credible explanation is that Elvis was from another planet, like in *Superman* or the New Testament. Elvis never even had to move a muscle, not even in his face—he always, from day one up till almost the very end, had that *glow*.

There was always something supernatural about him. Elvis was a force of nature. Other than that he was just a turd. A big dumb hillbilly a couple points smarter than his mule who wandered out from behind his plow one day to cut a record for his sainted mother and never came back, which he probably woulda forgot to even if he hadn't've been whisked up. Why shouldn't one physical corpus be capable of containing these two seeming polarities simultaneously? Especially if it's from outer space. Without even trying to or knowing he was doing it, Elvis caused more trouble, raised more hellfired ruckus than the Beatles, Stones and Sex Pistols all put together. Because of this, some people came up with the not altogether mistaken notion that he was subversive. He *was,* but like Burroughs's Nova Police his motto coulda been "We do our work and go." I mean, suppose he'd come outa the army and immediately started trying to be a badass again? Wouldn't he have ended up a pathetic old self-parody like Jagger? Most assuredly. In terms of sheer offensiveness and bizarritude, he was way hepper singing things like "Do the Clam." I mean, that ranks right up there with Sid Vicious's version of "My Way." Well, actually, you can't play it as often, but it sorta comes from the same place: *nowhere.* But nowhere is unassailable. Nowhere is Zen. And Elvis, like Sid in his way, was perfect. It was perfect he came outa the army to record a new version of "O Sole Mio" in much the same way that it was perfect the Sex Pistols should break up at the end of their first American tour. Both stances show great and similarly grounded integrity: we do our work and go. Having submitted to cryogenics the minute he entered the army, Elvis proved himself smarter than any of us had ever given him credit for being: he became Forever.

Perhaps Sam Phillips knew all this in front. Sun Records at its peak was like punk rock at its best, the premise and principle of American democracy brought right back home: I/you can do it too. Anybody can do it. All it takes is the spirit and a ton of gall. A quarter of a century later and *still* most people apparently don't realize (or, if they do, refuse to accept) this basic and transparently obvious fact. It's not about technique. It's not about virtuosity, twenty-five years at Juilliard, contrapuntal counterpoint, the use of 6/8 time in a Latin-tinged context. *This stuff is not jazz.*

This stuff is like playing marbles: aggies, greenies, steelies. This stuff is dirt bikes doing brodies: how long does it take to learn how to start up and ride one? Let somebody else fix the engine if it breaks down. This stuff is dirt. Everybody at Sun was white trash. The whole point of American culture is to pick up any old piece of trash and make it shine with more facets than the Hope Diamond. Any other approach is Europeanized, and fuck that—that whole continent's been dead a hundred years. Sid Vicious was the only time it came to life in a century. Whereas the American principle, what this country was really founded on, is *motion*. Energy, and using it to move on up or out and go and get somewhere, don't really matter where. Saddle up your pony and ride. Guralnick reports as much about the old Sun producer Jack Clement: that Jack's friends worry about him because he's crazy (only man I ever heard of had a tree with a swing attached installed in his living room so he can sit there swinging and staring and thinking up new forms of madness), some people suspect "he keeps talking simply for fear of what the silence might reveal," or, Guralnick: "Maybe it's just the journey, not the arrival, that counts."

Once the frontiers'd been crossed and a white bastard Europe's 86'd dregs-citizenry slaughtered the original landowners and took up trailer-park residency from sea to shining sea it was all over, nowhere to go but up, to the moon, as we did, and when we got there we played golf, just like the assholes we are, something I'm sure Elvis must have loved or certainly approved of, golfballs on the moon being not unlike mashed banana and peanut butter sandwiches three meals a day, so I suppose we'll go to Mars, except we found out there's no H. G. Wellsian nightmare lifeforms there, in fact there's nothing there, so we might as well go to Europe instead, helluva lot cheaper, but no, Elvis never did except for the army which wasn't his idea anyway, better just to keep going round in circles right here. Everybody should relax. Rock 'n' roll died when Elvis went down for his physical even if somebody forgot to tell Joey Ramone who sings "Nothin' to do and nowhere to go / I wanna be sedated" which was in later years Elvis's problem in a nutshell or more accurately gelatine capsule the fortunecookielike words of wisdom buffered by enough methaqualone to put the entire continent of Africa to sleep but not Elvis who used to lay in bed with the covers over his head getting fatter and fatter and more ethereal even in his gross corpulence ("He was no longer, it seemed, used to the air," Guralnick writes—*air*—reminding one of nothing so much as the hero of Huysmans's *Against Nature*, who after sampling all the decadent and sensual pleasures of society retreats to a little room where he steeps himself in ever more rarefied strains of artificial stimulation, one night opening up about seventeen different bottles of perfume and starting to sniff away at them, moving across the row from one exotic scent to the next sometimes next bottle sometimes way down the line sometimes all different from any others of the past few minutes sometimes repeating or returning to certain scent-motifs he particularly chimes in on, hittin' the note as the Allman Brothers used to say, thinking of this to my mind perfectly putrid and masturbatory indulgence as "a symphony of smells" he's composing but finally it all gets to be too much, he's overpowered by the fumes, sick, his brain reeling, his whole system reacting violently against such ghastly over-load, so he runs to the window, throws it open, breathes in the fresh spring air greedily, like a drowning man breaking the surface, and . . . falls to the floor in a wretched heap, helpless and half-dead because what he had not counted on was that his system had become so acclimated or adjusted or mutated to artificial stimuli that the original "natural" ones now threw it into chaos, panic and disease, which is to say that when he opened the window and breathed in, there was in the air a wisp of the smell of new flowers in the spring, dewfresh petals wafting, and after what he'd just subjected himself to the tiniest trace of said petals crunched him like a steamroller, threw his system into shock, dissolved his nerves, in short, the slightest wisp of nature even—or rather ESPECIALLY—in its purest, most pristine form, affected him like pure poison injected in the mainline, damn near killed him before the book was over, and when I read that book it reminded me more than anyone else of Elvis even though it was recom-mended to me by Richard Hell who said it was the best book he had ever read and when I asked him why he said it was because he admired the protagonist so much for his individualism and originality and integrity and all that: BUILD YOUR OWN WORLD AND BE, nobody's happy but maybe at least NO LONGER ALIENATED cause how can you be when nobody else is around course you're probably no longer human either or soon will lose what little grit and blood and marrow lingered on like that waxen old Elvis we all saw on that ghastly TV concert special of I guess one of his typical last stage shows in the waning days but then Madame Tussaud's ain't such a bad place to hang your hat for eternity and being a mummy is one way to live forever just like the Colonel said when some reporter asked him what was gonna happen now that Elvis was dead: "Why, nothin', son, it's just like when he was in the army!") so that even at his most grotesque there was still something of the Infinite about Elvis, something again perhaps extraterrestrial, even down to all the post-death indignities they submitted his poor corpse to I guess to get revenge for all those years everybody in the world wondered what the hell Elvis did all the time and nobody knew so now he's been demystified to the max as we read in the daily swillsheet how he died trying to squeeze out one more little turdlet sitting stool (god, that beats Lenny Bruce even, naked by his toilet with a needle hanging outa his blue arm! damn!) and the other nite on TV I saw Geraldo Rivera who is obviously a case of advanced ringworm it's just impossible to say whose body's and while hoping the unlucky host to said worm ain't all of us we get to watch the worm grill that poor ole Greek croaker who wrote all those scripts for Elvis and Jerry Lee and everybody else in town and is now a fall guy if ever I saw one and there was even talk of having Elvis's corpse dug up and the stomach analyzed for traces of drugs these two years on which led me to fantasize: Can you imagine anything more thrilling than getting to stick your hand and forearm through the hole in Elvis's rotted guts slopping whatever's left of 'em all over each other getting the intestinal tracts mixed up with the stomach lining mixed up with the kidneys as you forage fishing for incriminating pillchips sufficient to slap this poor sweating doctor 20,000 years in Sing Sing and add one more hot clip to Geraldo's brochure of heroically humanitarian deeds done entirely in the interests of bringing the public the TRUTH it has a consti-tutional right to know down to the last emetic detail which they in time get as you pull your arm out of dead Elvis's innards triumphantly clenching some crumbs off a few Percodans, Quaaludes, Desoxyns, etc. etc. etc. and then once off camera now here's where the real kick to end 'em all comes as you pop those little bits of crumbled pills in your own mouth and swallow 'em and get high on drugs that not only has Elvis Presley himself also gotten high on the exact same not brand but the pills themselves they've been laying up there inside him perhaps even aging like fine wine plus of course they're all slimy with little bits of the disintegrating insides of Elvis's pelvis

SO YOU'VE ACTUALLY GOTTEN TO *EAT* THE KING OF ROCK 'N' ROLL!

which would be the living end in terms of souvenirs, fetishism, psychofan-dom, the collector's mentality, or even just hero-worship in general. Notice I am leaving out such pursuits as necrophilia and coprophagy—there are admittedly some rather delicate distinctions to be made here, some fine lines to be drawn, but to those so insensitive as not to perceive them I will simply say that calling this act something like "necrophilia" would be in poor taste and if there was one thing Elvis always stood for it was good taste and maintaining the highest standards that money could buy so fuck you, you're just jealous, go dig up Sid Vicious and eat him, but if you do please save some for me because I'd like if possible just a small say 3″ × 3″ hunk out of his flank because what I want to do is eat the flesh under the skin, then dry the epidermis itself which isn't all that tasty anyway and slip it in the sleeve of my copy of *Sid Sings* as a souvenir to show my grandchildren and perhaps take out and wrap around my dick every once in a while when I'm masturbating cause a little more friction always helps get the wank achieved and sometimes I have found that when I literally can't get it up to jerk off because I'm too alienated from everything including my own cock if I take a scrap of dried skin from a dead rockstar—trade you an Al Wilson in mint condition well as mint as dead can be anyway for a Jim Morrison I don't care how shot to shit—it really seems to do the trick.

But I digress. Jerking off with some of Sid's track-riddled forearm could not even be called child's play compared to the exquisite sensation of eating those pills and gore out of Elvis. I mean, I read Terry Southern's "The Blood of a Wig" too, but that was written before the age of the celebrity, as Marisa Berenson told *People* magazine when they put her on the cover: "My ambition is to become a saint." *My* ambition is to become a parasite on saints, which shouldn't be too difficult, I mean they're supposed to get holier through physical mortification and all that, right? Plus I know about how Idi Amin used to dine on the flesh and drink the blood of his onetime enemies while lecturing their severed heads in a line on the desk in his office concerning the improprieties they committed while alive so I don't need to go get *The Golden Bough* just to prove to everybody else what I already know because it's simple horse sense which is if I eat a little bit of Elvis (the host, as it were, or is that mixing mythologic metaphors?) then I take on certain qualities possessed by Elvis while he was alive and walking around or laying in bed with the covers over his head as the case may be, and when these pills make me high they'll put me on the Elvis trip to end 'em all as I'll be seeing what he saw and thinking what he thought perhaps up to the last final seconds before kicking the bucket and if all of this works well enough as it most certainly will since I intend to be greedy when offered the chance of a lifetime and scoop out a whole giant rotten glob of his carcass that let's face it he's never gonna need again and I eat from deep in the heart of him as I fully intend to do, why, THEN I WILL BE ELVIS! I'll make several dozen unwatchable movies and that number plus a couple dozen more unlistenable albums! I'll know karate so I can kick out the eyeballs of my landlord next time he comes up here to complain I haven't paid the rent in three months! Like I'm sure he's gonna come complaining to Elvis about something as piddling as rent anyway! Ditto for Master Charge, Macy's, all these assholes hounding me for money

I don't have and they don't need: I mean, seriously, can you imagine *Elvis* sitting down with his checkbook and a stack of unpaid bills, going through the whole dreary monthly routine, and then balancing his bank account? He'd just go out and buy a car for some colored cleaning lady he'd never met before instead! Then Master Charge would tear up the bill saying "Mr. Presley you are a real humanitarian and since we are too we want to say we feel honored to have you run up as high a tab as you want on us."

Lessee, now, what else can I do? Well, concerts. Kinda boring, tho, since all I've gotta do (all I'm ALLOWED to do if I'm gonna not insult Elvis's memory by breaking with tradition) is just stand there holding a microphone, singing current schmaltz with no emotion, and occasionally wiping the sweat off my brow with one of a series of hankies hidden away in the sleeve of my White Castle studded jacket and then toss the con- taminated little rag to whichever female in the first few rows has walked more backs, blackened more eyes and broken more arms and legs in attempt to get up close to my godly presence. As my whole career has surely borne out, I believe with one hand on my mother's grave that aggressive persist- ence in the service of a noble cause should be rewarded. Still, all this, ah, don't *you* think it sounds kinda, well, *dull?* I mean, how many hankies can you throw out before you start to go catatonic? At least Sid Vicious got to walk onstage with "GIMME A FIX" written in blood on his chest and bash people in the first row over the head with his bass if he didn't approve of the brand of beercan they were throwing at him.

Sid got to have all the fun.

Let's see, there's GOT to be something else. Well, of course, of course, I can sit around gobbling pills all day, but ANYBODY can do that. You don't have to be Elvis to stay luded-out all the time; if you did, everybody in Washington Square Park is/was Elvis Presley. Which obvi- ously cannot be true, there can only be one, the King, me, not even "and," unless I decide to indulge in a little schizophrenia, but wait, I can't even be schizophrenic because I'm already catatonic and even if it were possible to have two variants of the same malady at once I don't think you should be greedy with your diseases. God knows there's few enough of 'em to go around and more and more people every day who wanna score one, any kind at all, just for some kind of change in the atmosphere. I may have croaked on the commode but I'm not anal retentive.

So. Shit. I thought bein' Elvis was gonna be *fun,* and here I am, stuck, ONCE AGAIN with "nothin' to do and nowhere to go," except now I am sedated beyond my wildest dreams, and that doesn't seem to be making a damn bit of difference. In fact, it feels just like being awake. Guess I could get one of my rifles off the shelf and shoot out a few TV picture tubes. Lemme get the *TV Guide* and see who's on I might wanna shoot: Hmmm, 6:55 Friday night. I've got five minutes left on which to knock off Carol Burnett, Oscar or Felix on "The Odd Couple," whoever the anchorman is on "New Jersey News" or the host on "Tic Tac Dough." There's a bunch of other local news shows just concluding, but fuck them, I can kill them another day. Well, I can't kill Carol or Oscar or Felix 'cause I like all those shows, and killing somebody in a TV show from New Jersey seems like stooping pretty low to conquer, like what's the point, while as far as "Tic Tac Dough" goes one game show host is as obnoxious as another, if I blasted whoever this john is it'd be no special treat, besides which if I killed *him* the other ones might get jealous 'cause of the publicity and start hounding me, and then I'd have to kill Monty Hall and Bill Cullen and Bob Eubanks and Hugh Downs and Chuck Barris and . . . aw, forget it, you can see what a hopeless course that'd turnout to be. I'd probably no sooner blow the smoke outa my barrel as the last one slumped behind his desk than knowing them damn networks I'd look in next week's *TV Guide* and see thirty-five brand new ones I never even heard of before all set and rarin' to go be slaughtered with new shows and everything. One person I definitely wouldn't mind killing would be Rip Taylor. If only "The $1.98 Beauty Show" was on. But it's not. In fact, I don't even know what night it's on. Maybe they canceled it while my back was turned, not too remote a possibility since it (my back) usually is. Maybe Elvis was bad when he was alive and got sent to Hell instead of Heaven—I mean, I definitely don't see his mom around here anywhere, or the brother that died. So I'm gonna have to spend the rest of eternity never getting a chance to kill Rip Taylor. Wait, not only that, but considering what kinda life Rip's probably led he'll get sent down here whenever he croaks from whatever's gonna do him, and HE'LL get to spend the rest of eternity torturing ME. Jeez, this is lookin' blacker by the second. It's now 7:10, which means that murder-wise I have my choice of Walter Cronkite, David Brinkley, and/or John Chancellor, whoever I pick from the cast of "M*A*S*H," Frank Reynolds, that guy who hosts "The Dating Game" or one of the contestants—ah-HA! "Bachelorette Number Two, do you—" BLAM!, anybody from "Happy Days," Fonzie, hmmm, two years ago maybe, now it's not worth the bother, same with "The Dating Game" really: you woulda wanted to kill Bachelorette Number Two in 1971, when you watched the show every day, but hell, by now I haven't seen it in so long I can't even remember what the host's name was/is—Jim Somethingorother. Or "Over Easy": Hugh Downs, Chita Rivera and her daughter. How dreary. Looking ahead to prime time, I find myself confronted with either Bill Bixby or Lou Ferrigno in the "Hulk" hour, except I always kinda liked both those guys for some reason and I bet (I mean, I *know*) so did Elvis; Shirley Jones; some nonentities on something called "B.A.D. Cats"; anybody on the Chicago Black Hawks, the Flames (whatever hockey town they hail from), the New York Arrows, or the Summit Soccer team way down in Houston—but shit, I never was much into sports, I wouldn't know who to shoot first so I guess I'd have to kill both teams whichever game I tuned in; the only guest on Merv Griffin I've even heard of tonight is Dr. Linus J. Pauling; wait, here, yes, this actually gets my blood up a bit: at 8:30 I can kill *Dick Cavett,* and Mary McCarthy too, depending on my mood by then. Only trouble is my mood by now has gotten so bad I don't feel like killing anybody, not even Dick Cavett, whom I've wanted to kill for years. I seem to have no will whatsoever, in any department or direction. I said catatonia? I think autism now. Perhaps both. Somewhere in the distance of the Bob Lind canyon of my mind I hear Paul Simon singing "I am a rock / I am an island," but it bears no significance or emotional impression positive or negative. Like nullsville, man. And nullsville is dullsville. I think maybe I feel more like a vegetable than a rock anyway. Broccoli, perhaps. In a frozen Stouffer's soufflé. Let's see: I can't eat. I can't sleep. I can't get high. I can't listen to music (it all sounds the same, besides which I made the best records of all time so what's the point?). I can't watch TV cause there's nothing on and if there was I don't have the will to get up, flick it on and maybe even have to (shudder) switch channels. I can't kill. I can't shit or piss. I can't get drunk because Elvis never did because he always remembered what his mama said about how alcohol made Daddy so mean but she never mentioned downers 'cause that's medication. I certainly can't read, except maybe some undoubtedly obscure martial arts text.

Is there anything left? Oh yeah, sex? Well, as I look around my palatial suite in Caesar's Palace here in Vegas then peek through the door and down the hall I see, oh shit, must be at least fifty busty babes that all look like they came outa the centerfolds or the Dallas Cowgirls or "Charlie's Angels." I used to like to jerk off to *Playboy* every once in a while, just about every night in fact, even the real plastic airline-stewardessy ones, before I was Elvis. Once I even jerked off at a picture of Farrah Fawcett-Majors. At the time I thought it was a really sick thing to do; it was fun. Now I could fuck or get blown by any of these broads and I haven't got the slightest bit of physical inclination, I feel about as sexy as a turnip. I mean I guess I could *make* myself, but what the fuck, you know? Besides, what does Elvis have to prove? What I can't figure out is why, when I used to really dig pulling my pud to pix of 'em in the magazines, and even had my special favorites that always got me hotter while there were others I always avoided because of the way they were posed or they just weren't my type somehow, it was just like girlfriends except lonelier, what I can't understand is why, now, here they all are in the flesh, I could even jerk off at 'em without touching if I had some kind of hangup, or send one out for a copy of *Playboy*, they all look exactly alike to me. The last time that happened was in 1973 when everybody on all the made-for-TV movies started to look like Stefanie Powers post–"Girl from U.N.C.L.E."

But Elvis don't sit around thinking theoretical psychosociological bull-shit like that, that's for sure. What does he think about? Beats me. Nothing, I guess. Nothing at all. Himself, maybe. But that's nothing. Like that Billy Preston song: "Nothing from Nothing Leaves Nothing." Jeez, Billy Preston, there's a hep dude, I bet he's sure havin' lotsa fun right now, wherever he is. I wonder if this is how Don Gibson felt when he wrote "Oh, Lonesome Me." But I don't write songs. I just sing 'em. Sometimes. But how can you even sing 'em when you don't know what any of the lyrics mean cause you don't have any feelings or experiences anymore or all feelings or experiences are equivalent—how can you call yourself an "inter-preter" when you've, uh, forgotten the language? So I guess I'm not a singer anymore either. Well, maybe there's some consolation there: that's gotta be the last one to go. Now I can turn into a test pattern. Oh well; sounds peaceful. And if that's the case I'm gonna sign off. Except I don't think I'll be resuming programming at six A.M. or any other time for that matter. I'd sing you the National Anthem, but I'm not a singer anymore, remember? I'm sorry. Wait a second, no I'm not; you're just as much to blame for this hopeless cipherdom as I am, since you made me the biggest star in the world, believed in me, pinned all these false hopes on me I couldn'ta fulfilled even if I'd understood what you meant, that asshole Peter Gural-nick and his friends: what the hell did they think I was, a slacker or something? Or even leaving the army out of it, what the hell did people like that really want me to do? Keep on singing rhythm 'n' blues? Why, so I could end up repeating the same tired riffs like Chuck and Jerry Lee and Bo Diddley and the rest of 'em left over from the fifties? So I could open for the Clash? Man, for*get* it. And fuck all the rest of you too, you "true fans" who bought any shit RCA slung out with my name on it and made yourselves love it or say you did or pretend to. *Having Fun With Elvis on Stage*, me babbling and sayin' "WELLLLL" for nigh on an hour, even I'd be embarrassed by an album like that, if I wasn't beyond embarrassment so long ago I can't even remember what it felt like. You think you're paying tribute but that's the world's *worst possible* insult. I'd rather you told me I was shit, some of the time, or even shit all the time. *Any*thing. But to say you love everything, indiscriminately, just because it was me or had my name on it—well, that just says to me that you never cared about the music from day one. You couldn't have, or you woulda complained *somewhere* down the line, like maybe by *Harum Scarum*, I dunno, they're all the same to me, too. But if you never cared whether I tried or not, then why in the hell should I? You rock critics and "deep thinkers," you were using me, projecting some fantasy of rebellion on me. I certainly wasn't rebelling against anything, ever. I dressed funny and wore my hair a little different when I was in school, but that wasn't rebelling, like Sam said, that was just . . . *me*. That was just a way of saying I existed, I guess. After I started to get big, I could *feel* it moving in the opposite direction—I don't know when it was, couldn't pinpoint a day, all I know is that, all of a sudden, at a certain point, pretty far before the army too, I started to stop being me. Because, well, everywhere I looked I started seeing me. Every singer, every kid on every streetcorner, everywhere. There was so much me goin' around it just started to look like *Playboy*. Yeah, I was still and always the leader of the pack, but that's not the point. The point is that something I started doing to make people know I existed started rubbing out my existence, a little at a time, day by day, I could feel it going, seeping away, steady and calm . . . and nothin' comin' in to replace it. And I knew nothin' ever would. Maybe if I'da been smart I shoulda gone right then and blown my brains out like Johnny Ace and then there only woulda been those few records and all the critics would be happy and the fans wouldn't know the difference and I'd be a legend. But I was a legend anyway; still am, even more than ever. Shit, I couldn't evena committed suicide! Not for real, because it wouldn't've been for any of the reasons real people use to commit suicide every day. It woulda been cynical, bad faith, trying to prove a point when I didn't have no point to prove. I don't want you to get the idea I'm feelin' sorry for myself. I'm not feelin' *anything* for myself, or anybody else. Except one thing. One last thing. I'm feelin' I wish you all would leave me alone. Go bother Engelbert Humperdinck. Or Gig Young, if you want somebody who's dead. Don't come 'round with your *National Enquirer* or your Peter Guralnicks and Greil Marcuses, not to mention your Geraldo Riveras. Just don't come 'round at all. 'Cause I was nothing for twenty years, and most of you couldn't tell the difference. And then I was dead, and you outdid yourselves thinking up new ways to finish off the job of leaving my corpse humiliated, pissed on, disrespected, degraded, demythified, lied about, deprived of every last shred of privacy or the most basic human dignities.

I'm sure you'll think of some more, and I'm not even that pissed off about it, 'cause that's just the way you are, the way I was: that's your version of *Having Fun With Elvis on Stage*. It's cool; I been there. Besides, I still do take some slight comfort in the fact there's something about me, some weird quality, that you haven't been able to figure out yet, none of you. I never could either. I guess I was something. The only trouble was that when I was somethin', I wasn't me, just like when I was me, I was nothin'. Oh, well. Life's like that. Write any kinda shit you want. I won't be reading it. I'm tunin' out.

The combined effects of the drugs and rotted bodily organs wore off about thirty-six hours later. I came out of a deep and not unrestful sleep feeling disoriented, displaced, vaguely depressed, emotionally numbed, but with mind and body in relatively sound state. After a couple of days I was even able to listen to music again, even his albums. There's just one thing that's different. If they exhume the body again, I don't think they should be worrying about drugs (*I* certainly wouldn't take any more drugs that came outa Elvis Presley's stomach!). I think they should take him down to a taxidermist's, and have him stuffed, like Trigger. I could say something like "and then have it placed on the steps of the White House," but that would be glib. The trouble is, while I *know* he should be stuffed and put on display somewhere, I don't for the life of me know where that should be. Because I guess he really doesn't belong anywhere, anymore, does he? Does he?

Dear East Village Eye: So far in your pages I have at different times learned
that both Richard Hell and John Holmstrom invented punk, presumably
also at different times. So I figured I might as well put my two cents' worth
in: I invented punk. Everybody knows that. But I stole it from Greg Shaw,
who also invented power pop. And he stole it from Dave Marsh, who
actually saw Question Mark and the Mysterians live once. But he stole it
from John Sinclair. Who stole it from Rob Tyner. Who stole it from Iggy.
Who stole it from Lou Reed. Who stole it from Gene Vincent. Who stole
it from James Dean. Who stole it from Marlon Brando. Who stole it from
Robert Mitchum. The look on his face in the photo when he got busted
for grass. And he stole it from Humphrey Bogart. Who stole it from James
Cagney. Who stole it from Pretty Boy Floyd. Who stole it from Harry
Crosby. Who stole it from Teddy Roosevelt. Who stole it from Billy the
Kid. Who stole it from Mike Fink. Who stole it from Stonewall Jackson.
Who stole it from Napoleon. Who stole it from Voltaire. Who stole it from
an anonymous wino whose pocket he once picked while the man was lying
comatose in a Paris gutter, you writers know how it gets when you're
waiting on those royalty checks. The wino stole it from his mother, a
toothless hag who once turned tricks till she got too old and ugly whereupon
she became a seamstress except she wasn't very good, her palsied hands
shook so bad all her seams were loosely threaded and dresses would fall off
elegant Parisian women right in the middle of the street. Which is how
Lady Godiva happened. Lady Godiva was a punk too, she stole it from the
hag to get revenge. And Godiva's horse stole it from her. Soon thereafter

said horse was ridden off to battle where it died, but not before the Major astride the horse stole punk from it. The Major was a serious alcoholic given to extensive periods of blackout running into weeks and even months, so he forgot he stole it. He forgot he ever had it. Forgot what it ever was or meant. Just like all of us. But one night in a drunken stupor he burbled out the age-old and Grail-priceless Secret of Punk to another alkie with a better memory. When the Major sobered up, the other alkie, a pickpocket and generalized petty thief, lied and told the Major that he, the pickpocket, had originally owned punk but that one night when he, the pickpocket, was in his cups the Major stole punk from him. The Major believed this. But later he got drunk and forgot all about punk again. So it might have been lost in one of the crevasses of history and John Holmstrom would be an aluminum-siding salesman door-to-door and Richard Hell would be pitching hay down from the loft of some midwestern farm where he was hired hand RIGHT AT THIS VERY MOMENT in which also I, creator of punk as I really shouldn't have to remind you, would not be a rock critic and sometime musician to the irritation of many and pleasure of some enlightened folk but rather a senior poohbah in the headquarters of Jehovah's Witnesses over in Brooklyn. Instead of reviewing Devo for the *Voice* I would be the author of the article "Springs—the Wonder Metal," published in *Awake!* magazine sometime in 1978. And that too would be something to be proud of.

from "Women on Top:
Ten Post-Lib Role Models
for the Eighties,"
a book proposal, 1981

I gotta pay credit where due: Andy Warhol set this whole process in motion, everybody tries to imitate him but they don't get the point. The point is that it's what's up front that counts. You ever see that old "Amos 'n' Andy" episode where the Kingfish tries to sell Andy a "house" looks like a fine unspandin brownstone, walkup the steps smell the roses pet the doggie then they walk in the front door but this hunka timber's doin' doubletime as *back door* too cause the whole house is a false front, and Andy look at de Kingfish and say, "Kingfish, dat de *fastastest* house ah eva been thru." "Ah know, that's whut's GREAT about it! It's MODERN! Got all the computer electronic dodads what comprise yo LAFSTAHL ma man, why look they serve ya up yer beer wash the dishes shine de TV screen. Why hell Andy, this here house'll even *fuck your wife for ya* if ya want it to! It's de lates' an' bestes' an' you gonna be de envy of yo block if you jez sighns right here and gimme the money bye I'm gone so long sucker" but Andy he be right proud o' that house, to him it was the Taj Mahal. He's still living there to this very day, makin' do. Andy Warhol didn't get the Nobel Prize for Literature for *a.* (in case you forgot that was dis book where buncha faggots hung around the Factory got themselves so jacked up on speed their eyeballs were bouncin' off Telstar and yakked about any diddleyshit that came into their heads for twenty-four straight hours, then they shut the tape recorder off, got a buncha wideeyed pink-vhecked li'l girl journalism majors to transcribe all this blather which they considered a privilege in fact would be willing to pay to do but they got it for free what the heck give the kids some slack gotta mind the karma what goes around comes around and if you come around me I'm gonna shoot your face on a vacation past the back o' your skull .44 Magnum but it's not me we're talkin bout it's andy's book which now was a thudding pile of pages of random street gibberish plus mundane appointments at unknown locations with people the reader doesn't know, they type it all up and even leave in the typos because Andy absolutely put his foot down on that one you know like I'm sitting at a typewriter right now and sometimes I make a mistake hit q instead of s for some damn reason because no bawd's puffick so when the book come out on Grove Press selling at ten dollars a copy you got to read things like ". . . yeah an' as I was sahin' to Florence Henderson the other nite: 'ghoyyoh bigkhkgkrwkgjbn,,snvnbnjhjdhejhoy9-4itu6hf,n,;nlrkkyi6uruyohkfj' " which you must admit does capture the tenor of the times and put this up against *Sophie's Choice* ask the audience to ring the buzzers which tome they'd lust to peep BZZZZZZZZZZZZ goes the big jackhammer and it's andy's *a.* all way way, a novel, by Andy Warhol who never touched it nor heard nor read a word of it but see that's the point YOU GET BETTER ART WHEN YOU LET SPEED-FREAKS OR ANY PASSING STRANGER FILL IN FOR YOU THAN BY ACTUALLY SITTING DOWN AND WORKING— WEEEEEEEEHHHHRRRRRRRUHKE?!?!? as Maynard G. Krebs always uesta say, hell man whutchoo doin here, youz oughta be loungin on de beach at bimini wid a big ole spliff danglin' outcha increasingly uncon-cerned lips an' sum faaahn dewy dappled frecklecheek dimple tanktop jes a-*cussin*' an' a-*fightin* demandin *reparations* its so too tight fo wut muchan-dise bez inside now aint you happy don't dis beat schlumpin' down widda headache and a heart of lead limp dick wouldn't lift one eyelid for dolly parton herself meanwhile thrrees company in the next room and there you scuttle and bash away blah blah blah words words words hey jack I got news for you nobody wants to read dat outhouse fulla "characterizations" "con-structions" "subtext" allat shit what are you foreign or somethin jus got off the boat from oslo okay i dig wanna buy some tuinals but meanwhile you might as well know they wouldn't flick a flea's ass off the coffee table to make widdis sofies choise horseshit give it up pack it in blow your brains out move to Jersey cuz you is plain stupid since as evabody knows evabody in de wholel dam world a writer you can check it on the birth certificates and they may read each other's works or argue about it or this or that petty career jealousies bullshit but lissen kid an lissen good cuz you look lak you mite someday go far in this corp'rate cartel internationelle if you just fuck my dawg an wife at the same time whise I jerk off an take pitchas hey i know you'rre runnin behind schedule well tell federal express to send YOU

a hooker fi' hunna buchs uz all I cn affurd sorrry slow month as andy'll tell
you cuz andy heah thats right I know him personally love ya baby bye he
the andy an if you gotta ask whut andy you so far out to lunch you dinin
on idaho cows backwards cuz ma man andy do be he de kiing o de block
an futhamoa we luv hims ass so much wez jez dee-LITED UP see jez lak
Coney Lisland to do him any an all mayahaps lil favors not to mentionn
all dat liftin an totin he bez de kahhhnness ghouoooooodisssss bossman we
dun eva cum unda fak we sided we gon plum make him our religion
meaning after all dint Tam magazin oh Paul Tilllich uh mebbe it wuzza
spooky the tuff lil ghos cmic book I f'git but anyway in wan a dem news-
papaz it daz say dar gawd iz daid so soomin he iz whuch seems mos lakly
given all available infomashun input well lissen what de hell man andy's
dandy andy's candy see he's even got a marketable logo much better'n at
jehovah azzole widdat bigbugugly beard a-fluerin evawar or jackson pollock
fo dat matta cats too rigid mus be german o sumpin no mam its andy pandy
gandy goose the moose on the loose what done blew Broos Sprinmgsteens
brainz out widdz twalv gayz shatgun right inna middle udda jawflappin to
de fek ole clance slickiss jig inna wat manz ban sinz chally pakka you
knowda rap about de flyin saucers how dey done brouhght dis jan-yew-wine
1928-mint Negro into the band all de way fum Marz gueshhha gotta
honeya jive turkey mandibles what bin you wanna make it in music cummin
outa jerseyland where mebbe dey shoulda chopped down sum all woods an
han dem juzzy moozez day walkin papuhs cuz when de moose git loose it
killl bruce so we gon ship em all to ethiopia whey dey dun sway an promise
sinin names on holy fishel writs whot do declares dey gon bless de beleaguered starving begging homeless masses ahv etiopia wid non*stop tweennny
fo owahs ą day* punk rock bradcastin wid heap more watts o power dan de
big o woolman fame cud eva claim man dey be *halin* dem sick an blin an
crippl an legles by playin abzlutly nawtin but de pres mos vital ital spirit
music consecrate de church today we gon play speshul sklusiv fo de hongry
masses we squattin spitchel brahood wid here ed bangler an de nozebleeds
de pork dukes de snivlin shits man luv dem jorg martin symphonic swooshes
in de bridge part o save yr hart fir mee az verzhund n remix at jelly ahm
sarry ah meant jerry lewis hizzef stipulated in de kontrak cuzzinz how son
Gary trad an e trad an e trad ad STILL neva cood cum up widda reasonable
facsimile o nontansebenseben headbang an bangandbanganbanganbangan
till day hadda kinna terminate de dat solly cholly well ah yoo know ah mean
sum folx sey what ole pop j's atteytude 'pon jewnyours' demise mita binna
tdda cold n heartles as day say in jane austen but hey man look at it dis
day de cat coont cut it no ma'ah whish weh yoo slas de pie I meean sheeit

iffin he cain git awp an jez brawnk out wid eben *wan* liddole
"TWURRRRNNGGG!" wid de Mekons who wuz so gracious az t'*nvite*
eez azs to jis kam op un JIM WID DE BAIN MAIN juz lak eny uda *no'mal*
tap satizen wadda dun, why din . . . i meen, datsit, fukim, case close but
hey thinka dis mebbe he bez up dea in rawknril hivvon rat now jez a-rappin
de boss christopher cross shit down wid IAN KUDDIS uv Ja Devazhin who
jez happen to recently also do de mouse ovv dis motel koil oah goil oah
whutcvah dcm cgghcad t s eliot n ez drankan putnuz muz no id iz kuz ey
god all de books yey eye gadda idea lez go uppin askem! Yeh sayhey ma
main man lungtam nawsea wutchoo do go hole up a likka so an' fuk it up
az per yewzyul an den dezide yalz gadda hide fo few daze cuzza heatl
beatcha tillya bristly bag o yogurt bones you be reddy you gladly confess
to killin sid vicioious or sum rilly enny udder ole dead rockat but heyman
lissen up we gon trunnl tupta xgau's house in a few minutes x-*who?* c'mahn
min yoo rawmemba dat time we poured a whole bottle a madawg twenn-
nytwenny down at rokriix bak atta paladium I think Mars waz headlinin?
ooh yaaaa i memba dat cat man wuz he snerd-OD oh wat? ya ya but memba
how we p'tinted we wez junkies anna maddaog was jes junkie puke runnin
downinsidea backa his shat you call dat a shat? wal at lug lag any udda
tee-shat ah eba saw aw c'mon man no sef-rispekin t-shut haz "STRAN-
GLAZ" plastad all akrass a franta heez chez? hmm, yeh gez yoo rat but
luk yu wan go say him wid me naw ennywheh? sho so day hawp a kab n
buzstazss ova t'sekint avanoue n twalv streaight luk iv luks de DEAN hizzef
iz home! an' not too busy what wit de teorahzin an palocaltackle thinkum
humphard to reseev um so ebidang kopiatik wutchjew boz wunt? quiz de
bag Bub wal sez Latnun wez bin tawkan in we disidead to let yoawulz be
di fannal ohbitraitor av dis barnun quesshun shoot sez de DEAN Slim take
ham it has ward in pool uh thuddy-ate kalibah rivoolvuh outan hiz lef hep
packet en poain't ut strat ut Bib's haid witch iv *yew* niew slim lak *aaaiieeee*
gnaw aive eez braiynz kersploop aoul obor de wall which bin kirrantly fitrin
fo de laz ot yas wan hooj pusteh ubba Geh Rates Rilly skeduled sam
sitorduoy backin may 1971 a miin shut—win sambaddie talls yuie taw die
somtang yoo du at rieght? o ef day zey "doan evah bimpus m'ahwllz
sourghwahr agin!" yud do thwit tue iz jazz cummon cartessy but diz iz alzo
drue dat daffrent sexshinz av de tawn gut dawfrint moo-rayze n moadez a
be-in an karyin yosevz psnly oi jiz woke awraiown in MAN MOI AWN
BAZNAZ, lawssenz sumbadiez heaven trubbl r fillin pearly r gattin mooged
ur sampan dun aie stup inn ayun p'latlee trah tu quail de dazdoibench.
hopanallah time av curse uh woan geet Caled mighsef netchilly

   so onywheh de liz tongue om guano seh barfour kluzzin ayoot das chipter, iz det uz azael, endy wiz riit. *a.* wez E bitter back den Sawfigh'z Jezz. Boy at tidie Ondine azza rule cquole kott, tax litza Obetrols in dan tux ubat uporih, zamdung woch a knaw gnitting eboit. Zo ef yeh Oz raidink zis, Arndarn, aien yeou hahve iny Obetrols, zen mae aw fiw on al bo yur frond var laff.

from
"Maggie May," 1981

Years later, flipping idly through his collection of ten thousand albums, he settled on an original mono copy of Sonny Boy Williamson's *Down and Out Blues* on Chess, slid it on the turntable, then lay back in his pasha's throne of a chair, contemplating the irony of it all: the wretched ragged wino on the cover of the LP, and what on earth he would do with a fourteen-year-old girl if she spread her legs before him, begging to be fucked. The wino might do better, he chuckled to himself. After all those *Vogue* mannikins, the would-be Bardots, next year's Lorens and closing-time pickups; with some of them he'd been so drunk he'd never be able to say with absolute certainty that . . . no, there was just no way. Right now he'd rather be sipping this hundred-year-old brandy and digging Sonny Boy running down those same old lines he first heard when he was living on mashed potatoes than fuck *anything*. Sonny Boy was juicier than Brooke Shields would ever be. It had been better to sit and starve, nursing his desperation till some kinda break came his way. When it came, it wasn't the kind of break he'd had in mind. Which only figured.

It was 1966. There she was, the Perfect Slattern, propped atop that barstool ugly and coarse as only far-gone alcoholics can be, forty if she was alive but still looking all there in a leathery kind of way that surprised him, that turned him on, but here *he'd* somehow ended up, ditched by a friend who unlike him had enough money to keep on drinking, and he looked at her and she at him and a pact was thereby sealed before a single word was spoken on either side—now is that true love, or what? Mutual convenience perceived through alcoholic fog was more like it. He walked over and slid up onto the empty stool next to her, and she took one look at him—his hair, his clothes, his hangdog face—and immediately knew who was buying the drinks. She asked what he'd have, he ordered a shot of rum and a pint of Guinness. He wanted to court blackout or at least unaccountability before he had a chance to think about what he might be getting into. He drank so fast even she was a little surprised, laughing and drawling something like, "Surely I can't look *that* bad—Christ, I just came back from the powder room. Or is Art really *that* agonizing?" And she threw back her brass mane, opened those full lips and laughed again, a true healthy harde-har this time, nothing self-effacing or ingratiating about it. She had him, and she knew it, and somehow his position as Henry Miller–style roué without a sou to his still unfamous name, living off his wits and special Way with the Ladies, did not seem to save much face or cut too far into her cynicism. He was just too pathetic, anybody could have him for a meal, but she was the one willing to take him out of sheer strumpet benevolence if nothing else—and since she now owned him dick to dorsal he might as well get an equivalent eyeful of his Owner: she looked good. Damn good. Better, in fact, at least to him at that moment, than all those damn ersatz Twiggies flitting around Carnaby Street on Dexedrine scripts and boyfriends in bands with first albums just breaking the U.S. Top 100, the kind of girl you saw everywhere then and he'd fucked enough of to know he didn't really like them, because anorexia somehow just failed to light his fuse, ninety pounds of speed-nattering Everybird, never read a book in their collective lives beyond *Shrimpton's Beauty Tips,* less soul than Malcolm Muggeridge's mother, just sitting there waiting for someone to happen but sufficiently plugged into the Scene to let them in on which name it was gonna be hip to drop next week. He always thought when he fucked them he oughta come away with purple bruises on each hip, war trophies of the 'orrid bone-bangin' he'd endured just 'cause some poof on telly told them all that you just could *never* be too thin. . . .

Now, here, next to him, sat a middle-aged slut with bulging reddened alkie eyes, leering through rotten teeth, just beginning to go to fat in a serious way. He began to get a serious hard-on, and he wondered for a second if he had some kind of Mother Fixation, then decided that he couldn't care less. He got harder with the decision to stand his ground, incest be damned. Looked straight at all of her, as she at him: he estimated size 38 tits, beginning to sag a bit but that was all right, the way of nature wa'n't it?, globes that heaved up from a rather lowcut frock even for that neighborhood, and like the rest of her those breasts might reek but retained just a pinch of that pink, plump, girlishly buxom cremecast of milkmaid tenderness, and gazing rapt and rigid he could not help but wonder awe-struck at just what manner of pagan secrets might lie deep in the pit of cleavage. Surely there was *something* down there, one had but to dig breastplate-deep to dredge up treasures untold (the Twigs, of course, had no tits whatsoever and were all prissily proud of it), perhaps jewels and musks she'd carried all the way from the narcotized dens of the mystic East, where she'd spent her girlhood tremulously awaiting the needs of some fat sheikh who was so stoned and overstocked fuckwise he never even got *around* to her, so in revenge she stole into his inner sanctum and purloined his most prized rubies, opals, amulets and blocks of pure hash and opium, hiding them in the handiest place, and though the master didn't catch her at theft he did find her encroaching on his hophead den and in punishment booted her ample ass clean out of his fleet of tents and into the molten Sahara sands, a whitehot sea where she'd've roasted like a squab had she not hitched a ride from missionaries, whose camel deposited her on the outskirts of Tangiers, where she sold her virgin essence to some stogie-smelly Yank robber baron who came quick anyway, but after he OD'd on absinthe she picked his pockets clean, netting not only enough money to keep her off the streets and in the bars for a while but a ticket to London via Luxury Cruise, in the course of which she enjoyed a brief affair with the son of a famous American expatriate or so he claimed, but then he apologized for his rather pallid passions explaining that Dear Old Dad had bequeathed him a palpable preference for boybutt. She didn't believe a word out of his mouth and they both had the time of their lives getting drunk like Boer War vets on the anniversary of the Big Battle, forgetting all about sex for the nonce. Landing on Blake's native soil, she made a beeline for the seediest part of London Central, renting a crummy room she decorated with a reproduction of Man Ray's famed *Box with Two Peaches in the Sky* taped up on one wall which cheered her up no end.

Man Ray might have been a gay porno star as far as his knowledge extended. He didn't know said lithograph was worth twenty-five pounds if it was worth a shot on the house. On the other hand, she had never heard Otis Rush's original 78 rpm rendition of "Double Trouble" on the Cobra label, which he just happened to be the proud owner of. Clearly it was a match made in heaven, especially when he looked down and discovered himself delighted at the sight of one peremptory ripple of flab around her middle. That hula hoop of fat, he knew there was definitely no turning back now, so downward yet anon did slither his ogling orbs to grow themselves all wet at the sight of two more than amply supple legs in black fishnet stockings crossed under the hem o' that minidress, the whole thrilling vista tapering in most sublime tribute to Jehovah's very handiwork in two black patent leather shoes with stiletto heels could slice a porkbutt clean asunder. And amazingly enough, she wanted none other than that scrawny excuse for a failed fop HIM!

By now they'd practically consummated a week of orgiastic gymnopedes via eyes alone, so she paid up quick and out they scooted. Fairly *ran* down the block and up the stairs, through her door, where then she did after all think to stop and ask, "Like my Man Ray?"

"What's that? Some billboard for a new poofter play?"

She charitably ignored this idiocy, choosing instead to trip and shove him backwards onto her scummy rumpled bed, the sheets and blankets not washed in weeks because she was too busy at the wine to remember them so they stank like sick goats but little he cared being drunk and lust-wracked too, so they commenced to make what Shakespeare, who could get at least as down 'n' dirty as say Texas Alexander when so he chose, once called "the beast with two backs." An apt description in this case, because the pair set to rutting like hogs been penned apart all winter, or dogs sprung from sexually segregated pounds (a pup-population control measure once actually tried in America, resulting in one lockup fulla Rovers crawling around the room all day leaving bowwow-jizz all over the floors, and another wherein the bitches thus imprisoned and deprived set up such a tempest-trough of yipyap yelpings and piteous yowls not unreminiscent of chalk squeaking on blackboards that the whole idea was abandoned overnight and a platoon truckload of panting Fidos imported special to the Lady Bowzers for a fullscale K-9 orgy just to shut 'em the fuck up) (happened in Keokuk, Iowa, case you wondered where the locals'd be fool enough to concoct such a scheme in the first place), they were hungry, and nosh awhile they did, groinwise that is, grinding away in to-the-hilt gimme-glee sloshed swill-sploshes of Eau de Poozwax Straight Up & Mulching Mit More Spizz-Overflow than whole popovs with some o' them Twiglets occasioned—it splashed across the grimy walls and soaked through the putrid coverlets, one rampant rivulet running down the bed cross the floor under the door down three flights of stairs and all the way out into the street where it conjugated unnoticed with TB sputum, not that the two lovers in question noticed any such minor details inasmuch as by that time they were too busy eating each other just toothpick-shy of outright cannibalism, after which they did it doggie-style and rocked so mighty they damn near broke the bedposts, the springs meanwhile playing at least five different Bartók string quartets and "From the Diary of a Fly" at once, causing an eighty-nine-year-old widowed pensioner in the next room past the wall which was about as thick as the cover off a copy of *Uncle Scrooge* ca. 1948 to seriously consider attempting to make his way down the stairs, a feat he had not accomplished in a decade and a half, so as to thereafter hit the street and see if he himself could purchase the last hit of whoopie he'd ever know except even allowing for the stairs he was still thinking WW II prices which'd mean he couldn't afford much beyond a quick whackoff into an old handkerchief while peering through a peephole at some grainy loop or two of (sign on door claimed) Mexican lezzies havin' at each other orally which mighta been still a heap better'n nothing (I tried it once on 42nd St. and it was great, but felt filthy afterwards so never went back) except Pops here ain't even really had it up since the Rosenbergs were burned so what the fuck. . . .

When they were done dogfucking they sprawled back awhile to rest and pant and contemplate just exactly what they mighta forgot to try. Licking assholes? They talked about it but agreed it was finally neither's style. Mild B&D/S&M? Well, both were tired. So they tried something really daring, truly *avant*, beyond the pales of known thrash: they snuggled up for warmth, and hugged and kissed, with full passion but also gently and tenderly, sometimes just barely grazing each other's liptips (which *really* reactivated the lust-pustules in both bodies), for about twenty minutes. They kissed. Like kids, which was what he in fact was, and made her feel like all over again, which was the best feeling she'd had in years if not ever. When fully reprimed, they fucked once more, a long, slow, languorous workout in nothing but the Missionary Position, and when at last they came it seemed as if some timeless primal river was unleashed headwaters between the two as they writhed in one slow sliding tangle of YES from the core to YOU and no other . . . it was almost like some sort of, well, *religious* experience, mystical somehow, certainly elemental, the mindless melding of two principles always drawn together yet always warring everywhere, no confluently conjoined once in lifetime-memorable rapture among all manner of fucks high and low and every pitstop in between but this was one of the few ever that anybody's lucky enough to get which really actually on some intangible certainly beyond verbalization level *matters* . . . what you keep on looking for every time you lie down, and suspicion or nerves or reminiscence of some past lover who warn't so hot or drug-numbness or outright hatred or simple bone-weariness or god knows whatall else seems to come between you and it every time damn near . . . and True Love has *nothing* to do with it, on one level it's nothing more than pure chemistry, though on a level a high degree of in-front mutual trust helps plenty, and finally maybe it's just dumb luck: THIS TIME.

When it was over they lay in silence for upwards of an hour, lost in commingled dreams, drained beyond movement, finally he sat up and said: "What's your name?"

She looked at him in silence for a full minute before answering. "Thanks a lot, SHITHEAD. That'll do for you as far as I'm concerned. As far as mine goes, just for that you'll never know. Now get dressed and get the fuck out of here."

So he did, a little sheepishly to be sure. He wanted to apologize, but felt so, well, dazed and confused right then, that he had no idea how to even begin to try. He knew he had done something stupid, ugly and thoughtless, but he hadn't really meant anything by it, it was simply a product of his inexperience, which of course mortified him even *more*, till he felt he'd better get dressed and go or he was gonna wind up sitting there paralyzed. He'd never in his life felt more like a little boy, just as she had never felt more used, fucked and then slapped down, put in what any cur of a male would be sure to think of as her rightful place, if for no other reason than that she was poor and single. She hated him, and all men, at that moment, and there was nothing in the world that could have changed that at the time.

When he was fully dressed, he stumbled across the bed, nearly breaking a leg and spilling across the floor, but no, he made his feet, though he still felt too wretched and ashamed to stand straight up all the way, so he kind of hunched across the room, hesitating by the door. He turned a bit, but was afraid even to look at her.

"Get out." It was the voice of a sidewalk as it hits a drunk in the face. Except he was no longer drunk. He felt it, every dollop of loathing, contempt, finality. Sick in the pit of his gut, moving with the spindly gait of somebody staggering away from an automobile accident, he turned the knob on the door and let himself out. She turned her face to the wall, which was oily and stained in places and where she faced it almost black with the accumulated dirt and lives of so many people, most of them down-and-outers, over so many years, and she cried hard, bitter convulsive tears that seemed to come tearing out in great chunks like the face of some cliff smashed away by . . . what? One too many assholes? Solitary middle age with no real prospects in sight? The sudden sensation that it just might be the sum total of her life, for this was all she had managed to piece together in over four decades, and what in god's name did she have to look forward to? Who wants a fifty-year-old hooker who's particular about her services (no S&M, no showers, no really kinky stuff of any sort) in the first place? Or get in on the ground floor of some new, "straight" business . . . yeah, sure. Even waitresses had to show some list of past employments. All she had to show, really, was a succession of men: two failed marriages, countless lovers, most of them as callous as this one had turned out to be or worse, various marginal forms of employment (go-go dancer, topless waitress, hooker, massage parlor, call girl . . . it all boiled down to the same thing), no family contacted in decades, no kids, not even a pet, no library or record collection amassed over the years that could now be presented to herself as some kind of evidence proving she knew not what . . . nothing. Alcoholism. A lifetime of self-con, pretending she was some schoolgirl on a spree when everybody else her age was married, employed, or both. She was so ill equipped for real life, she reflected, that she wouldn't even know how to commit suicide properly. Fuck it up no doubt. She laid her face in the black place where the two walls met, while more sobs heaved up from her very guts like boulders. In the next room, somebody turned up a radio playing some awful, maudlin song; they didn't want to have to hear her.

He staggered on down the street, still in shock, found his way home, sat down and tried to piece it all together. On one level it was all so simple, on another it was just too abrupt a jolt from too great a height to too miserable a sink. That plus the knowledge that he'd hurt someone, and he did have some though hardly a complete idea just how badly, and it was the person that on that day of his life he wanted most in the world to avoid hurting. Again he felt himself overwhelmed by feelings of helplessness and self-hatred. He sat like this for hours, barely moving a finger joint, almost in a trance, as the darkness fell over the city and filled the room. Finally, around ten P.M., he got up and turned on the lamp. Then he sat down again. He knew that punishing himself this way, to such masochistic extremes, he was only reconfirming, again and again, the very conviction of immaturity which had, aside from the pain he'd inflicted, made him feel that way in the first place. But he was young and male and selfish enough to be more concerned with whipping himself and turning it into a grand melodrama than with what she must be going through. *Well,* he thought ruefully a couple of hours after turning out the light, *at least here's another song for you.* Which of course made him feel even more ashamed. He fell into a fitful sleep, sitting up in his chair. He dreamed that he was a dog pawing the legs of passing women, all of them classy, fashionable, gorgeous, and looking up he saw the sneers on their faces: "Stupid mongrel mutt, go piss on somebody else's leg." One kicked him, and he went limping away. No one in the streets would even look at him, not even the beggar children: he was a mange-ridden stray.

She did not sleep. All night and all the next morning she sat on the bed, after the last tear had choked out, and stared at absolutely nothing. In the early afternoon she moved one limb. Then another. A bit at a time, she physically collected herself. For what she was about to do she hardly needed a mind. Finally she looked in her purse: £6. She snapped it shut, stood up with it in her hand, and walked out the door which she did not bother to lock. Down the stairs, down the street, into another bar. It was a bar where lots of low-rent johns hung out, and she was going to be broke again soon. She took a stool and ordered a drink. And another. And another.

When he awoke he felt stiff and sunbaked, sitting up like some mummy in a chair. He remembered everything, and the self-loathing had not abated, but at least now he was capable of planning and executing some course of action. For some reason he trusted himself just a hair more than last night. He left his apartment and headed straight for the bar where they'd met. When he didn't find her there, he walked out and headed down the street, looking in every bar along the way until he came to the corner. Then he walked back, checking every bar on the other side. He didn't drink.

Three hours later he walked into a dim small bar on a side street, he saw her, hesitated, then clumsily approached. Her back was to him; she was looking down into her glass of wine. Standing behind her, he said, "I'm . . . so *very* . . . very *sorry* . . . I didn't mean it . . . I mean . . . I just didn't know . . ." The more he talked the worse he was. With all the dignity of the longtime alcoholic who knows she's drunk and couldn't care less because unlike in the movies there are worse things in the world, namely, almost everything else in the world, she turned to face him. In the deadest voice possible she intoned: "You-have-got-some-fucking-nerve." She looked at him; he couldn't meet her gaze. She grew almost waspish: "Wasn't yesterday enough? I'm not gonna give you the rest of your kicks by beating you. Although I will say you are a miserable whelp and one of the poorest excuses for a man I've ever met. But you know what? You're not even the worst. Don't kid yourself. You're just another creep on the street. Now go wallow in somebody else's miseries. I'm sure there's a candidate just down the bar." She paid for her drink, making sure to leave a tip, picked up her purse and walked out.

He didn't see her for two weeks. She felt better after the confrontation, but surprised herself with the realization that she also felt sorry for him: he really *didn't* know what he was doing. He really *was* just a kid. She was taking a lifetime of sons-of-bitches out on him. Not that he didn't give every indication of quite likely growing up to be one fully as practiced at true brutality as the rest. It was just that, somehow, even as she sensed his selfishness, she couldn't help being touched at least a little by his confusion, his genuinely repentant albeit masochistic manner, and her own inclination to give him the benefit of the doubt. *Why?* she kept asking herself. And finally concluding: *Maybe just because you have at this point absolutely nothing else to do with your life.* Which, once she'd articulated it, was obviously as pathetic a reason for doing absolutely anything as any of his. *Fuck it,* she thought, tricked her landlord and a couple of others she forced out of memory as soon as the episodes were done, and started drinking again, moving slowly from bar to bar at her own unset pace.

He hadn't been able to look a woman, any woman, in the eye since she'd told him off in the bar when he'd gone to find her. For several days he sat in his room, finally he called a friend and told him the whole story. "C'mon," laughed the friend, "she's just a whore. Don't be a sucker." "Fuck you," he said.

Crass as his friend had been, he'd come away knowing one thing: she was no more perfect than he, and he'd been putting her on a pedestal purely in the interests of his masochism. Whether or not she might actually be a prostitute was a matter of no moral judgment to him one way or the other. If he had suspected she was one, it had been a secret excuse to romanticize her. Slowly, somehow, without further contact, he began to perceive her as a human being. As all that fell into place, his anger at himself assumed a more fitting perspective. Finally, he saw that even his groveling apologies—perhaps in a way *especially* them—were at bottom selfish. She'd been right. For some time now, he'd been in the habit of treating women with casual unconcern—like shit. It was an act that worked more often than not, but it also ensured that he'd always end up with the same kind of woman, and ultimately alone. Now that he had encountered somebody he was capable of caring about, he'd exploited her in a way that was probably even worse—to expunge his guilt over all the others he'd mistreated, to put himself in their place, to know how it felt to be treated just that shabbily. He also felt that, if they could ever clear all this up, there might be some possibility for . . . what? Something more than what he'd been accustomed to. On the other hand, it might just be that all it had amounted to was an incidence of random lust, proof of which lay in the very fact that the instant they'd tried to verbally communicate, all hell had broken loose. He wondered at times if he shouldn't just forget the whole thing, or take it as a lesson learned and go on with his life. But gradually he came to realize that one way or another she was almost all he ever thought about. Which might mean that this was just a particularly twisted teenage crush, but he had to find, see, and at least try to talk to her again. For better or worse.

She'd been on the bottle long enough to have long since lost track of the days. In one bar she ran into a guy she'd once lived with, a comparatively decent sort, who'd given her some money. "Take better care of yourself," he said evenly but with real concern. "You're too good a person to go out this way." She asked him what the fuck he cared. "I guess I probably don't," he admitted, "except insofar as we were once lovers; if I cared for you enough to live and sleep with you then, part of that must still exist now. You see what I mean? I don't know if I loved you. But I did care. And I still care, and maybe I always will. I don't know what's happened to you and I don't think I want to, but do me a favor and try to pull yourself out of this downslide. You know that's a coward's way out, and I never would have been attracted to a coward in the first place. You're the same person and so am I. I don't want anything out of you now except that you maybe show some of the spunk that drew me to you in the first place. I mean, what the fuck? Why kill yourself over some asshole? Why give him the satisfaction? Just START is all I'm saying—put one foot in front of the other, and keep doing it. Things'll get better, not today or tomorrow, but bye and bye. You'll see. I've been down there too." He laughed. "Otherwise, terminate the soap opera with some style: Go get a pistol out of the nearest fuckin' pawnshop and BLOW YOUR FUCKIN' BRAINS OUT!"

They stared at each other for a long moment. Then both laughed at the same time, not loud and hearty by any means, but for real. It was her first real laugh, since . . . well, yeah, since all that. "I'll even loan you the money," he said. They laughed again. Between his sense of humor, the pep talk, his shaming her for being maudlin and giving yet another creep any satisfaction whatsoever, plus the basic knowledge that at least one other person in the world actually cared with no strings attached, she came out of it.

"Let's go fuck," she said.

"No," he said. "Not today. Nothing personal."

"Okay," she said, and stopped drinking.

They embraced and kissed lightly, without tenderness or passion. They walked off in opposite directions. She had absolutely no idea what she was going to do with herself. It was enough merely to feel good, to nourish some resolve however vague. She went back to her apartment and thought about her options for the rest of the afternoon. There certainly weren't all that many of them, but how many did most people have? Fuck it. The first thing was to make some firm decisions, second thing to stick to them. Set her life in order. She picked up pad and pen and made a list:

(1) Sober up. Stay that way.

(2) Don't fuck anybody else for money.

(3) Don't fuck anybody you don't really want to.

(4) Find some sort of straight job.

(5) No more self-pity, no matter what happens.

That was enough. It took her three days to sober up. She faked an application form and got a shit job filing papers in an office building. Temp work termed permanent. It was hell. But she just did what she'd always done when she was fucking for money: shut off her mind and let Bach or Mozart play instead. Bit by bit, day by day, she regained her self-esteem. Even made friends, of sorts, on the job. Of course none of them were the kind of people you could really *talk* to—they were all women, and they all actually thought being a secretary was going to lead somewhere, or they just wanted to get married, and generally spoke in banalities of their lives and the things they had just bought or were planning/hoping to buy. She made one male friend who lasted exactly a week and a half, until he made a crude and clumsy pass at her over lunch, and when she politely refused, he began to sulk. After that he wouldn't talk to her. Fuck him. One day she realized she had been celibate for over two months. At night she read or listened to the radio, what she could stand of it, which was very little, or watched TV, what she could stand of it, which was very little, mostly old movies and news. She thought about her life. It hadn't been so good, in fact much of it had been an outright nightmare. But then she thought about the women she worked with, and their lives, with or without men, what they had amounted to so far or possibly ever could: they were so timid they might as well never have been born. She was better off with the nightmares. She'd learned a few things. When that thought hit her, she couldn't help laughing out loud.

Meanwhile he sat in his apartment, thinking about her when he wasn't dwelling on his own problems or mentally combining the two. He was still determined to find her, but she seemed to have disappeared from the bars. Nobody seemed to have a clue as to her whereabouts. One day he thought, *I wonder if she is dead,* and a chill ran through him. He was still writing songs, but none of them were about her. He wasn't ready yet—or he was afraid. The songs weren't about anything in particular. He knew he was stagnant, knew he had to do something with his life and his music, but had no idea what.

Months passed. One day he turned a corner in the middle of London and almost bumped smack into her. They were both startled, then both laughed in spite of themselves. It had been too long for high dramatics of any sort. "Well, well," she said calmly, a bit too calmly she thought. "Of all the ghosts in this town. And just how are you? Still fucking women just so you can shove them facefirst in the dirt five minutes after?"

She was surprised at the lack of malice in the way she said the words. Somehow they felt almost obligatory; somehow, she knew, she wanted to talk to him. About what, she had no idea.

He blushed. That was when she knew why she wanted to talk to him, and why she felt just the slightest bit foolish for making the little speech she'd just concluded. "I . . ." he began, and stopped. Still an adolescent. They looked at each other. "Let's go get a cup of tea," she said.

They sat down in a restaurant around the corner and stared at each other a while longer. To her, it felt downright comical. Still, she knew just how much she was enjoying the power she was now holding, the feeling of totally controlling the situation with a man for once in her life. She didn't like the idea of letting that go. At least she knew she didn't want to right this minute. *But what the hell did that mean?* She had no desire to hurt him; if anything, she felt playful. But that too seemed a kind of unnecessary mockery, in spite of her memories. She wanted to talk to him, she repeated to herself. If only she knew where to begin.

He began. "I was a terrible fool. Please forgive me."

"Stop." She was beginning to get irritated already.

"No, no, you've got to listen. Please. I was wrong and I hurt you. And then I compounded it later."

"That you did."

"Well, at least I can tell you that I know all that now."

"Congratulations." She was being too cool, too terse, it was some form of overcompensation, she knew it. What she didn't know was why. Which meant that suddenly she was no longer in control. And given *this* state, that left a real mess: two cartoon characters, trying on balloons. No, that was forced cynicism. She didn't know what she felt. One thing she did know: she had been on automatic pilot for what seemed like an eternity. This was like two babies stumbling across a playpen towards each other more than anything else, but even *that* was more than anything she'd felt with anyone else in so long that . . . she was fascinated, pulled in, and she didn't know why. She kept telling herself the whole thing was stupid—she should just get up and leave.

"I've thought about you a lot."

She didn't say anything. She had thought of him as little as possible.

"I've also been trying to find you for months. Not to ask any kind of absolution, but . . . you made me understand certain things about myself. When you weren't even around. I guess that sounds selfish, but . . ."

"Yeah, especially considering humiliating me was your ticket to Total Enlightenment." She grew impatient again. "Look, I know you're young. But I've just been through too many assholes in my time. Maybe to someone else, especially a girl your own age, it would have meant less. Maybe to some it would have meant nothing. People have that attitude a lot these days. I—"

"I don't either. Maybe what you're really saying is that I have nothing to offer you. Aside from whatever you might have to offer me."

"Well, I could give you pointers on the etiquette of how not to treat women like shit, for starters. The next person you fuck might appreciate that."

"What can I say? You've got me over a barrel. I blew it. I can't even apologize anymore. All I can say is one thing: Will you go to dinner and the movies with me this Friday night?"

"Why on earth should I do that?"

"I honestly don't know. I might not if I was you. I'm just asking. You can say no."

"Dinner and the movies—how charmingly *teenage.*" She knew her sarcasm was flat, stalling for time.

So did he, finally. "So stop playing around: what's your answer?"

She looked at him. "Yes."

Now neither held the cards. "What is this?" he asked, simply and sincerely.

"I swear," she sighed, "I haven't got the *slightest* idea. If I did I'd be glad to tell you."

"Maybe it's good. This way."

"What's good?"

"I don't know."

"This conversation is absurd. The tea's gotten cold. I have to go, I'm late getting back from my coffee break." She gathered her things and stood up. "See you Friday night. You know where I live. I'm generally home after six o'clock; other than that, I'm not particular about time. Just don't come barging in in the middle of the night, ever. I've been through that one once too often. And *especially* don't come barging in drunk, ever. Which reminds me, I'm trying not to drink now. Just thought I'd let you know. I don't mind going to bars, but don't expect me to get wasted on anything with you."

"Okay."

She walked out. He tasted his tea. It *was* cold. She'd left him the check. He paid, left a tip, and walked out.

She had trouble concentrating on her work. It was just that it was so *boring.* So, ultimately, were Bach and Mozart, at least when you had to hear them inside your head. Here she was, a woman in her forties, with a Friday night date with some rock 'n' roll teenager. She didn't even like rock 'n' roll.

Friday night he showed up at exactly 6:10 p.m. "What kept you?" she joked.

"Huh?"

"Nothing. So, what's on the agenda? What's the movie? What kind of exotic meal you got planned for us? A foreign restaurant, I hope? And will I be expected to fuck you in return at the end of the evening?"

He didn't say anything; he looked hurt. Instantly she regretted the last sentence that had come out of her mouth. "Look, all I meant is that I'M BORED OUT OF MY SKULL. I WORK IN A MORGUE. You're a teenager, they're supposed to be up on all the latest kicks. Well," she tried to joke, "SHOW ME SOME KICKS. I'M A DESPERATE WOMAN."

He didn't know she was joking. "You work in a morgue? Really?"

"No. I wish I did. It's a morgue for dead papers—writs, subpoenas, wills, old lawsuits, on and on and on. Dead bodies would be a definite improvement."

"Oh."

He was nervous. So was she, but in a different way. Clearly, each wanted something different out of the other. Somehow they just kept missing. She decided to try a more direct approach. The most direct.

"What do you want from me?"

He didn't answer for a couple of minutes. "I'm not really sure, except . . . I think somehow it has something to do with—don't laugh now—*soul.*"

"Who's laughing? I'm flattered. But then, I'll take just about anything I can get these days. Soul. Why me?"

"That's a lot harder to answer. Maybe because . . . you're the sort of person who would joke about your job by describing it as a morgue, or wish it was instead, or maybe it's just that . . . I think you want something from all of this—meaning all this around us, life, work, whatever—that you're not getting. And you're not gonna stop struggling. Or," he laughed, "at least *complaining* until you get it. Or at least find out what it is."

"What if I'm not missing anything? What if there's nothing there *to* miss?"

"You aren't the type to settle for a good answer when I finally managed one, are you? You gotta push it to the next level of impossibility. In fact," he laughed again, "I wouldn't be surprised if you turned out to be impossible all the way around. Maybe," he stared at her for a long moment, not kidding at all and both of them knew it, "that's the last word with you. Maybe that's how you get your kicks after all. You get your kicks by seeing to it that everything remains impossible. And I don't even mean anything so banal as you and I. I mean a serious effort, conscious or not, in futility as a way of life."

She hadn't been ready for that. It was too close to the exact center of her most basic fears. All she could do was own up. "You're right. I'm into absolutely nothing. Waiting around to die. So what's a bright, talented young lad like you doing with the likes of me?"

"I don't exactly know, just yet. Why should I? Maybe I agree with you. Maybe I think you don't want to believe your own arguments. But I don't want to turn this into a philosophy seminar. I'll tell you this: I'm not in love with you—"

"That's good—"

"—I just like being around you. And I think by now I've earned the right to ask you at least one question: Just why in hell do you wanna be around the likes of me? Some dumb kid who doesn't know whether he's coming or going, loves and even writes and sings music you hate—like you said the other day, we have absolutely nothing in common. So why did you say yes? And why do I get the feeling that this whole conversation amounts to more of the same? JUST WHAT DO *YOU* SEE IN ME, HUH?"

"I . . . can't honestly say. When you're as old as I am you'll understand better, and I don't mean this to sound condescending, what I mean when I say that 99% of men, that I ever encountered at least, are 100% shits. The odds don't look too good, given my age, my work, my financial situation, my marital status, how many children I've contributed to our ever-expanding social future, my history as regards booze and the like—any way you look at it, I'm a bad bet. I hope you appreciate I'm telling you the truth."

"You're also deliberately leaving out all the emotion."

"That's because I don't feel any yet."

"That's a lie."

"No it's not. I haven't felt any in a long, long time. I shut all of it off. You kids can afford to throw that emotion stuff all over the place—us older folks, especially women, are rather more spent. And I don't fit in anywhere. Never have. I never will. You, on the other hand, have a whole 'generation' to back up any horseshit you get yourself into. You're lucky, but I'm not jealous. You'll end up one of two ways: just like me, or just like the rest of the people on my job. Either way you'll be unhappy. This 'generation' stuff is just a con to try and sell you something. I know, I've seen it before, the same catch phrases. But the last word is I'm desperate. And THAT'S"— here she bore down almost with a vengeance—"WHY I'M SPENDING

FRIDAY NIGHT WITH YOU INSTEAD OF ALONE WITH A BOOK, OR THE RADIO OR TV I NEVER PLAY."

"So you're desperate. So are millions of other people, but they're not with me. You are. How come?"

She felt cornered. "Because . . . I'm just narcissistic enough that when I look at you, I see some of me looking back, and I like that. I want a yes man—"

"Ah, come on—"

"Okay, then, I want a mirror. Or somebody who shares some of these feelings you call futile. I want to talk like this, even if we're both just digging one big hole that leads nowhere, as I strongly suspect, I've been starved for talk like this for longer than you can imagine. Most people never do it, and when I start to—"

"I know—"

"They get weird."

He looked her in the eye. "That's 'cause they're afraid of you. Because the very fact of you raising the questions threatens the very foundations of their lives, what they live for and why."

"Don't you DARE deny how scared you are of me—"

"Yeah, but that's different. . . ."

"So what? Maybe we're wrong and they're right. Maybe we should just shut up and go buy something."

"Okay—whaddaya want?"

"Absolutely nothing anybody's selling, at least not at any price I can afford. Two months on the coast of Spain might be nice. How about *you?* *Surely* there's some new rock album you're just *dying* to own."

"I already bought it, the day it came out."

"Well then, a new stereo."

"Old stereos are better, at least for the kind of music I usually listen to, and I already got one."

"A new guitar."

"Already own two."

"Strings."

"Thirty-four pence apiece."

"Amp."

"When I have more money."

"Clothes."

"Why? Soon as you get caught up they change all the fashions so you just have to start all over again."

"That sounds exactly like something I would say."

He grinned. "Maybe that answers your question of why we should be together."

"Or why we should stay away from each other at all times."

"Face it: we're both snobs."

"We don't like anybody or anything—"

"That's 'cause nobody and nothing is good enough for us—"

"Or so we *think*—"

"So here we are, pretending we're right and they're wrong—"

"When really we both know better—"

"If we don't they'll be letting us know real soon."

"Would you rather spend the rest of your life in prison or the nuthouse?"

"That's a rough one. Gimme some time. Neither."

"My answer exactly."

"But what's gonna happen when we get to the point—"

"Wait, I already know what you're about to say—"

"When we both think the same thing—"

"Always—"

"So we no longer need to talk at all?"

"I guess we'll just have to wait and see."

"Either that or find out what we can't stand about each other and go our separate ways."

"All right. So we've agreed about all the things we HATE—so much so we don't even need to discuss them. . . ."

"Yeah . . ."

"Yeah, well, what about the things we actually *like?*"

"What about 'em?"

"Well, JUST WHAT ARE THEY? I mean, *I wanna see an itemized list.*"

"Can't be done."

"Why not?"

"Guess."

"We don't like enough things to fill out the fingers of one hand much less a whole sheet of paper."

"Right again."

"Though there is one thing . . ."

"Yeah . . . ?"

"Well . . . I'm kinda hesitant to bring it up . . ."

"For God's sake, WHY?"

"Because . . . well . . ."

"Are you talking about what I think you're talking about?"

"Uhh . . ."

"You are. After all we've been through."

"Yeah, but look at it this way: when the rest of human experience is totally worthless, and we see eye to eye to such an extent we can barely talk, that leaves just ONE THING."

"Hmmm . . . and what if that runs out too?"

"It won't."

"Why?"

"Trust me."

"Why?"

"You've got nothing better to do."

"True enough."

"Hey."

"What?"

"Let's fuck."

"I thought you'd never ask."

From that night it began to seem as if they measured their time more in terms of when and for how long they had to be apart than when they saw each other. They became so attuned to each other's thought patterns that conversation did indeed sometimes become all but superfluous. Yet, curiously, that was all they lived for. Or so they thought. So he thought. There was never the slightest doubt in his mind.

After a few months, she began to have second thoughts. They were *too much* alike. Lovers brought something unexpected, some tension to the relationship that made it click, cook and change. This was more like brother and sister. Which she never told him, but she increasingly found less than dizzyingly erotic. It was simply too pat. Yet there he was, as happy as she had ever seen anyone be in her life. Her reservations made her feel guilty, and the fact that she didn't voice them compounded the guilt. She was hiding plenty from him, more all the time in fact. She couldn't stand the thought of him being unhappy. If things continued on their present course she was going to end up bored out of her fucking mind. She was beginning to feel like his mother: precisely because she understood all this and he didn't. Whereas he felt like a 100% fulfilled LOVER, if not a flatout husband.

One thing was clear: they were not communicating. He just thought they were. He was living in a dream that she had the power to break in a moment, with a word. She had never heard of anything more unfair in her life. And what was most unfair about it was that it was nobody's fault.

There were no villains, no excuses, no nothing, and she was going crazy. Something had to give. There was no solution, short of death. And she was not prepared to die. He was healthier than anyone else she knew. Why shouldn't he be: she, as he'd put it so often, repeating the phrase till she could scream, "completed" him. Completed him. Was that even fair to him, assuming it was true? What sort of life could he possibly have, when both of them were so alienated, and the crucial difference was that she had had over forty years to acclimate herself to it, even view it with a certain wry detachment, whereas he, being a child of the sixties with all that that entailed, thought there was no reason on earth why he should acclimate himself to anything? Why shouldn't they just be happy? Wasn't that what it was all about? Hadn't they found it in each other? *But we aren't* supposed *to be happy,* she wanted to scream.

She thought about it all the time. How could he not notice? Had he gone senile? Maybe his whole generation was senile, with their Beatles and drugs and notions of happiness as some inalienable birthright instead of an occasional holiday that sneaks up on you while you figure out a way to fuck it up. She was just too set in her ways. Whereas he could bend to anything, and did, regularly. Which was one of the main reasons why she was beginning to feel like a mother. Who the hell was she to remake and define his whole life? Yet that was seemingly exactly what he wanted. What else was there for him? It was sickening. Once they were alike; now they were both her. One was more than enough.

One day she sat down and made a list of possible solutions:

(1) *Commit suicide. Then he would be free.* Unacceptable. As pointless as life was, she had no intention of checking out until absolutely necessary. Besides, who was to say that he might not kill himself in grief immediately thereafter, becoming her shadow even in death?

(2) *Confront him. Tell him she couldn't stand it anymore. Then ask for his advice.* Trouble was, she suspected he wouldn't have any. He had externalized his own emptiness to the point he thought she was perfect. Perfect. Some joke that was. A forty-six-year-old divorcee and intermittent alcoholic subject to chronic depression and conviction that life is meaningless and empty, an individual with zero interests, no skills, shit job, ex-hooker, no children, now carrying on an obviously deeply sick relationship with a boy almost twenty years her junior, half her age. Maybe she had let the whole mess get started in the first place simply as a hedge against the fact she'd never had children. Now she had a son. Whom she fucked. Who imitated her in every way he knew how. Lord help us. If this was perfection, give me a country of miscreants, mutants, psychos, and cripples.

(3) *Demand they break up.* Break his heart. Deprive him of his sole reason for staying alive. HURT HIM. And herself as well, no doubt about it. Back to the office and the papers and slimy men making hideous propositions over chili dogs? The coffee klatsch? Bach and Mozart, even? She'd rather kill herself. *She* would have nothing to live for in that case. Yet somehow she got by before him. How? She could not remember.

(4) *Force herself to develop some new outside interest which was sure to alienate him.* A cult? Antirock crusade? Right-wing politics? Jesus freaks? The Chamber of Commerce? Fascinating Womanhood? She would rather learn bass (as he had in fact even on occasion urged her, for Christ's sake) and join his damn rock band. And she hated his singing as well as his songs. She would rather be dead.

(5) *Kill him.* At least if she did it right he'd never know what hit him, never know unhappiness for the rest of his life. But she had no right to do this. Besides, it would break her heart; she would kill herself first. Besides, she couldn't stand the thought of either prison *or* the mental ward.

(6) *Simply disappear.* Pull a Judge Crater. Somehow that seemed the most cowardly way out of all. And more than likely, they'd end up back together.

It was a single word which made up her mind for her. One morning she awoke, turned her head on the pillow, looked at him sleeping so blissfully beside her with one arm wrapped around her naked body and even a sleeping hand cupping her breast, and she thought: *I am his guru.* GURU. That was the end. To be anyone's "guru" was more than she could bear, whatever the consequences. It was funny how life worked. Nothing had changed. Just one word. But that word made all the difference in the world. For her it was like "Hitler" or "nigger" or any of those other buzzwords that set alarums raging in the human heart. She would murder a busload of schoolchildren in cold blood before she would be even one single human's "guru." Just looking at him there on the pillow, she wanted to vomit.

But what to do? Stealthily she crept out of bed, padded into the kitchen, and over a cup of coffee plotted. Out of six possible escape hatches, no single one of which was satisfactory, perhaps she could contrive a combination kiss-off that might work. Yes. She dressed, making sure to keep as quiet as before so he'd sleep on while she plotted, then drove the car to the liquor store, where she bought a half-gallon of Johnnie Walker Black. Arriving back home, she began to mix it with the coffee, fifty-fifty. Drank it down pretty fast. By the third cup she had hatched fifteen more schemes, each more outlandishly unworkable than its predecessor. By the time he awoke, she was drunker than she'd been in years, plotzed, zonked, a mess. She checked the bathroom mirror: yep, it'd done the trick. She looked *fifty* years old if she looked a day. Keep this up for a week and she'd be a hundred. How could he possibly want to fuck that, much less idolize it?

He walked into the kitchen and blinked, still half asleep but palpably shocked: "What are you DOING?"

"Whaddaya mean, waddami doin? I'm having a li'l *fun,* thaz wad I'm doin'. Wat the fugh's it to ya, anyway?"

She knew this wouldn't be enough. He commenced to grill her: "Is anything WRONG?"

"YA DAMN RIGHT SUMTHINZ WRONG. LIFE STINKS, TAZ WAT. I TRIED TO ENJOY IT, BUT IT WUZZA LIE. I'M GONNA DRINK UNTIL I CROAK."

Jeez, was this corny. But he was buying it. Was there no depth to which her respect for him could not sink?

"But . . . but . . . everything was going so well . . ."

"YEAH—SO *YOU* THOUGHT. I *HATED* EVERY SECOND OF IT." Well, there was certainly enough truth in this. "I'M JUST TOO SET IN MY WAYS. NOT YOUNG LIKE YOU. GWAN AN' LIVE. I WAN' DIE."

"But WHY? You've got ME; we've got EACH OTHER."

"BIG DEAL." Better soften the payload a bit. "All we are is MIR-RORS of each other. We used to be two IN . . . INN . . . N-DIV-VIJAWLS . . . NOW WE'RE JUST ONE . . . *LUMP* . . . not even hardly HUMAN. . . ."

He began to cry. Well, tough shit. "But we've shared so *much*—so many *ideas,* made so much *good love,* enriched each other in SO MANY WAYS . . ."

"YEAH, THAT'S WHY I WANNA DIE, JERKOFF . . . ain't no YOU or I anymore . . . just WE . . . face it: WE ARE BORING AS SHIT. Wanna drink?"

"NO. I want . . . god, all of a sudden I don't know. . . ."

Time to up the ante with a little gross-out: "I DO. YER RIGHT ABOUT THE LAV MAKING AT LEAST"—yanking her dress up and panties down, ripping the latter in the process, spreading her legs as crudely as she could—"HOW 'BOUT A LI'L POO-ZEE? C'MON, BUSTER BROWN—LESSEE YA *LAP THAT CUNNY UP* . . . or"—in world's absolute worst Mae West impression—"PIPE ME YER WAGSTAFF, BIG BOY, I WANNA FRESH LOADA A.M. JIZM RIGHT *HERE.* . . ."

He was getting physically ill. On the other hand, so was she. This project obviously called for more extreme measures. She ran out and jumped into the car, drove it 90 mph to a shabby house well known as headquarters of the local Hell's Angels chapter, and invited them all back to the house for a gangfuck. This was asking for serious trouble, but anything was better than being Baba Ram Dass. Fourteen of them came roaring after her. When they arrived back at the homestead, she lay down in the middle of the living room floor, hiked her dress again, and hollered, "C'MON BOYS . . . FIRS' COME FIRS' SERVE . . ."

They didn't look any too eager—but then he like a damn fool had to go and try to protect her Maidenly Honor. He picked a fistfight with them. They beat him to a pulp, one of them demanded a blowjob from her, she refused, sirens began to be heard in the distance, they all did the quickest disappearing act she'd ever seen outside the movies. She drove him to the hospital. While he was laid up in there three straight weeks, she hired one whore after another to go into the ward disguised as nurses and seduce him. It didn't work until she spiked his orange juice with a triple dose of street acid: she sent three different girls up that day, and he fucked, sucked and orificially jimjammed his little brains loose. With the third one of the day she pretended to innocently wander in on them—"WHAT IS THIS? I THOUGHT YOU *LOVED* ME?"

"I *DO*, I *DO*," and damn if his hard-on don't wilt outa guilt. The hooker stalks out in disgust while he grovels, begging forgiveness till it reminds her so much of the first time he ever pulled that act, way back in the beginning, she wants to puke. Instead she whips out a copy of Garner Ted Armstrong's *The Plain Truth* and begins to hector him at the top of her lungs, liberally peppering this gibberish spew with extensive quotes from said publication, the whole rant to effect that if ONLY he would SEE THE LIGHT of JESUS CHRIST OUR LORD he'd forget about them wicked wimmin forever. By now he's practically catatonic. Meanwhile she's taking more swigs of Johnnie Walker Black, holy rolling and mouthing scatological rants all mixed up together at the top of her lungs, till it brings half the hospital staff down on them, who toss her off the premises immediately.

In fact, she is denied entrance to the hospital for the remainder of his stay. So every day by messenger she makes sure he's sent copies of *The Plain Truth*, Gerald L. K. Smith's *The Cross and the Flag*, *Communism, Hypnotism and the Beatles*, *The Watchtower*, and *The Journal of Krishna Consciousness*, as well as more hookers in nurses' uniforms, drug dealers disguised as staff doctors, forcing every sort of street dope on him from acid to speed to Placidyls to methadone, slimy strangers who regale him with long involved tales of all the sexual hijinx she's supposedly been pulling with 'em while barred from his hospital ward.

By the time his broken bones are healed he's ready for the nut ward, but she carts him home, and all he'll say is: "We gotta have a talk." At last.

So they sit down in the kitchen. He leans forward over the table, looks her square in the eye, and says: "I realized one thing in the hospital: you're right. I don't know what you're up to, but whatever it is, I haven't felt this good in years, broken ribs and all. As Crowley said: 'Nothing is true; everything is permitted.' So, from here on out, we are libertines."

This is more than she can take. The whole thing has backfired. There's only one way out: find some way to make him a rock star, get him a hit record and out on tour, then maybe she'll be free. . . . So she pulls out her ace in the hole: "Well, look, I've been reading *NME* a lot while you were laid up, especially the classifieds, and it says here the lead singer of this band is splitting, the band needs a new, dynamic individual type lead singer to break them in America. I think that might be you. . . ."

"Might. Trouble is, one of those Angels stepped on my Adam's apple—my voice sounds like shit."

"Well, hell, look—do yourself a favor, go on down and try out for it anyway. What've you got to lose?"

Answer, of course: nothing. What she's got to lose is one king-sized albatross, as he gets hired and the rest is history or what passes for it. He ends up one of the biggest superstars in the world, while she goes back to the bars and stays alive on the occasional check for not all that many bucks he sends along. . . .

Now, you'd think after she went to all that trouble for him, practically made him what he is today, that he'd be more grateful, but he's not. One day he shows up with an acetate, looking kinda sheepish, and says: "I thought it only fair you be one of the first persons to hear this. . . ."

She takes the *St. Matthew Passion* off the box and slaps on this circle of black plastic without even a label. What is it? Whadda YOU think.

When it's over, she very calmly takes it off, hands it back to him, pours another tumbler full of Johnnie Walker and says, cool as you please: "Well, I certainly gotta hand it to you: you've come full circle: from SOB by mindless nature to re-educated rather sweet fella, which I guess never really suited you inasmuch as your entire personality disappeared into mine and you became merely an adjunct of my apathy, clear through to your present status as SOB who knows just exactly how big a slime he is and is gonna clean up off it I have no doubt."

"Yes, and I owe it all to you."

"Well, not exactly. Though the thought is certainly touching. I'm not sure exactly who you owe it to, but please leave my name out of it. Just send a check every now and then. . . ."

"Good as done . . ." He slides the acetate back in its sleeve and splits pronto, a little nervously methinks. But so what? You'd be nervous too if you had to go through life worrying that somebody might spill the beans on you at any moment. She's not about to do so, of course, because she couldn't care less as long as she never has to listen to it, and he keeps sending what after all is only her fair share of the royalties for, uh, "inspiring" his biggest hit. As long as he does and she keeps her mouth shut in public, he's happy, she's happy, the record industry's happy, and all's well with the world.

Of course, she still laughs about it: "Yeah, poor old guy . . . only man I ever knew with real potential. Trouble is, if he'd've told the truth in that stupid song, not only would nobody've bought it, but instead of World's Foremost Casanova Tinseltown Division he would today be a mere drugstore clerk in South Kensington. His sex life would be more satisfying, as I'm sure he recalls it was for a while there. I guess in the end it all boils down to a matter of priorities: would you rather be the ship or the cargo? He made his choice, I made mine, and I hope you've all made yours. Cheers." And she raises her glass again.

PART SEVEN

Untitled

from Untitled Notes, 1981

from Untitled Notes, 1981

LESTER BANGS: My whole life had been leading up to this mystical act of Oneness or attrition or atonement or some sick dark impulse: I spent five dollars and seventy-five cents on a copy of *Sucking in the Seventies*.

PAUL NELSON: *REALLY? Another Rolling Stones greatest hits album except this time they're lousy? WHY?*

I don't know.

You could have called up Atlantic for a copy.

I know, but for some reason I didn't want to, besides *never* wanting to talk to most of those people. But this was something other. It had been sorta eating at me for days, the constant knowledge that sooner or later I was gonna fork over the bucks for that sucker. It'd leer at me off the record store walls, knowingly. Finally one Friday afternoon I just walked down into the street, over to 8th Street, and bought it.

You mean "bought it" in the sense of the Warren Zevon song?

Well, it sure felt good. I particularly enjoyed the air of deliberation with which I did it. I mean, we're joking, but on another level, if you think about what it represents, it's totally *sick,* and the assumed innocuousness makes it even worse, like Valium addiction might be more insidious than heroin. I knew it was a piece of shit the first second I saw it. So do the Stones, of course, why else'd they call it that, though I don't imagine they expected to lose the sales. But they really rubbed our noses in it this time, even more than usual, worse than *Jamming with Edward* by a mile— remember that little letter to the buyers Jagger sent out with that one? No, I think I wanted to debase myself in some chickenshit, wretched little way, which of course you always expect in some form or another from the Stones. There was a ritualistic quality about the way I thought about it all week, and then took such methodical pleasure in going and doing it. I stood in Bleecker Bob's and looked at the song titles, some of the choices they'd made, and how they were programmed so you already knew you'd never be able to listen to a side all the way through, you'd have to get up every time right in the middle and move the needle over to avoid some little four minutes of irritating lameness they obviously made sure to put right there so it'd cause maximum inconvenience—I mean, I've heard of people paying to be beaten and whipped, but can you imagine what we must have come to when people will go like johns and *pay* to be inconvenienced?

Boy, are you deluded. You think too much. Do you honestly believe the Rolling Stones put more than five minutes, probably not even one of them but some corporate lackey, into consideration of what was gonna go on that LP?

Sure.

I think you're trying to pretend it's Metal Machine Music.

No, no, look: what we're talking about is the essential relationship between an artist and his audience, how that relates to their ego addictions and our consumer junkiedom playing off each other, and how the nature of the relationship keeps changing in all these interesting ways. I admit I'm more perverse than most people—maybe. But maybe not. The fact is, when the record comes out, if you're a fan, you'll find a way to like it. It's kinda like buying a gila monster for a house pet. After that there's only one of two things it can do: fade under your environment's unsuitability for gila monsters till it curls up and dies, or thrive on your detritus till it grows big and strong enough to one day come over and bite you. But when it does, you don't even die: you just pretend to! Actually you've been waiting for this all along! Because now you brag to your social set that you've got its disease! Which of course confers instant social status. You're not gonna turn into a gila monster yourself, but at least you can tell yourself that you're a little more like one.

For five years at *Creem* part of my job was to interview a different rockstar every single month of the year, let's see, at twelve stars a year times five that's sixty Culture Heroes in all, plus all the rest who just happened to be passing by backstage or whatever! Wow! What an education!

I remember riding to the gig with Rod and the Faces in an over-crowded limo where we drank and swapped stories laughing about what cretinous creeps 90% of the other "stars" we'd met in this biz were. People like Ian Anderson, who told me that John Coltrane was just a jerkoff who played nothing but garble-garbage, or Carl Palmer, who said Charlie Mingus was a lousy bassist and a fool besides. I'll tell ya, these characters some of 'em what they know about music is truly amazing. Ian Anderson, when he informed me that jazz was "a hoax being perpetrated on the public." But really, on a very basic level almost every musician I have ever met has been just as bad. It's one thing to demand technical excellence if you're Duke Ellington or Charles Mingus for that matter for shit fucking sure but as I get so tired of repeating to bigoted jackasses year after year it has nothing whatsoever to do with rock 'n' roll. This notion did not start with "punk rock." I'm not sure exactly when it started. Doesn't matter anyway. I do know that, for instance, when John Lee Hooker started out nobody could play drums on his sides because his rhythms were so eccentric they were considered by one and all impossible to follow and however compelling the performer just plain obviously wrong. Everybody, damn near, who's worth a shit gets subjected to this sooner or later (if they're lucky it's sooner and folks wise up later, or later, or later yet). It happened to Bird, Ornette, Coltrane, Miles, Cecil Taylor, Bob Dylan, Phil Spector, Jim Morrison, the Velvet Underground, the Stooges, the Dolls, the Ramones, the Sex Pistols, the Clash, Richard Hell and the Voidoids, Television, Patti Smith Group, Suicide, MC5, and the Faces in my lifetime, to name just what obvious names spill off the top of my head. Every one of them. Nowadays everybody and his brother saunters around intoning the sacred words "Velvet Underground," and every cheapjack-nihilism band who can't play and don't do that or anything else with any style gets called "the new Velvet Underground." Now, what I've long suspected is that the people today dropping "Velvet Underground" all over the place are the EXACT SAME PEOPLE who in 1967–8 woulda called 'em what they got called then, Faggots Who Couldn't Play Their Instruments, and that furthermore none of these namedropping assholes actually sit around *listening* to "Sister Ray," for fucking *pleasure,* ever. I finally started checking out people's record collections, just routinely when I walked in anybody's house pulling out their copy of *White Light/White Heat* (of course EVERYBODY has it, because it's so hip to have) and sliding it out of the sleeve. Yep. Almost nobody I ever meet has ever much played the damn thing. In fact, nearly all the copies in folks' homes look *virgin,* like they got played maybe once, right after they were purchased, maybe then not all the way through, and then filed.

Apparently nobody ever bothered to inform nine-tenths of musicians that music is about feeling, passion, love, anger, joy, fear, hope, lust, EMO-

TION DELIVERED AT ITS MOST POWERFUL AND DIRECT IN
WHATEVER FORM, rather than whether you hit a clinker in that third
bar there. I frankly wouldn't expect most musicians to be able to figure this
out for themselves, as you'd think absolutely anybody could, because it is
a fact that nine-tenths of the HUMAN RACE never have and never will
think for themselves, about anything. Whether it's music or Reaganomics,
say, almost everybody prefers to sit and *wait* till somebody who seems to
have some kind of authority even if it's seldom too clear just where they
got it to come along and inform them one and all what their position on
the matter should be. Then they all agree that this is gospel, and gang up
to go persecute whatever minority might happen to disagree. This is the
history of the human race, certainly the history of music, and it don't
matter whether it's Mom and Dad in 1955 listening to Perry Como and
telling you that Elvis was a no-'count hillbilly hollerawin' raggedy nigger
gooze, or all the kids I went to high school with who thought they were
so hip because they went out and bought Doors albums but snickered down
along with Uncle Frank Zappa (a despicable wretch morons actually call
"composer" instead of "rip-off artist," walking human offal if such matter
ever lived) on the Kingsmen and later Count Five and Question Mark and
the Mysterians. When I was in a teen band playing the local bowling alley
in 1966, I got to blow harp on four or five songs every night: "Goin' Down
to Louisiana," "Blues Jam," "I'm a Man," "Psychotic Reaction" and I
forget, and I noticed at the time that these guys just LOVED to play "I'm
a Man" and pretend they were Jeff Beck, but they always groaned when
we had to run through "Psychotic Reaction," and while I had no technical
knowledge of music it did seem like they came awfully close to being THE
SAME SONG. (Okay, throw in a little "Secret Agent Man" on "Psychotic
Reaction.") I played harp exactly the same in both. But it was understood
that "I'm a Man" was the admittedly almighty Yardbirds, or (if these guys
were that hip) the unquestionably authentic and righteous bluesbustin' dad
of rock 'n' roll Bo Diddley, who has certainly filled out his albums with some
slices of timeless musical merit—"Yakky Doodle," "Say Man," etc.—but
who the fuck were Count Five? Just a bunch of zitfarms from San Jose
about like the band I was in, that's who, so fuck 'em. Which of course
meant that my fellow bandmembers considered themselves worthless, but
I never bothered to bring this up.

I saw the '64–'65 Kinks perform live on TV on "Shindig" once, and
can testify that at that time Dave Davies couldn't play—when it came up
to Solo Time in their big hit "All Day and All of the Night," he staggered
and stumbled all over himself. It was a little embarrassing. Then there was

the time in 1965 I saw the Byrds open up for the Stones in San Diego. God, were they awful. I didn't buy their first album for six months on the basis of that performance alone. Vocals, rhythms, guitar solos, harmonies, you name it—those cats couldn't hold together a song to save their lives. Years later I found out that in fact McGuinn was the only one who played at all on the first Byrds album, the rest was all standard high-priced hack L.A. session guys, the best money could buy to be sure, Louie Shelton or people like that, but still hacks. So then how come that album's a classic that sounds almost as fresh today as the day it was released? Beats me. All I know is that when the Dark Ages, my little band at the bowling alley, had to do "Psychotic Reaction" each night, that was how they treated it: as some-thing they "had" to do, just run through the paces to keep the audience happy, because it was a hit. They felt exactly the same way about "96 Tears."

I roomed with some of these guys for a while in 1968, and one night just before I went to bed I put on the "Dreamy Side" of *Oldies But Goodies Vol. 1* on the Original Sound label, and the next day I asked the bassist in the Dark Ages how he'd liked it. "Yeah, you put that stuff on at the perfect time," he laughed. "It put me right to sleep!" It was only classic doo-wop, but y'know I think the real fly in the ointment probably was those liner notes on *Freak Out*, where Zappa sneered that stuff about "having to play 'Louie, Louie' in lousy bar bands" or some such—I think that fucked up an enormous amount of people's thinking. All it really says, of course (unless as I grant is possible in the light of *Cruisin' with Ruben and the Jets* Zappa really liked "Louie, Louie" and was misunderstood) is that Frank and all the boys in the band had that Tired Old Session Man/Bar Hack mentality, that drab mood Fogerty conjured up so well in "Lodi," which is a point at which the dues paid and final pointlessness of it all render the musician unutterably tired, surly, and above it all to the once-unthinkable point of actually hating music itself of just about any kind. Now, the Mothers looked like a buncha such cats in the first place—a little older, balding here and there, etc.—and for every Jeff Beck there's ten million bitter old session men who've finally stopped giving a damn and are just picking up a check. You think somebody in that kind of mood is going to let the likes of the Sex Pistols get away with anything? Forget it. They hate 'em even more, because it's in front that the punks in whatever form or era DIDN'T pay their dues; it'd be unnatural or weirdly Christlike if these guys *didn't* hate 'em. Meanwhile, you should have seen the looks that'd come over the faces of my '68 roommates, who laughed at doo-wop but played Cream every day, when I put on *White Light/White Heat,* which I did every day. They let me know they thought I was a closet queer. Why else would anybody listen to such shit?

I didn't go around shoving my prejudices down everybody's throat. I just endured Cream every fucking day, "Spoonful" and all the rest of that whiteheap bigdealsowhat. And you'd think it'd only be fair for them to endure Velvet Underground, Count Five, *Oldies But Goodies,* the Fugs, the Godz and I forget what other godawful racket I doted on. But they wouldn't let me have my equal portion of obnoxiousness. My music was "bad," and theirs was "good." And maybe that's why I've ended up doing what I've done so far with my life, which Bob Quine called me up one day and summarized: "I've figured you out. Every month you go out and deliberately dig up the most godawful wretched worthless unlistenable offensive irritating unnerving moronic piece of horrible racket noise you can possibly find, then sit down and write this review in which you explain to everybody else in the world why it's just wonderful and they should all run right out and buy it. Since you're a good writer, they're convinced by the review to do just that—till they get home and put the record *on,* which is when the pain sets in. They throw it under the sink or somewhere and swear it'll never happen again. By the next month they've forgotten, but you haven't, so the whole process is repeated again with some other even more obnoxious piece of hideous blare. . . . You know, I must say, I have to admit that's a noble thing to devote your entire life to."

He nailed me. Since 1969. But with the one proviso that I genuinely *like* all those same plates of horrid blare and play them for pleasure myself, it just occurred to me that maybe the whole reason this stuff happened to become my life was that original traumatic incident back there with those hippies: I've been trying to get revenge on those assholes ever since.

Culture heroes. Lou Reed and I had some fun for a while baiting each other in public, though it was also true that at the time he was for me what Dylan'd been in 1966 or whenever—*Numero Uno.* THE MAN. I learned some fairly unpleasant things about him and got snubbed and treated like some wretched groupie in public a few times when I was only practically his fucking press agent, keeping more than a few people (or so they've told me over the years) interested in him at a time when they'd otherwise've been prepared to write him off entirely. I'll go as far as to say that I think the stories I wrote about Lou in the mid-seventies were all better art than the records, any of them, he was making at the time.

But really that's neither here nor there. What applies is that I don't finally and factually think that Lou Reed has too many evil bones in his body. When in that bigdeal actually quite fun 1975 "fight" interview he told me that I used to be a good writer but now was wasting away in posturing jive he did me a favor that 99% of my best "real" friends sure as hell never got around to, because it was the truth and if somebody hadn't snapped a finger in front of my eyes and delivered a few well-placed words the kind of self-parody not to mention self-destructiveness I was making a point of specializing in so I could be Charles Bukowski Jr. or somebody would have eventually destroyed me as both a writer and a person. As it happened, I can think of about three people who bothered to point this out to me at the time. One of them was my girlfriend. One was Lou Reed. And one was a woman photographer who was only telling me that he'd been right when he'd said those things to me the night before.

Most often the code of the road is to encourage the absolute worst behavior possible or imaginable in the young "genius." I have had the very same people who goaded me on in these buffooneries every day sit in hotel rooms and talk about me as if I wasn't even present but was such an idiot savant that I didn't merit inclusion in the human race. But I was lucky. Around the time Lou Reed said those things to me I was engaging about four times more in grossout proto-punk Legs McNeil self-promotion than I was profiling the ostensible subjects I was supposedly writing about each month. They were all entertaining pieces—in fact, there are a lot of people who think to this day that I did the best work I'll ever do while at *Creem* and since moving to New York have turned into an increasingly embittered, gimme-a-break moralist, occasionally amusing but increasingly bitter old washed-up hasbeen. Fuck 'em. I got lucky: this bullshit became my life while I was ensconced in the relatively decidedly pissant environs of *Creem*, so once I woke up I made it out and can say that though I have my days just like everybody else I still think I have a future.

Index

Permissions
Acknowledgments

ABOUT THE EDITOR

Greil Marcus is the author of *Mystery Trains: Images of America in Rock 'n' Roll Music.*

letter and enclosure,

postmarked Las Vegas, Nevada,

received by Dave Marsh, February 1986

Wayne
Newton

MEMO

DATE Feb 6

TO· Dave Marsh

COPY TO

FROM· above

SUBJECT· mail forwarding

Have no idea why this came to me, assume it will not be happening
again in future. I have far more important matters to deal with.

Since you're reading, might as well tell you about the new Springsteen
"dark" medley I'm closing my shows with: "Dancin' In The Dark," "On
The Dark Side" and "Darkstreets."

Love that "one soft infected summer me and Terry became friends"
line. I thought "Daddy Dontcha Walk So Fast" was poetry, but
not compared to tying fate between our teeth, you know?

FROM THE CLOUD OF

Lester Bangs

Dave--

Boy, what a new year's surprise! Rick Nelson! Turns out
he's a decent cat. And that reunion between him & Oz
even brought tears to Baby Huey's eyes (my best friend
on this celestial island).

Turns out Oz has a real jones for these milkshakes with
Heavenly Hash ice cream. Tried to get me & Huey to scarf
some but we wuz flyin' on meth and couldn't even watch
him shovel it up. Rick was teachin' the Singing Nun the
chords to "Garden Party."

Can't find your address anywhere up here, but I know you
& the boss are tight, so I'll send it straight to Vegas and
let him forward it to you. Later.

$-LB$

PS--What is this fucking "M.T.V." Thought for sure it was
some new drug, but Rick says no it's not. Then he thinks
for a second and says, "You know, Lester, maybe it is at
that." Said if it had been around in '69, Stones'd have
to make a "video" of "Gimme Shelter." I say huh?